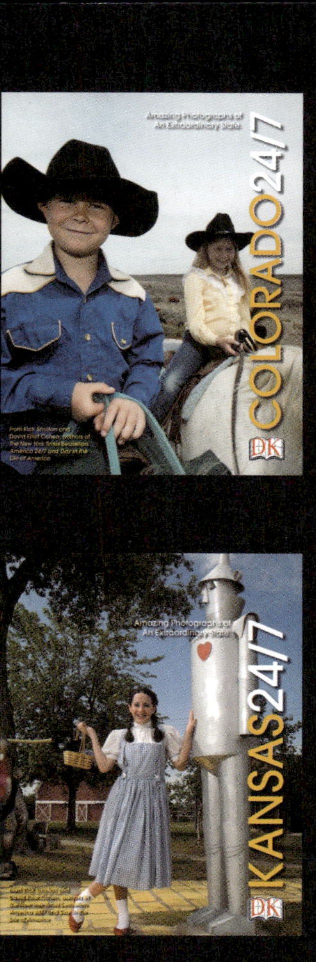
COLORADO 24/7
KANSAS 24/7
DK
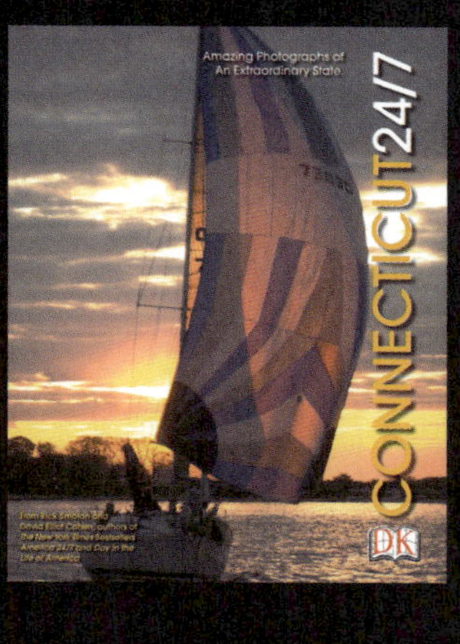
CONNECTICUT 24/7
DK
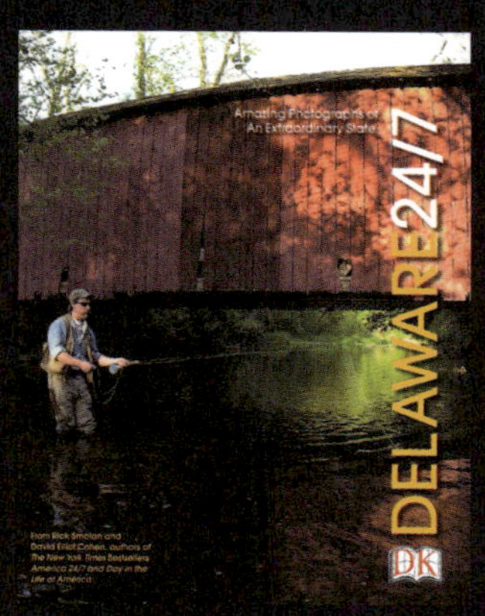
DELAWARE 24/7
DK
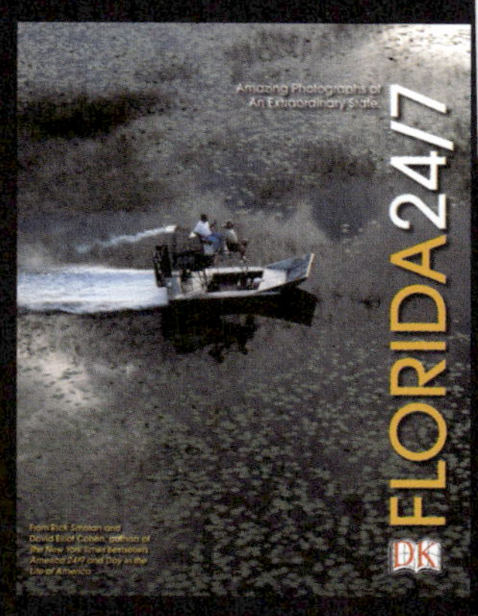
FLORIDA 24/7
DK

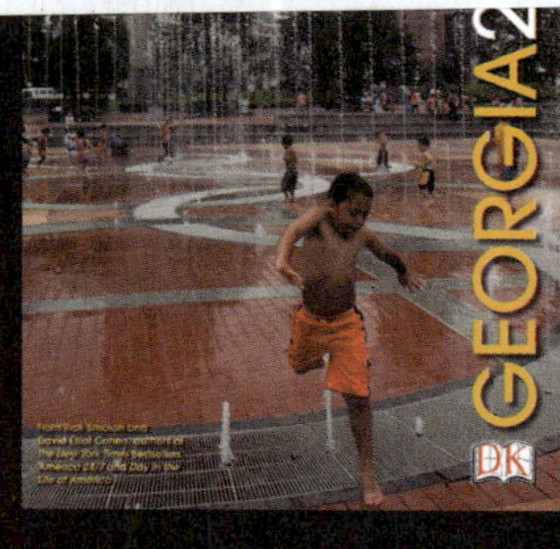
GEORGIA 2
DK
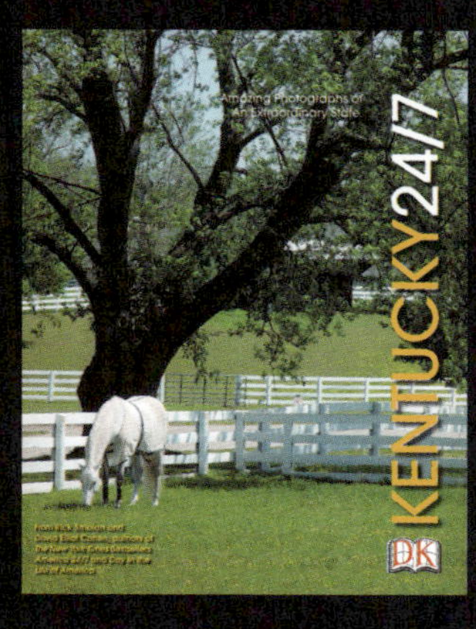
KENTUCKY 24/7
DK
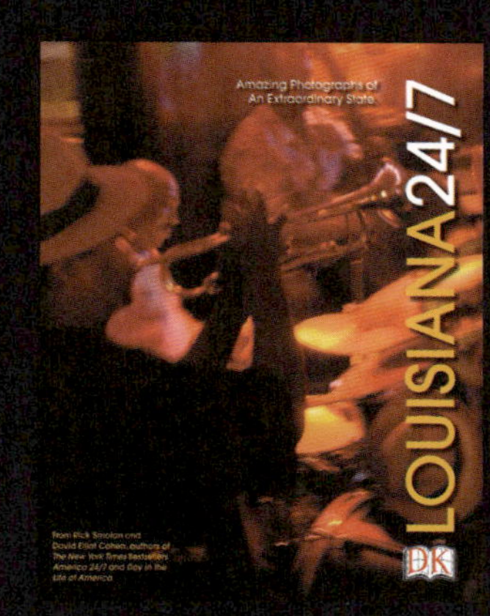
LOUISIANA 24/7
DK
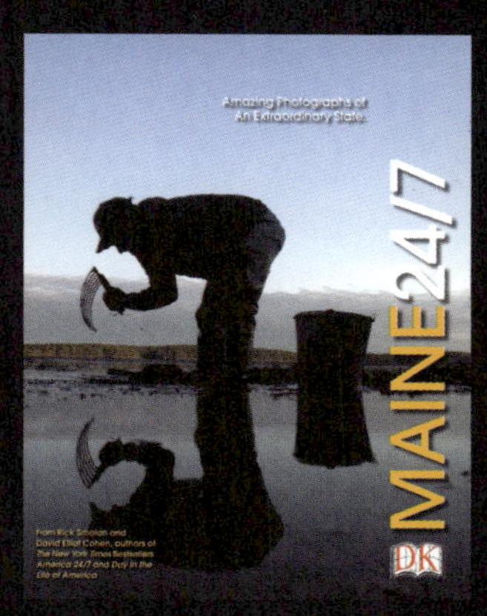
MAINE 24/7
DK
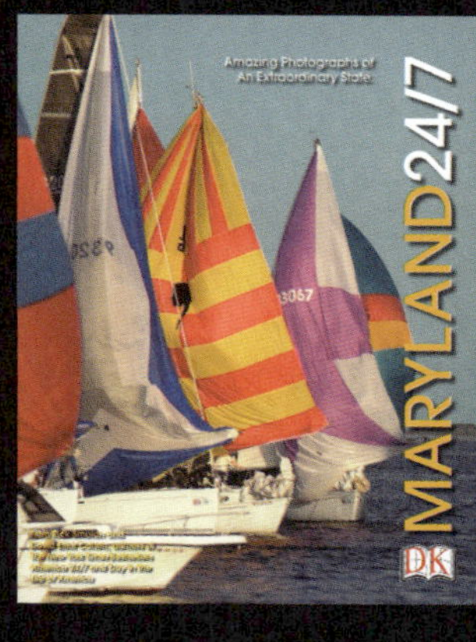
MARYLAND 24/7
DK
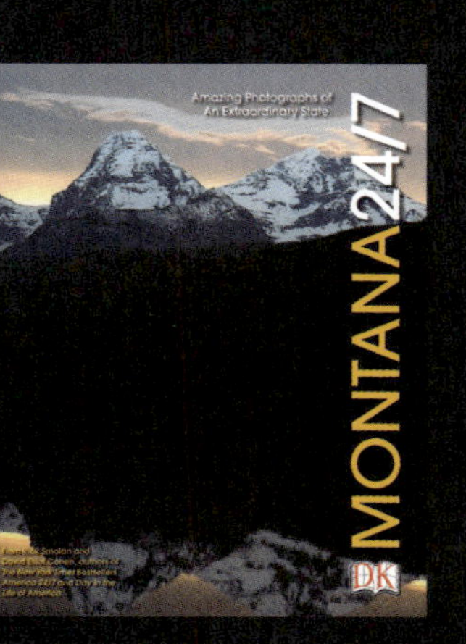
MONTANA 24/7
DK
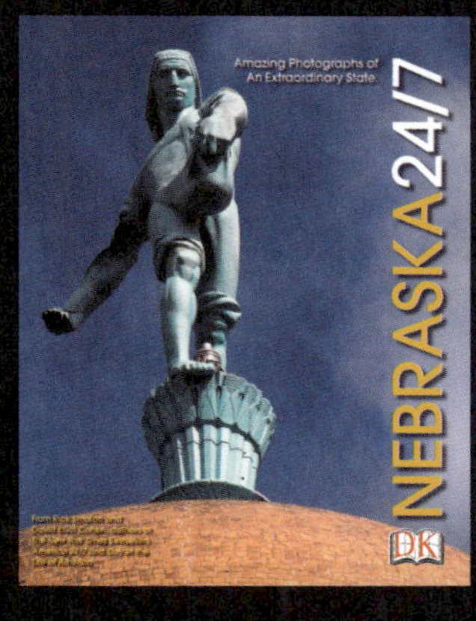
NEBRASKA 24/7
DK
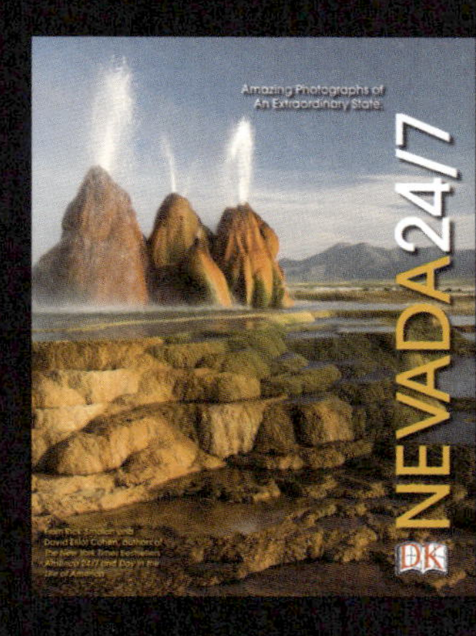
NEVADA 24/7
DK
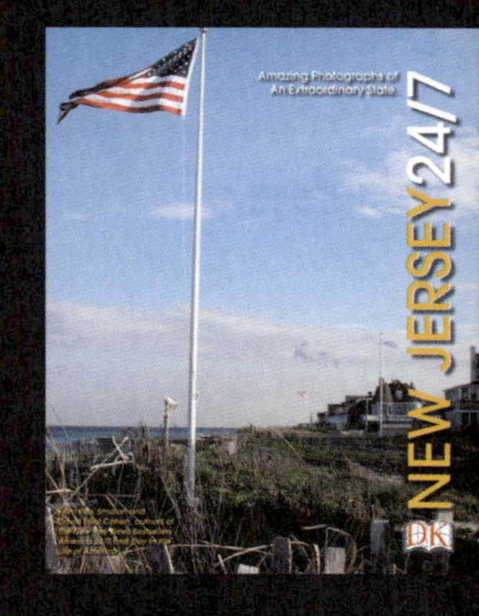
NEW JERSEY 24/7
DK
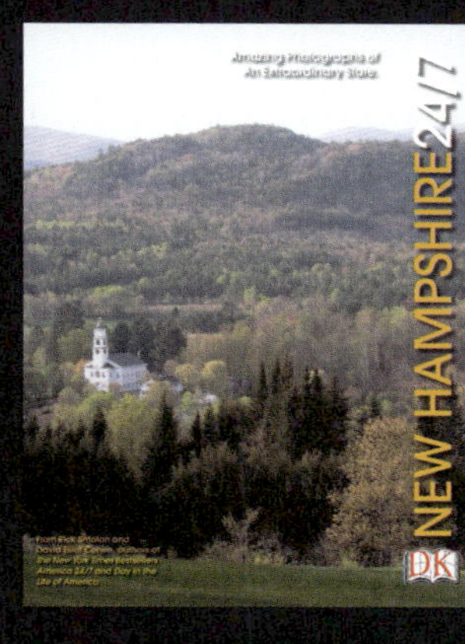
NEW HAMPSHIRE 24/7
DK
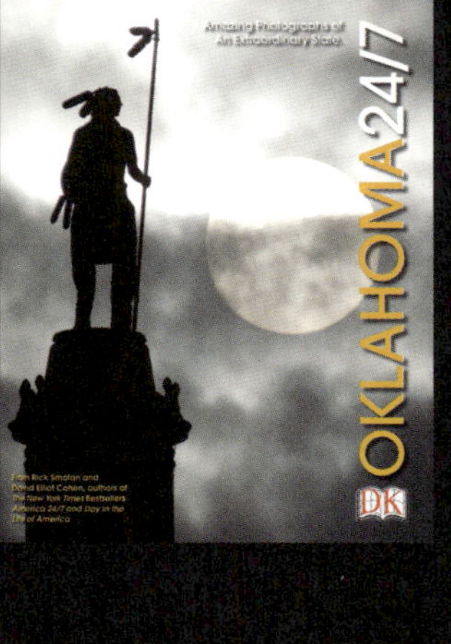
OKLAHOMA 24/7
DK
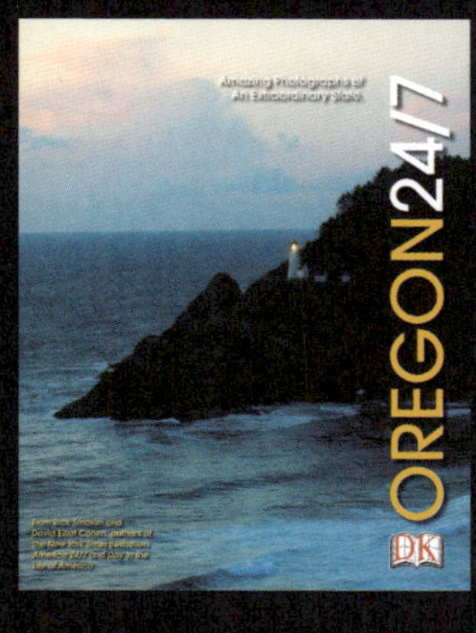
OREGON 24/7
DK
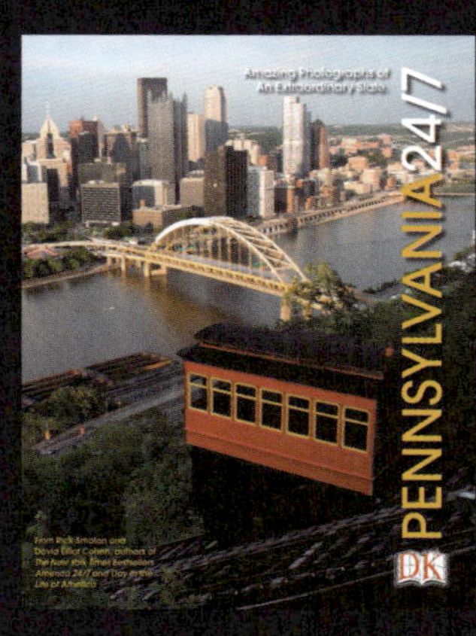
PENNSYLVANIA 24/7
DK
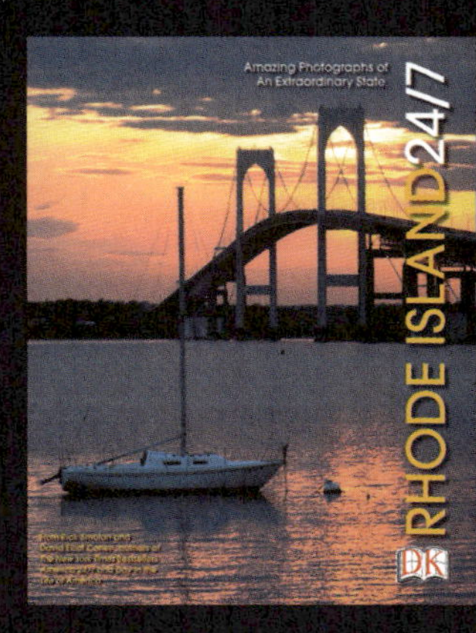
RHODE ISLAND 24/7
DK
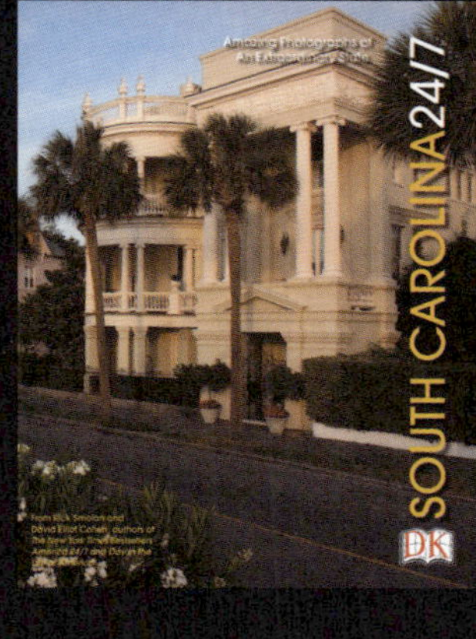
SOUTH CAROLINA 24/7
DK
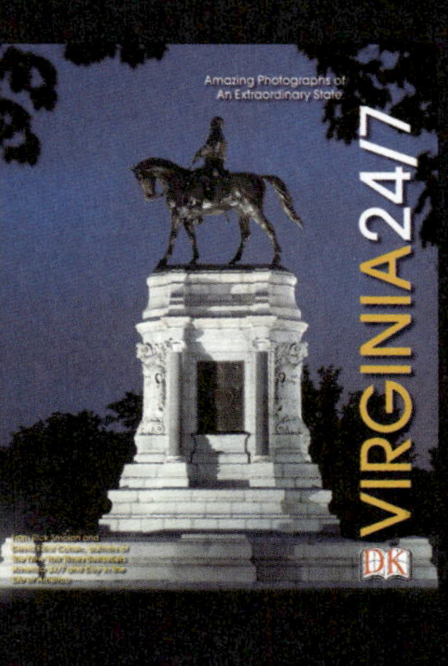
VIRGINIA 24/7
DK
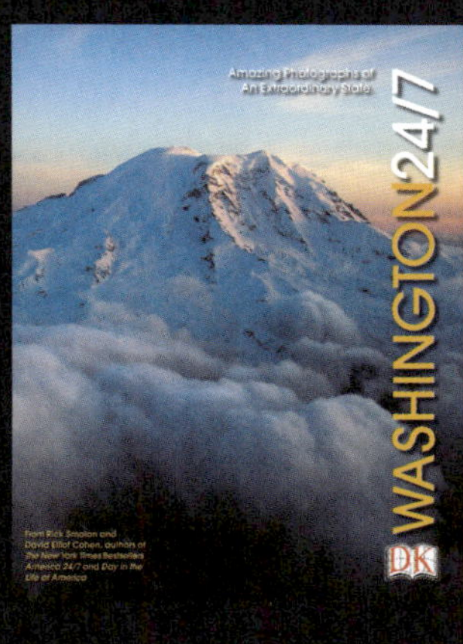
WASHINGTON 24/7
DK
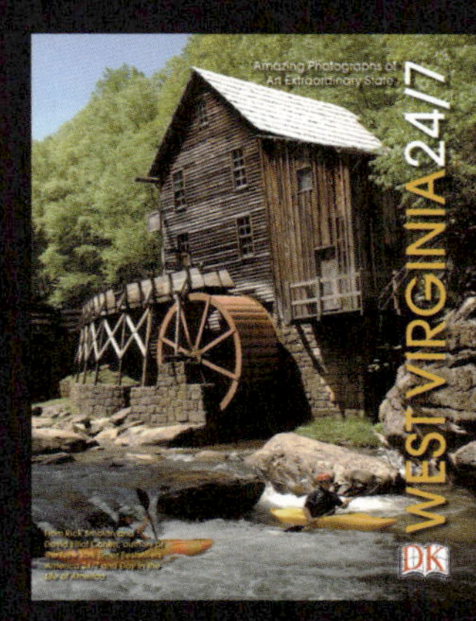
WEST VIRGINIA 24/7
DK
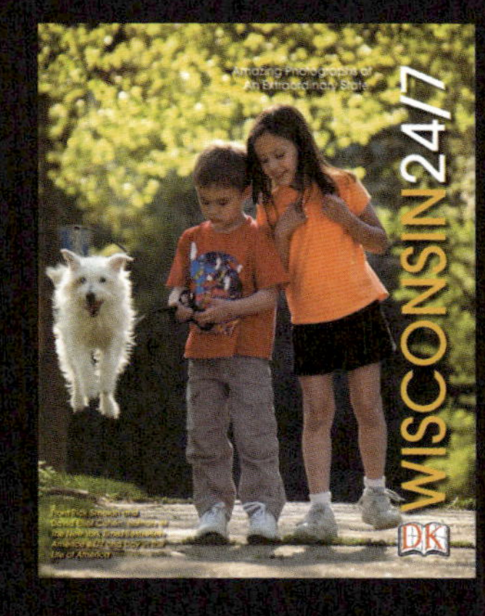
WISCONSIN 24/7
DK
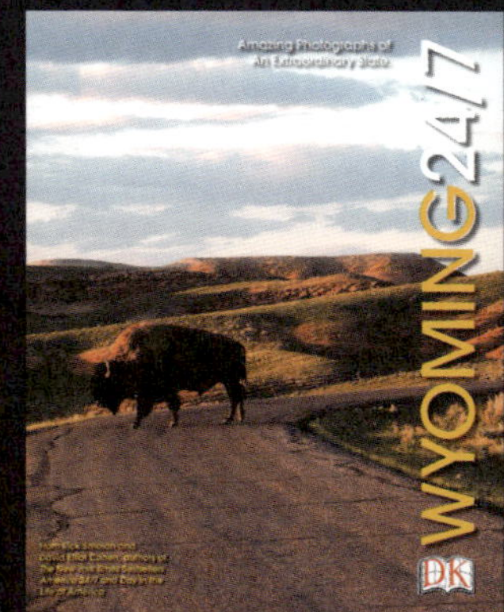
WYOMING 24/7
DK

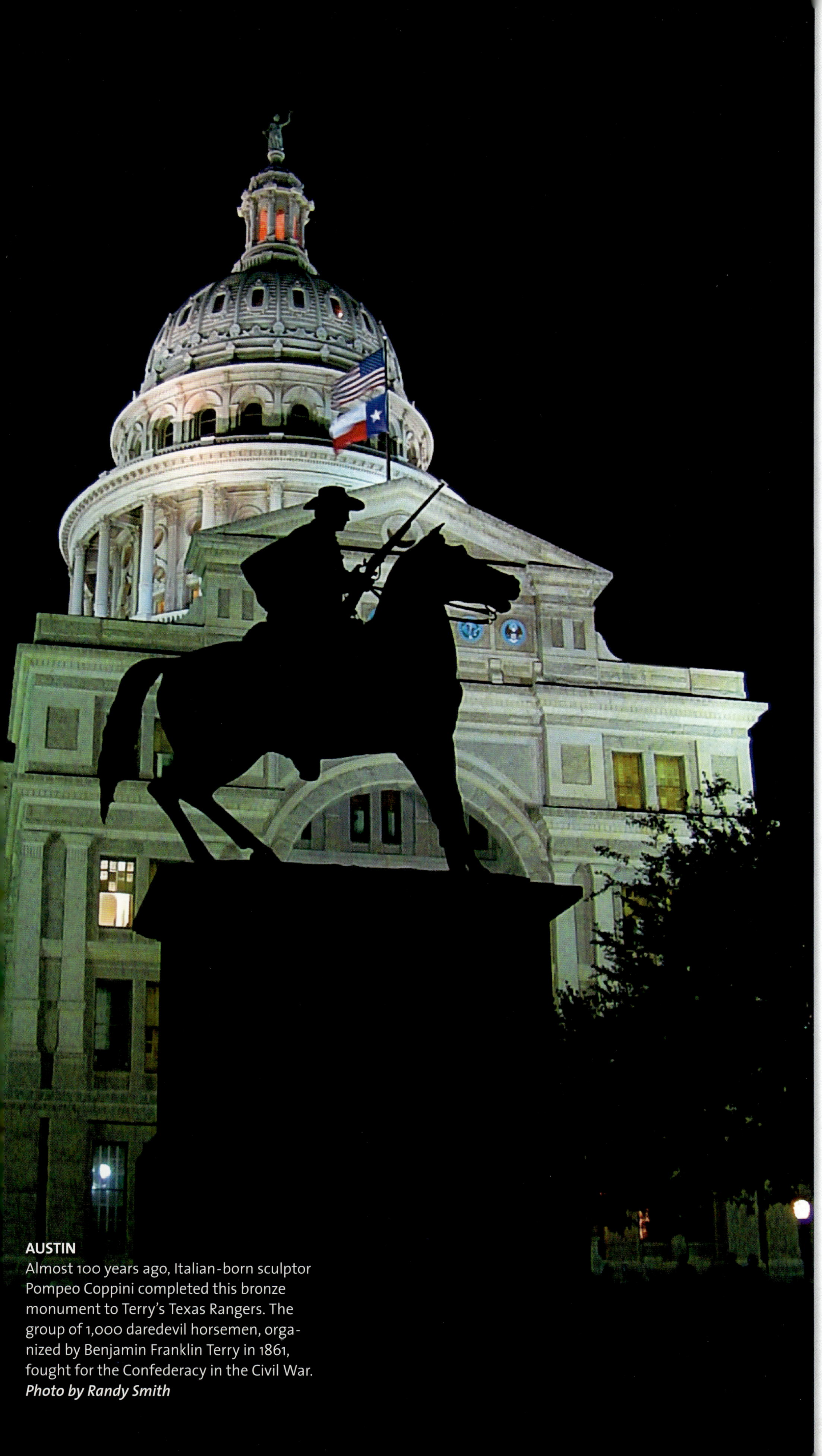

Texas 24/7 is the sequel to *The New York Times* bestseller *America 24/7* shot by tens of thousands of digital photographers across America over the course of a single week. We would like to thank the following sponsors, the wonderful people of Texas, and the talented photojournalists who made this book possible.

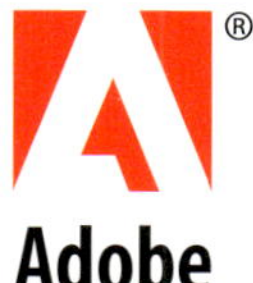

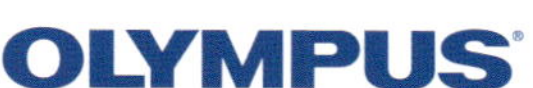

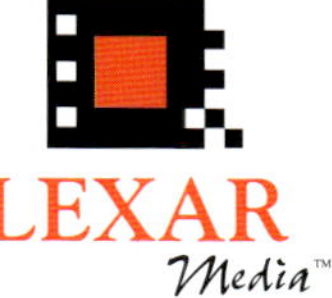

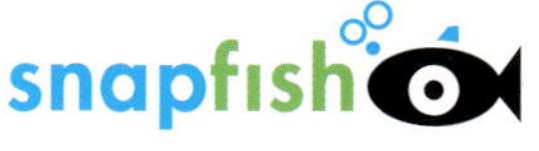

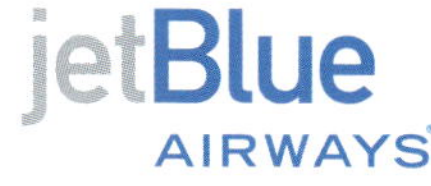

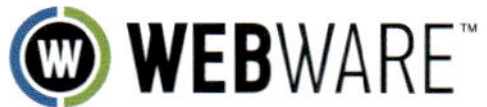

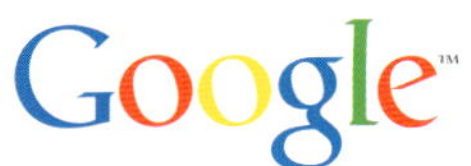

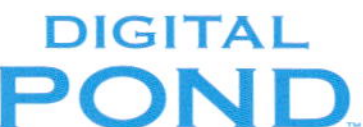

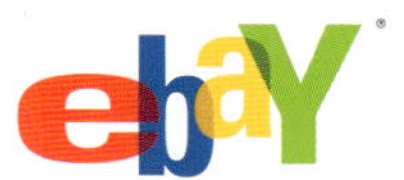

AUSTIN
Almost 100 years ago, Italian-born sculptor Pompeo Coppini completed this bronze monument to Terry's Texas Rangers. The group of 1,000 daredevil horsemen, organized by Benjamin Franklin Terry in 1861, fought for the Confederacy in the Civil War.
Photo by Randy Smith

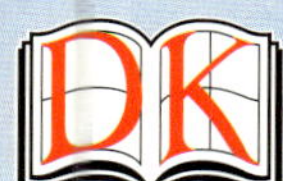

LONDON, NEW YORK, MUNICH, MELBOURNE, and DELHI

Created by Rick Smolan and David Elliot Cohen

24/7 Media, LLC
PO Box 1189
Sausalito, CA 94966-1189
www.america24-7.com

First Edition, 2004
04 05 06 07 08 10 9 8 7 6 5 4 3 2 1

Published in the United States by
DK Publishing, Inc.
375 Hudson Street
New York, NY 10014

DK Publishing, Inc. offers special discounts for bulk purchases for sales promotions or premiums. Specific, large-quantity needs can be met with special editions, personalized covers, excerpts of existing guides, and corporate imprints. For more information, contact:

Special Markets Department
DK Publishing, Inc.
375 Hudson Street
New York, NY 10014
Fax: 212-689-5254

Cataloging-in-Publication data is available from the Library of Congress
ISBN 0-7566-0084-7

Printed in the UK by Butler & Tanner Limited

First printing, October 2004

DALLAS
The Houston Street Bridge, running one way from downtown Dallas to Oak Cliff, has been carrying traffic across the flood-prone Trinity River since 1912. For a very short time, it was the world's longest concrete structure, and a 13-year-old Clyde Barrow once lived in a shantytown beneath its arches.
Photo by Peter A. Calvin

TEXAS 24/7

24 Hours. 7 Days.
Extraordinary Images of
One Week in Texas.

Created by Rick Smolan and David Elliot Cohen

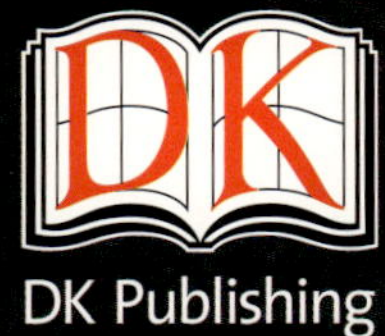

DK Publishing

About the America 24/7 Project

A hundred years hence, historians may pose questions such as: What was America like at the beginning of the third millennium? How did life change after 9/11 and the ensuing war on terrorism? How was America affected by its corporate scandals and the high-tech boom and bust? Could Americans still express themselves freely?

To address these questions, we created *America 24/7*, the largest collaborative photography event in history. We invited Americans to tell their stories with digital pictures. We asked them to shoot a visual memoir of their lives, families, and communities.

During one week in May 2003, more than 25,000 professionals and amateurs shot more than a million pictures. These images, sent to us via the Internet, compose a panoramic yet highly intimate view of Americans in celebration and sadness; in action and contemplation; at work, home, and school. The best of these photographs, more than 6,000, are collected in 51 volumes that make up the *America 24/7* series: the landmark national volume *America 24/7*, published to critical acclaim in 2003, and the 50 state books published in 2004.

Our decision to make *America 24/7* an all-digital project was prompted by the fact that in 2003 digital camera sales overtook film camera sales. This technological evolution allowed us to extend the project to a huge pool of photographers. We were thrilled by the response to our challenge and moved by the insight offered into American life. Sometimes, the amateurs outshot the pros—even the Pulitzer Prize winners.

The exuberant democracy of images visible throughout these books is a revelation. The message that emerges is that now, more than ever, America is a supersized idea. A dreamspace, where individuals and families from around the world are free to govern themselves, worship, read, and speak as they wish. Within its wide margins, the polyglot American nation manages to encompass an inexplicably complex yet workable whole. The pictures in this book are dedicated to that idea.

—Rick Smolan and David Elliot Cohen

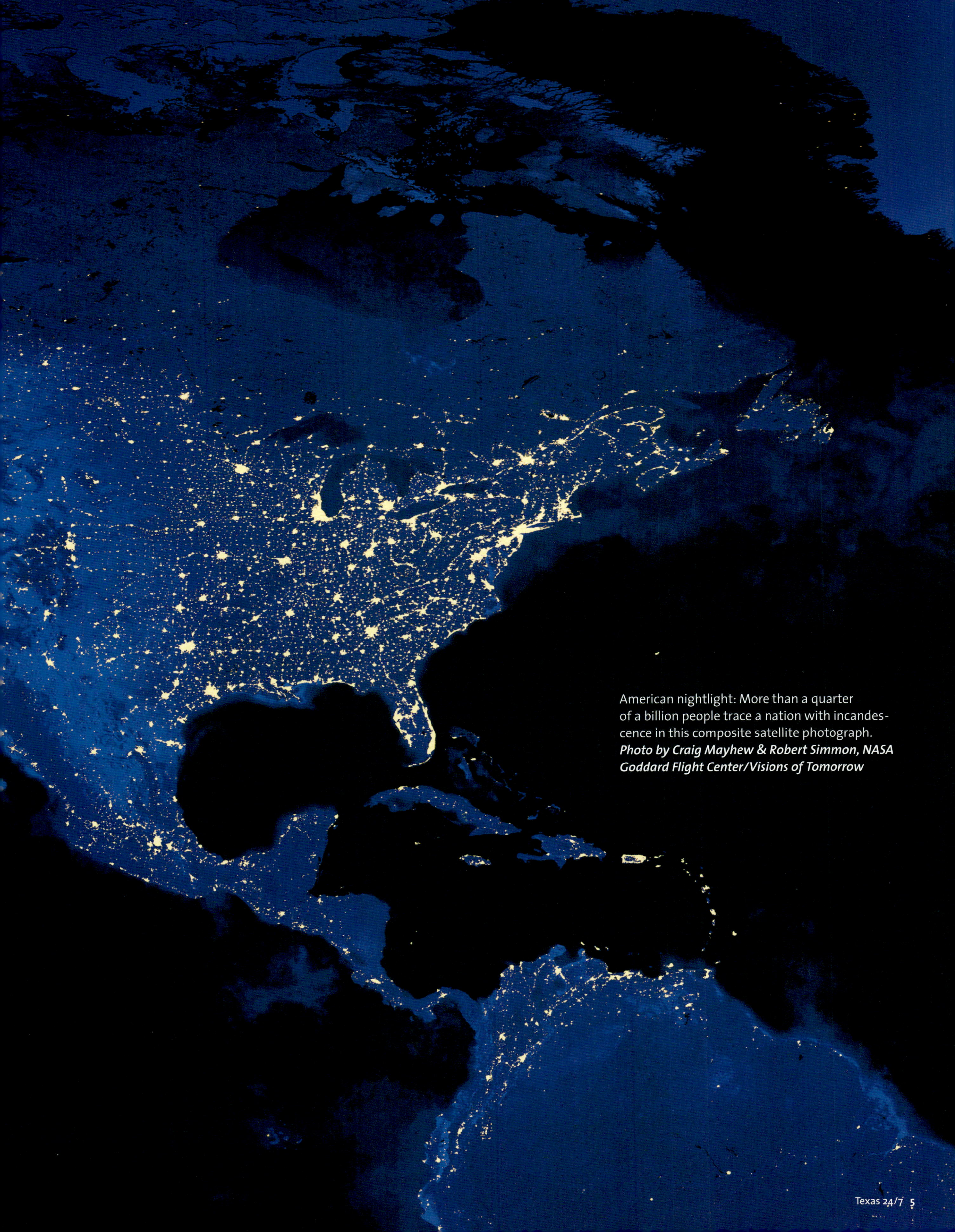

American nightlight: More than a quarter of a billion people trace a nation with incandescence in this composite satellite photograph. ***Photo by Craig Mayhew & Robert Simmon, NASA Goddard Flight Center/Visions of Tomorrow***

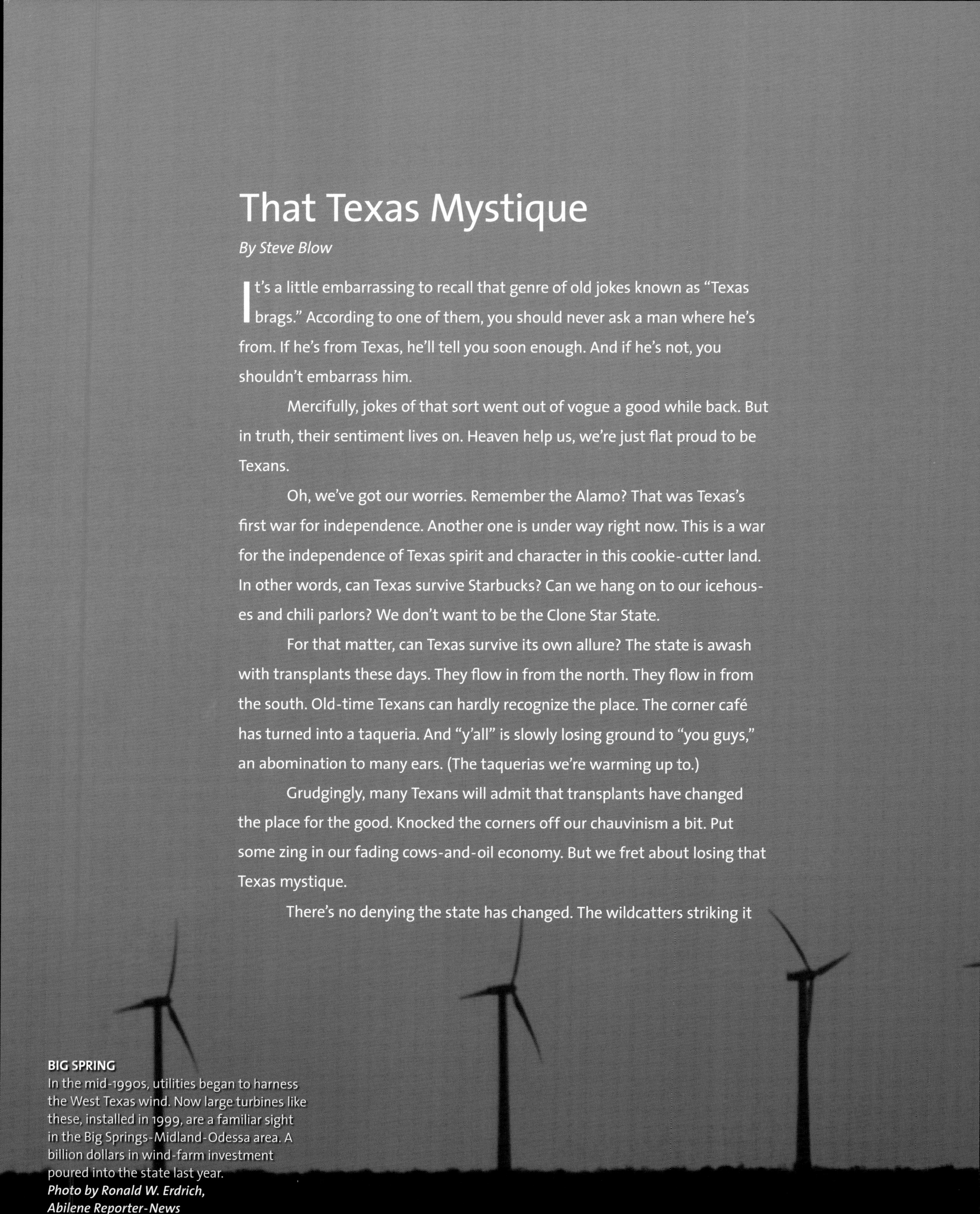

That Texas Mystique

By Steve Blow

It's a little embarrassing to recall that genre of old jokes known as "Texas brags." According to one of them, you should never ask a man where he's from. If he's from Texas, he'll tell you soon enough. And if he's not, you shouldn't embarrass him.

Mercifully, jokes of that sort went out of vogue a good while back. But in truth, their sentiment lives on. Heaven help us, we're just flat proud to be Texans.

Oh, we've got our worries. Remember the Alamo? That was Texas's first war for independence. Another one is under way right now. This is a war for the independence of Texas spirit and character in this cookie-cutter land. In other words, can Texas survive Starbucks? Can we hang on to our icehouses and chili parlors? We don't want to be the Clone Star State.

For that matter, can Texas survive its own allure? The state is awash with transplants these days. They flow in from the north. They flow in from the south. Old-time Texans can hardly recognize the place. The corner café has turned into a taqueria. And "y'all" is slowly losing ground to "you guys," an abomination to many ears. (The taquerias we're warming up to.)

Grudgingly, many Texans will admit that transplants have changed the place for the good. Knocked the corners off our chauvinism a bit. Put some zing in our fading cows-and-oil economy. But we fret about losing that Texas mystique.

There's no denying the state has changed. The wildcatters striking it

BIG SPRING
In the mid-1990s, utilities began to harness the West Texas wind. Now large turbines like these, installed in 1999, are a familiar sight in the Big Springs-Midland-Odessa area. A billion dollars in wind-farm investment poured into the state last year.
Photo by Ronald W. Erdrich, Abilene Reporter-News

rich today are young high-tech entrepreneurs like Michael Dell and Mark Cuban. Republicans fully control state government for the first time in 130 years. Houston, a city that is infamous for its lack of zoning, has a revitalized downtown—thanks to some savvy, just-in-time city planning. Fort Worth just opened a nationally acclaimed modern art museum. And Big D has a flourishing rail transit system, of all things.

Texas is a much more citified place now. Draw a triangle with Houston and San Antonio at the bottom and Dallas-Fort Worth at the top, and you've roped two-thirds of the population in just a little sliver of the state. We still love our ranching-and-roughnecking image, but the fact is that most Texans now ride herd over a cubicle. When we boot up, it's on a computer.

But that doesn't tell the whole story, not by a long shot. That urban triangle may represent the economic heart of the state, but it doesn't begin to capture the enduring, epic heart of Texas. That lies out to the east, in the cathedral-like quiet of East Texas's piney woods. It lies to the west, in the barren, heart-breaking beauty of West Texas. It's the lonely highways of the Panhandle, the lively fiestas of South Texas, and the shrimp trawlers out on the Gulf.

These are just some of the things we cherish. The pages that follow feature many more. Texas is a thousand miles across. And it's that many more from top to bottom. There's no measure of all that we hold dear, deep in the heart of Texas.

Steve Blow *is a metro columnist for* The Dallas Morning News. *He was born in Tyler, Texas, and will be buried there.*

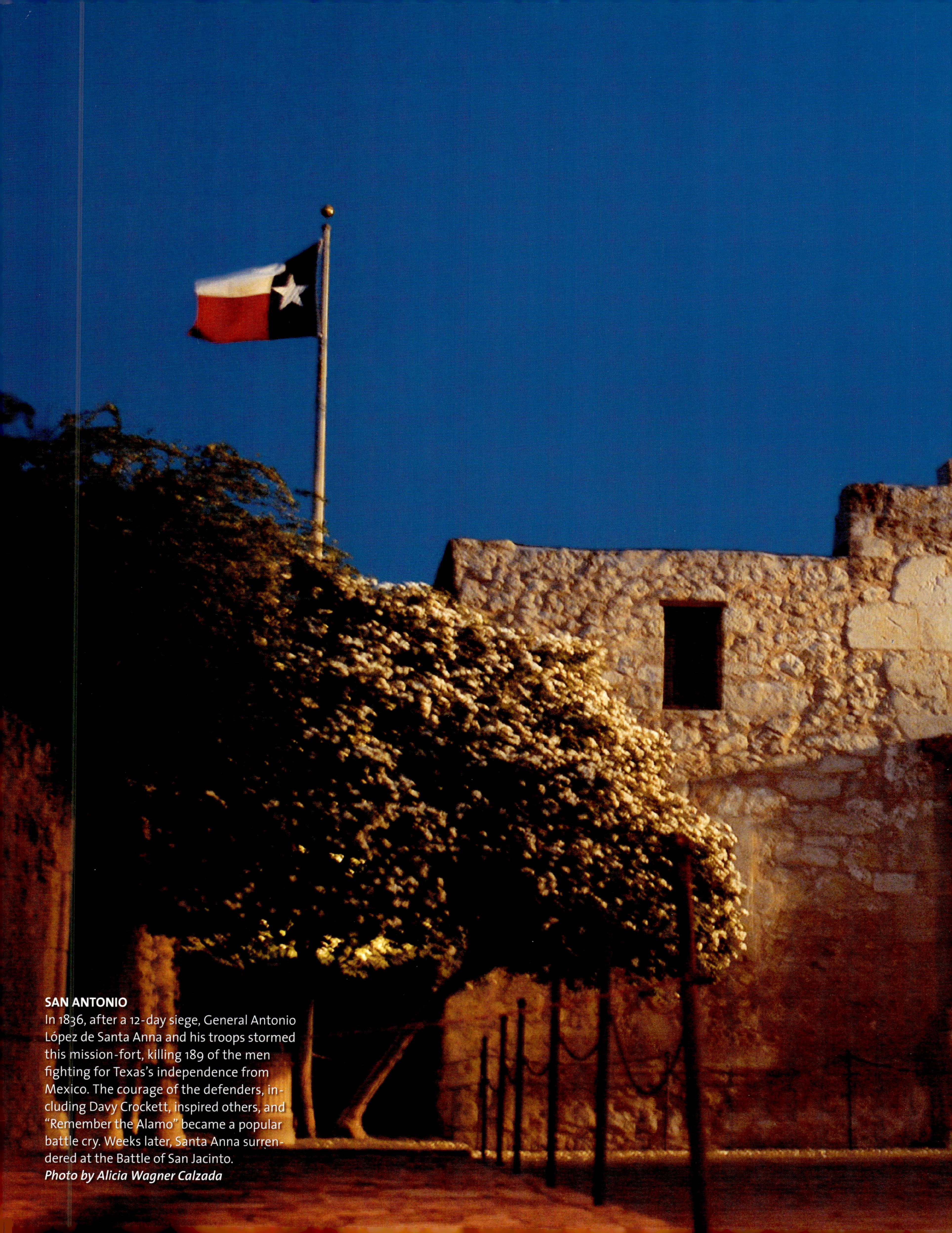

SAN ANTONIO
In 1836, after a 12-day siege, General Antonio López de Santa Anna and his troops stormed this mission-fort, killing 189 of the men fighting for Texas's independence from Mexico. The courage of the defenders, including Davy Crockett, inspired others, and "Remember the Alamo" became a popular battle cry. Weeks later, Santa Anna surrendered at the Battle of San Jacinto.
Photo by Alicia Wagner Calzada

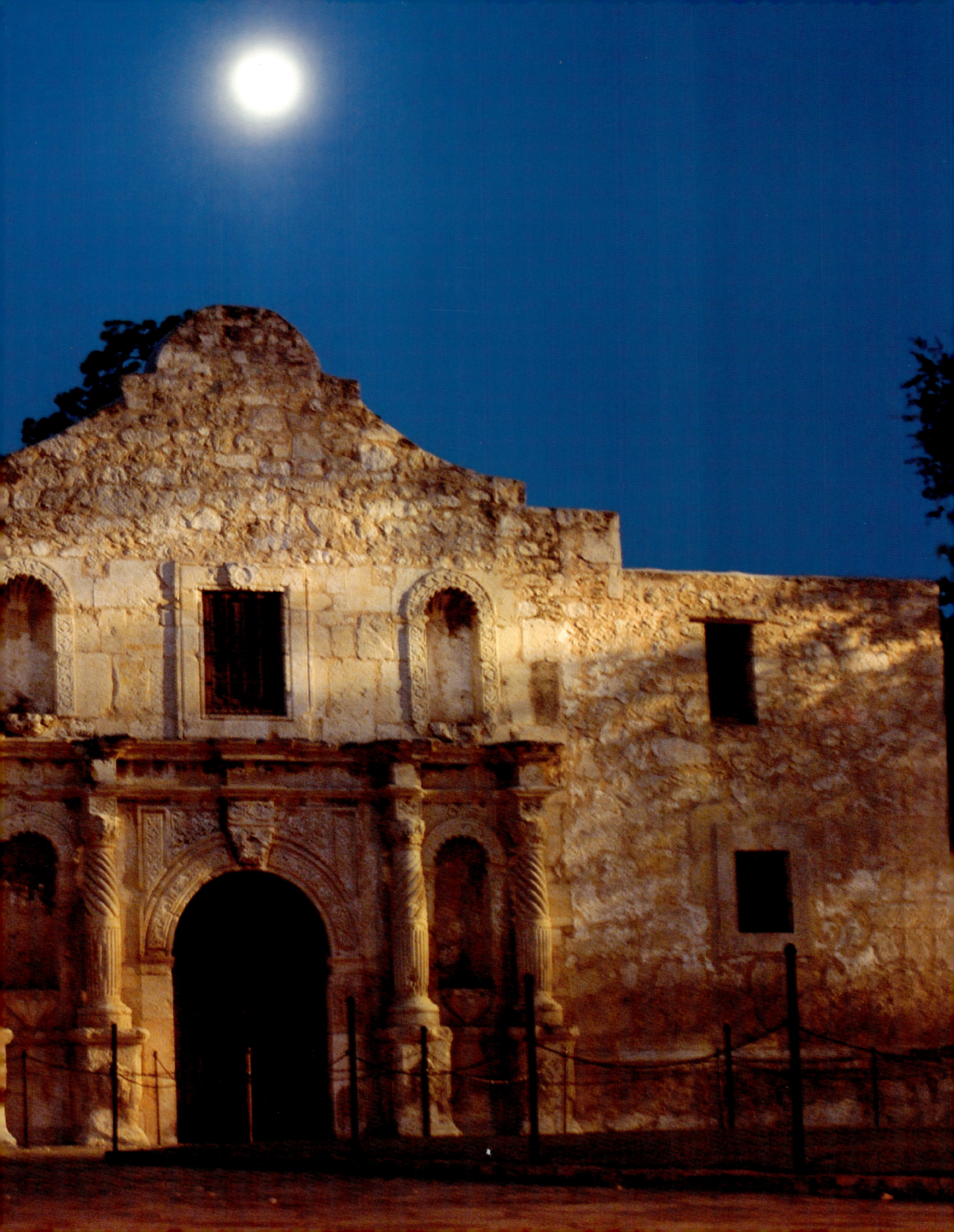

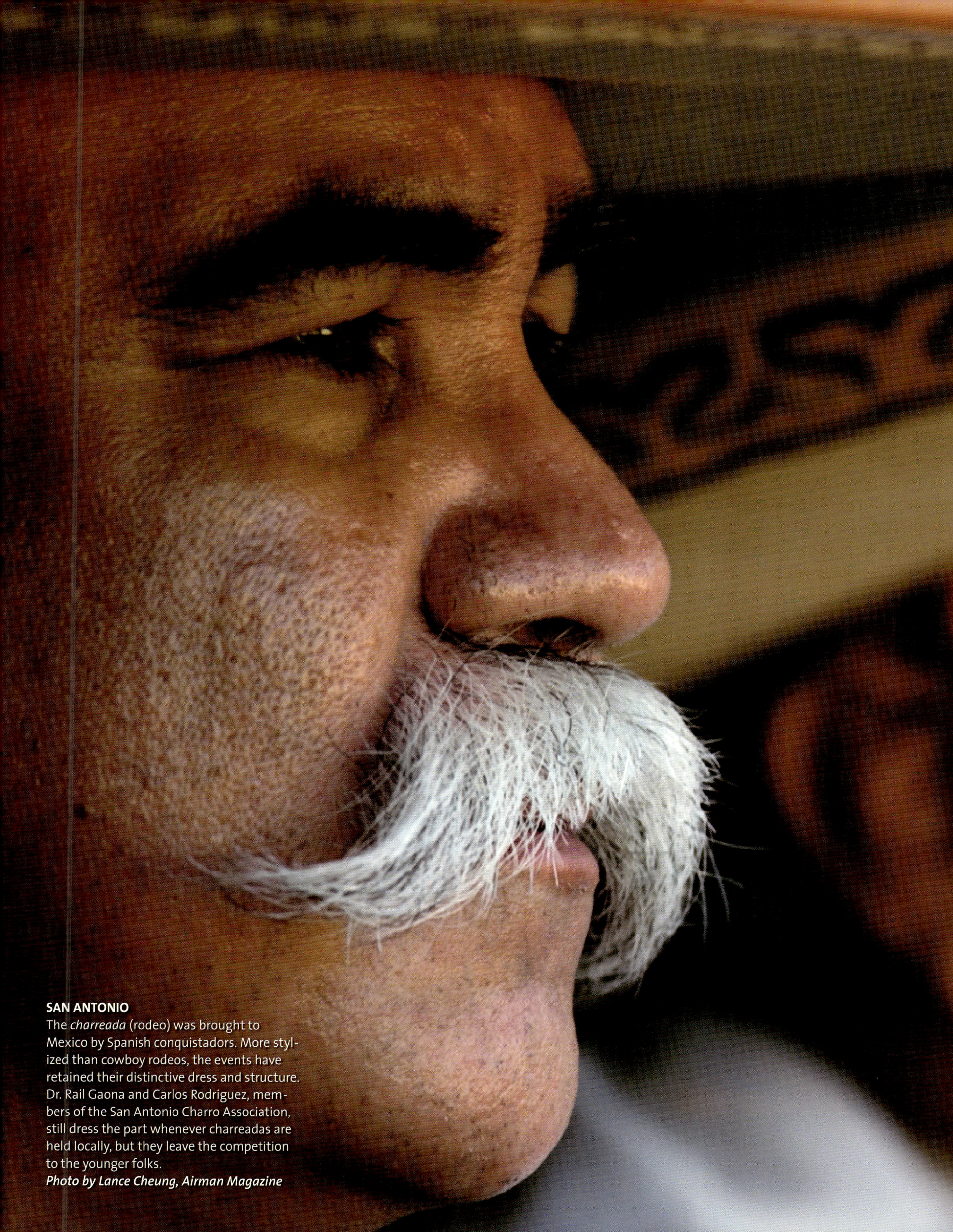

SAN ANTONIO
The *charreada* (rodeo) was brought to Mexico by Spanish conquistadors. More stylized than cowboy rodeos, the events have retained their distinctive dress and structure. Dr. Rail Gaona and Carlos Rodriguez, members of the San Antonio Charro Association, still dress the part whenever charreadas are held locally, but they leave the competition to the younger folks.
Photo by Lance Cheung, Airman Magazine

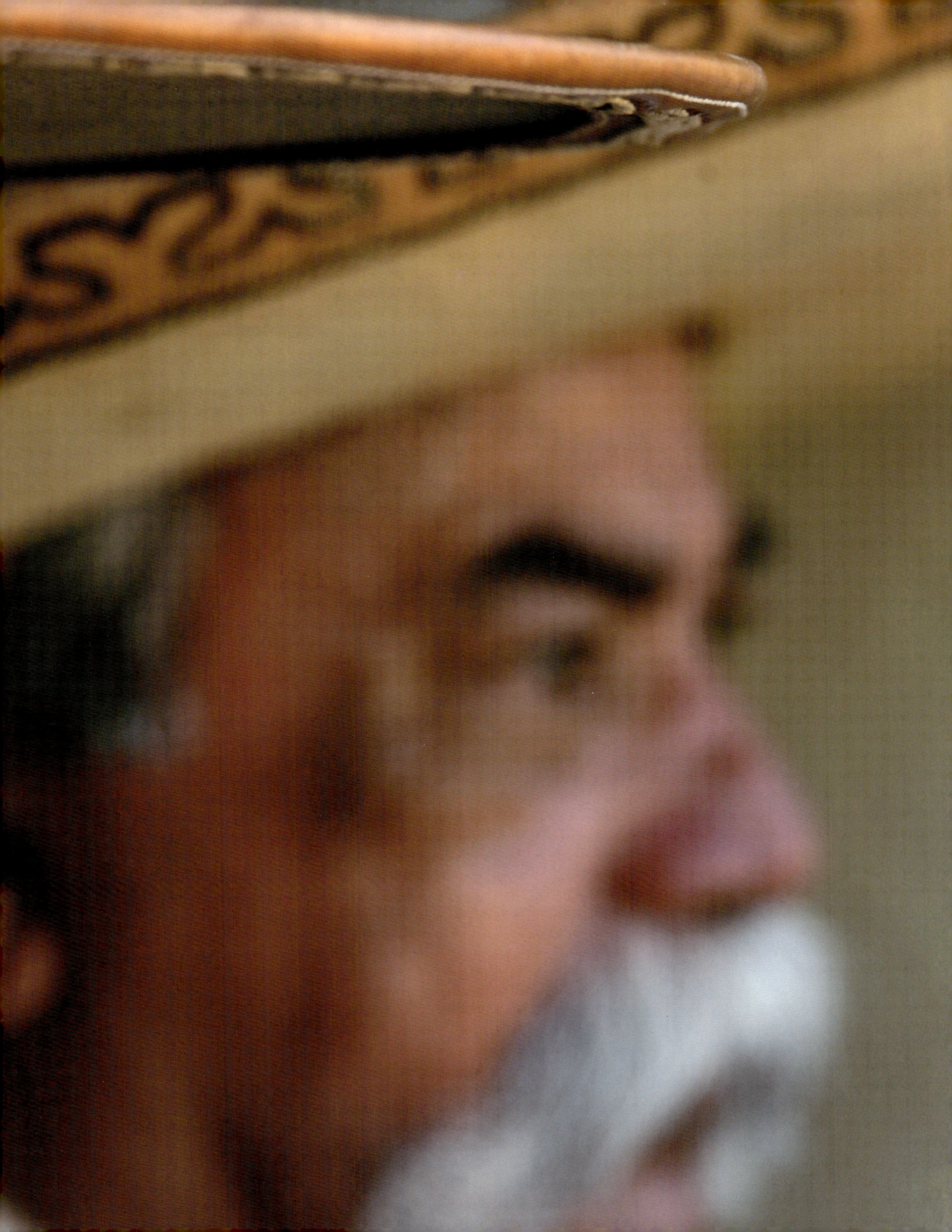

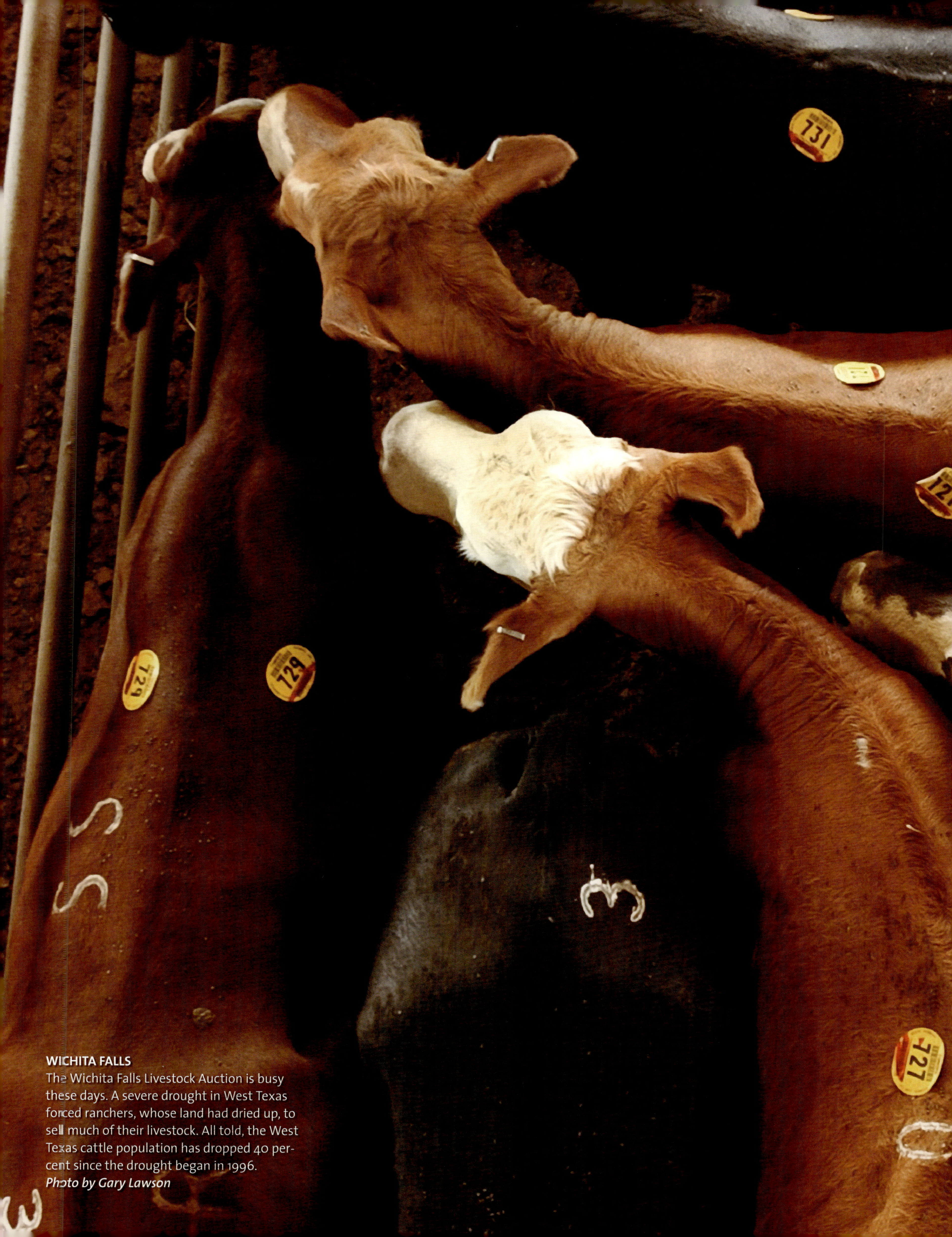

WICHITA FALLS
The Wichita Falls Livestock Auction is busy these days. A severe drought in West Texas forced ranchers, whose land had dried up, to sell much of their livestock. All told, the West Texas cattle population has dropped 40 percent since the drought began in 1996.
Photo by Gary Lawson

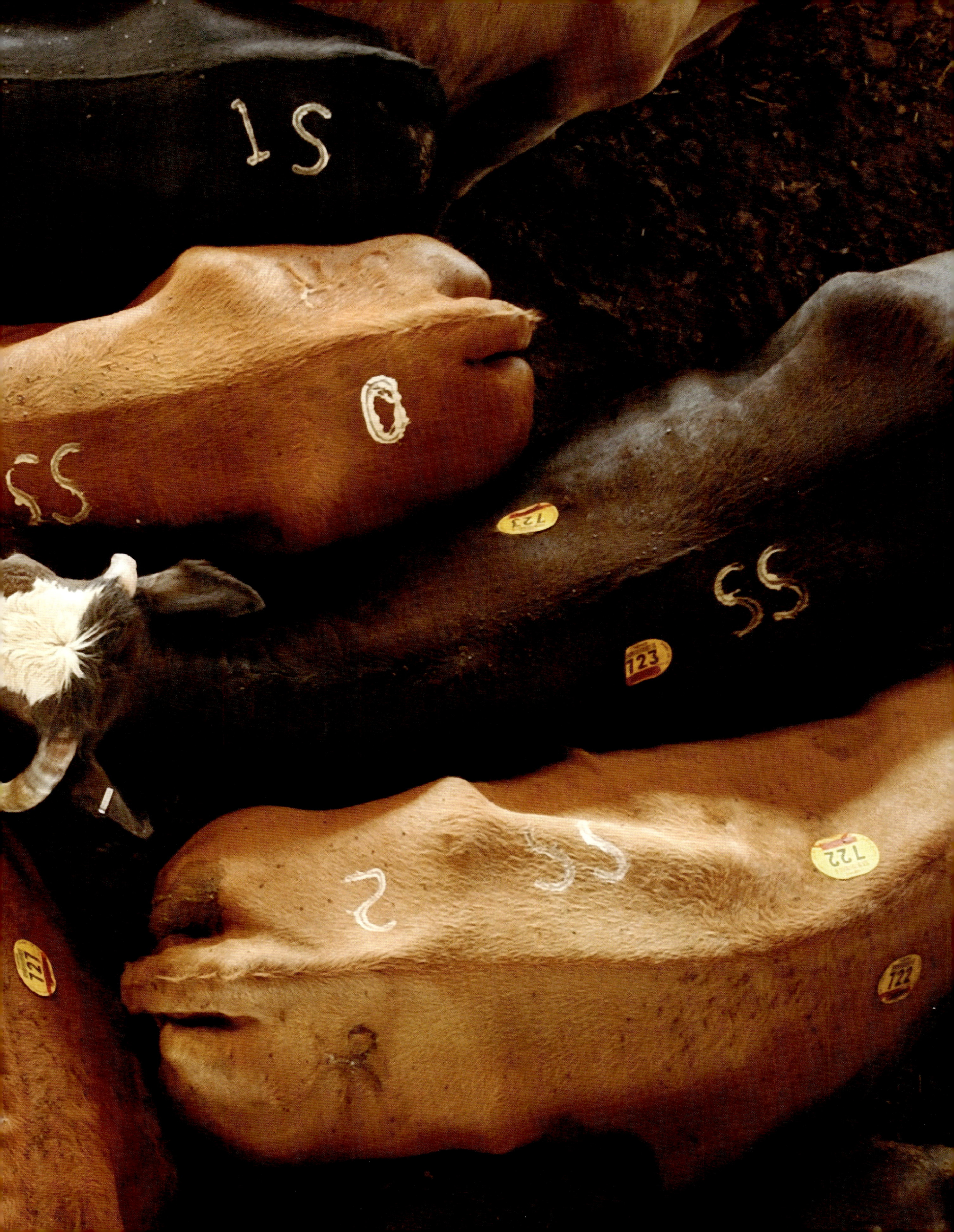
723
722
727

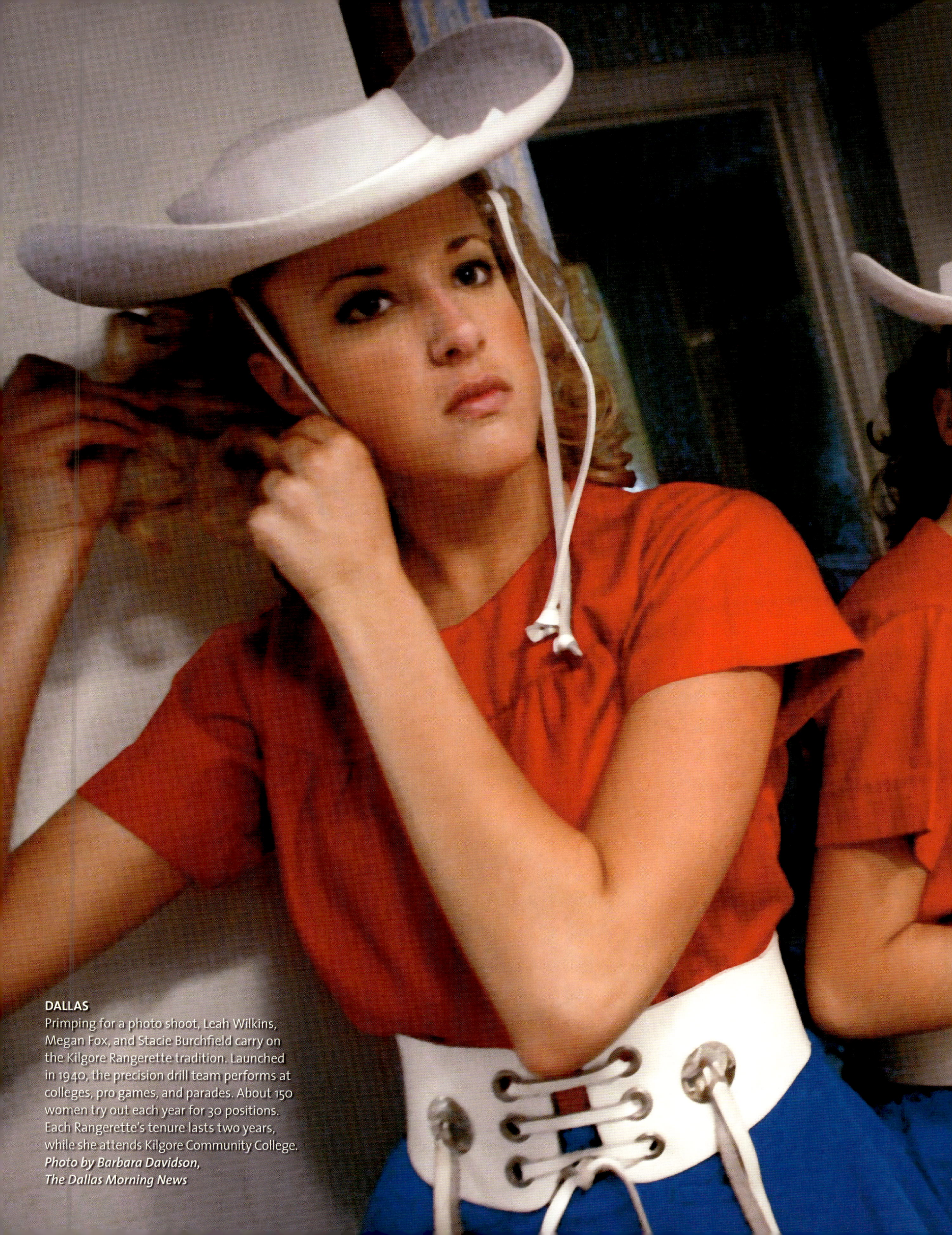

DALLAS
Primping for a photo shoot, Leah Wilkins, Megan Fox, and Stacie Burchfield carry on the Kilgore Rangerette tradition. Launched in 1940, the precision drill team performs at colleges, pro games, and parades. About 150 women try out each year for 30 positions. Each Rangerette's tenure lasts two years, while she attends Kilgore Community College.
Photo by Barbara Davidson, The Dallas Morning News

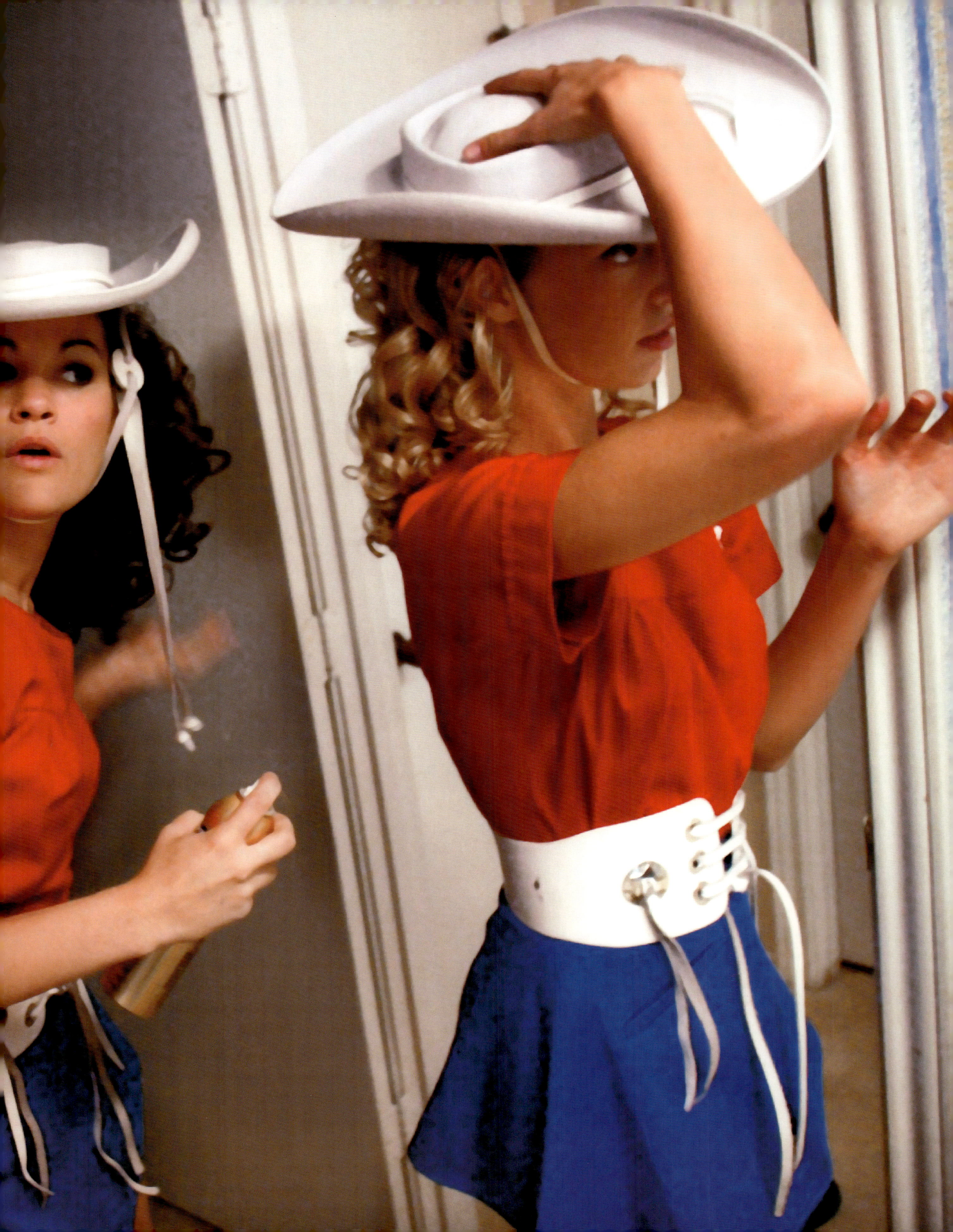

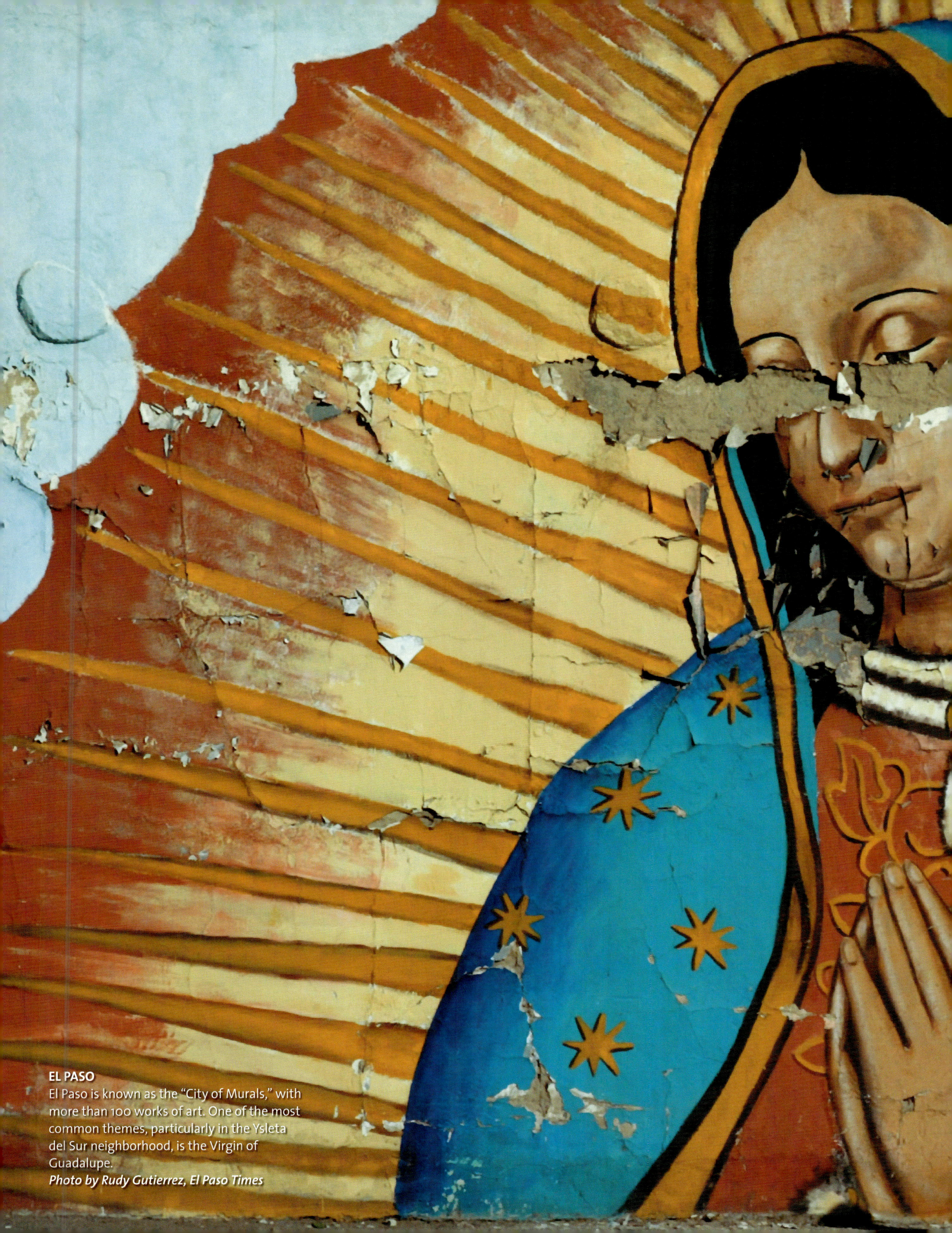

EL PASO
El Paso is known as the "City of Murals," with more than 100 works of art. One of the most common themes, particularly in the Ysleta del Sur neighborhood, is the Virgin of Guadalupe.
Photo by Rudy Gutierrez, El Paso Times

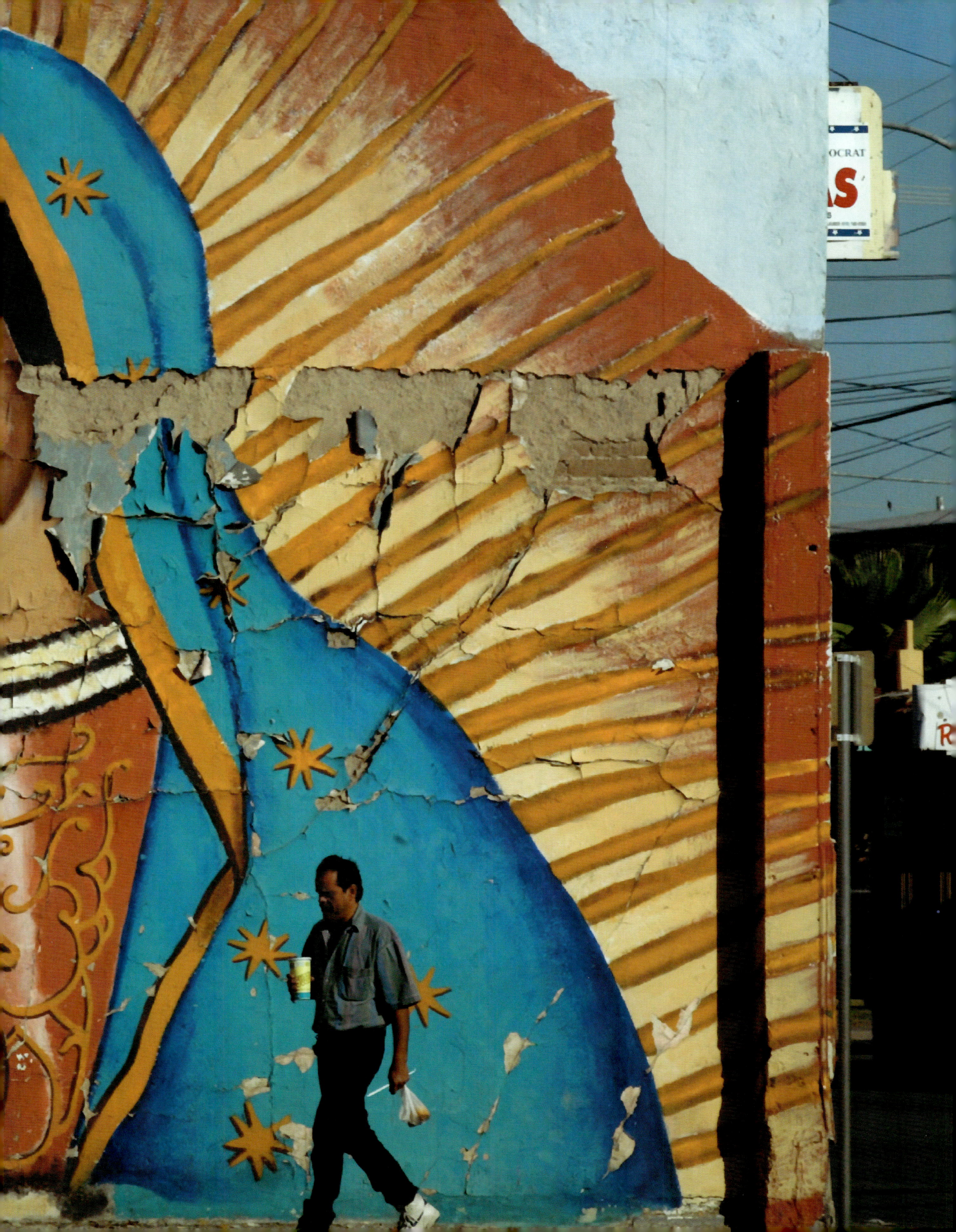

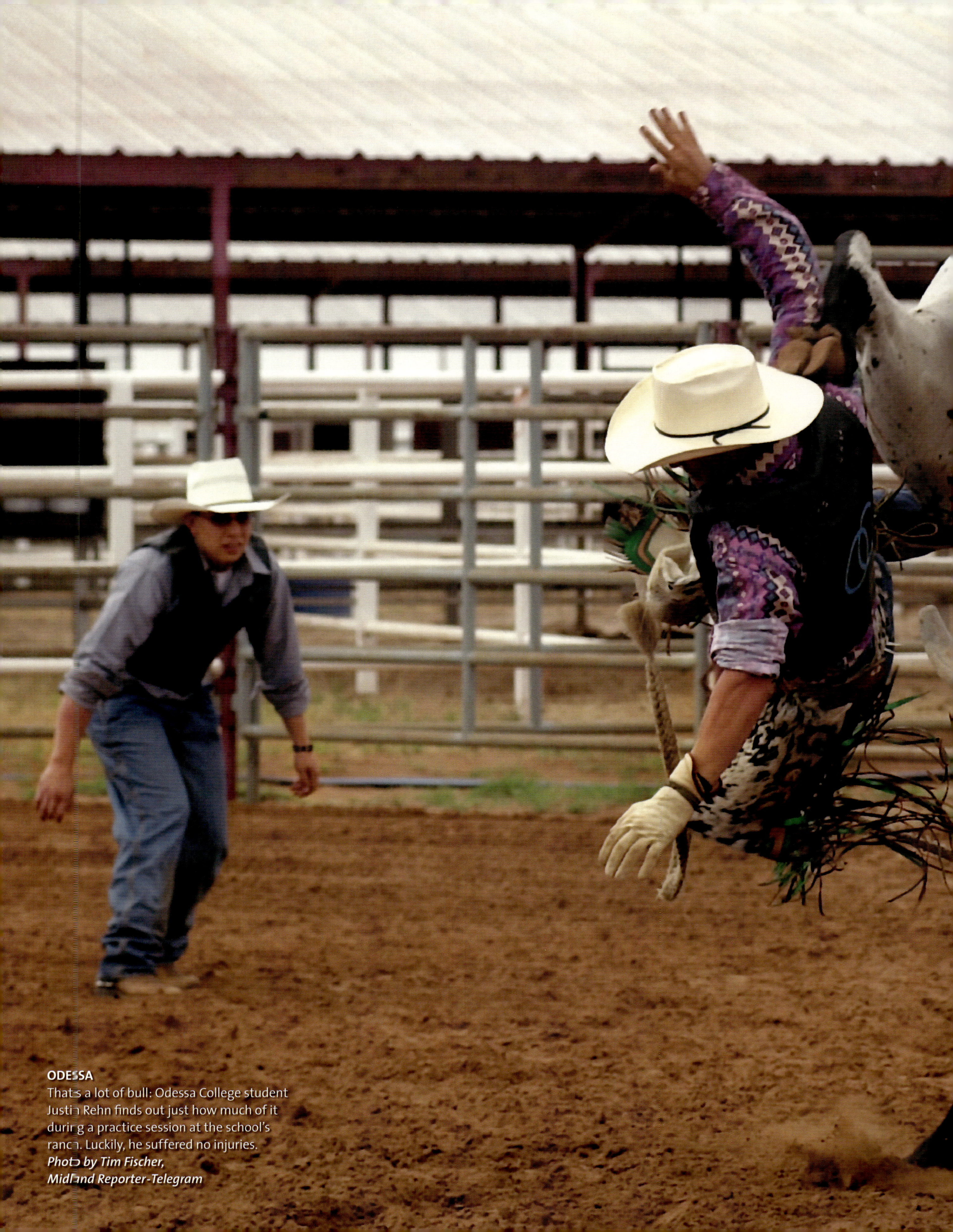

ODESSA
That's a lot of bull: Odessa College student Justin Rehn finds out just how much of it during a practice session at the school's ranch. Luckily, he suffered no injuries.
Photo by Tim Fischer, Midland Reporter-Telegram

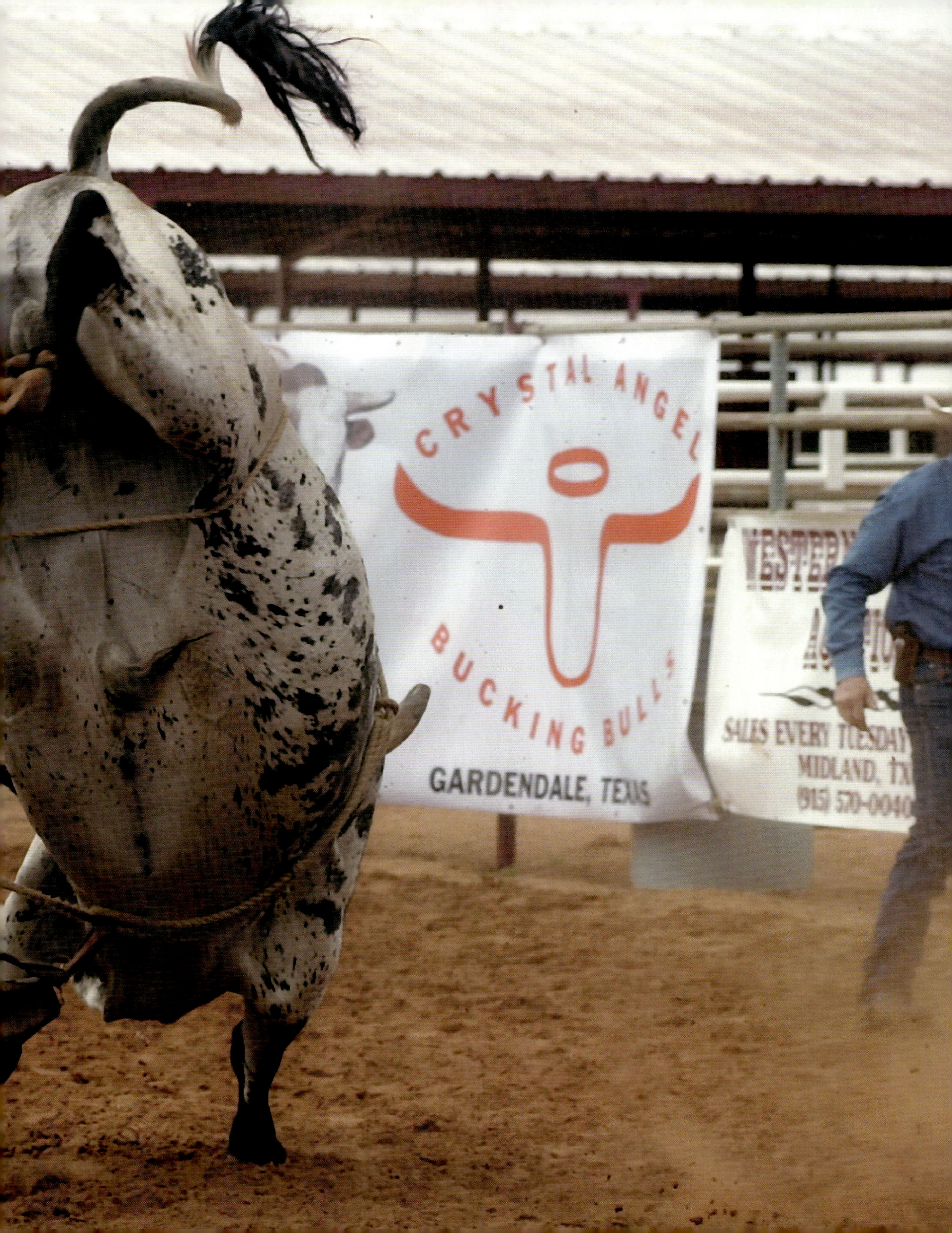
CRYSTAL ANGEL
BUCKING BULLS
GARDENDALE, TEXAS
SALES EVERY TUESDAY
MIDLAND, TX
(915) 570-0040

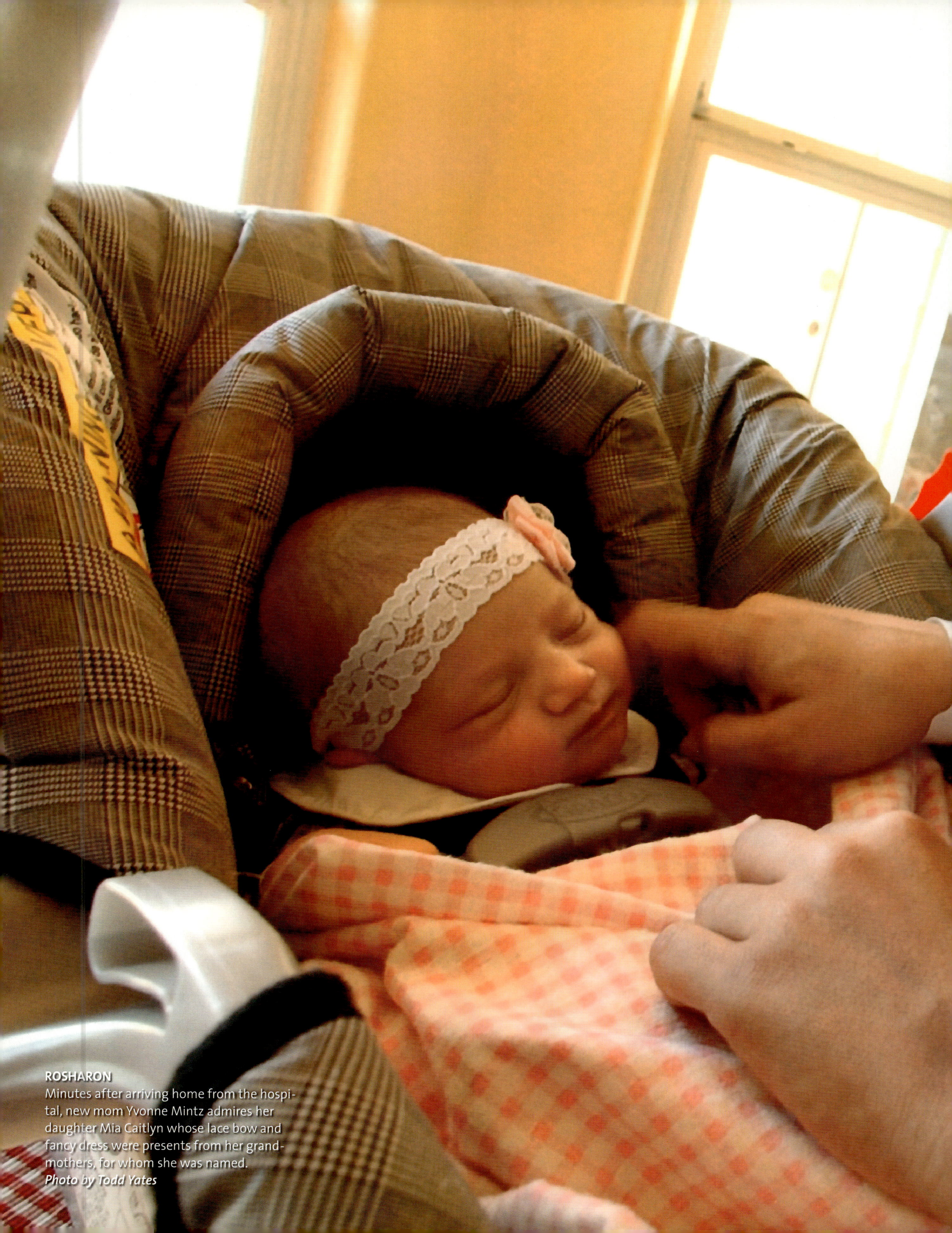

ROSHARON
Minutes after arriving home from the hospital, new mom Yvonne Mintz admires her daughter Mia Caitlyn whose lace bow and fancy dress were presents from her grandmothers, for whom she was named.
Photo by Todd Yates

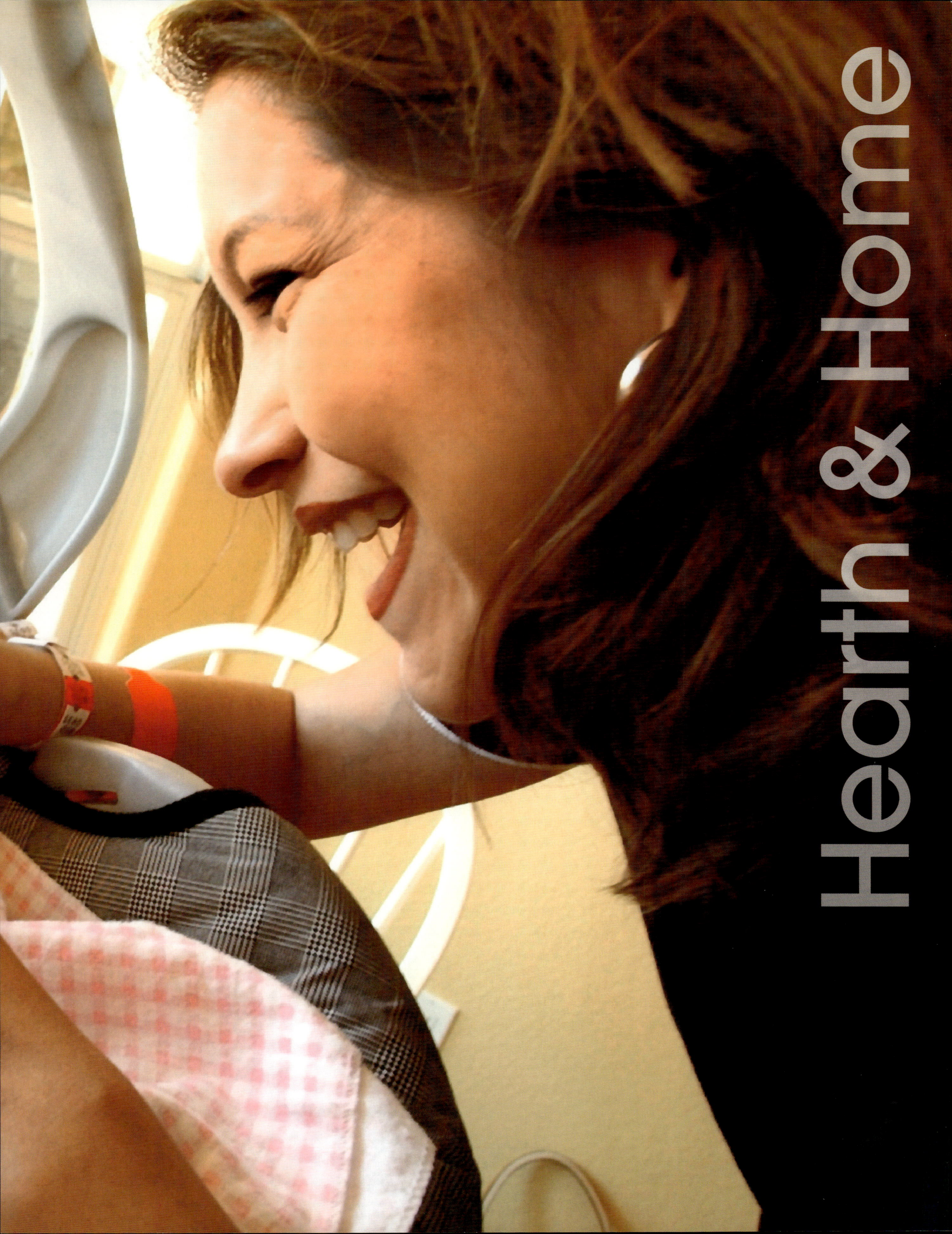
Hearth & Home

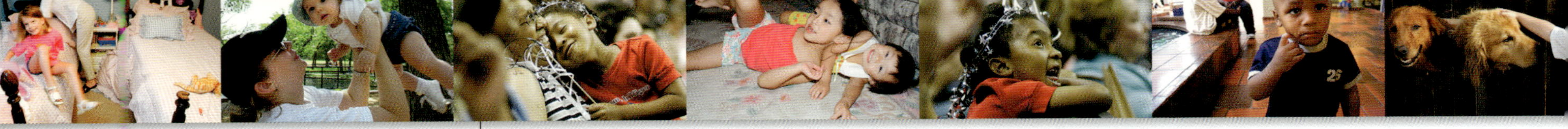

SAN ANTONIO
Girl's night out: Sandra and Dominique Preyor-Johnson snuggle during a WNBA game between the San Antonio Silver Stars and the Los Angeles Sparks at the SBC Center.
Photo by Alicia Wagner Calzada

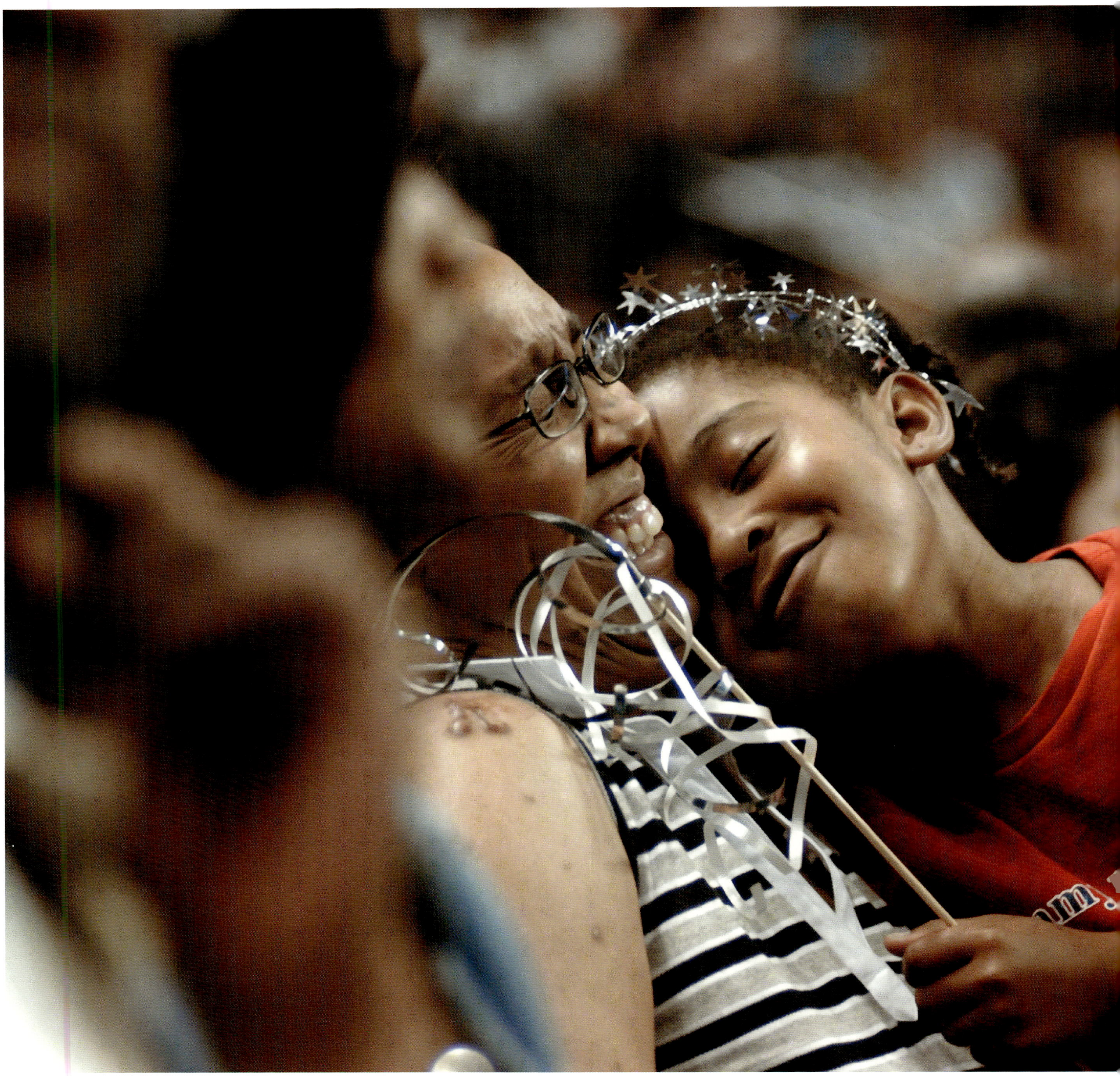

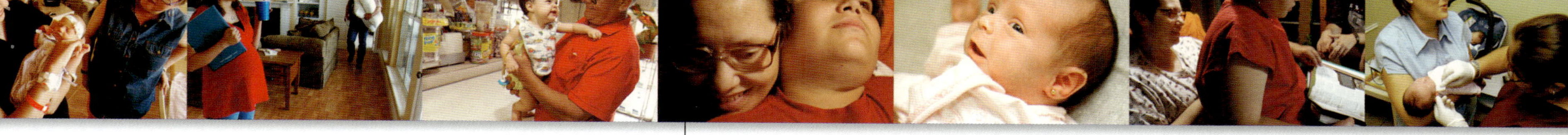

ABILENE
Maryanne Martin, who has been fighting ovarian cancer for five years, received a transplant of her own stem cells in 2000. While not a cure, the treatment helped jump-start her immune system, giving her more time with her family. "If I can get him raised, I'll be happy," says Martin of her youngest son Jonathan, 14.
Photo by Ronald W. Erdrich, Abilene Reporter-News

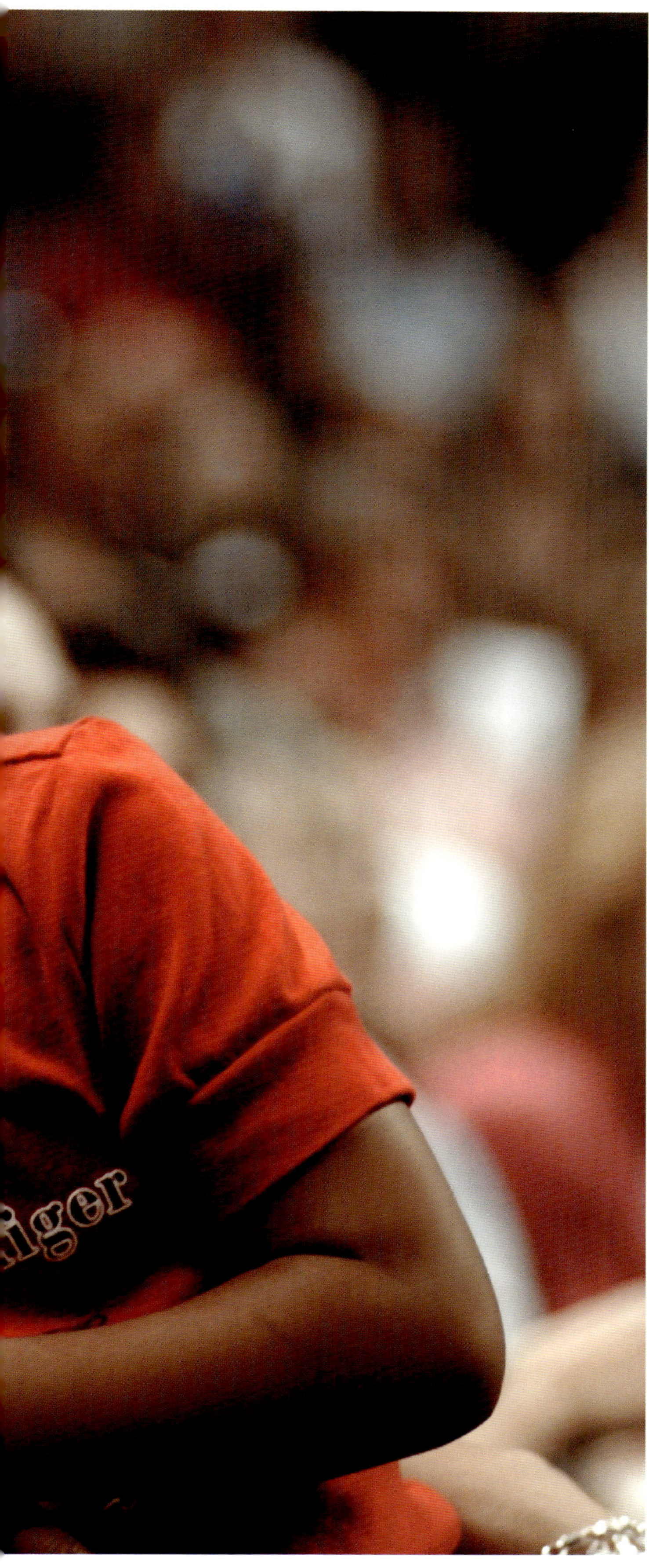

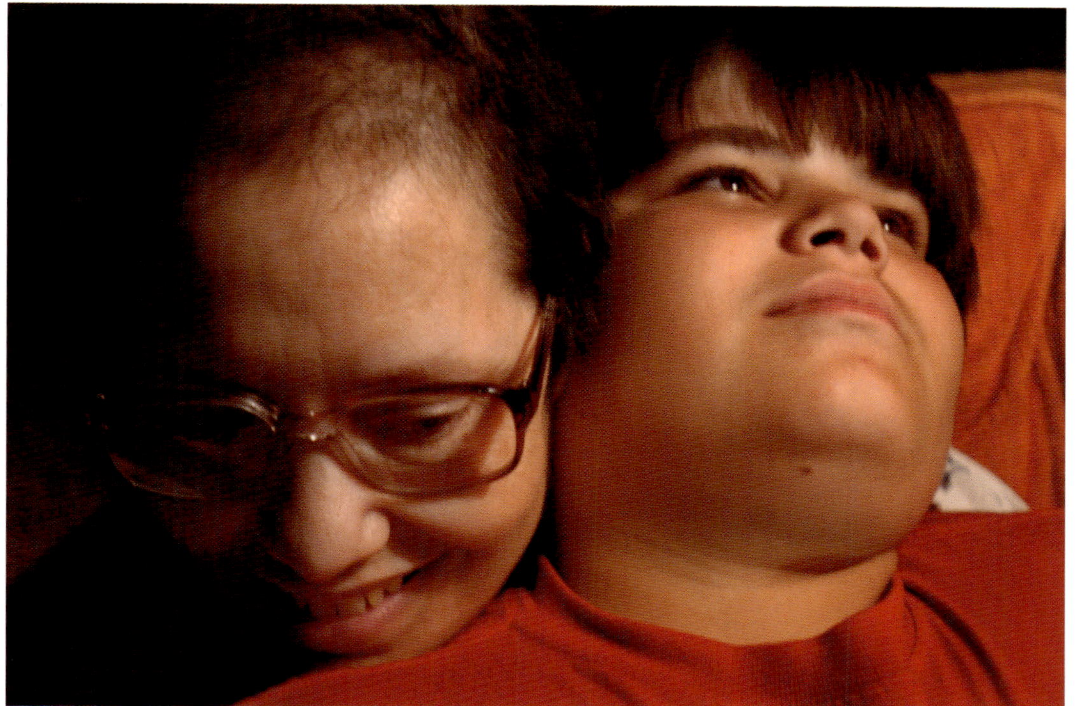

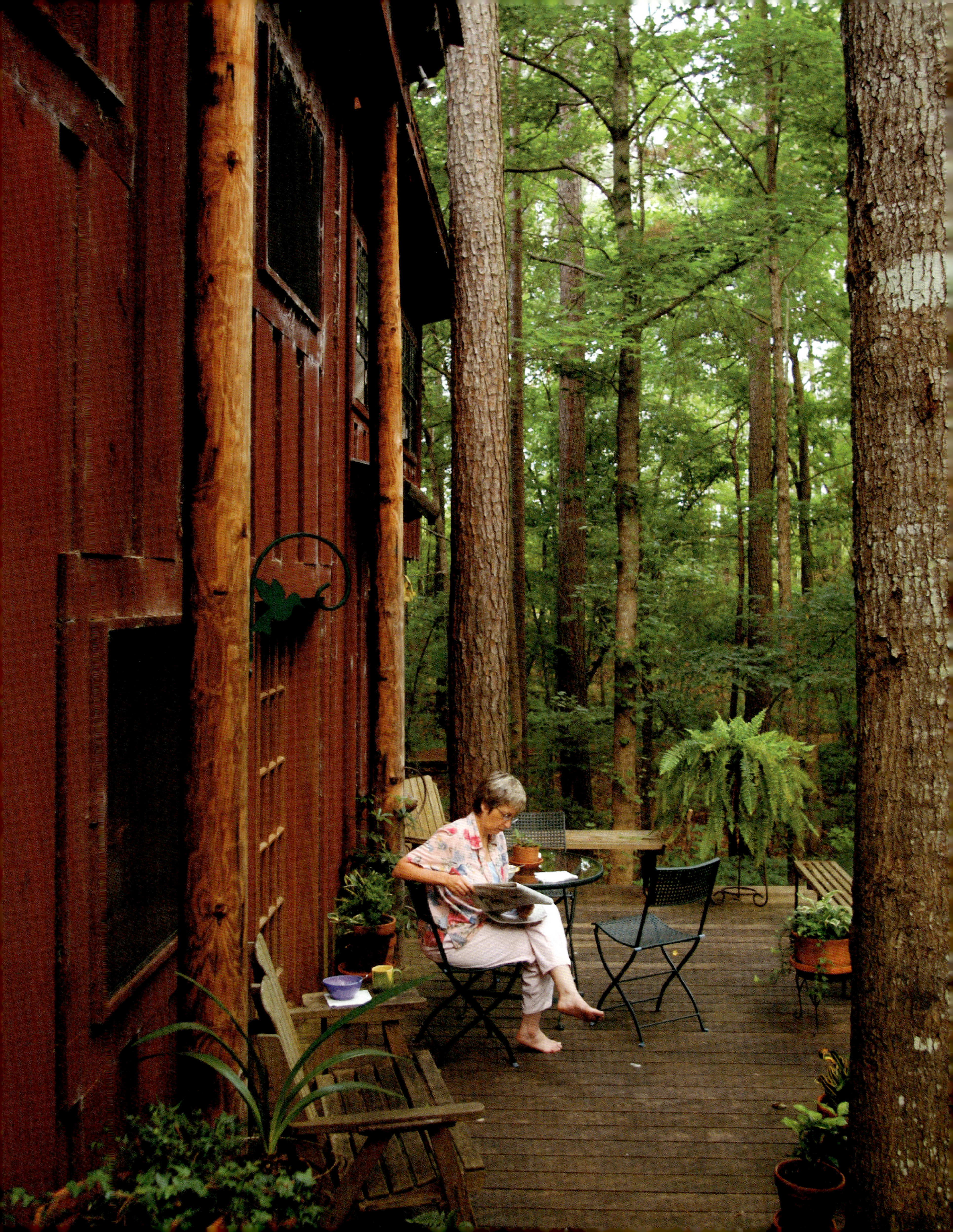

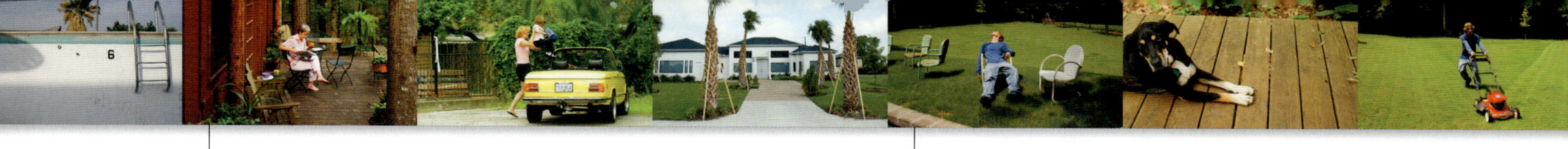

NACOGDOCHES
Before heading to work, Becky Mayo reads the morning paper on her back porch, surrounded by loblolly pines. Mayo is a lecturer at the School of Social Work at Stephen F. Austin State University.
Photos by Scogin Mayo

DALLAS
One mow time: Nathanael Mayo is in charge of keeping the lawn at his family's Oak Cliff residence looking tidy. The teenager kicks back after mowing the half-acre plot.

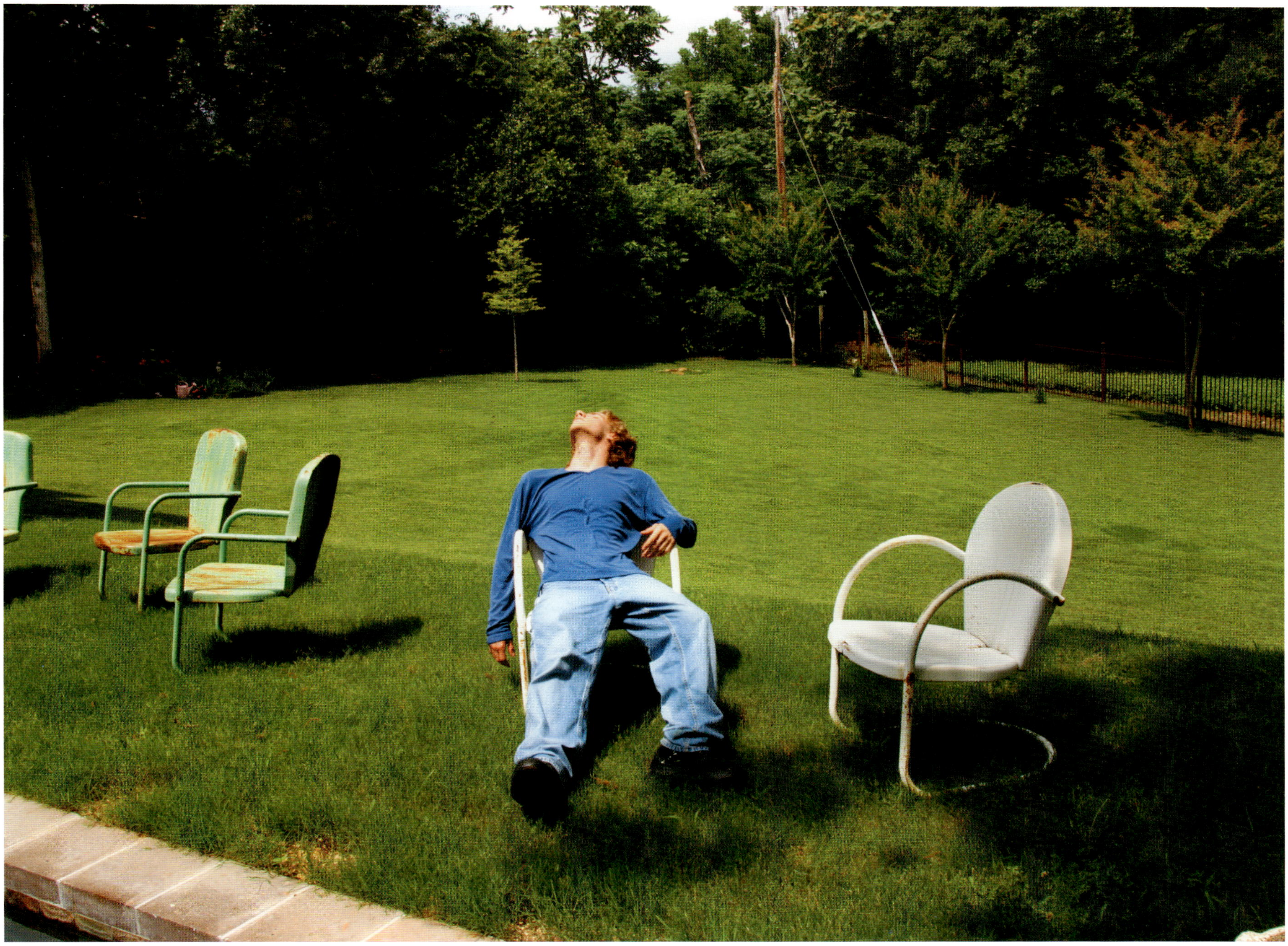

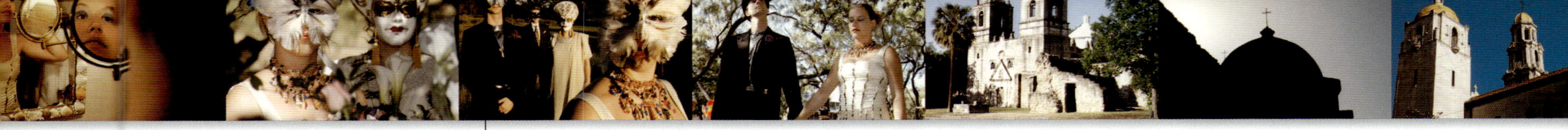

MARBLE FALLS
"I had a dream about the wedding and everyone was wearing masks," says Gwen Strickland (right), explaining her masquerade-theme wedding. Strickland held evening craft parties in the weeks before the ceremony where family and friends could make their masks. Stickland's mask is a butterfly. Husband Tom Kiehne (left) fashioned his from plaster and silver paint.
Photo by Steven Noreyko

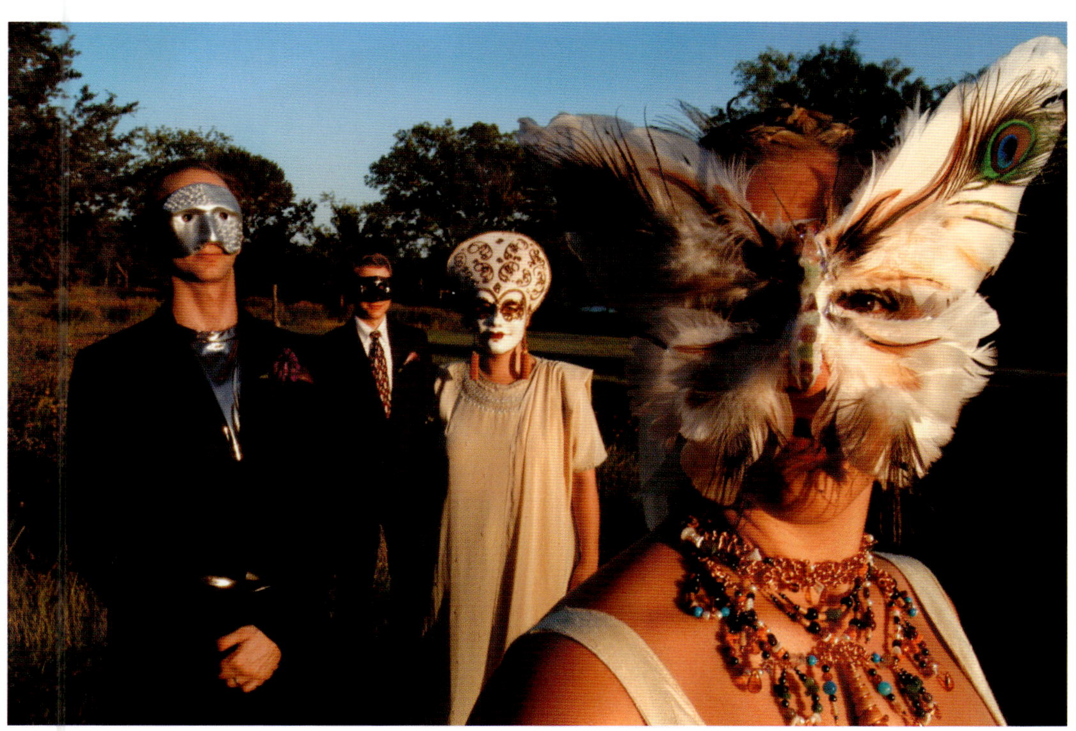

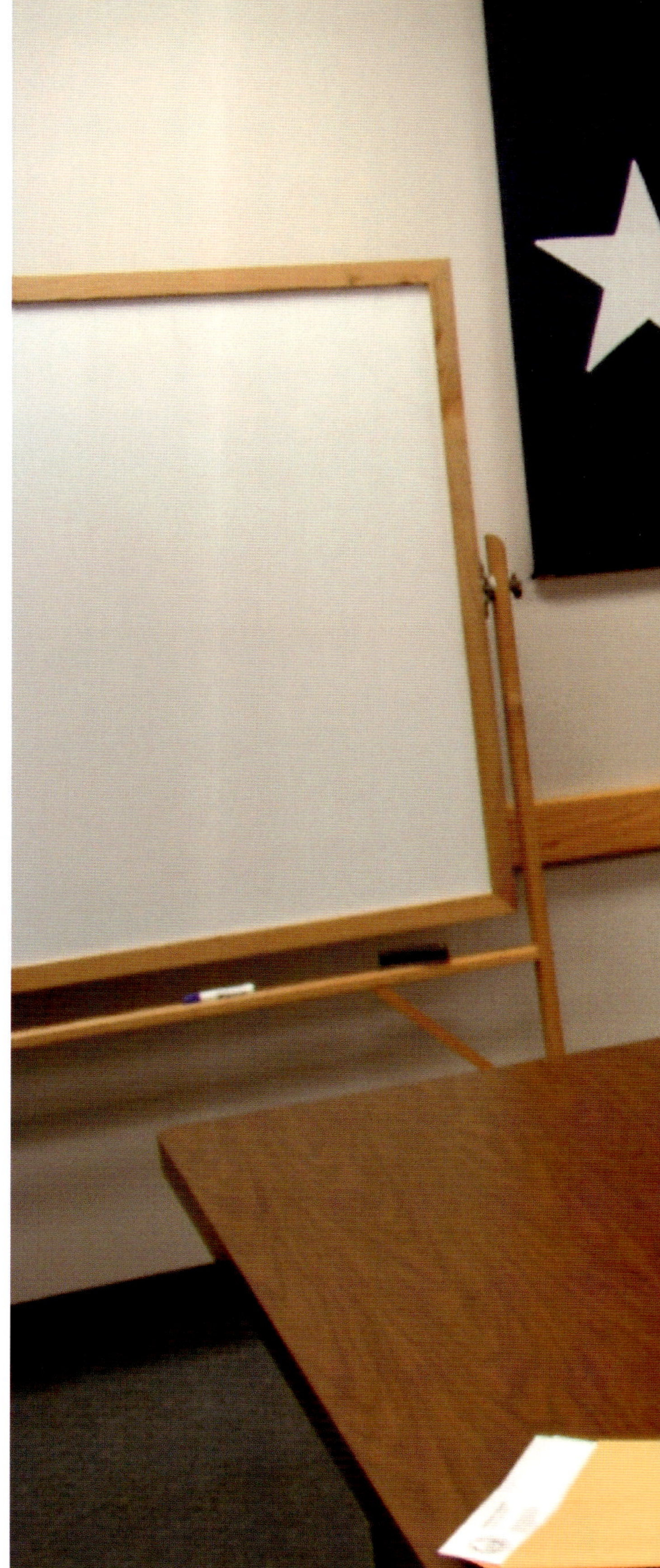

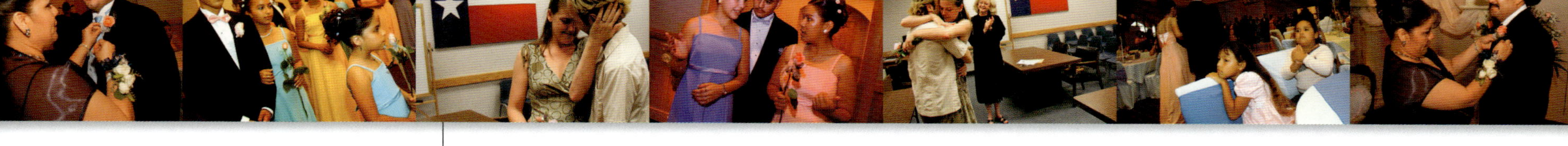

AUSTIN
In March of 2002, Tamara Trent, a Texas native and jewelry maker, met Carles Zanetti, a drummer from Genoa, Italy, at the SXSW music festival in Austin. She spoke no Italian and he was just learning English, but she saw something in his eyes that went beyond words. Fourteen months later, they embrace before their wedding.
Photo by Penny De Los Santos, National Geographic, Freelance

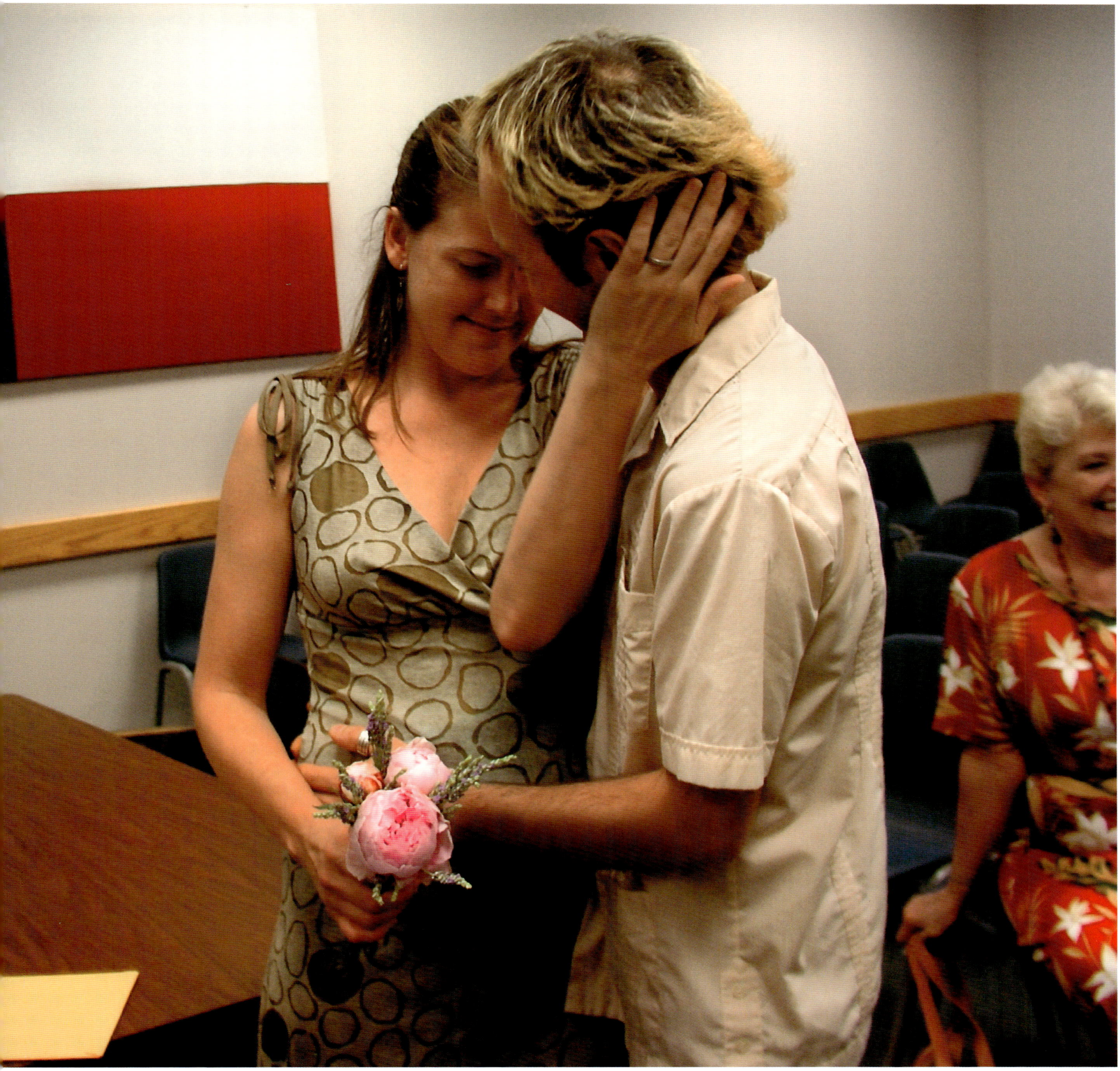

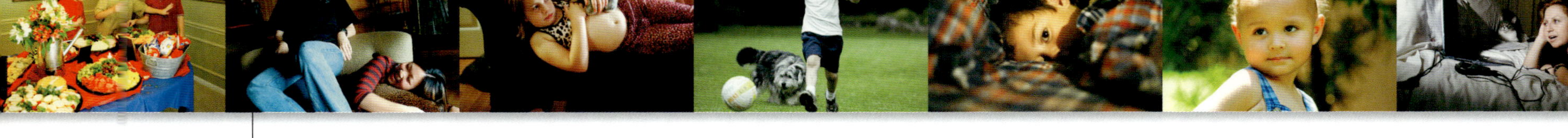

RICHARDSON
Although recent graduate Joyuan Kao and her sister, freshman Jolene, both attended UT Austin for a semester, their busy schedules as radio/TV/film and fashion design majors respectively did not give them much time to see each other. Now home for the summer, they spend endless hours catching up.
Photo by B'Lan Kao

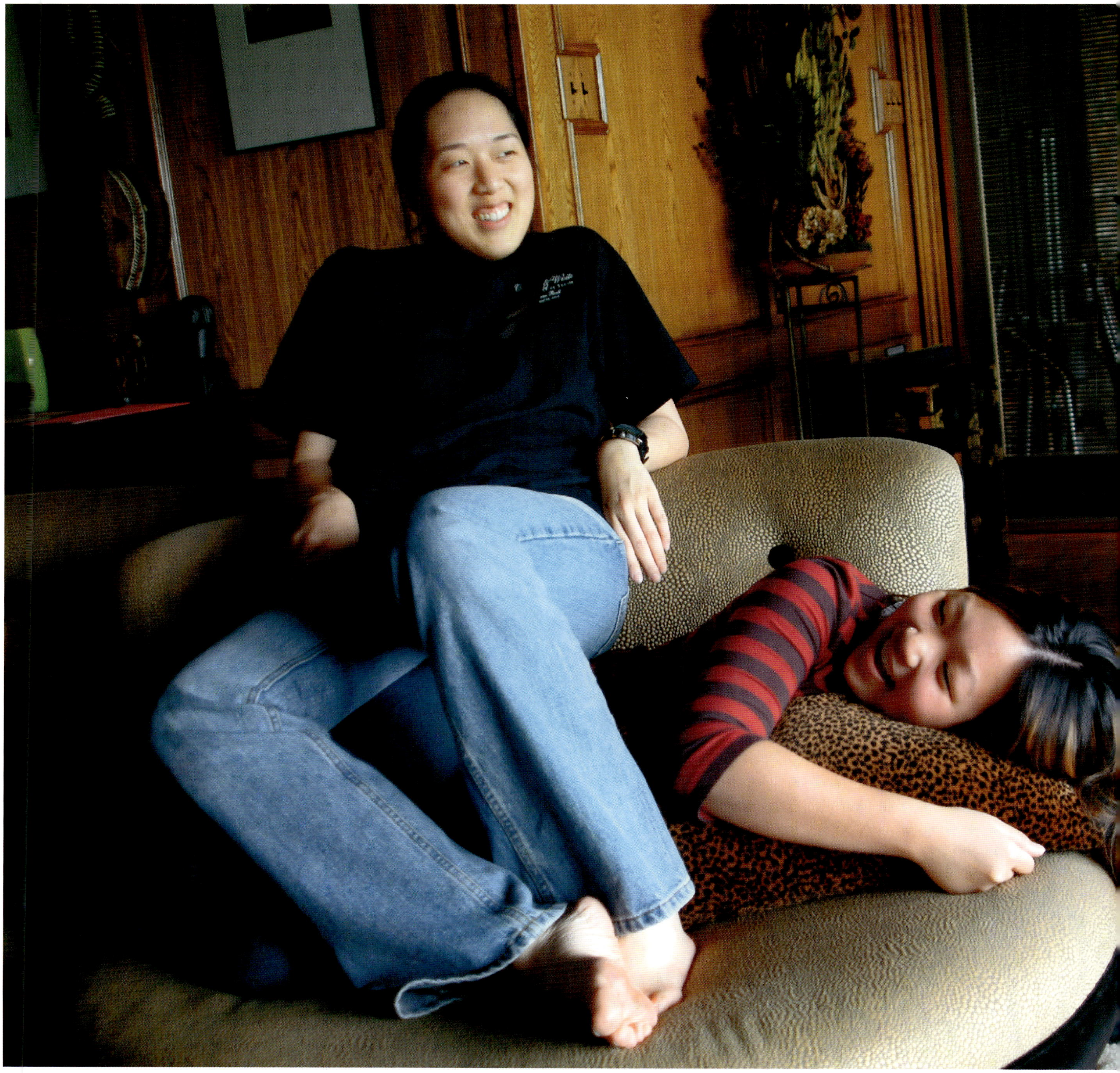

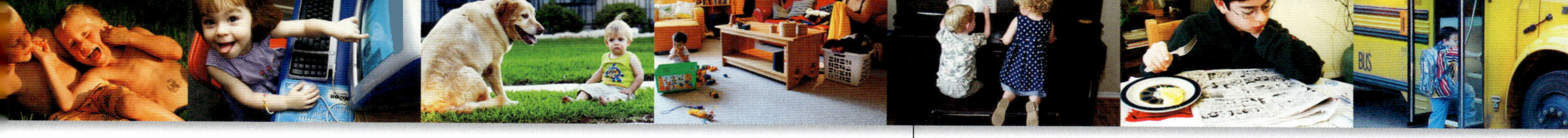

DALLAS
Ben Hurley, 3, chooses to "play" piano with Cadyn LaBounty rather than hang with the other kids who are outside on the bouncy.
Photo by Danny Hurley

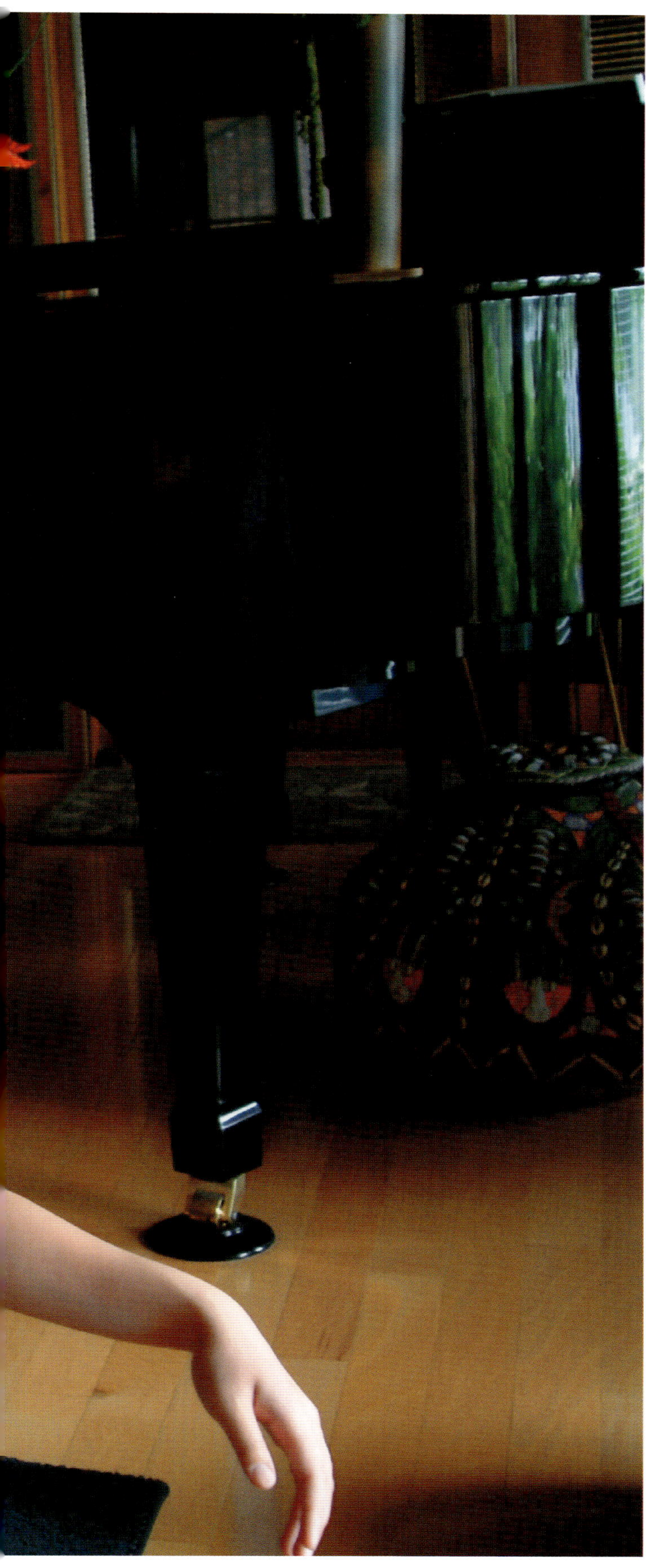

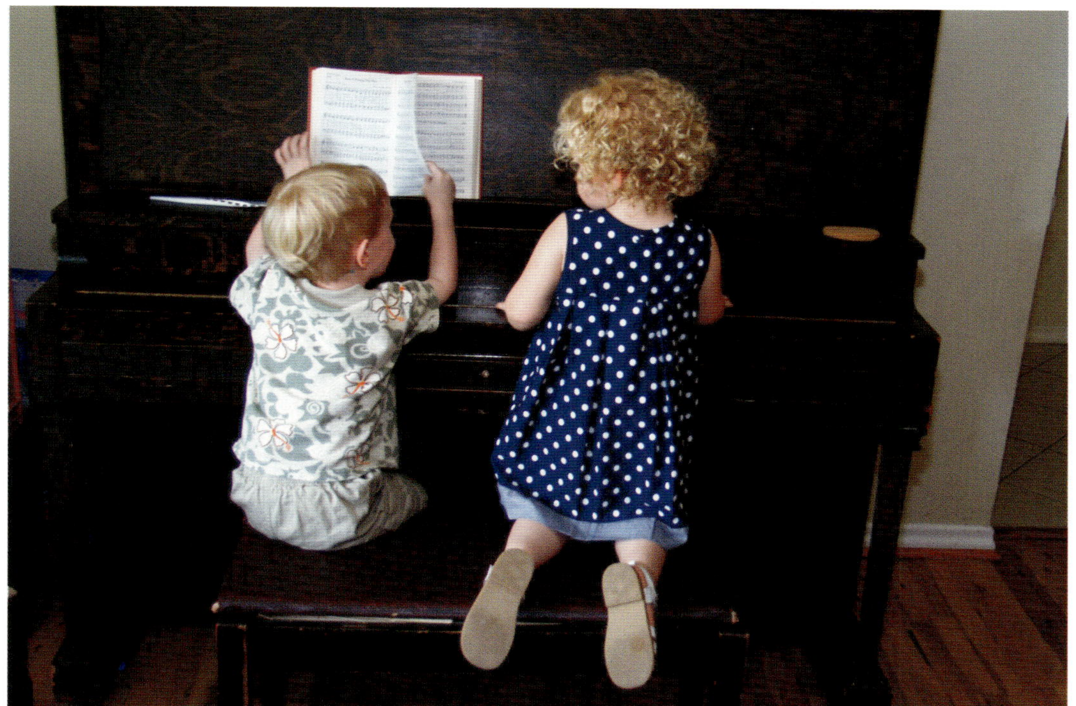

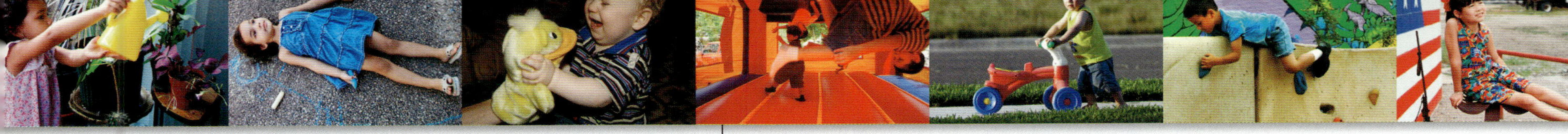

KYLE
Amateur acrobats Marcos Reyna, Alan Ruiz, and Joe Ryan Gomez practice their flips in an inflatable fun house rented for their friend Alejandro's birthday.
Photos by Rodolfo Gonzalez

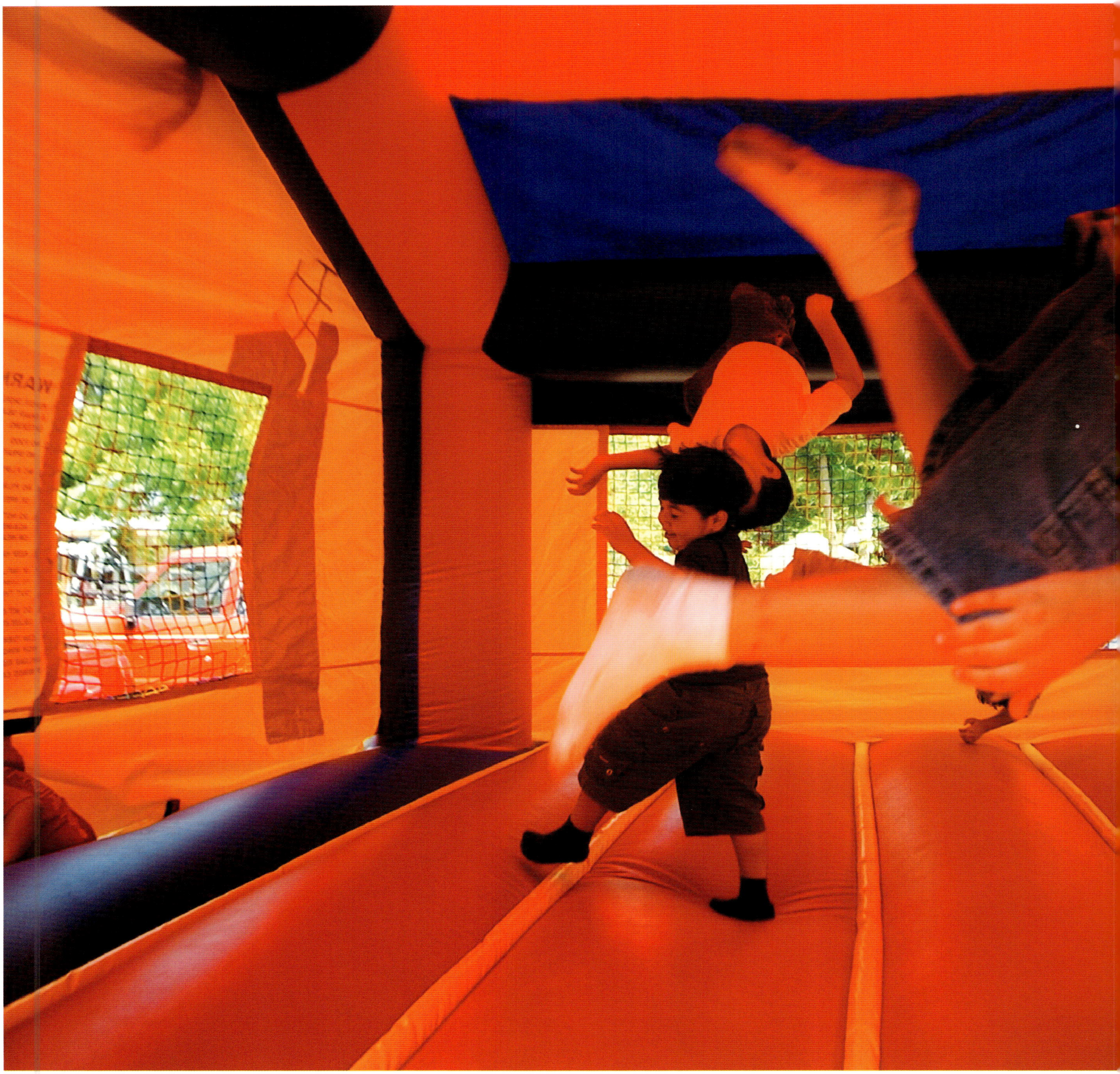

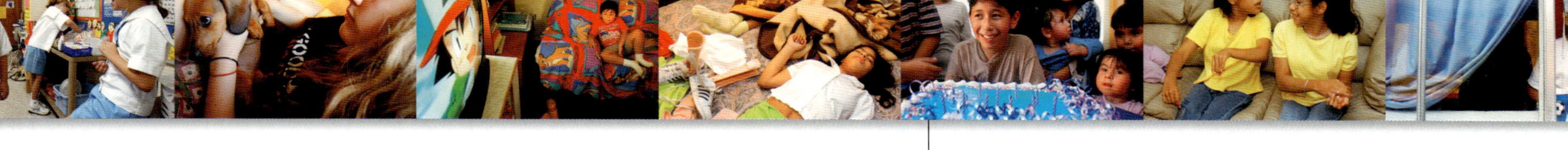

KYLE

Alejandro Beltran (center) beams after blowing out his candles at the start of his 11th year. The birthday boy, whose family emigrated from Mexico four years ago, is surrounded by friends and relatives—Joe Ryan Gomez, Alan Ruiz, Maria José Beltran, Isabel Martínez, Brandy Morales, Marcos Reyna, and Angel Gustavo.

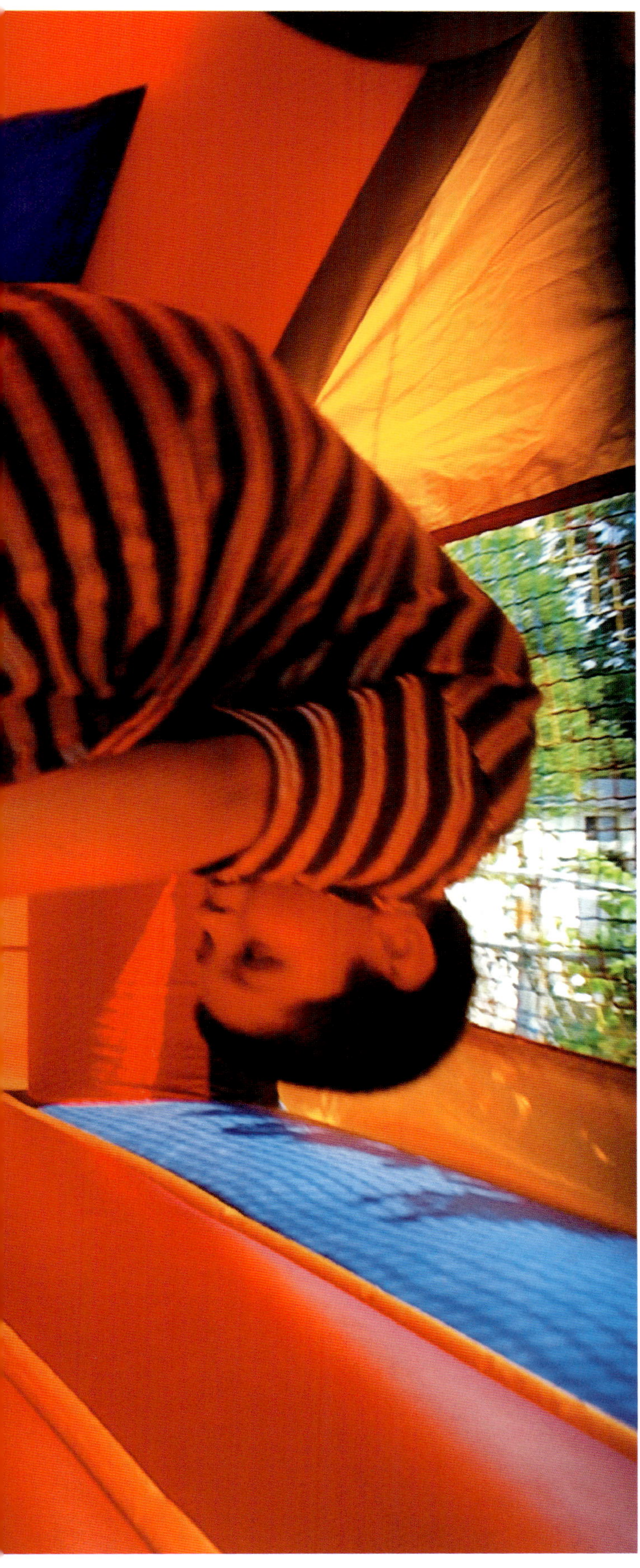

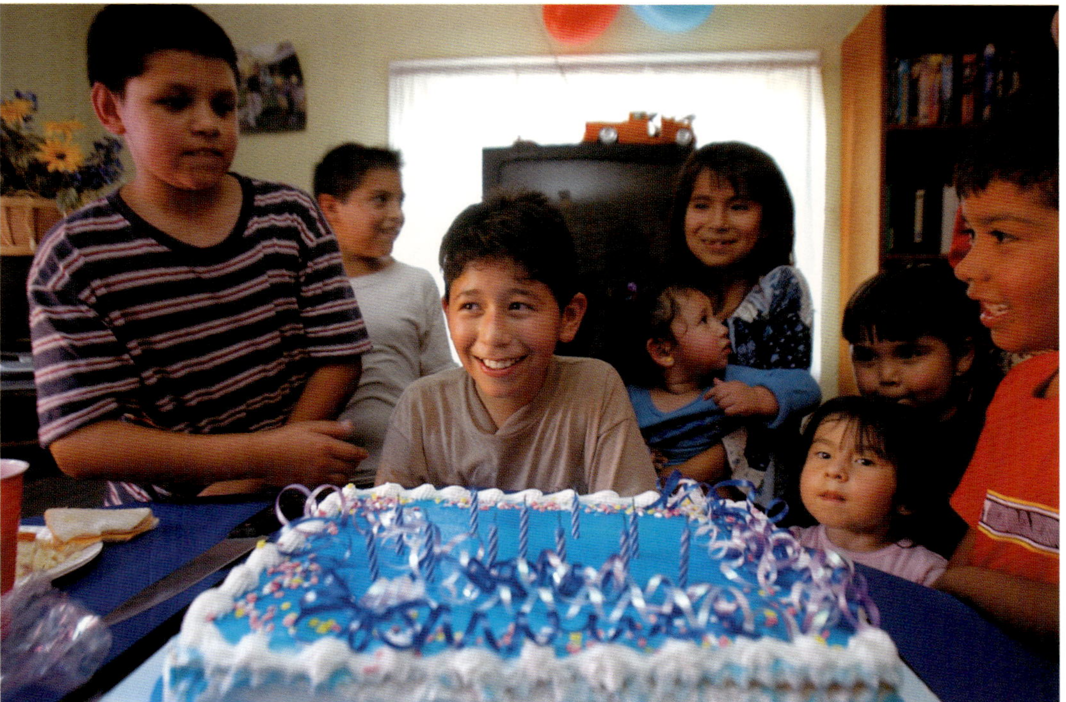

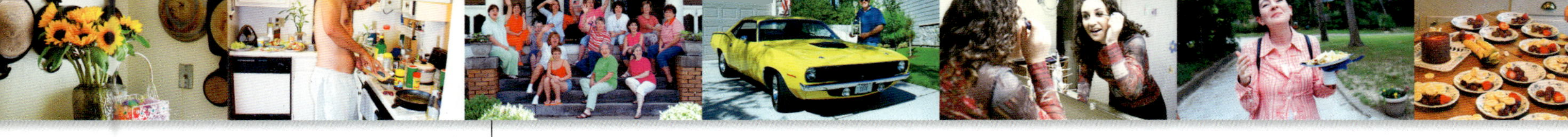

GRANBURY
The sleepy town of Granbury, 30 miles southwest of Fort Worth, wakes up with a bang on Fridays: Tourists arrive in droves to check out the historic town square with its 19th-century buildings. They stay at quaint bed-and-breakfasts like the Iron Horse Inn, which is home this weekend to a group of teachers from Whitehouse, Texas.
Photo by John Ater, www.johnater.com

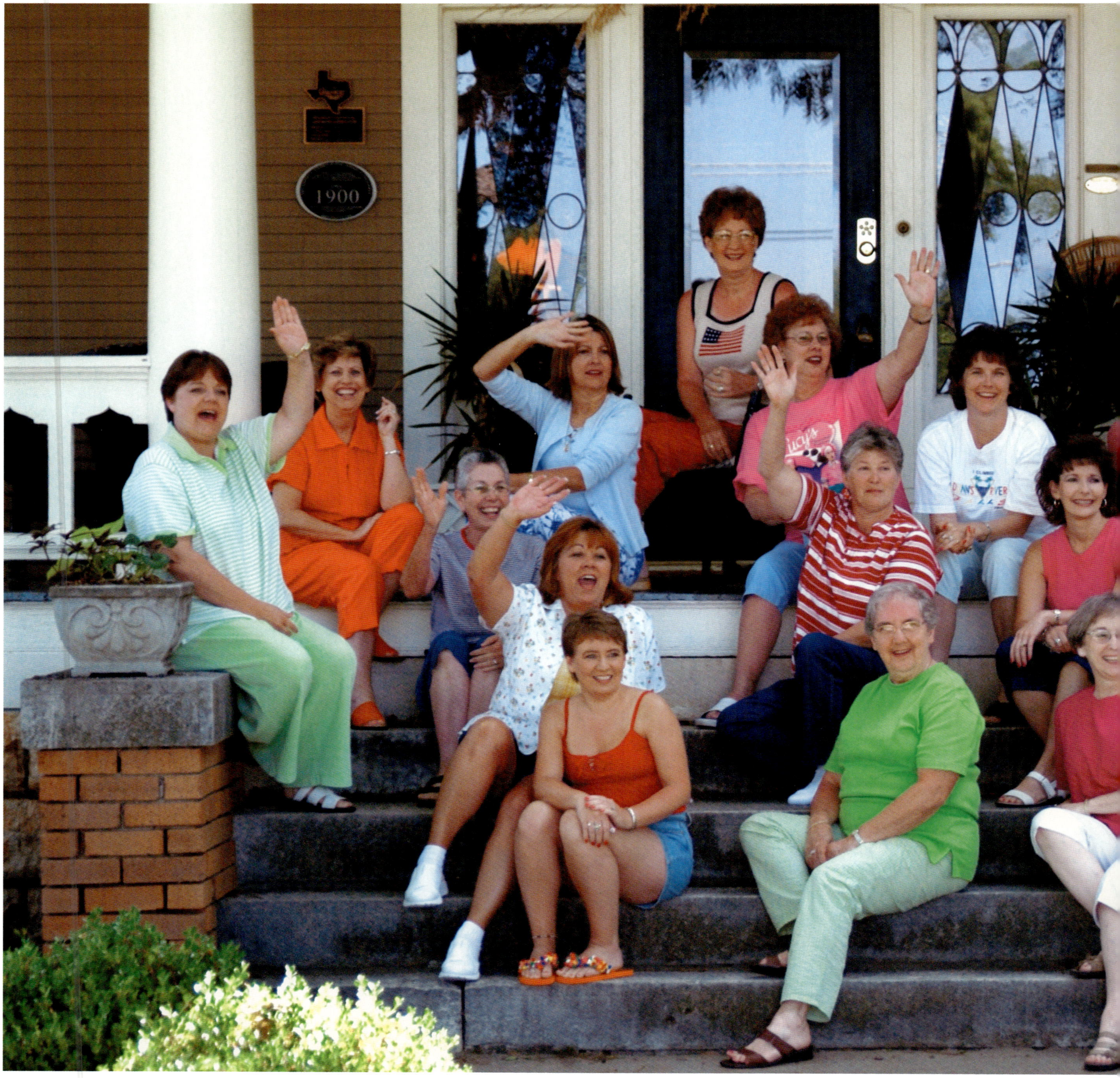

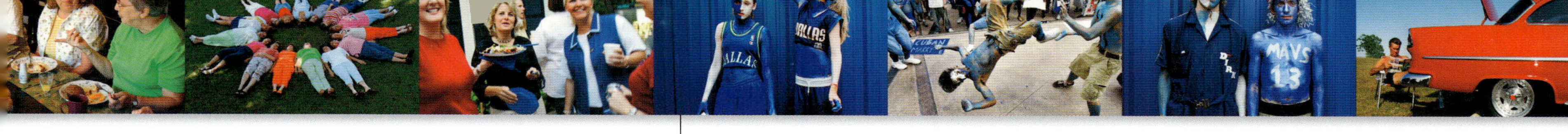

DALLAS
True blue: Dallas Mavericks superfans Morgan Ream, 14, and Audra May, 13, make a colorful attempt to win tickets to an upcoming play-off game. The duo competed against other Mavericks zealots in a pregame contest at the American Airlines Center (where the Mavs take it to the hoop) and won.
Photo by Barbara Davidson, The Dallas Morning News

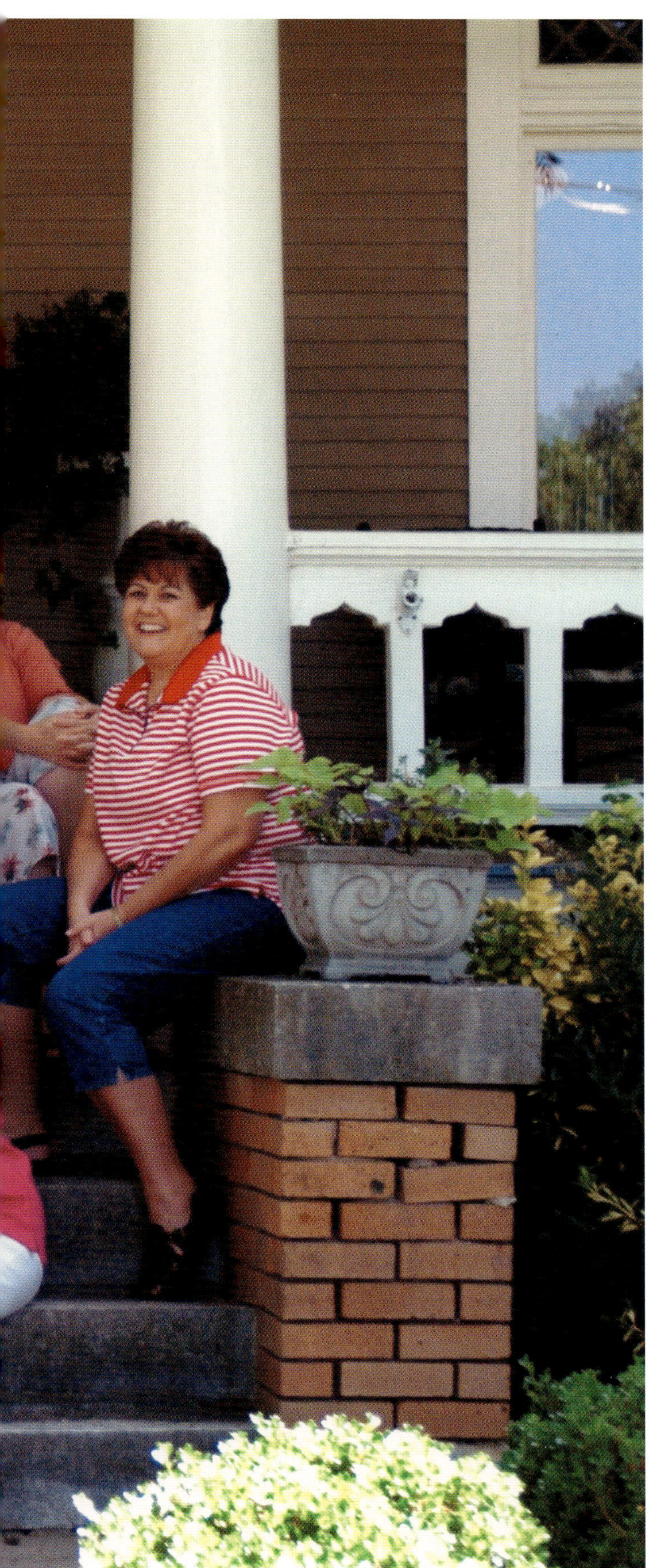

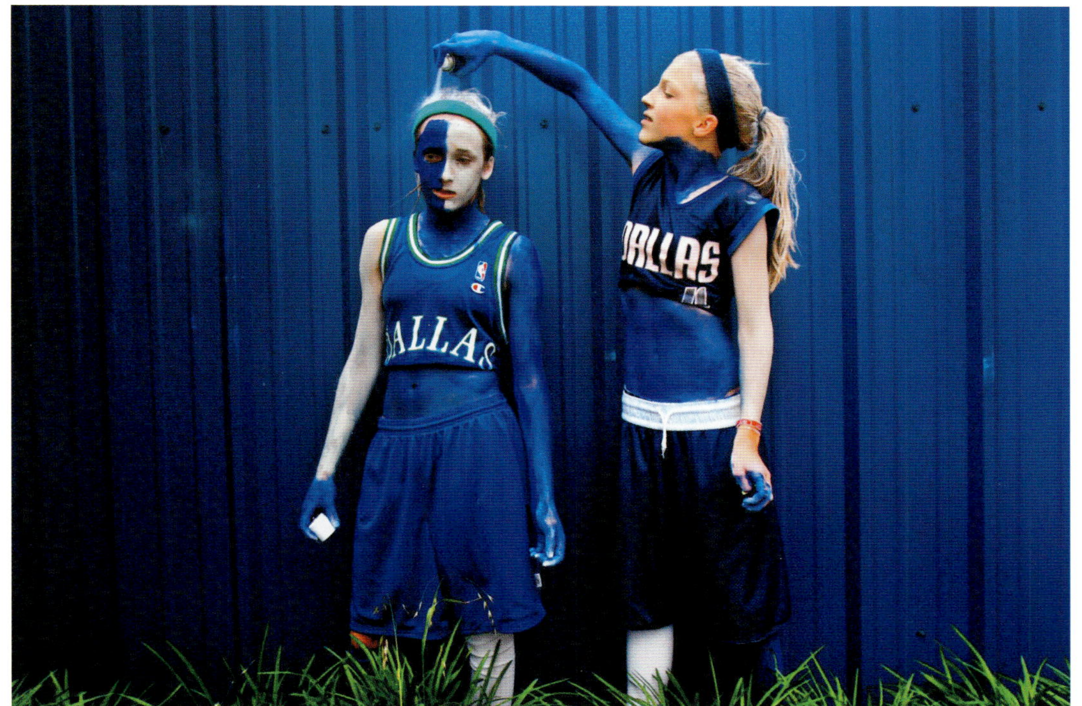

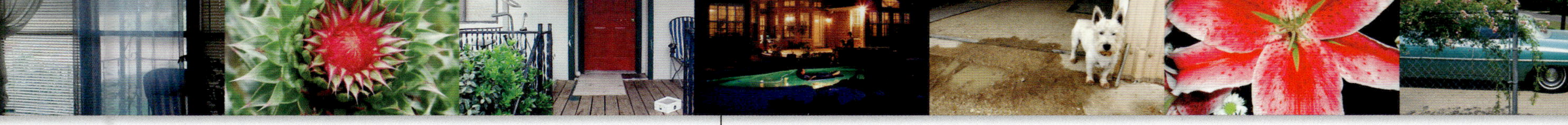

RICHARDSON
On a warm Texas night, Dave Porter floats in his pool while chatting with his sister-in-law Diane. Porter moved to Texas from Wisconsin in 1983 to work as a manager for a telescope manufacturer. He and his wife share their new, 3,100-square-foot home with three golden retrievers.
Photo by Gary W. Porter

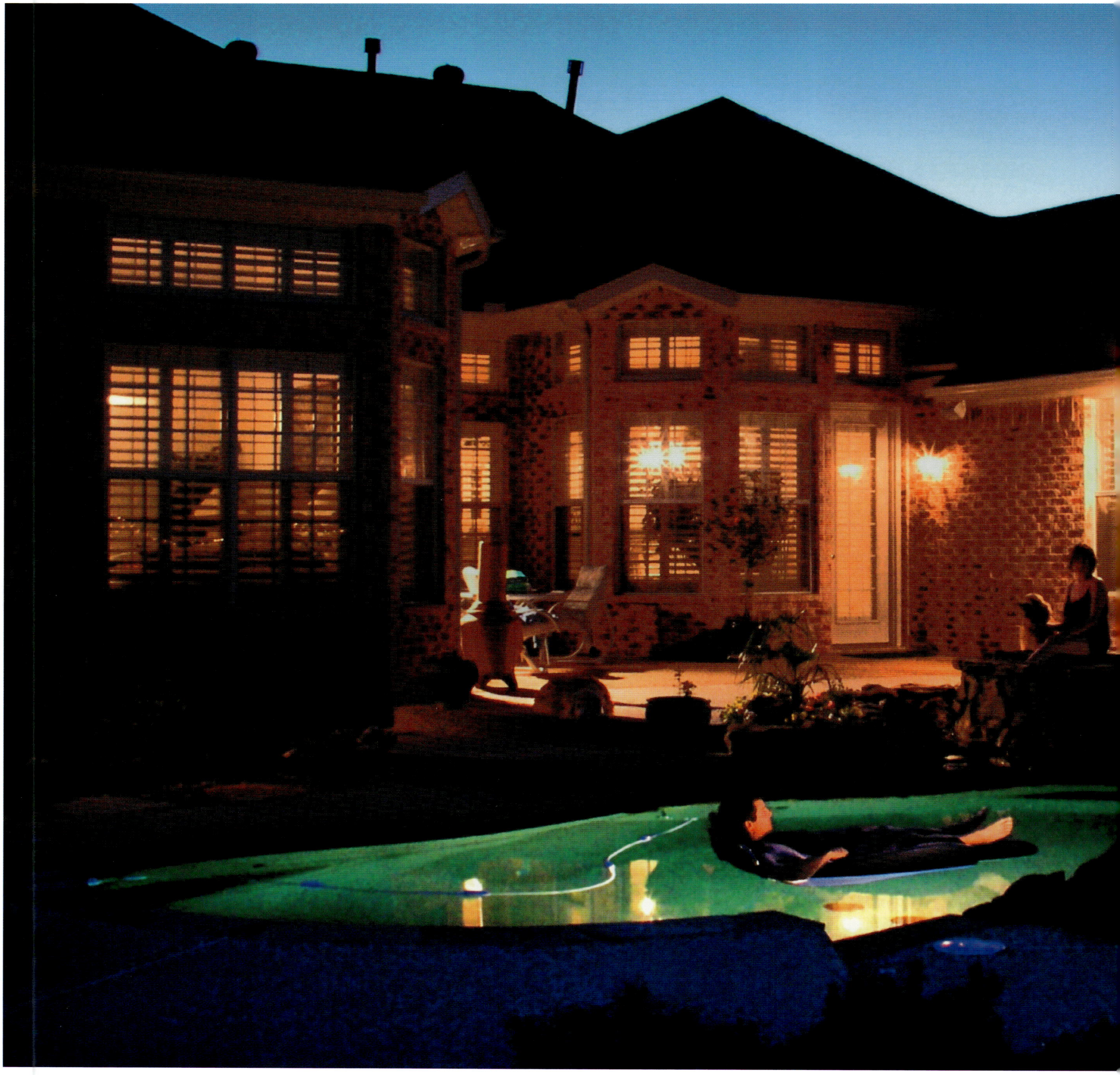

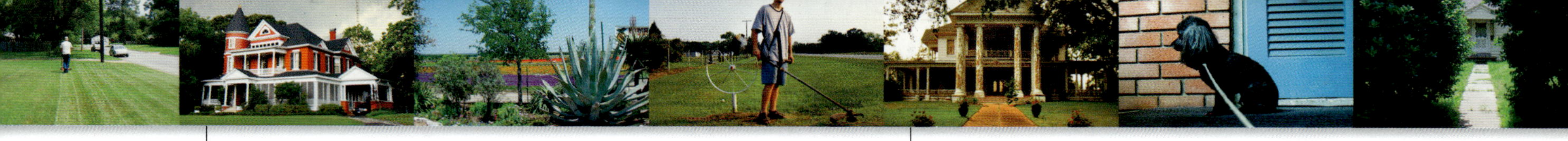

PALESTINE
The Hearne House was constructed in 1896 by businessman John Randolph Hearne, and the Queen Anne-style home is still in the family. Its current resident is 101-year-old Esther Hearne, widow of John's son Ben. Esther's longevity and eccentricities—she bought a brand new Cadillac when she got a dent in her old one—has made her almost as famous as the home.
Photo by Scogin Mayo

PALESTINE
This home at 601 East Hodges Street was built in 1911 by Judge James Perry, one of Palestine's earliest settlers. The house is now owned by James Boone, a local attorney. It is one of 1,700 historic homes in what is known as the "Queen City of East Texas."
Photo by Scogin Mayo

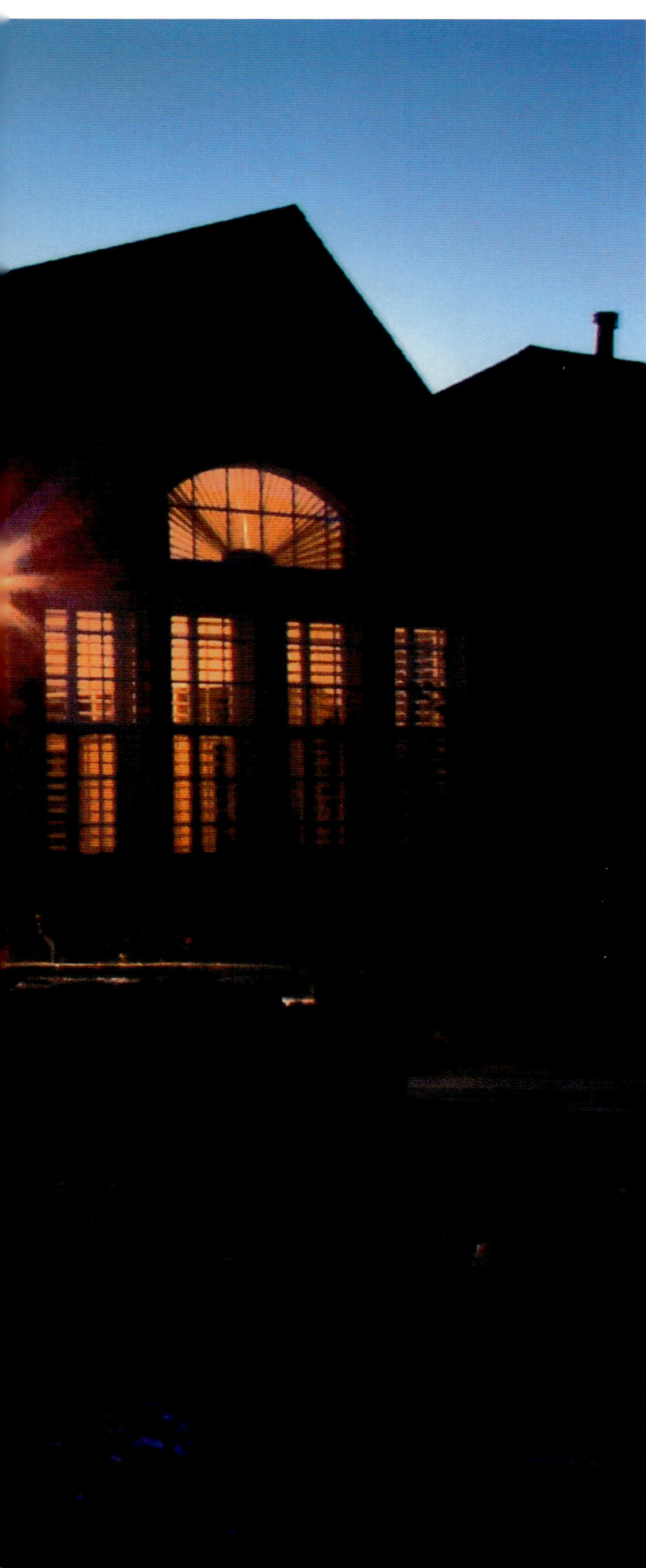

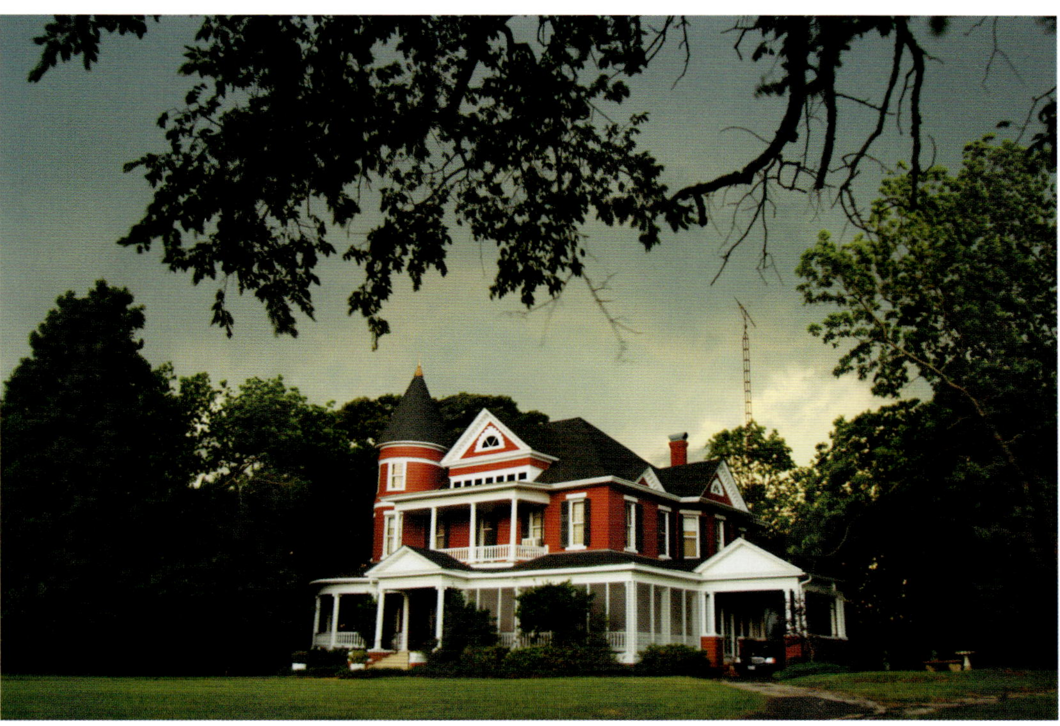

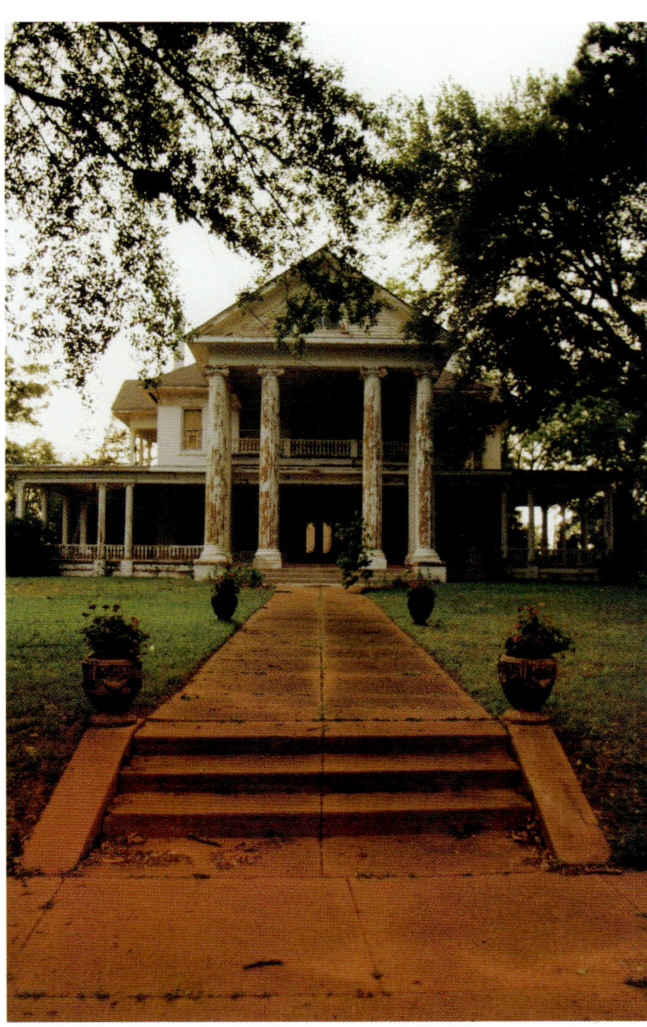

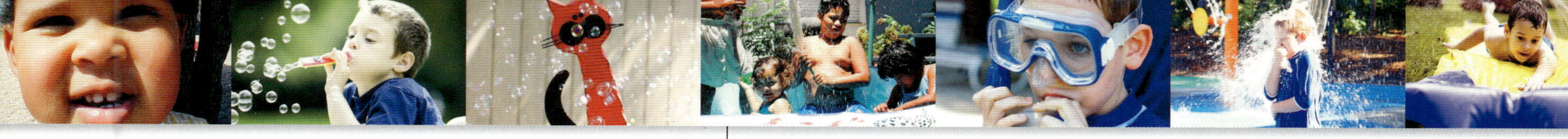

SAN ANTONIO
Ebony Calzoncit (front left) and cousins Felipe, Miguel, and Milagros Lopez escape the scorching heat of the East Side streets—and the congestion of their two-bedroom duplex that is home to a family of nine.
Photo by Dee G. Crawford

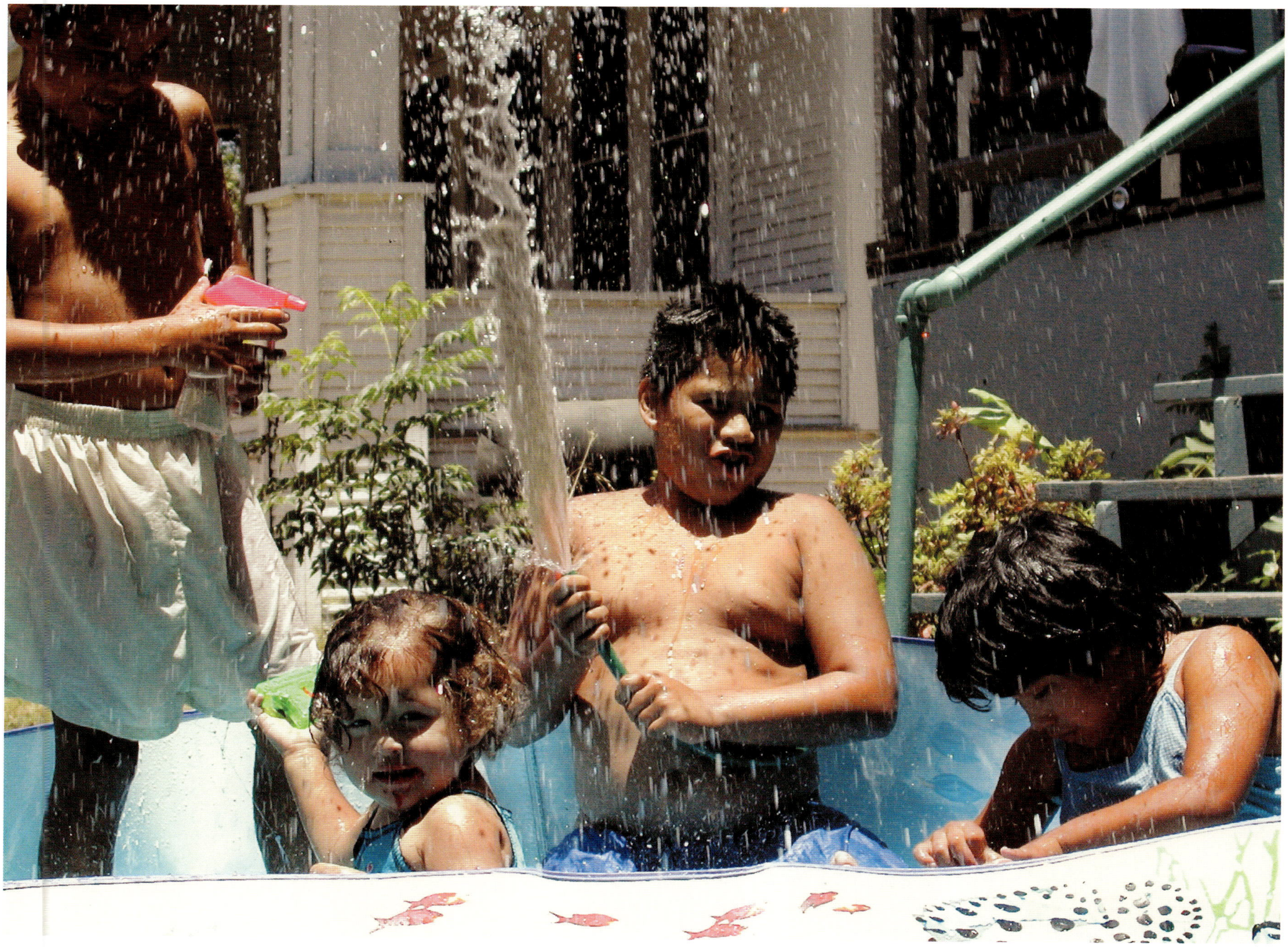

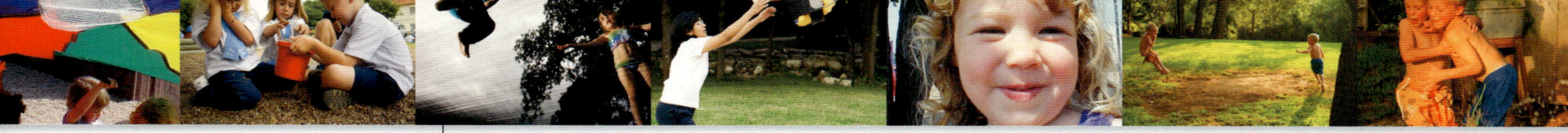

RUSK

Dylan and Delaney Starkey play made-up games on their backyard trampoline. In "alligator," one lies down and tries to grab the one jumping over. Now that they're playing "spiderman," Dylan gets to show off his karate moves.

Photo by Les Hassell

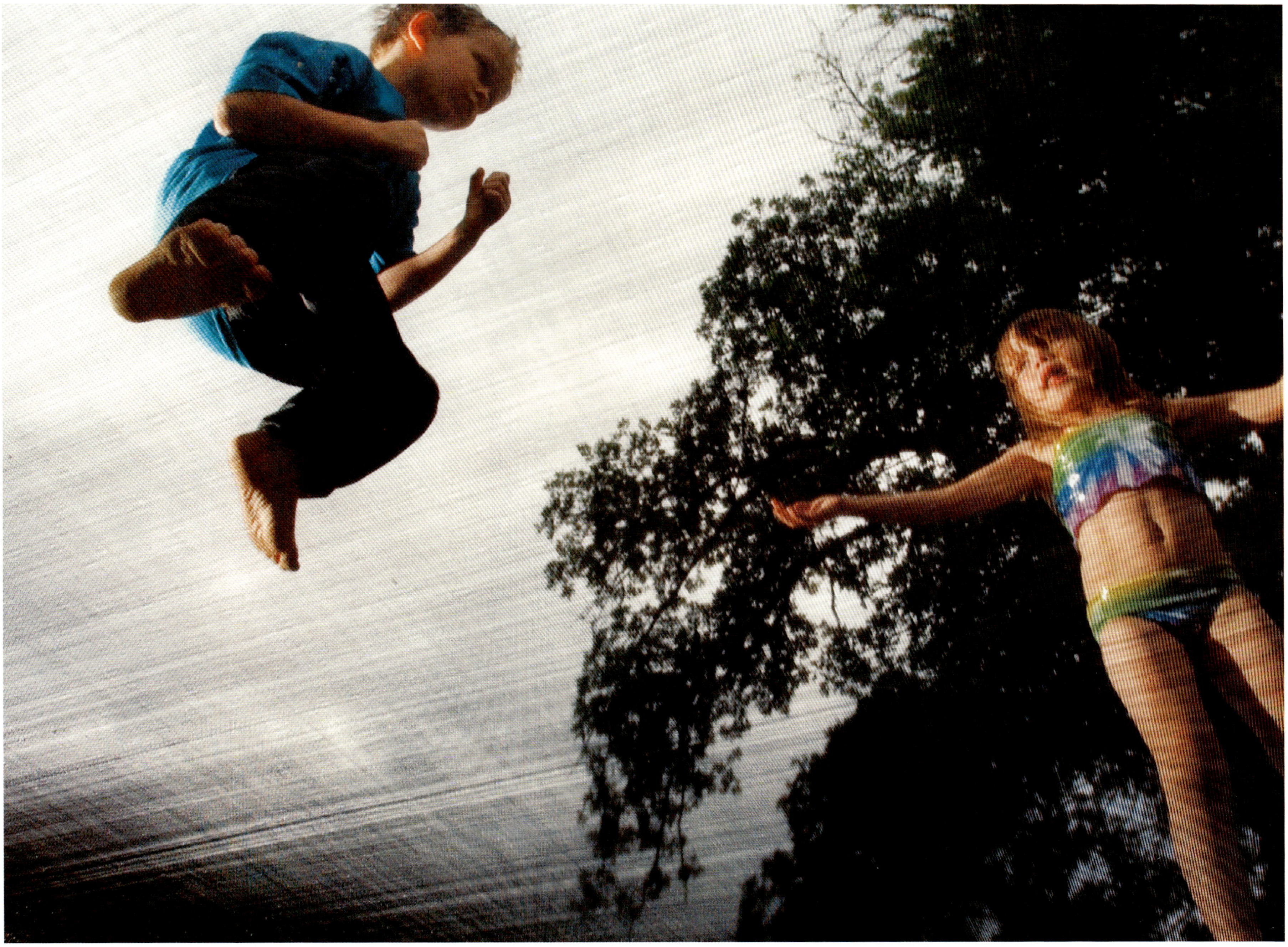

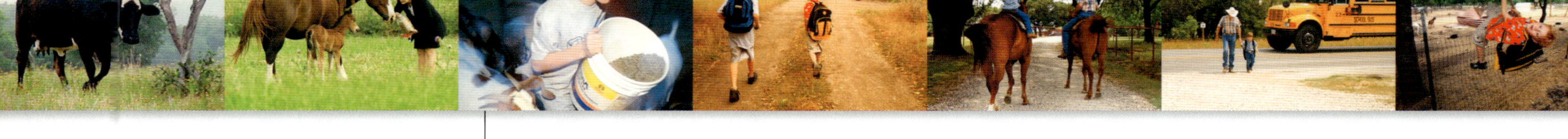

KYLE

Every morning before catching the school bus, Michael Wittkopp feeds his family's goats. The Wittkopps raise 100 goats, which they breed and sell to other farmers throughout the country.
Photo by Rodolfo Gonzalez

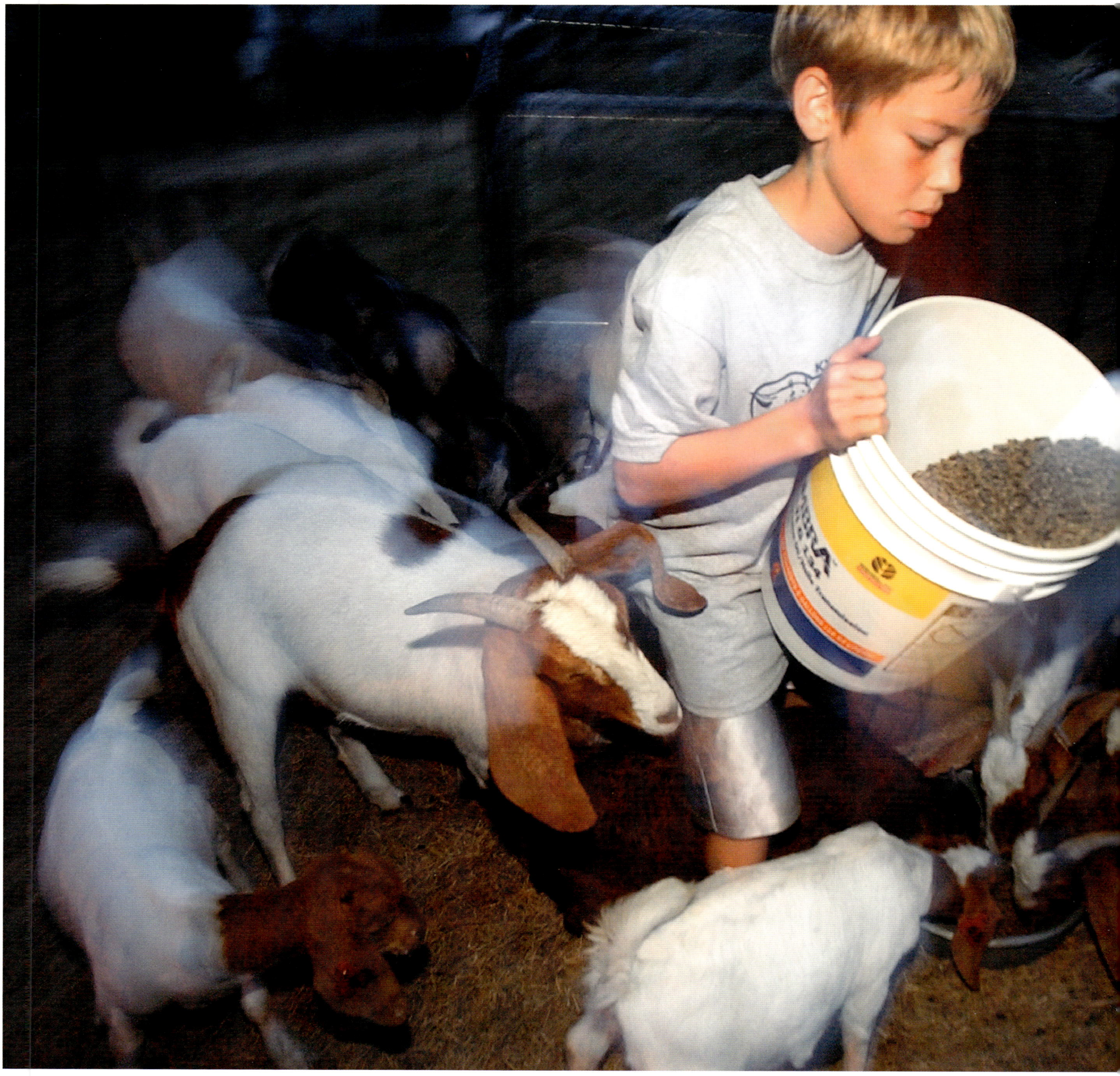

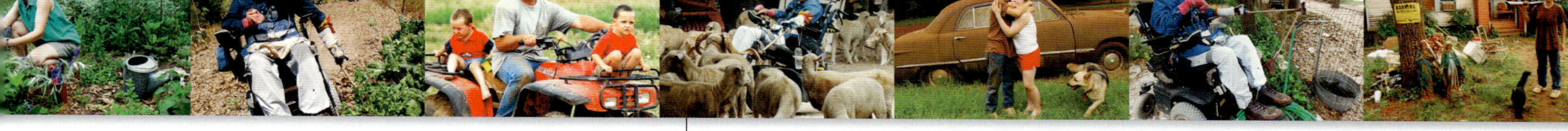

BOERNE

Bluette Duennenberg taught biology at Sul Ross Middle School for 30 years until a drunk driver crashed into his car. He now lives in town with a friend. Another friend takes him out to his farm every day, where he tends to his sheep and garden. "My parents raised me here, so it gives me a sense of peace," says Duennenberg.

Photo by John Davenport, San Antonio Express-News

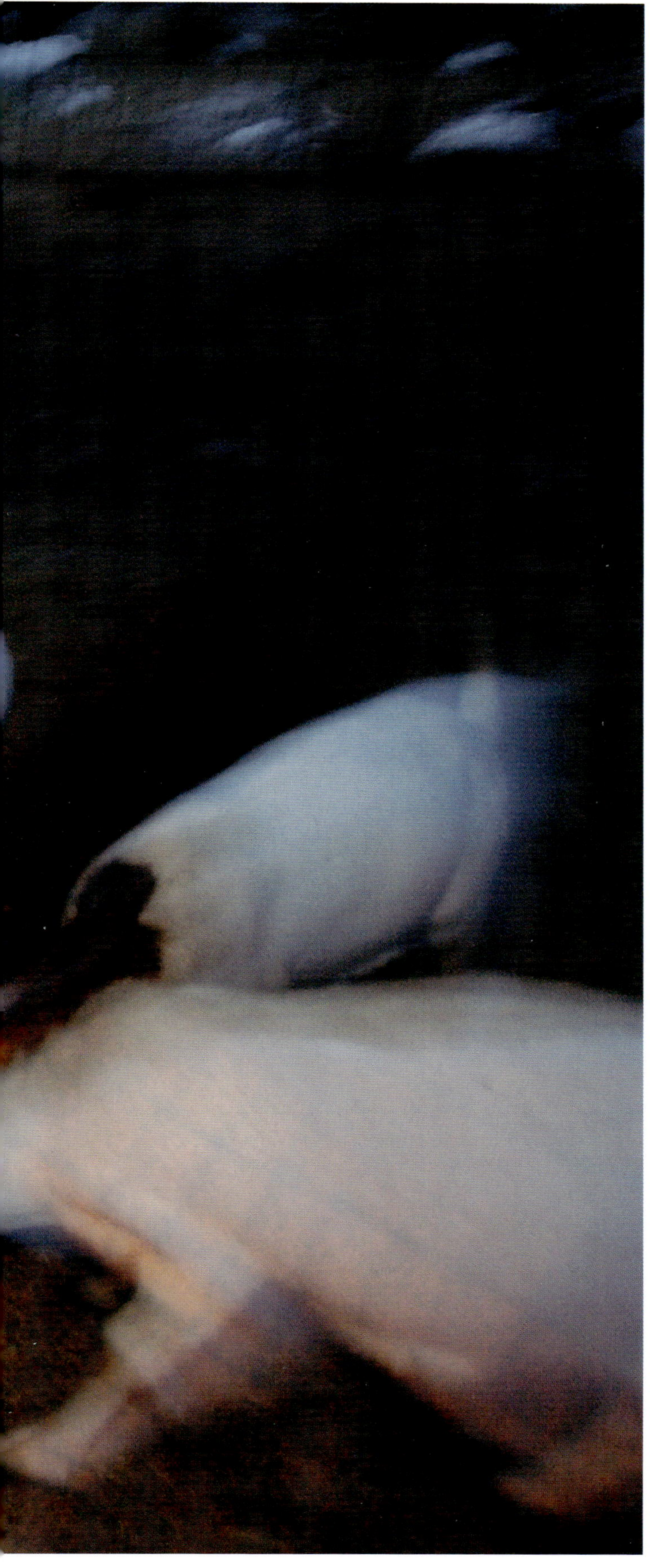

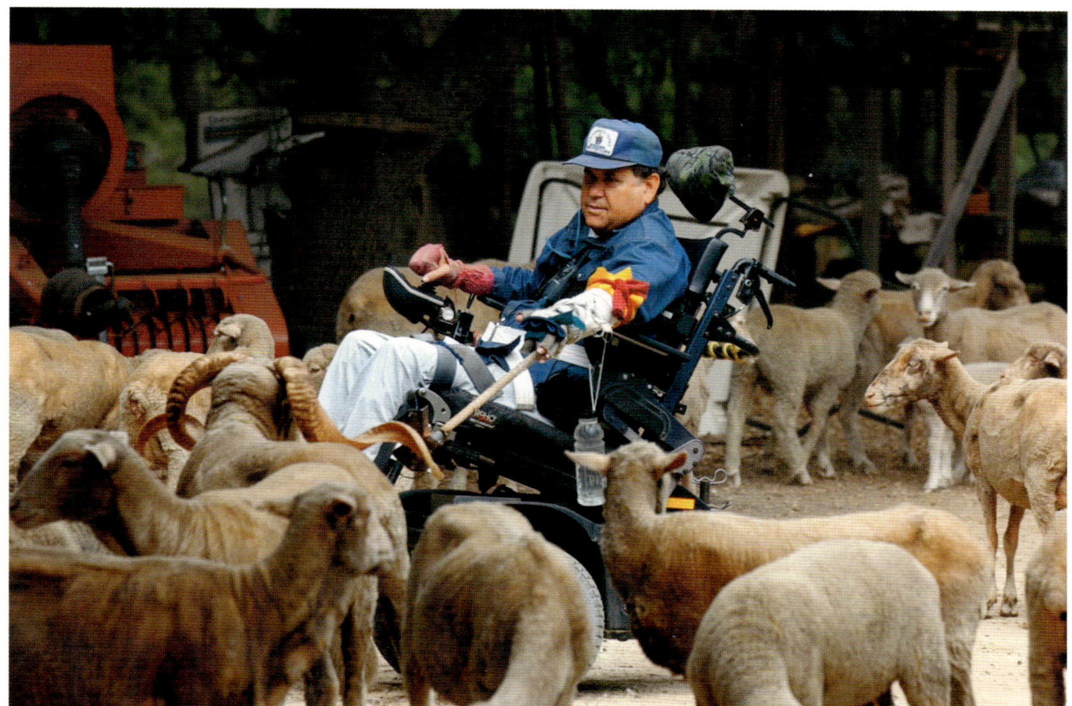

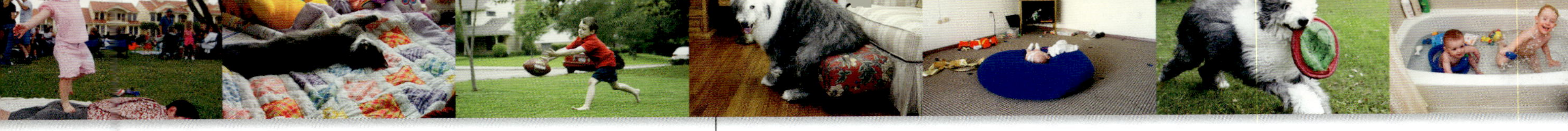

DALLAS
Daisy, an Old English sheepdog, taught herself to sit on a stool for relief from arthritis of the knee. The disease is a common problem for this breed. "Nevertheless, she is good-natured and active," says owner James Smith. "She still tries to herd the kids."
Photo by James D. Smith

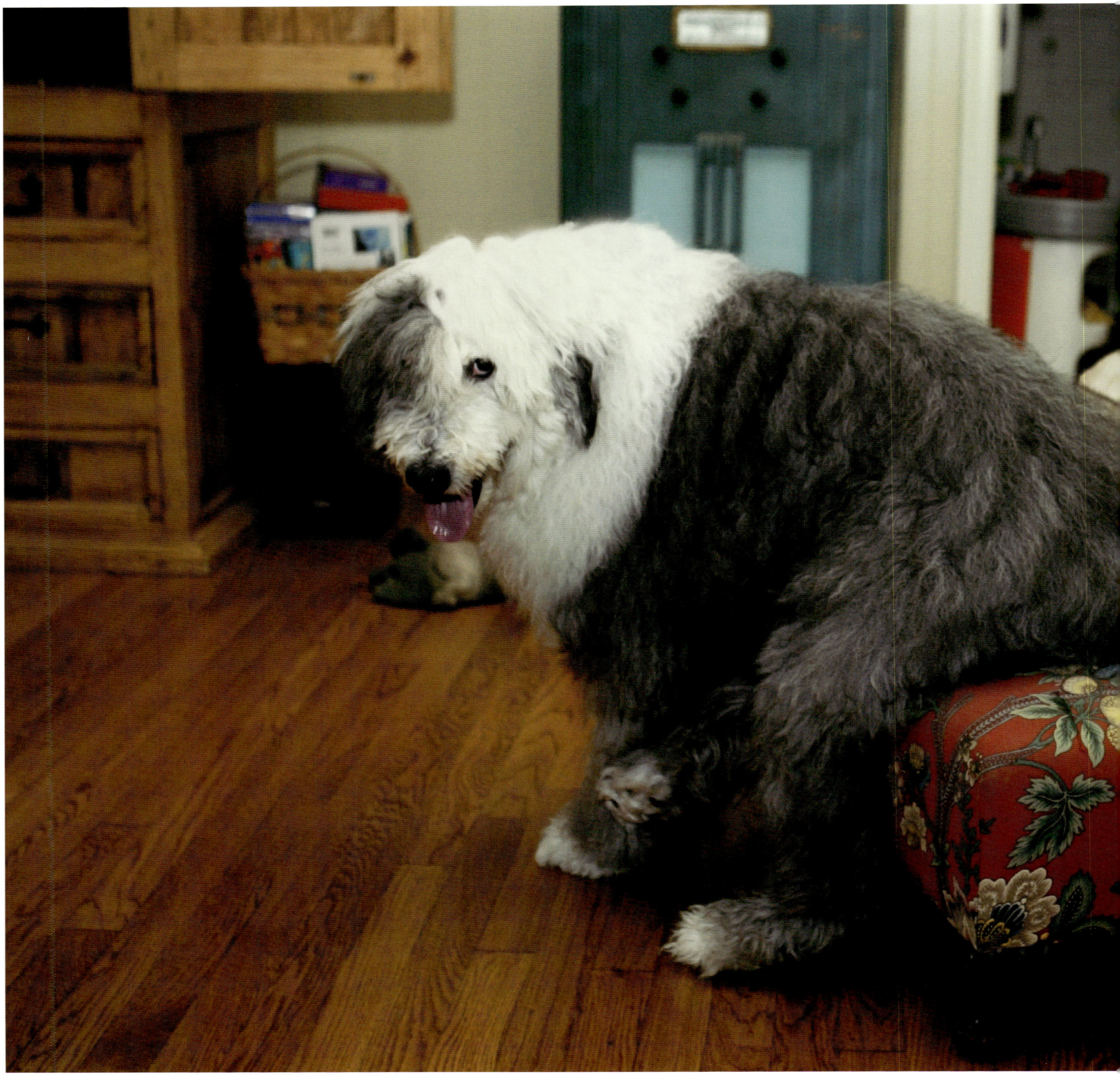

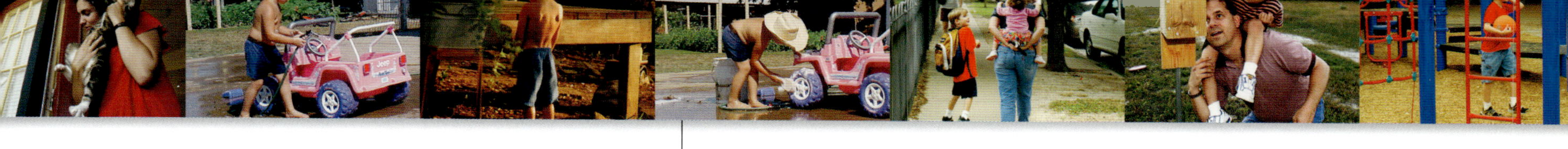

KINGSLAND
Five-year-old Michael Adler, known as "Bubba," saw this Jeep at a garage sale with his parents. He didn't care that it was a Barbie model, only that it had four wheels.
Photo by Lana Morgan Adler

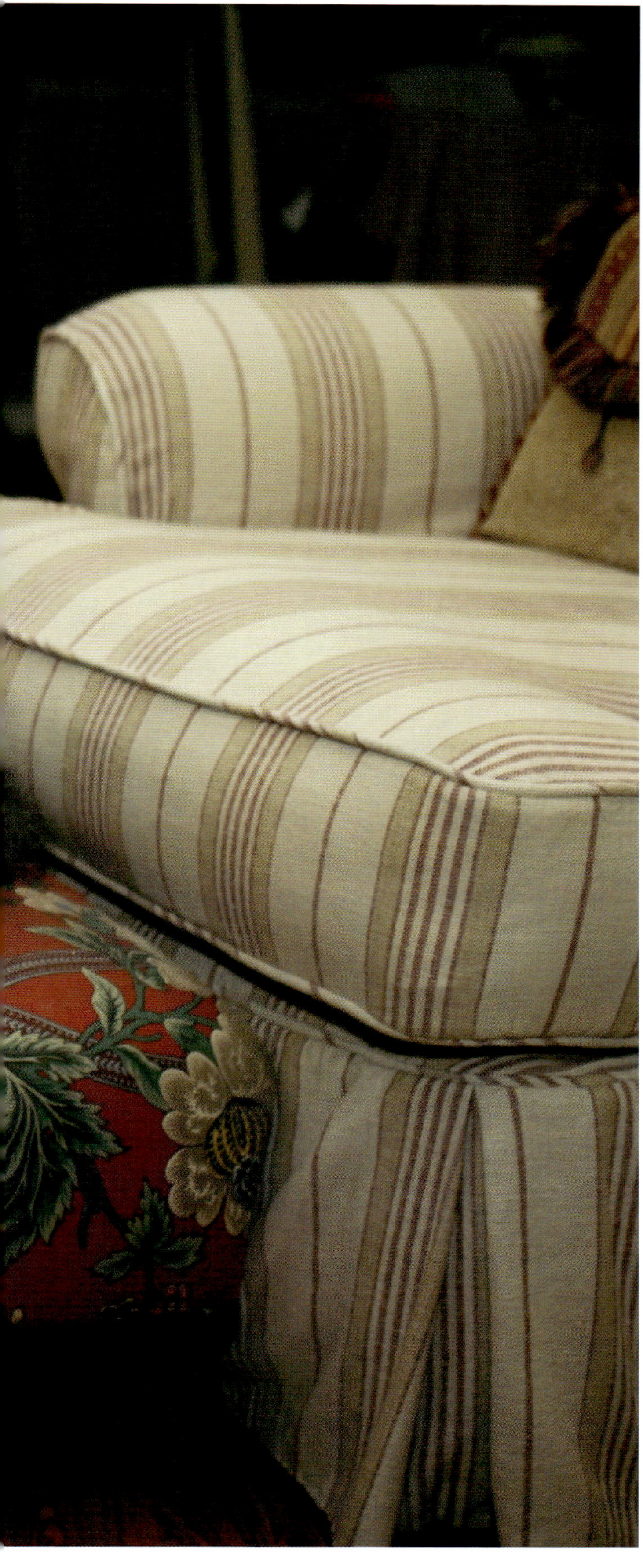

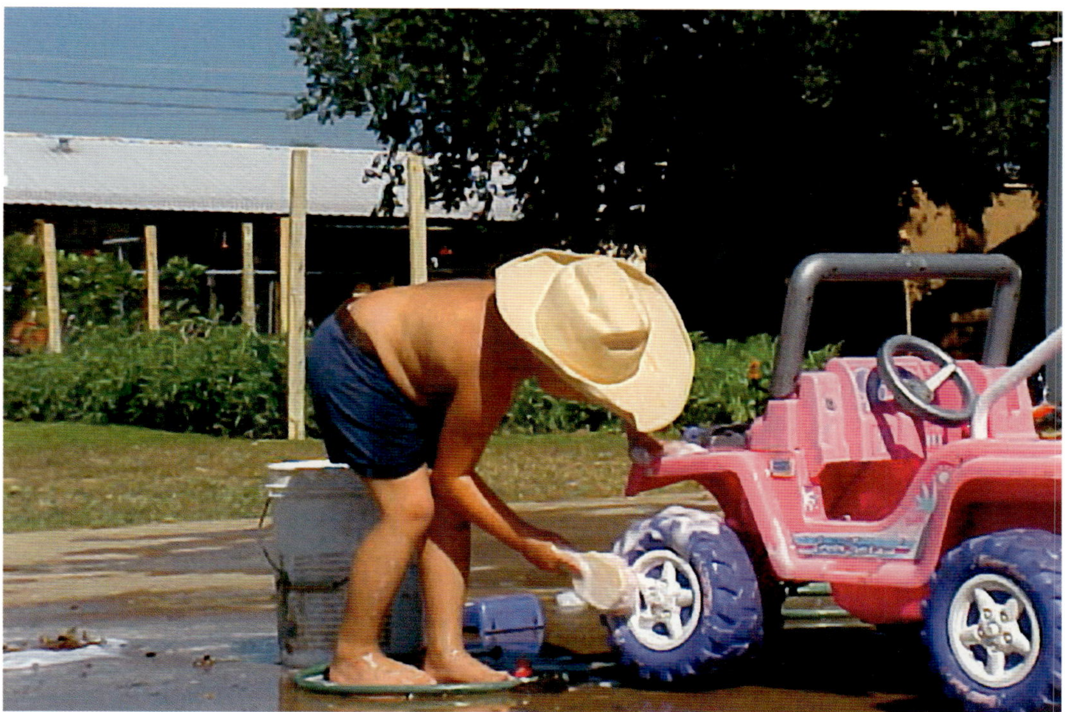

The year 2003 marked a turning point in the history of photography: It was the first year that digital cameras outsold film cameras. To celebrate this unprecedented sea change, the *America 24/7* project invited amateur photographers—along with students and professionals—to shoot and, via the Internet, submit digital images. Think of it as audience participation. Their visions of community are interspersed with the professional frames throughout this book. On the following four pages, however, we present a gallery produced exclusively by amateur photographers.

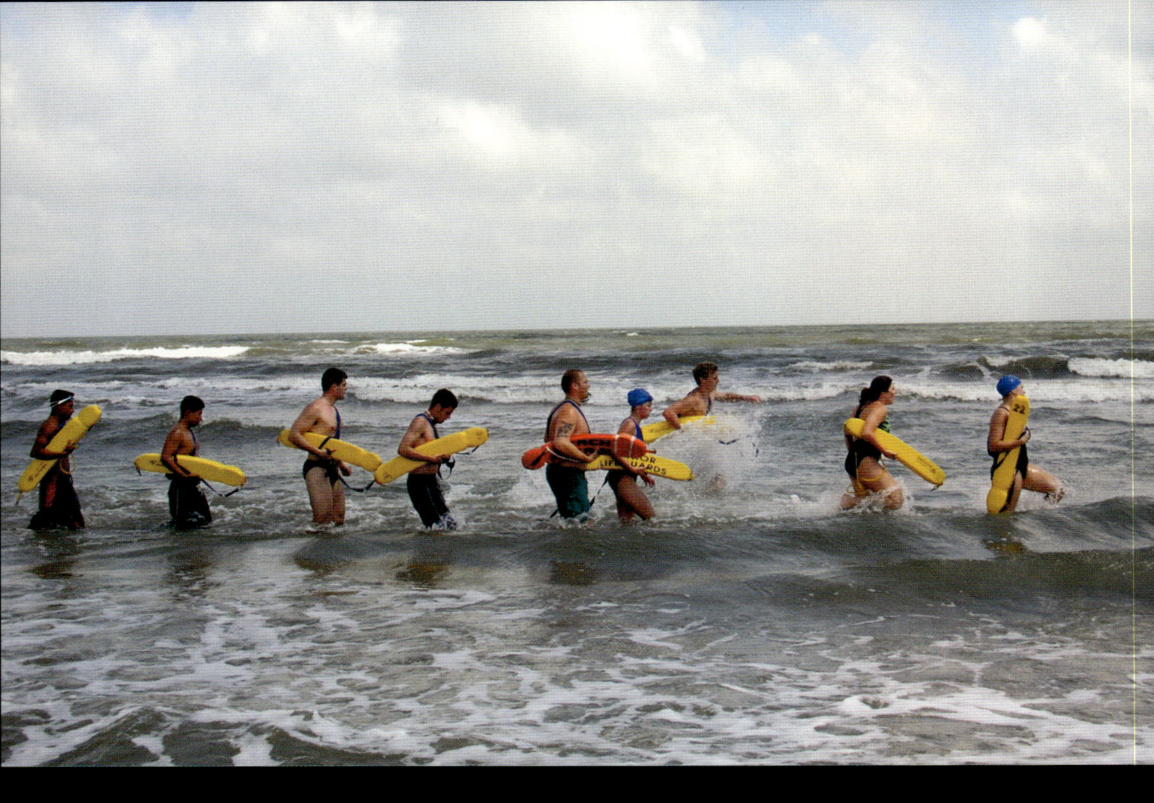

GALVESTON Wanna-be lifeguards for the Galveston Beach Patrol build up stamina in the surf. The drill? The last one left behind runs to the head of the line as it keeps moving. ***Photo by Ronald Harmon***

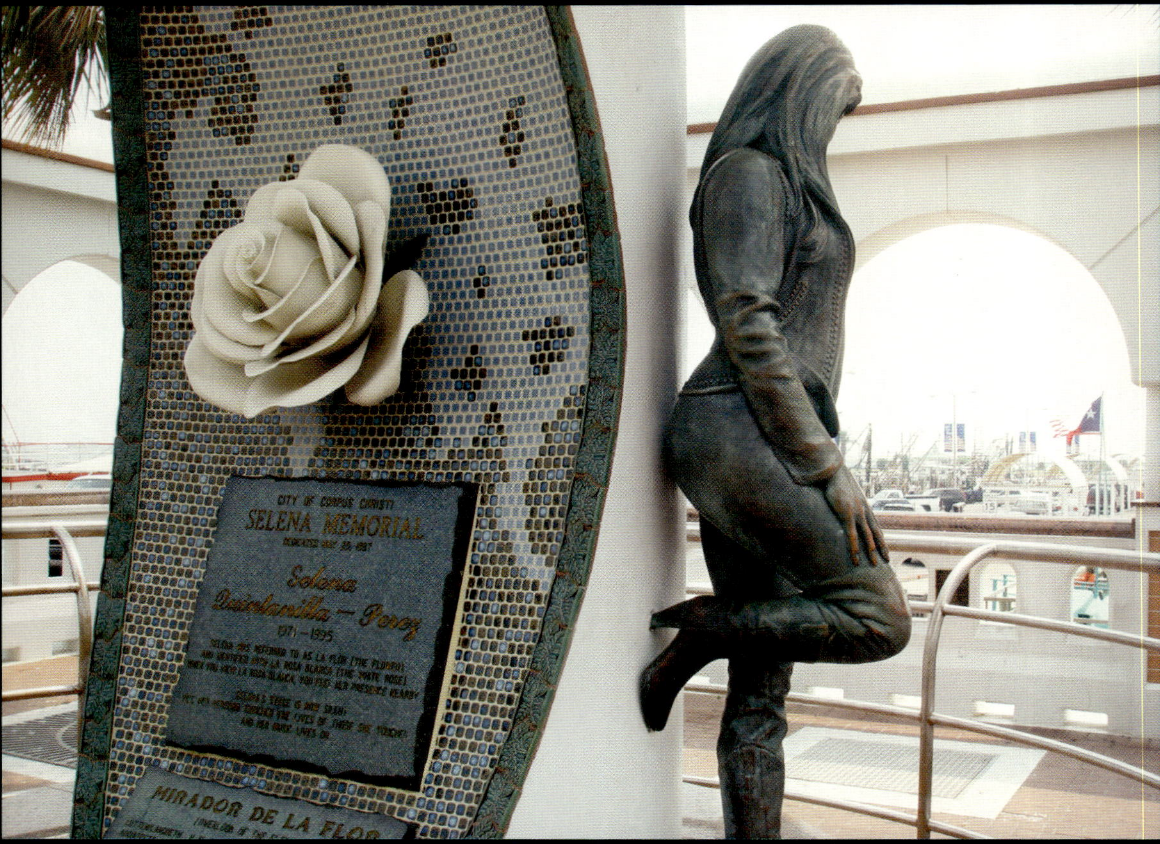

CORPUS CHRISTI A curvaceous statue commemorates Tejano singer and Corpus Christi resident Selena. The 23-year-old had just won a Grammy and was becoming a crossover star in 1995, when she was killed by a member of her staff. ***Photo by Rey Cortez***

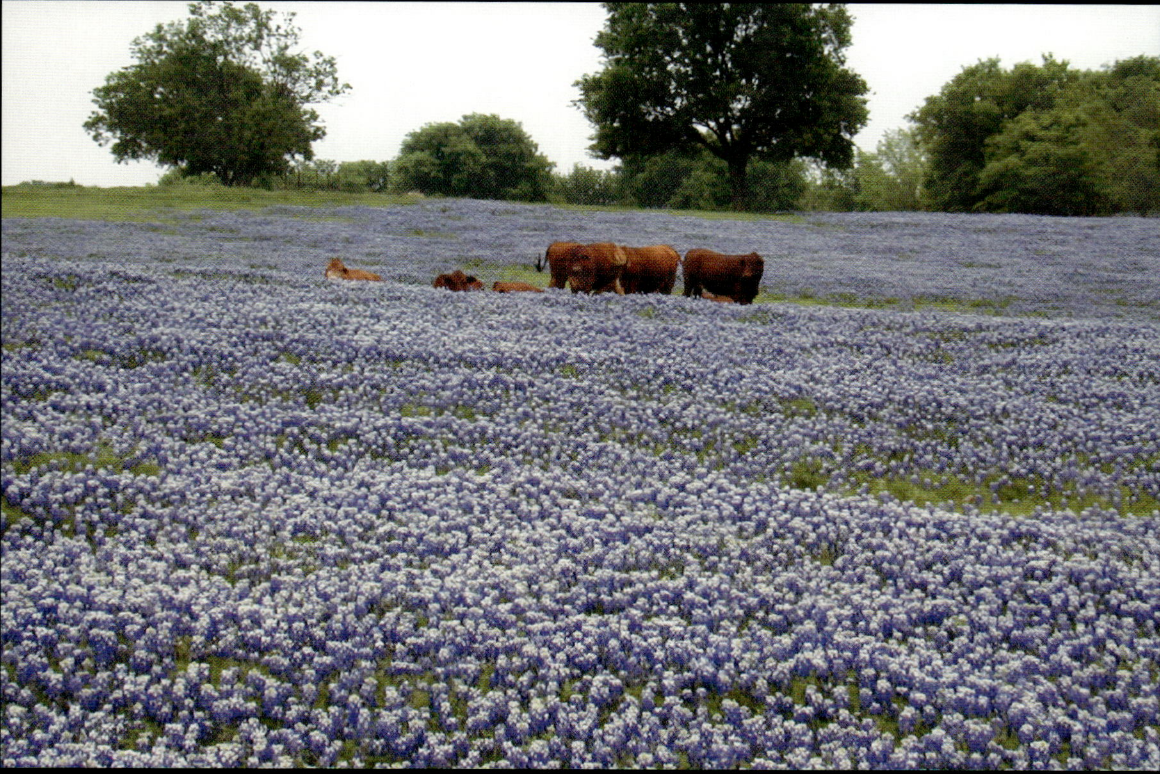

ENNIS With its flower-studded trails and sea blue fields, the "Bluebonnet City" of Ennis is home to all five species of the Texas state flower. ***Photo by Steve Soza-Gorham***

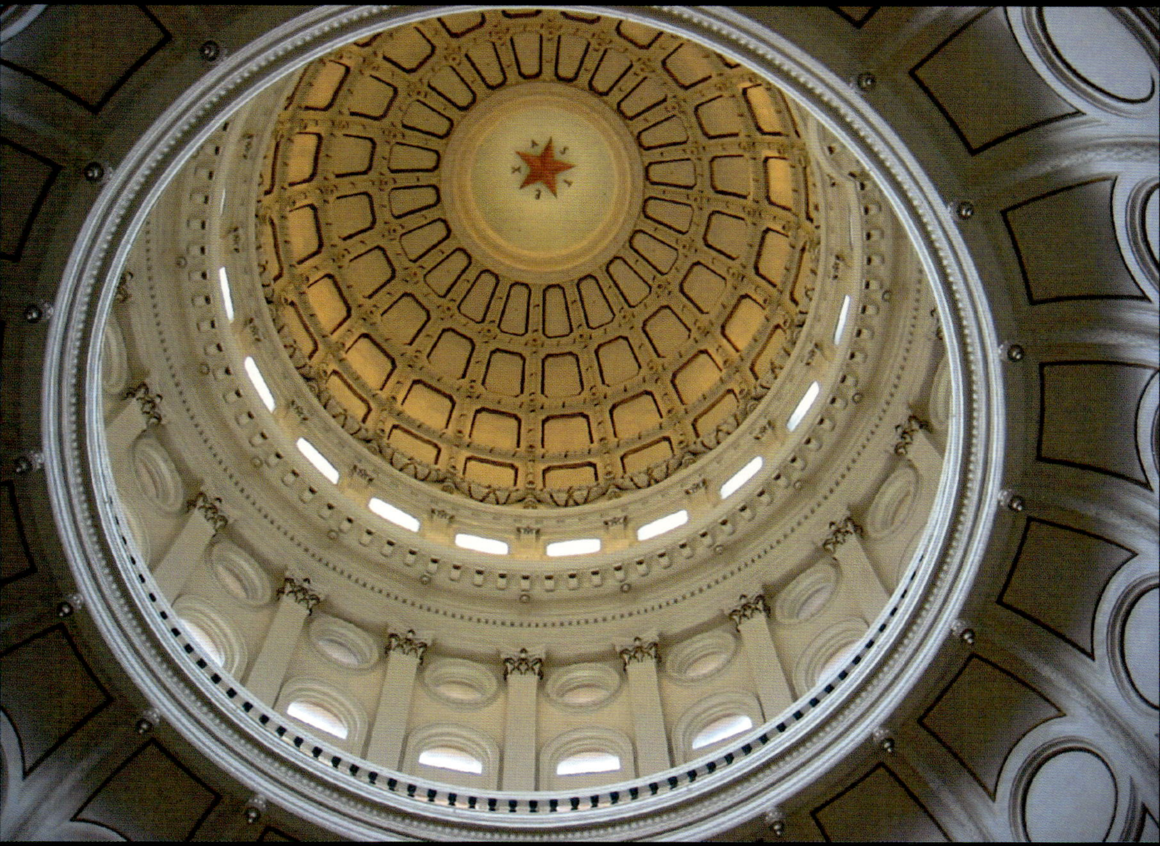

AUSTIN The Lone Star at the top on the Texas State Capital rotunda may look small, but it's not. It's eight feet from tip to tip. ***Photo by Rae Lynn Tipping***

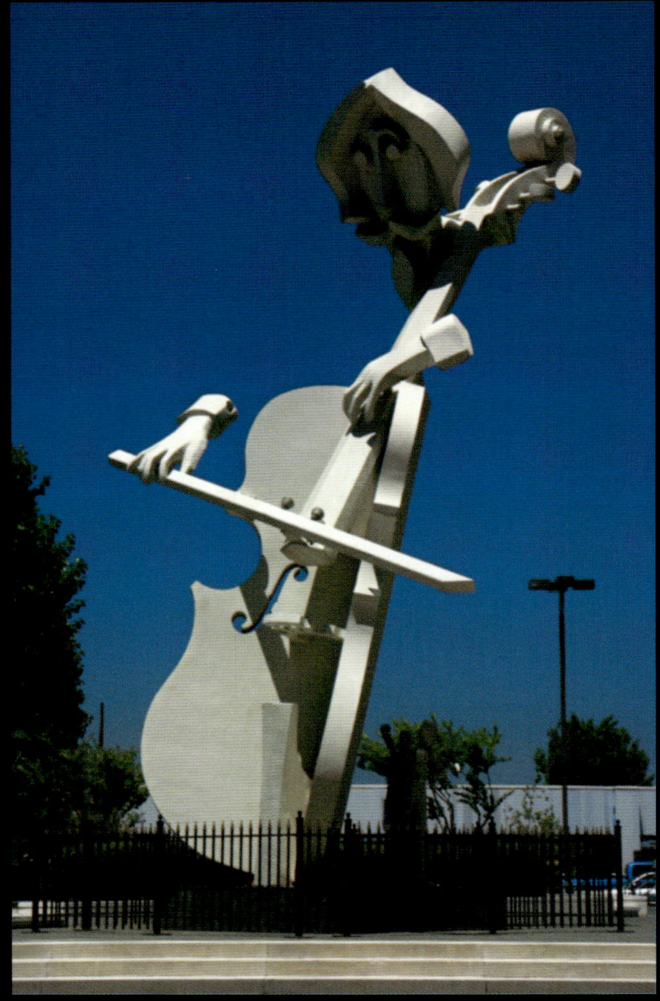

HOUSTON Sculptor David Addickes's 21-ton *Virtuoso* gives a touch of humor and grace to downtown Houston's Lyric Business Centre. ***Photo by James Benton***

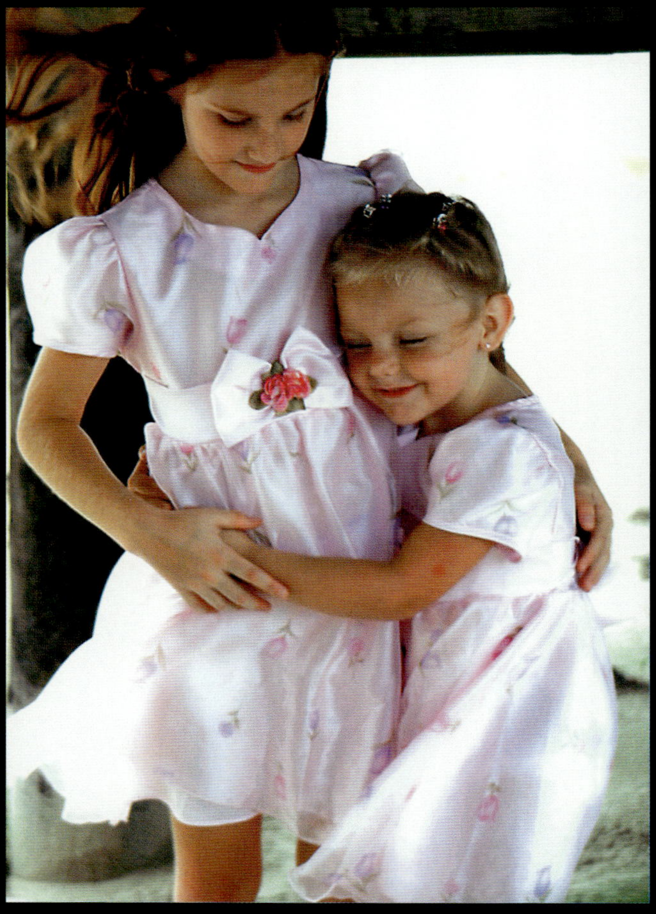

GALVESTON Sister love: Five-year-old Analysa Edmiston looks up to older Alissandra, 10—and is not shy about demonstrating her devotion. ***Photo by David Cazier***

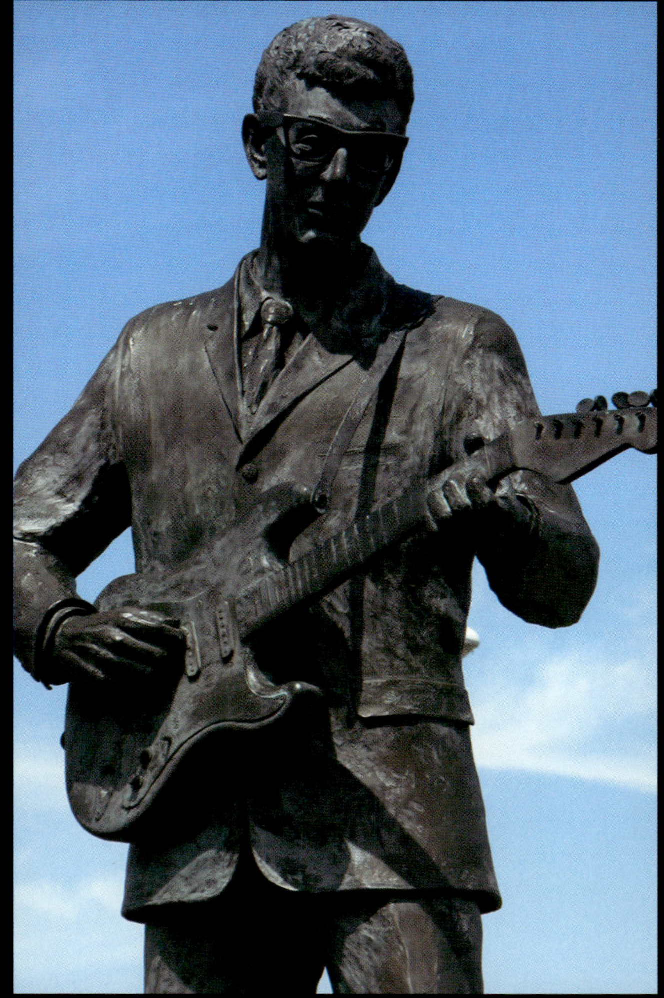

LUBBOCK Buddy Holly, native son of Lubbock, was immortalized in 1980 with an 8-foot 6-inch, 2,500-po bronze statue, located across from the Lubbock Memorial Civic Center. ***Photo by David Johnson***

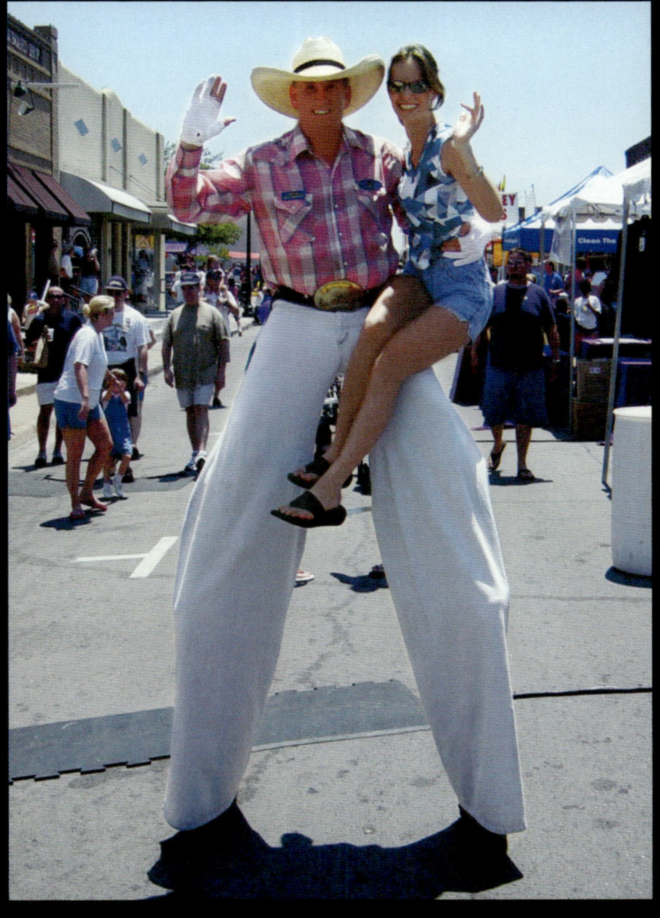

GRAPEVINE Thanks to the "official hug therapist" at the town's Main Street Days arts and crafts festival, Michelle Cummings has an uplifting experience. ***Photo by Peter Christensen***

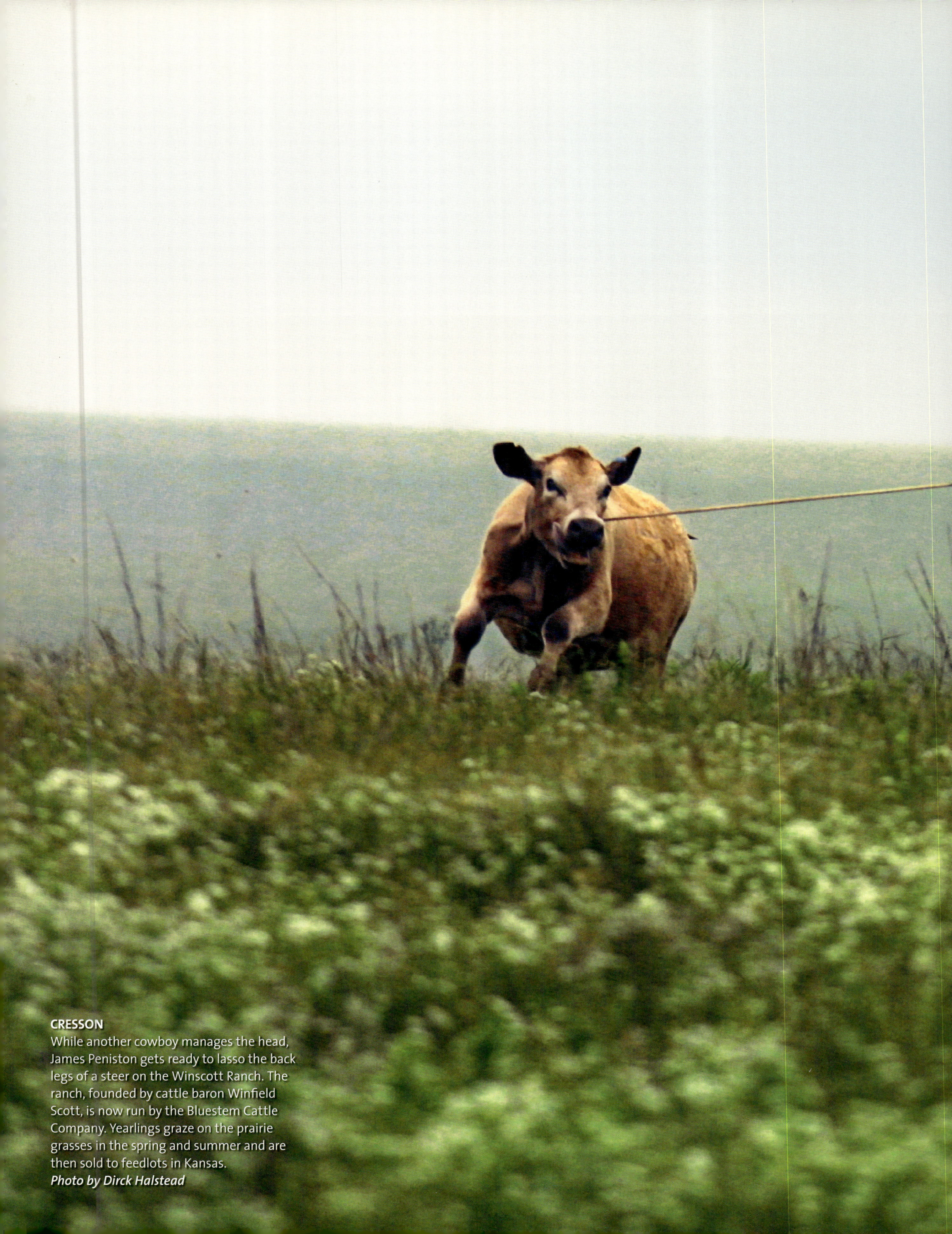

CRESSON
While another cowboy manages the head, James Peniston gets ready to lasso the back legs of a steer on the Winscott Ranch. The ranch, founded by cattle baron Winfield Scott, is now run by the Bluestem Cattle Company. Yearlings graze on the prairie grasses in the spring and summer and are then sold to feedlots in Kansas.
Photo by Dirck Halstead

Hard At Work

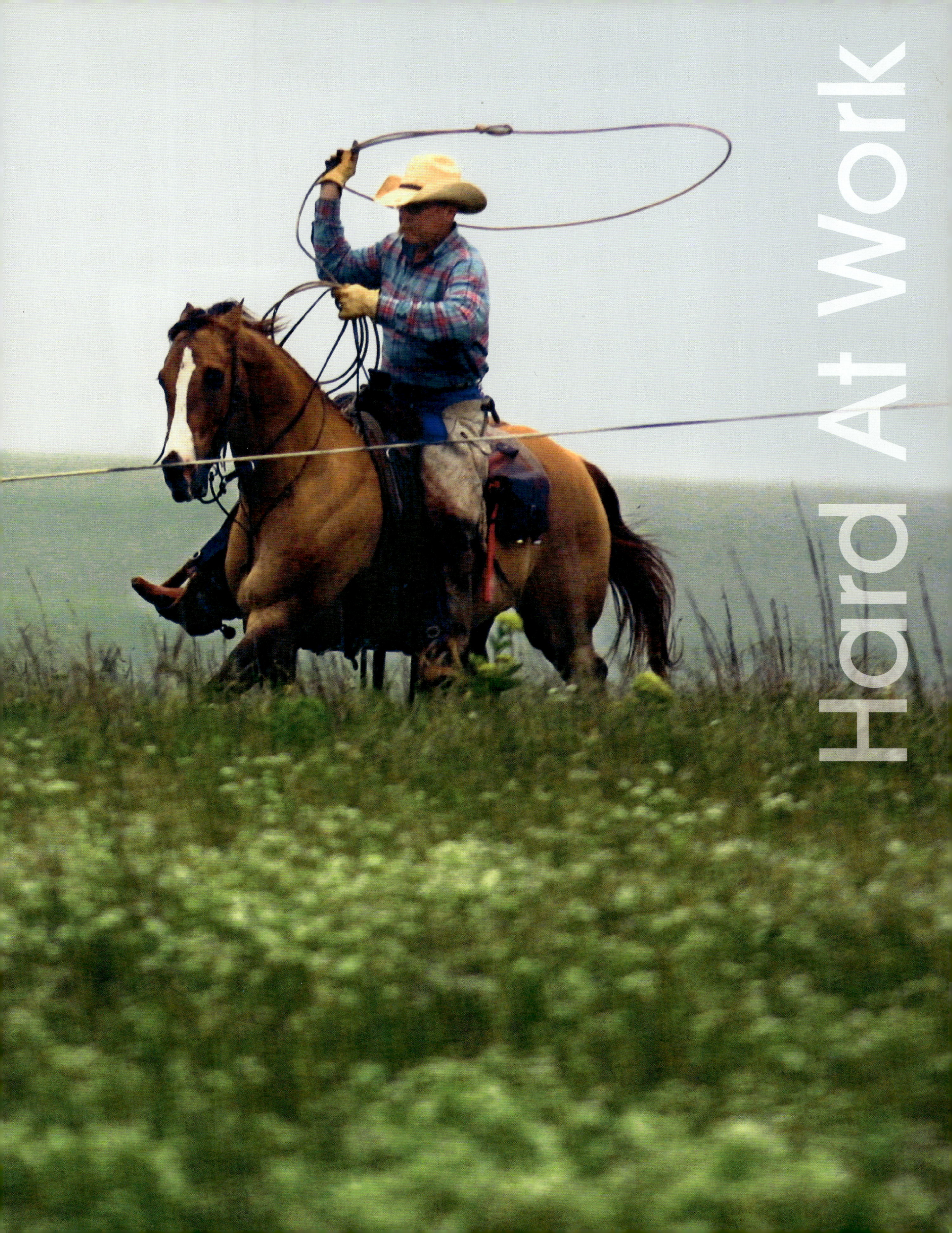

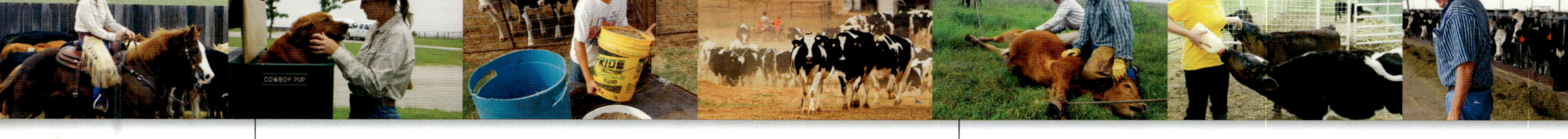

CRESSON
This "dog box," as rancher Vicki Bass calls it, provides Cowboy with a privileged perch for his trips around the property. The golden retriever doesn't help with the herd, but he's more than happy to chase the many flocks of birds.
Photos by Dirck Halstead

CRESSON
While James Peniston holds the hind legs and another cowboy makes sure the "header" rope stays taut, Vicki Bass and Troy Hoefer mark a cow. After steers have been roped and inspected, they are marked with colored grease pens to indicate any ailment (usually hoof rot or pink eye) and the treatment they've received.

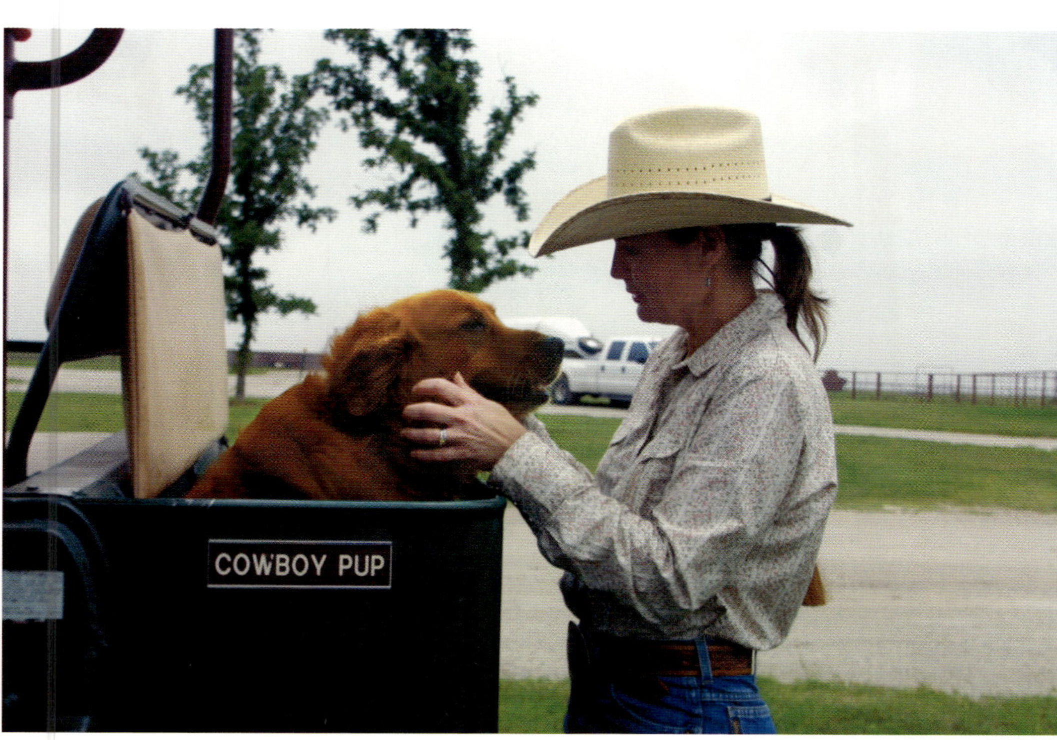

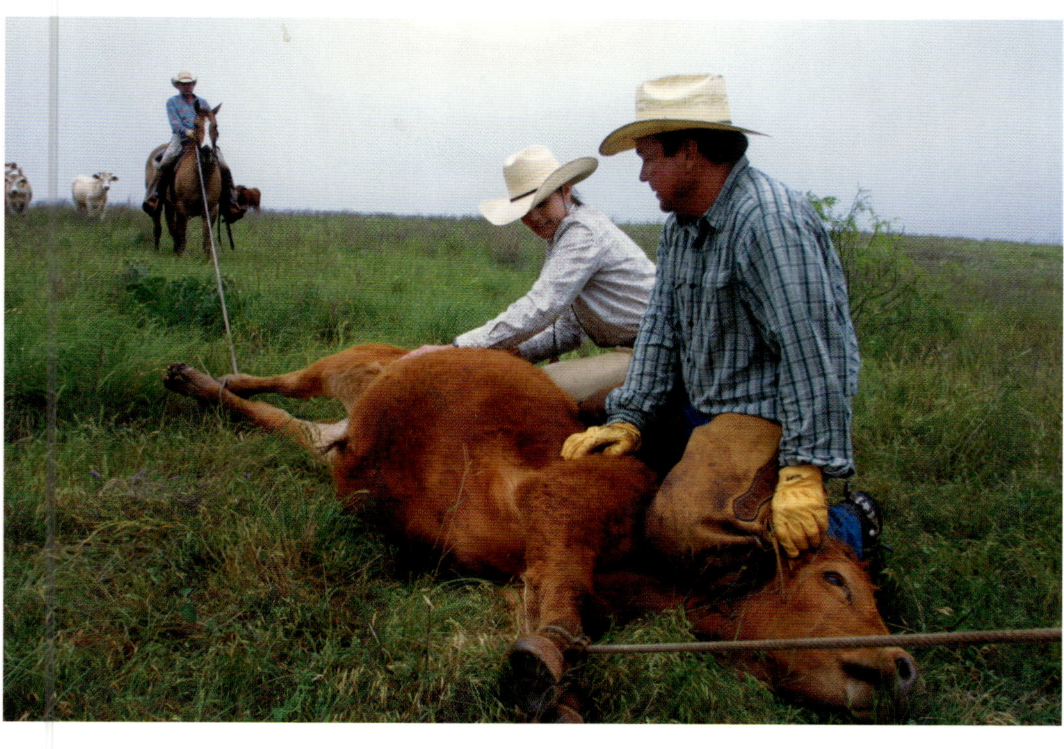

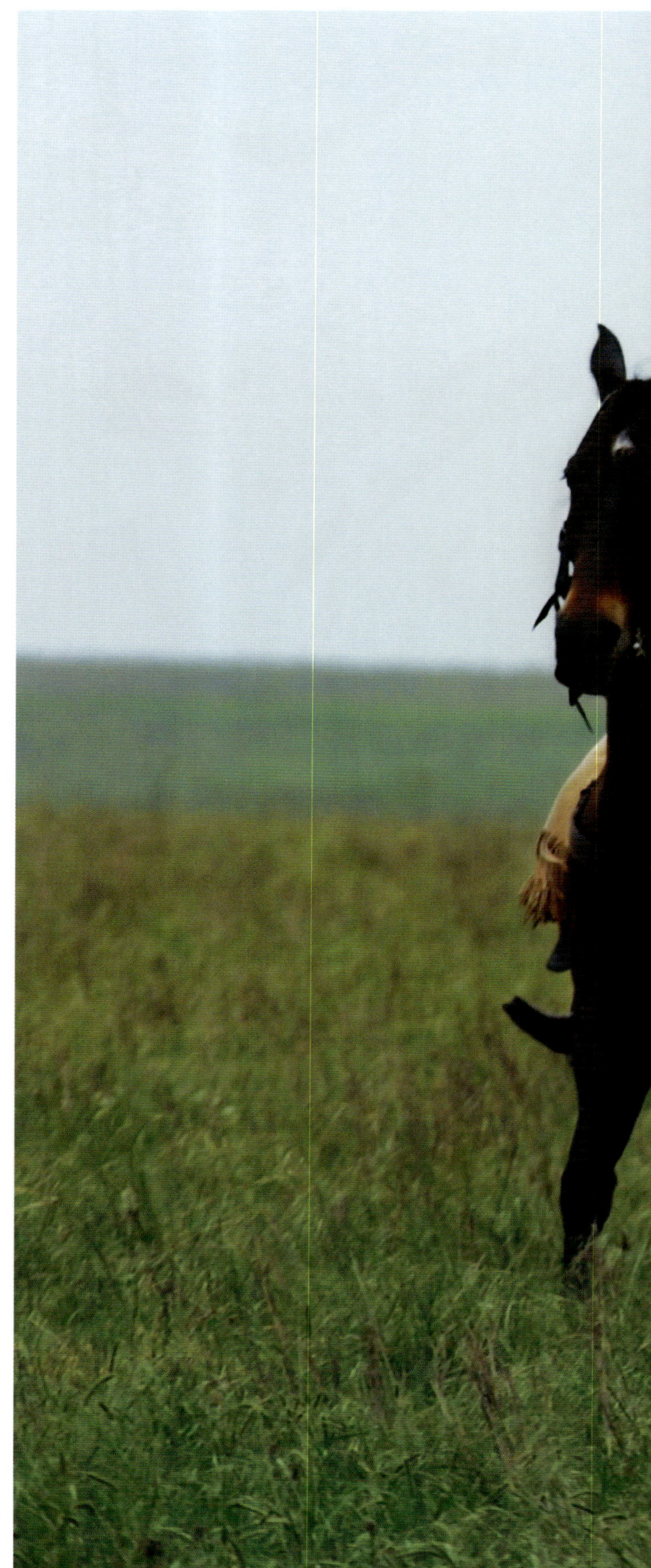

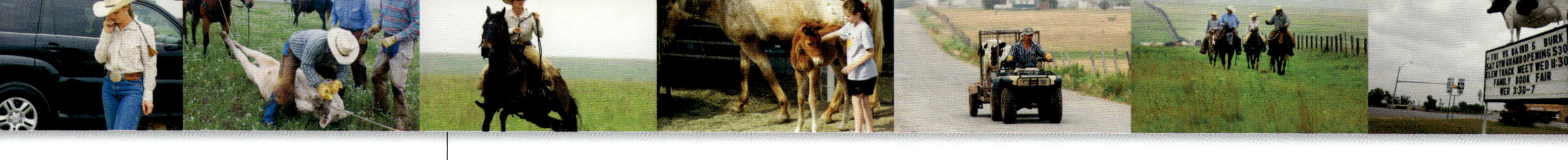

CRESSON

An ocean of bluestem grass, which used to grow as high as a man's shoulder, according to local journals from the 1800s, surrounds Vicki Bass and her quarter horse Zack. Though ranch work keeps Bass busy, she also competes in cutting horse shows.

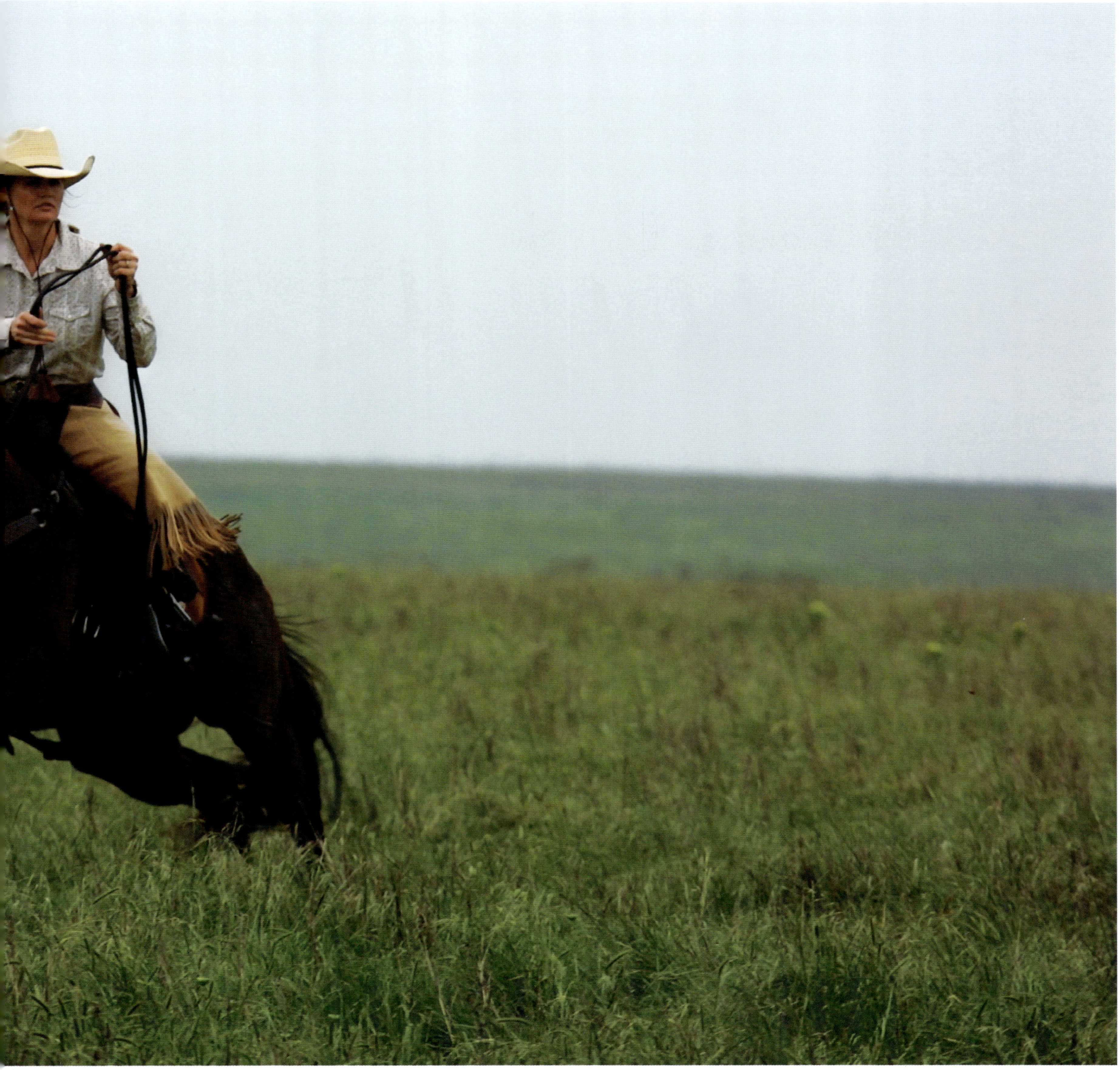

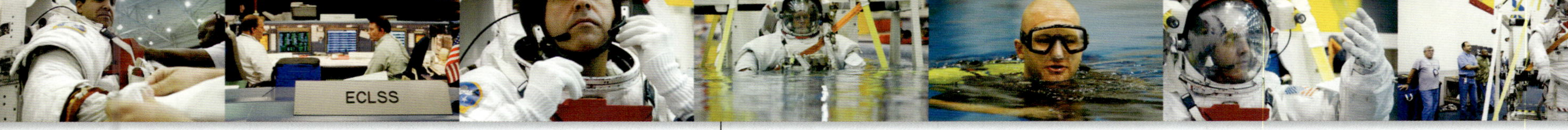

HOUSTON

Army Colonel and NASA astronaut Patrick Forrester wears an Extravehicular Mobility Unit spacesuit as he trains at Johnson Space Center's Neutral Buoyancy Laboratory. Weightless conditions in space are duplicated in the lab's 40-foot-deep pool, which helps Forrester, a veteran of two space walks, practice repairing the exterior of the International Space Station.

Photos by Joshua Trujillo

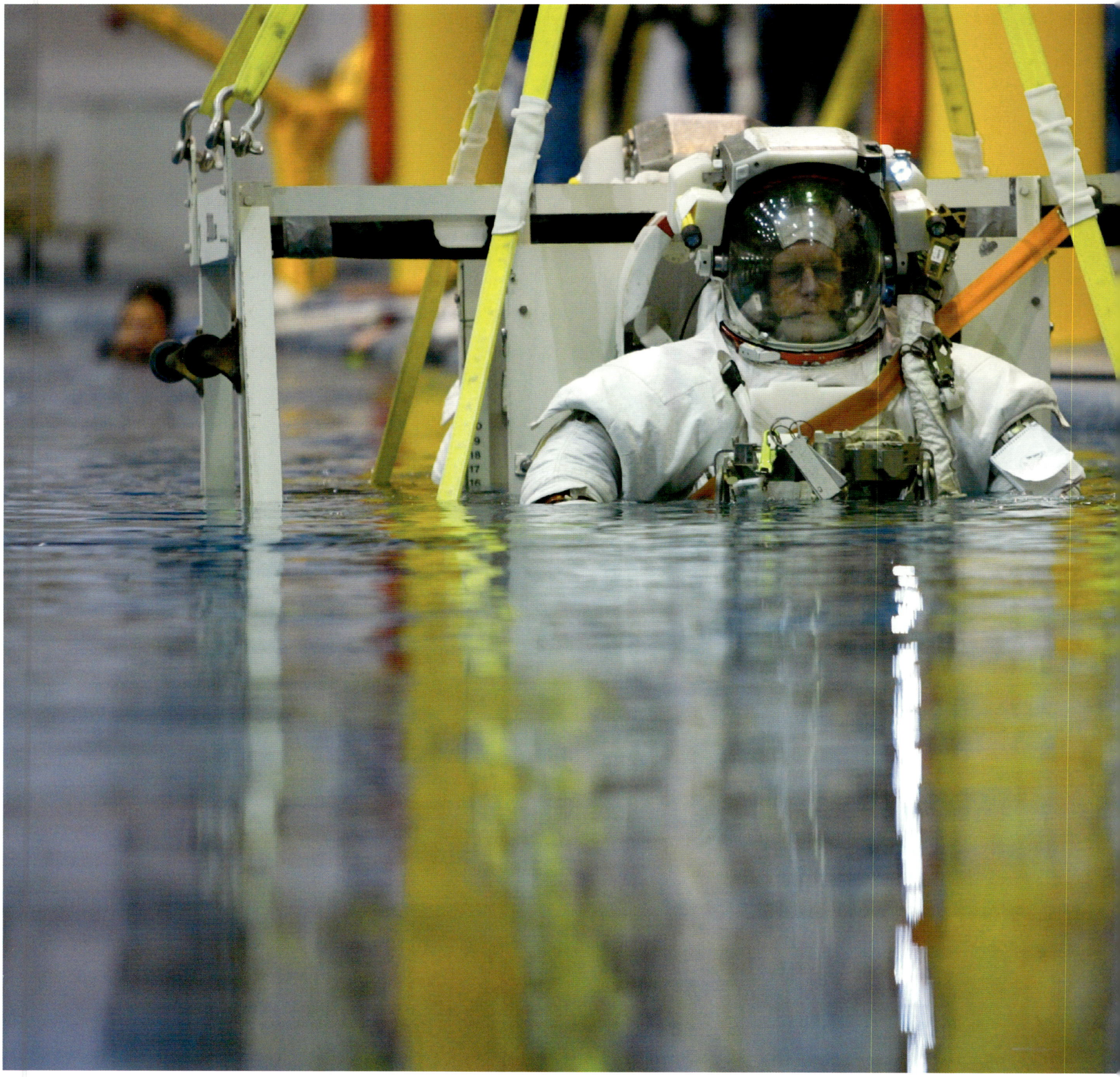

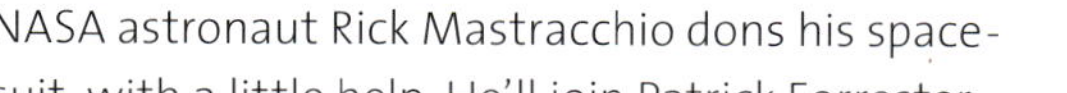

HOUSTON
NASA astronaut Rick Mastracchio dons his spacesuit, with a little help. He'll join Patrick Forrester in the lab's pool to train for future shuttle missions. An experienced space traveler, Mastracchio was aboard the Atlantis during a 12-day mission that prepared the International Space Station for arrival of its first live-aboard crew.

HOUSTON
Randy Hubbard talks with science officer Edward Tsang Lu and flight engineer Yuri Ivanovich Malenchenko at Johnson Space Center's Mission Control. The two astronauts were launched from Baikonur Cosmodrome in Kazakhstan on April 25th to replace the existing crew on the International Space Station. The two are expected to spend six months in space.

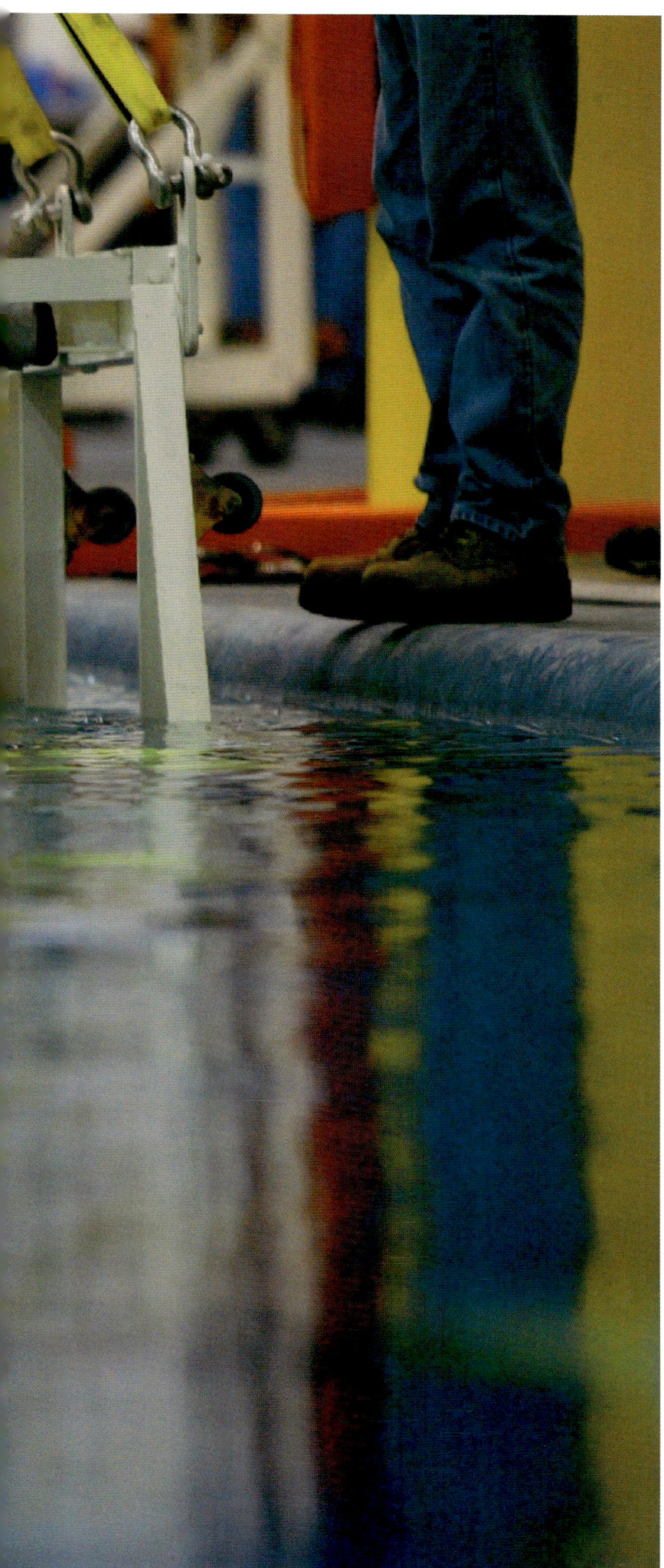

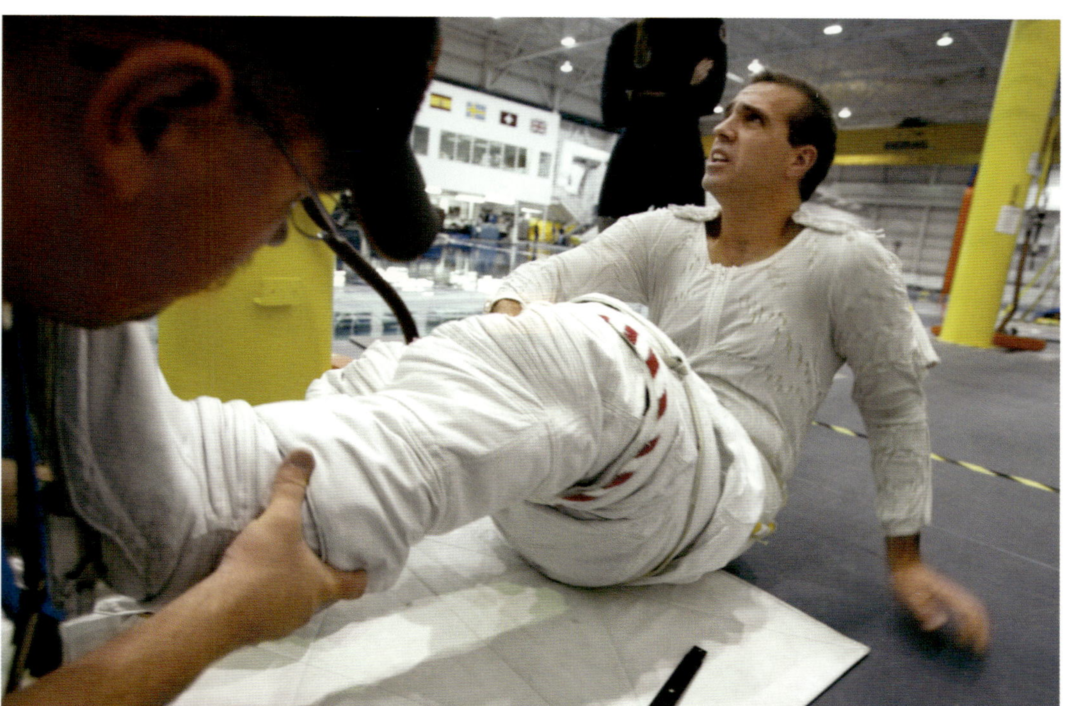

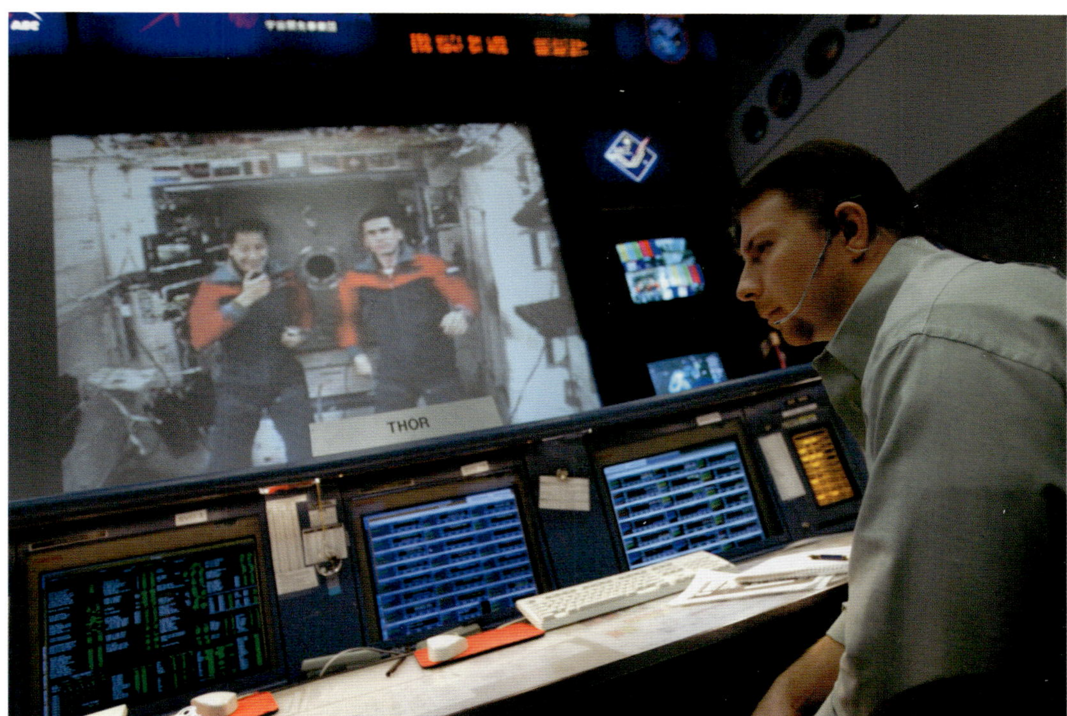

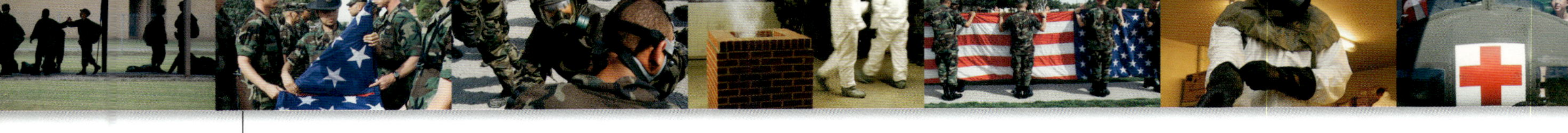

FORT BLISS

Every day at dawn, as the sun turns the Franklin Mountains pink, an American flag is raised over Ft. Bliss in El Paso. At 5 p.m., the flag is lowered, folded, and stored for the following day's ceremony. Flag detail rotates among the Advanced Individual Training units. Today, it's the duty of the 56th Air Defense Artillery.

Photo by Rudy Gutierrez, El Paso Times

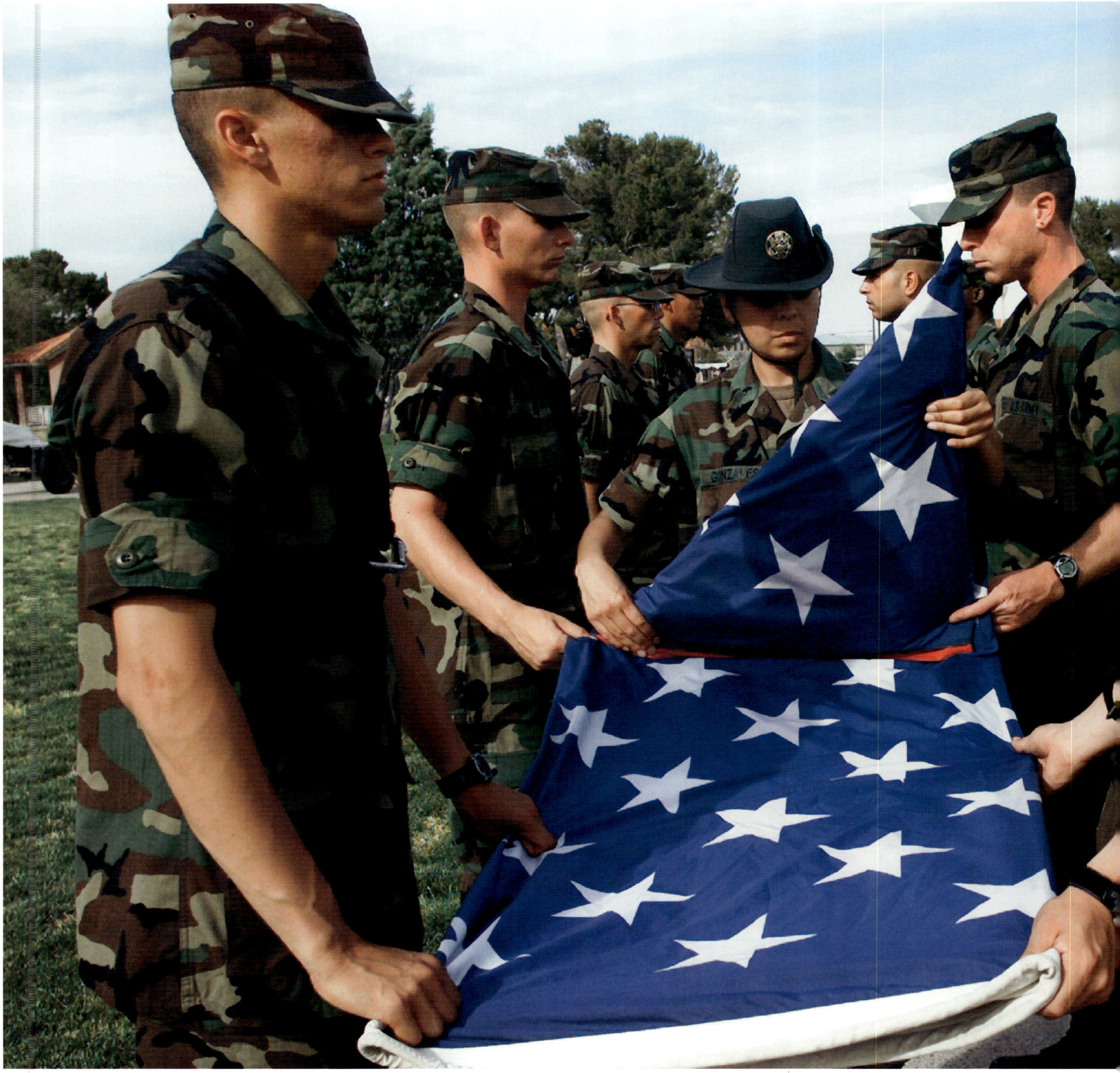

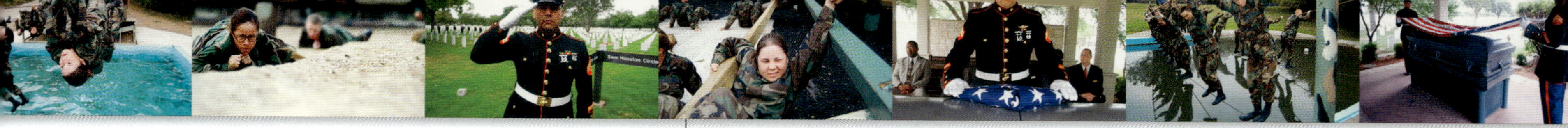

LACKLAND AIR FORCE BASE
During basic training, Kelley Larsen completes the low-rail section of an obstacle course that's part of confidence building and physical conditioning. At the end of the six-week basic program, female graduates must be able to run two miles in 21 minutes, complete 38 sit-ups in two minutes, and do 14 push-ups in two minutes.
Photo by Alicia Wagner Calzada

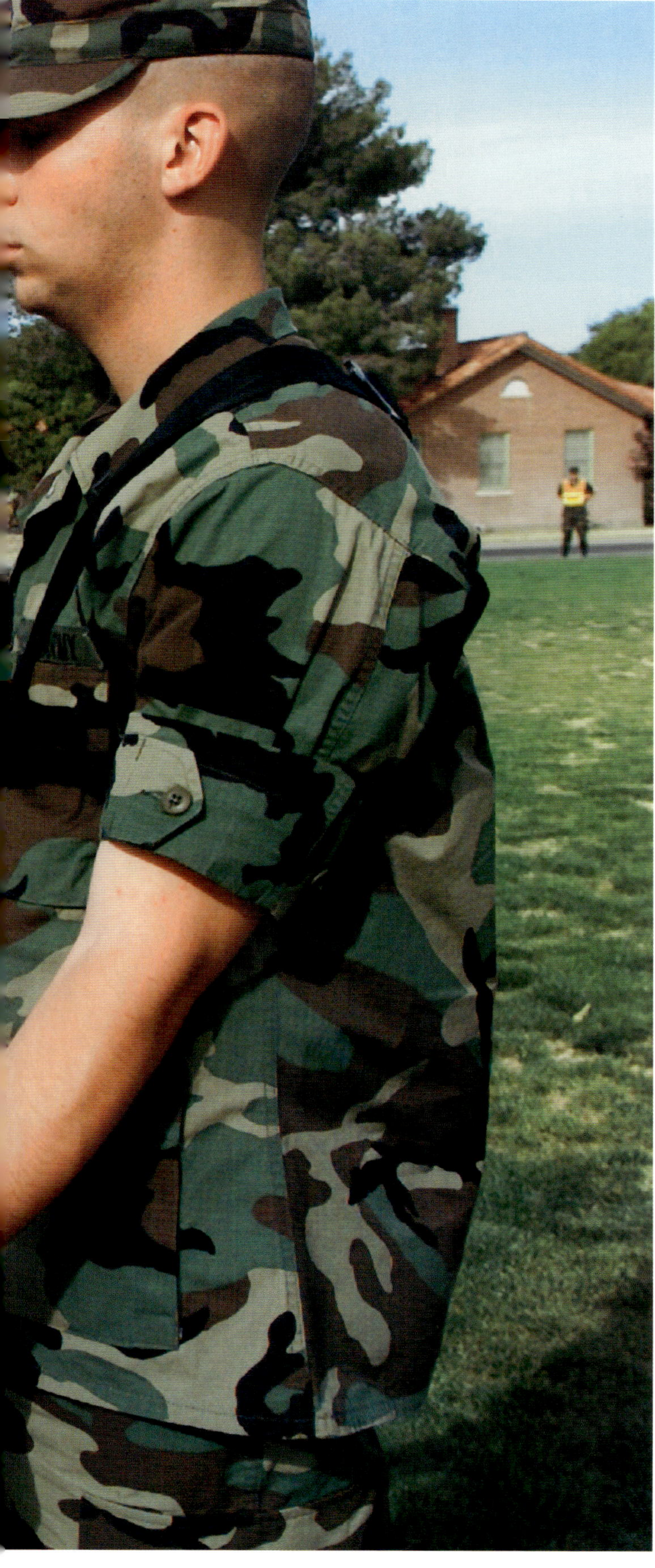

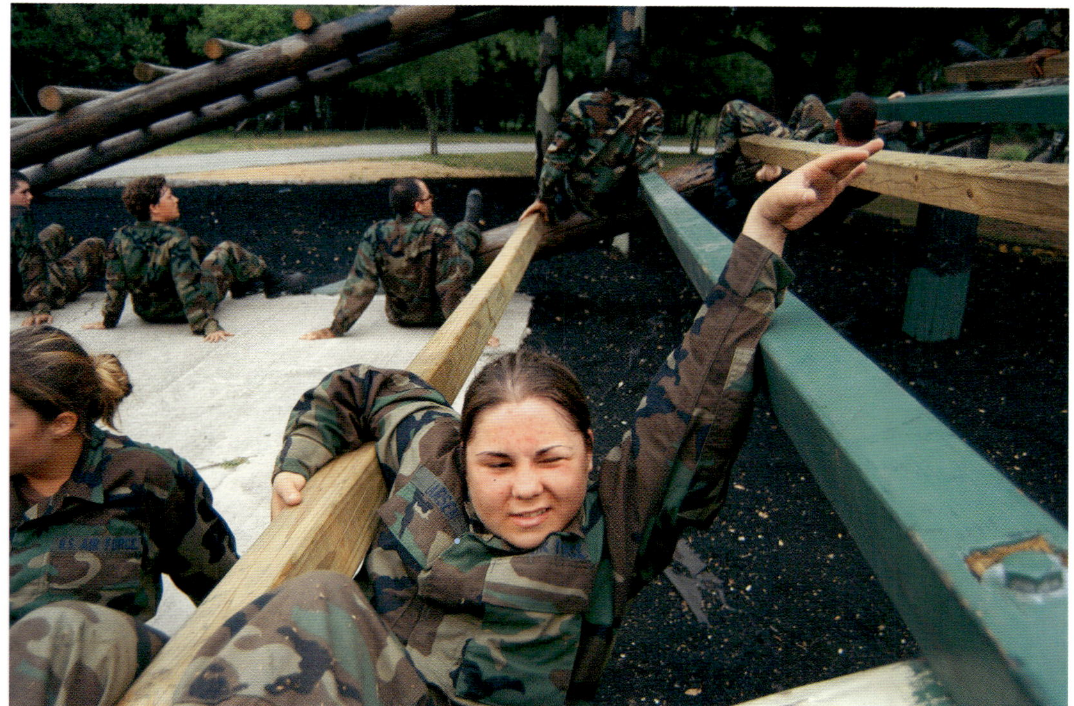

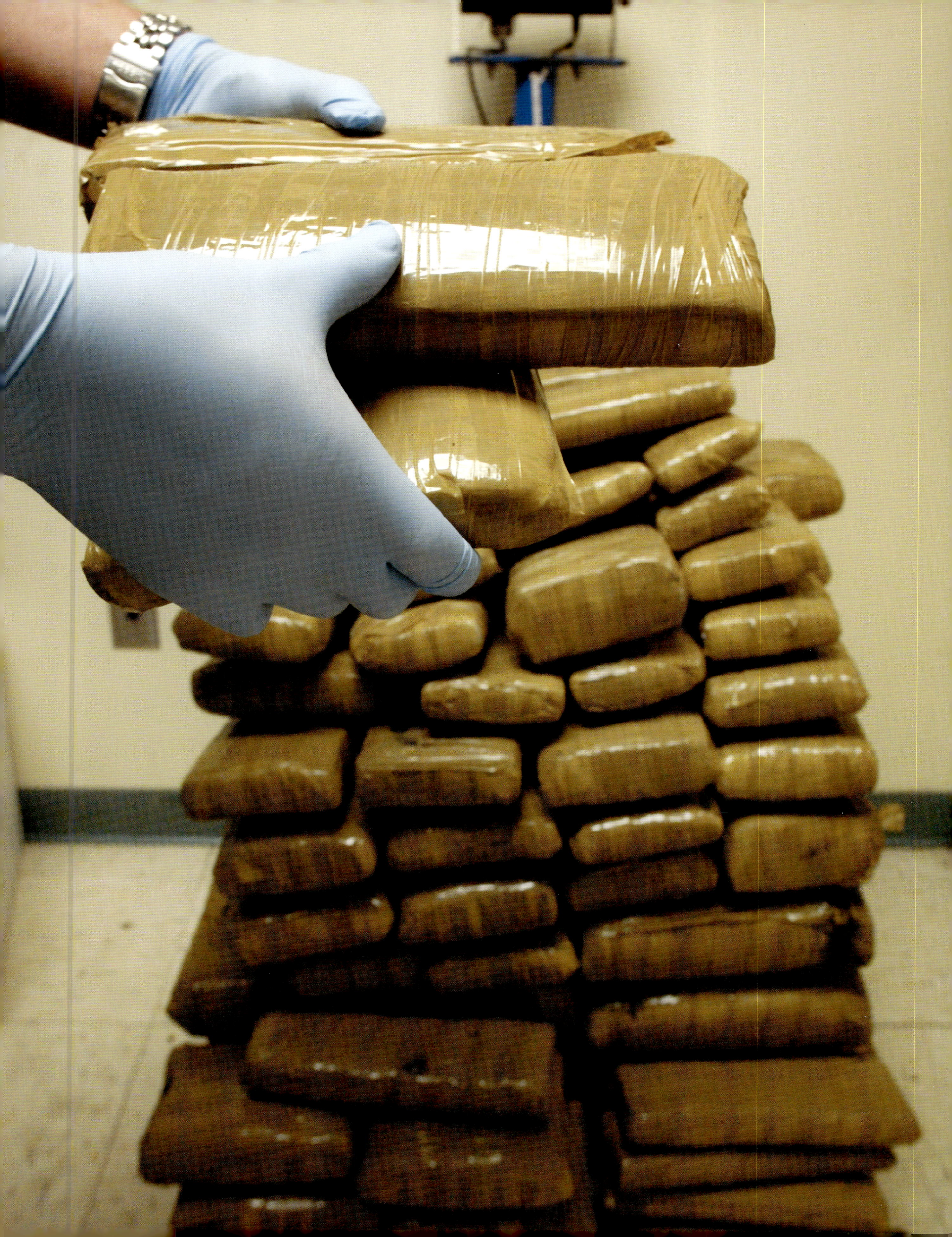

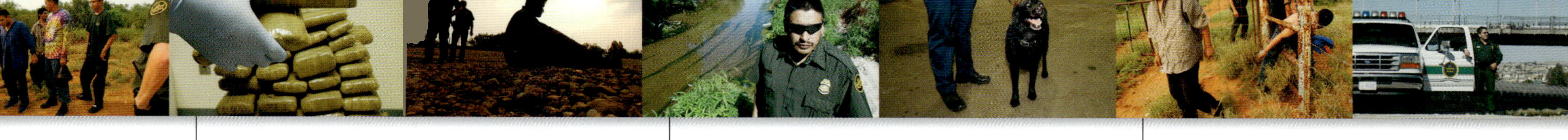

EL PASO
Weighing the evidence: About 240 pounds of marijuana were found in a car's floor compartments at a border crossing. The driver, a 19-year-old Juarez woman, was charged with importation and intent to distribute a controlled substance. A record 335,000 pounds of marijuana were seized by El Paso border agents in 2003.
Photo by Rudy Gutierrez, El Paso Times

EL PASO
Cameras, helicopters, and boats are used to monitor the U.S.-Mexico border, but agents like Caleb Vidaurri are still crucial, especially along unfenced parts of the Rio Grande River. Over 88,800 illegal immigrants were apprehended in 2003 in the El Paso district, which covers nearly 300 miles in New Mexico and west Texas.
Photo by Rudy Gutierrez, El Paso Times

LAREDO
Caught by U.S. Border Patrol while attempting to board a van on the Camino Columbia Tollroad, these Mexican immigrants will be sent back home after being booked. In an average week, 1,700 immigrants are apprehended between Nuevo Laredo and Laredo while crossing the U.S.-Mexican border.
Photo by Jerry Lara, San Antonio Express-News

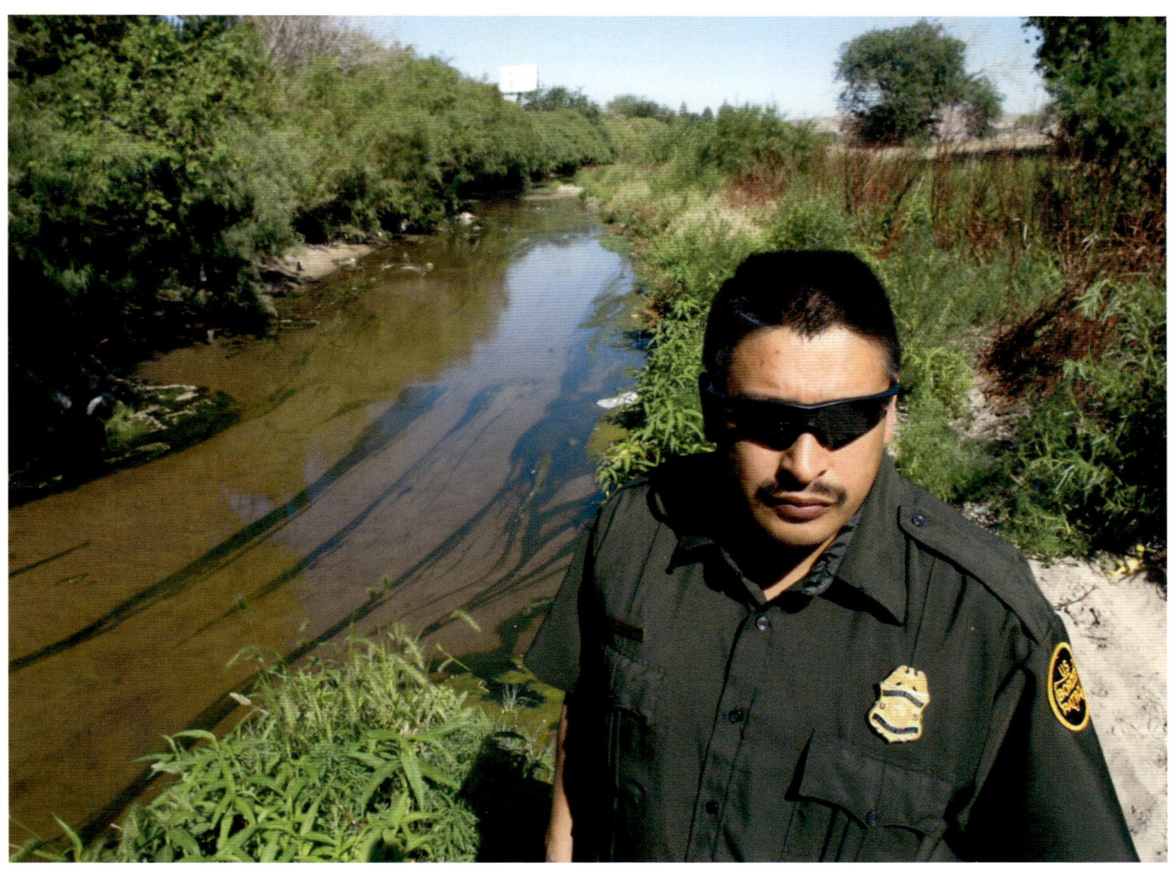

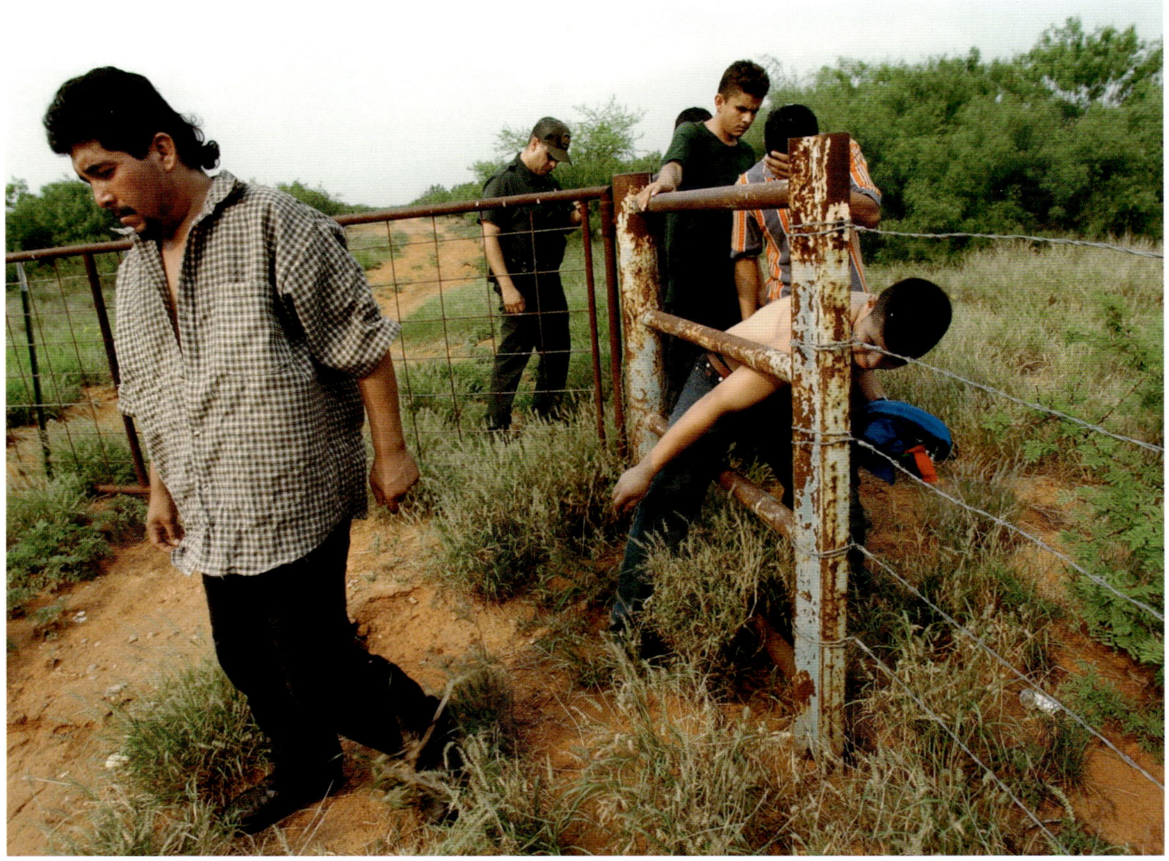

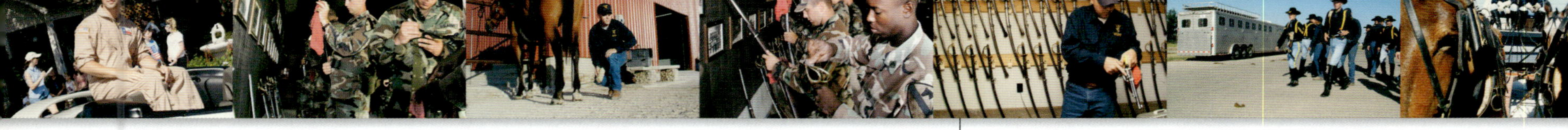

FORT HOOD

U.S. Army Sergeant First Class Daniel Tramell cleans a .45-caliber revolver in the armory of the 1st Cavalry Division's Horse Cavalry Detachment. Created in 1972, the unit is composed of 37 active-duty soldiers. At parades and ceremonies, they demonstrate the horsemanship and weapons skills of the 1880s-era mounted troopers.
Photos by Craig Robinson

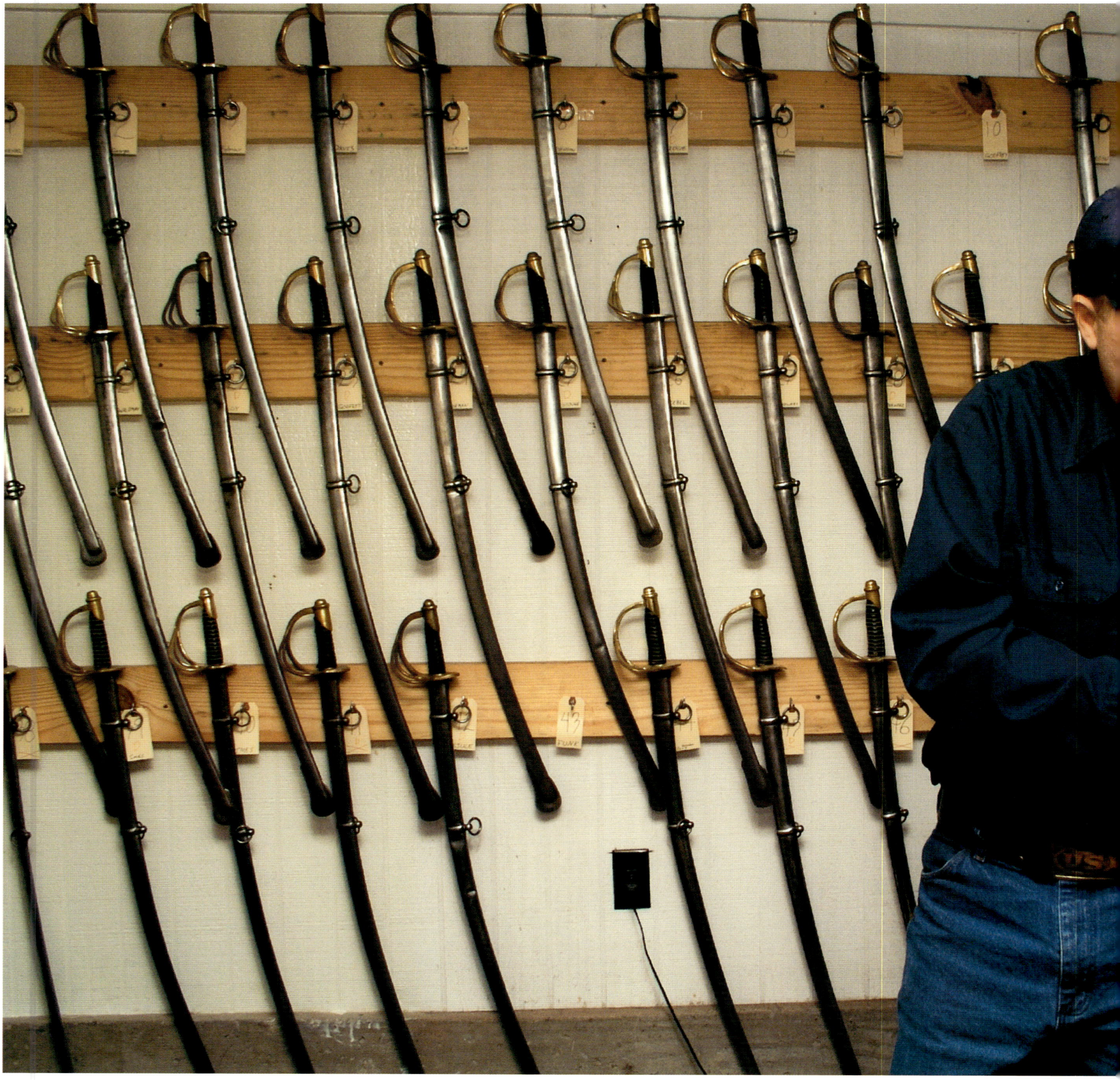

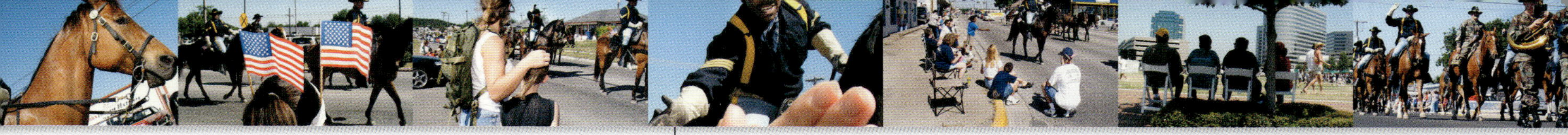

COPPERAS COVE

A soldier from the 1st Cavalry Division's Horse Cavalry Detachment (the last mounted unit in the U.S. Army) shakes hands with a young fan during the annual Festival of the Five Hills. The roots of the famed "1st Cav" Detachment go back to 1855 when they patrolled the western frontier.

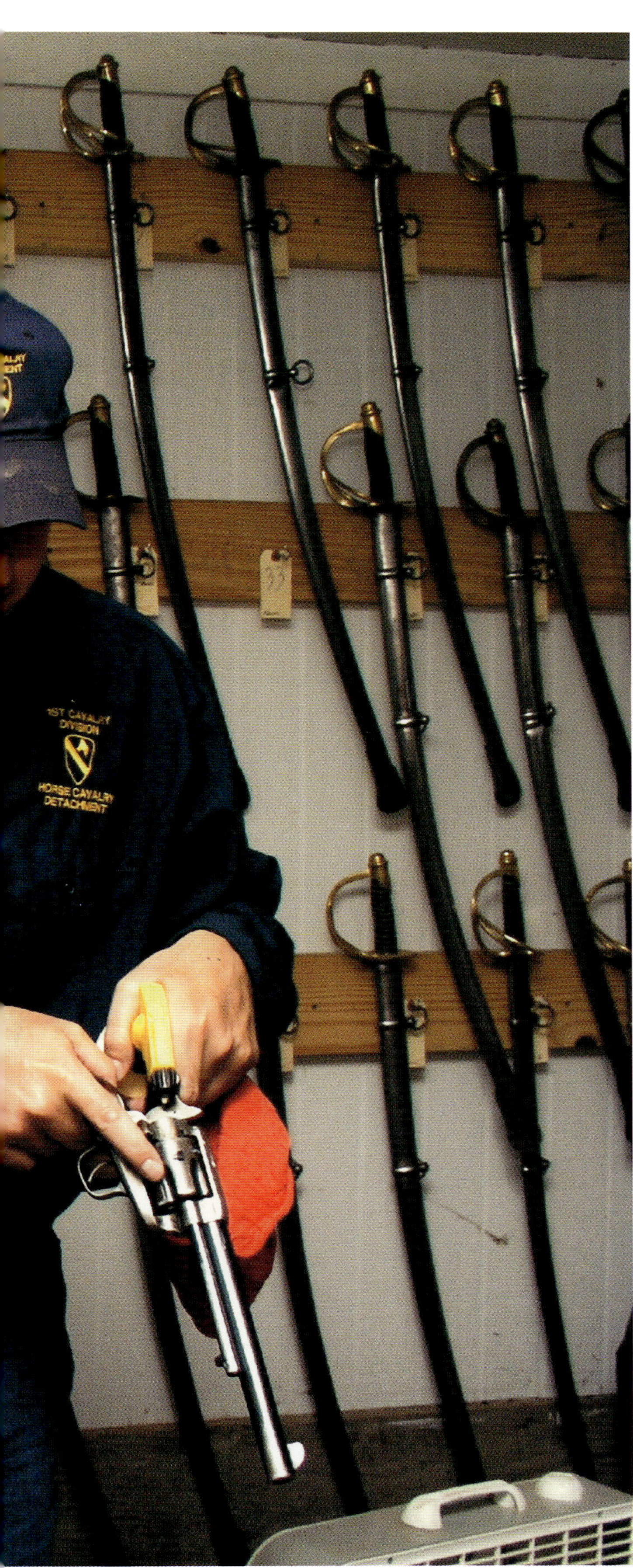

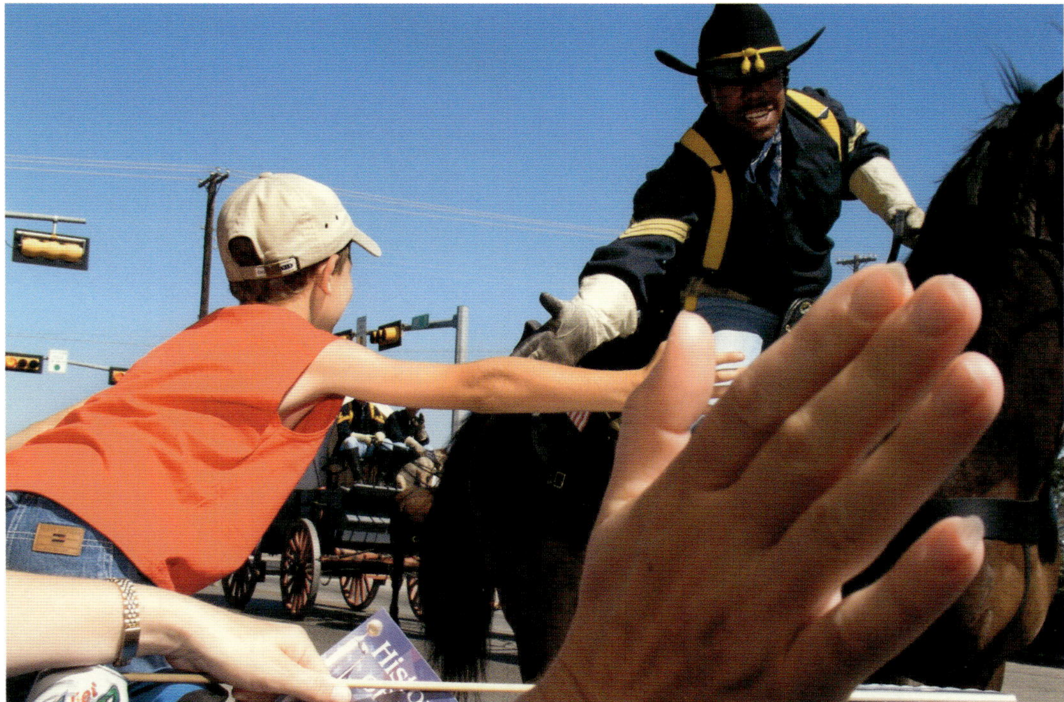

CROSBY COUNTY

A cotton farmer works his fields on the high plains east of Lubbock. In recent years, the record heat has taken its toll on King Cotton. Around Lubbock, cotton depends on irrigation, and it's difficult to keep enough water on the plants because of the high temperatures. As a result, farmers planted 1.2 million fewer acres in 2002 than in the previous year.

Photos by Sean Meyers Photography

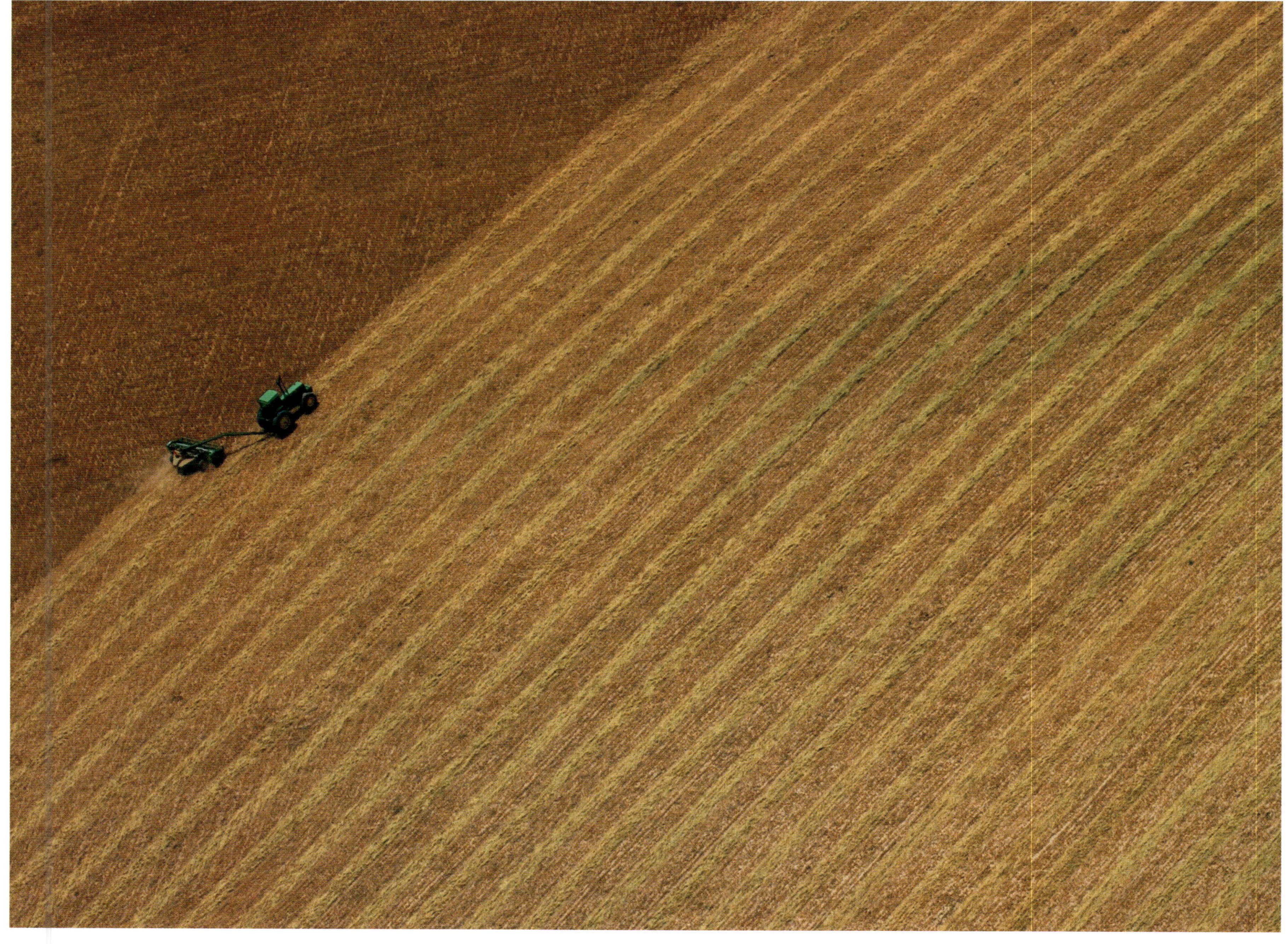

LUBBOCK
Oil derricks dot the Texas Panhandle's landscape. The Lone Star state contains about 25 percent of the nation's 21 billion barrels of "proven" oil reserves. Since 1991, Texas reserves have decreased by 20 percent, which means the crude oil below is rapidly disappearing.

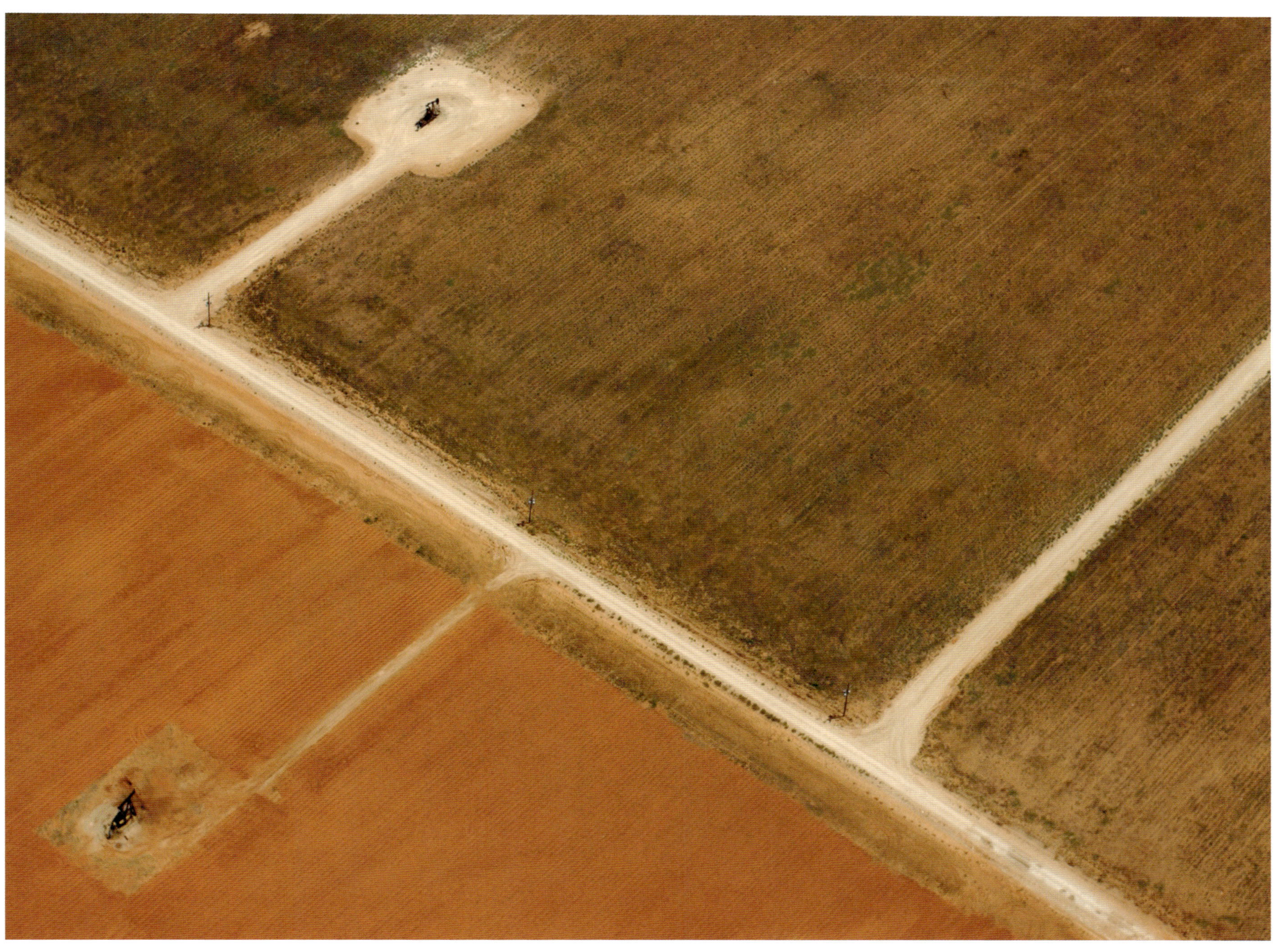

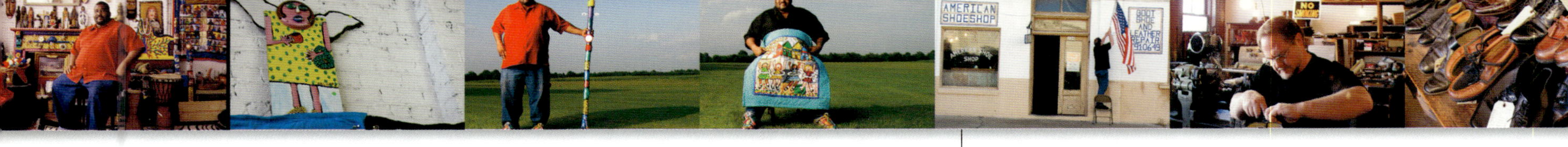

TEXARKANA
Richard Davis hangs a flag outside his downtown American Shoe Shop, as he has done every working morning for 22 years. The 113-year-old business has been in the Davis family since 1958.
Photo by Chris Dean

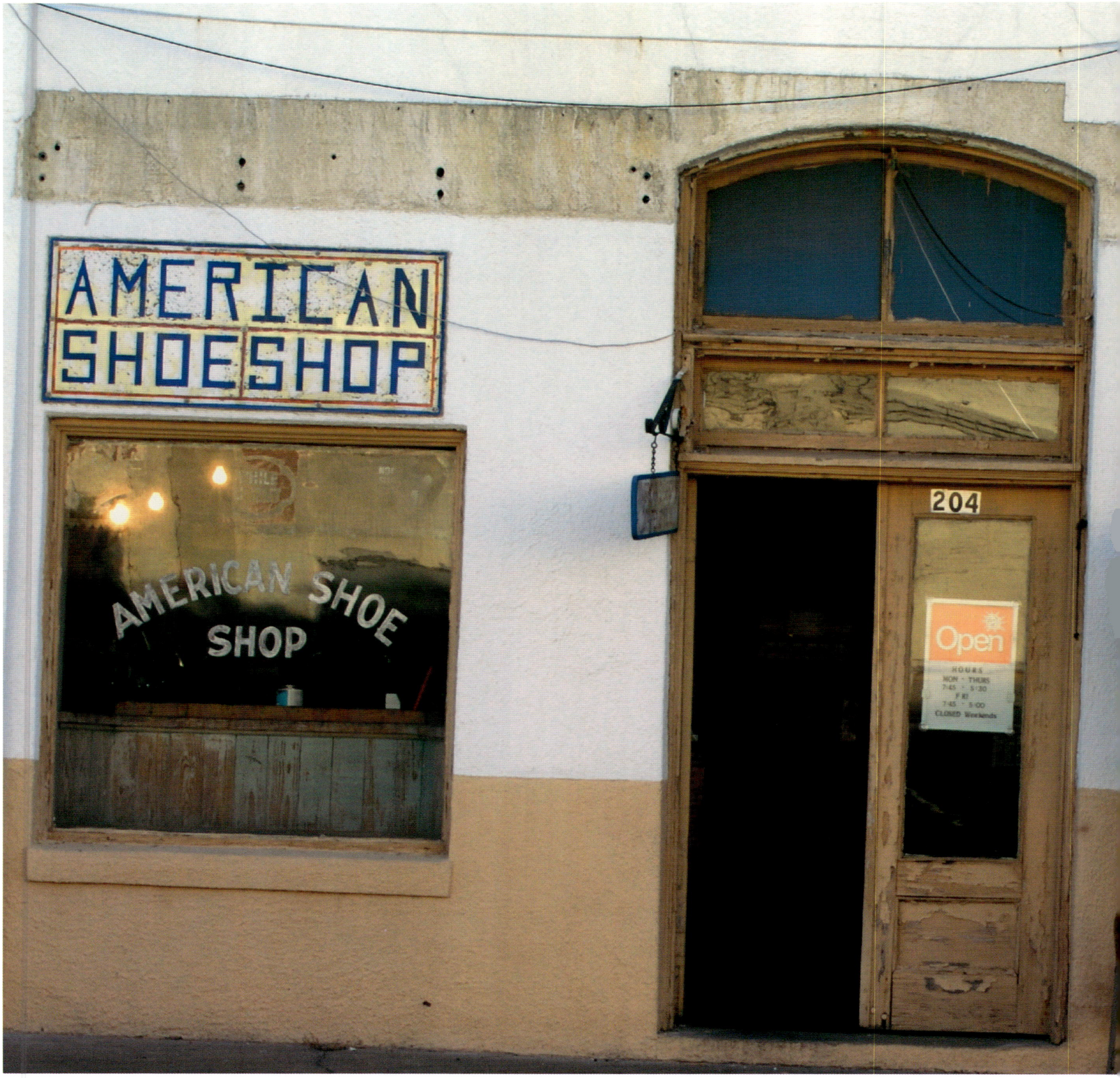

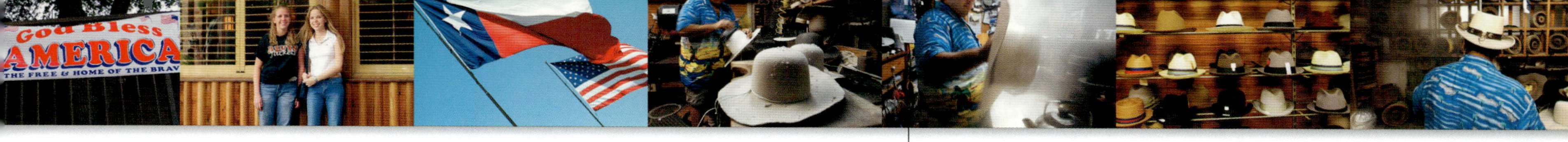

BUDA

At Texas Hatters, they make some mighty big hats. For 77 years, three generations of founder Manny Grammage's family have been shaping cowboy hats, fedoras, derbies, and Panama hats for everyday Texans and celebrities like Willie Nelson and Clint Eastwood. General Manager David Torres shapes a straw cowboy hat.
Photo by Rodolfo Gonzalez

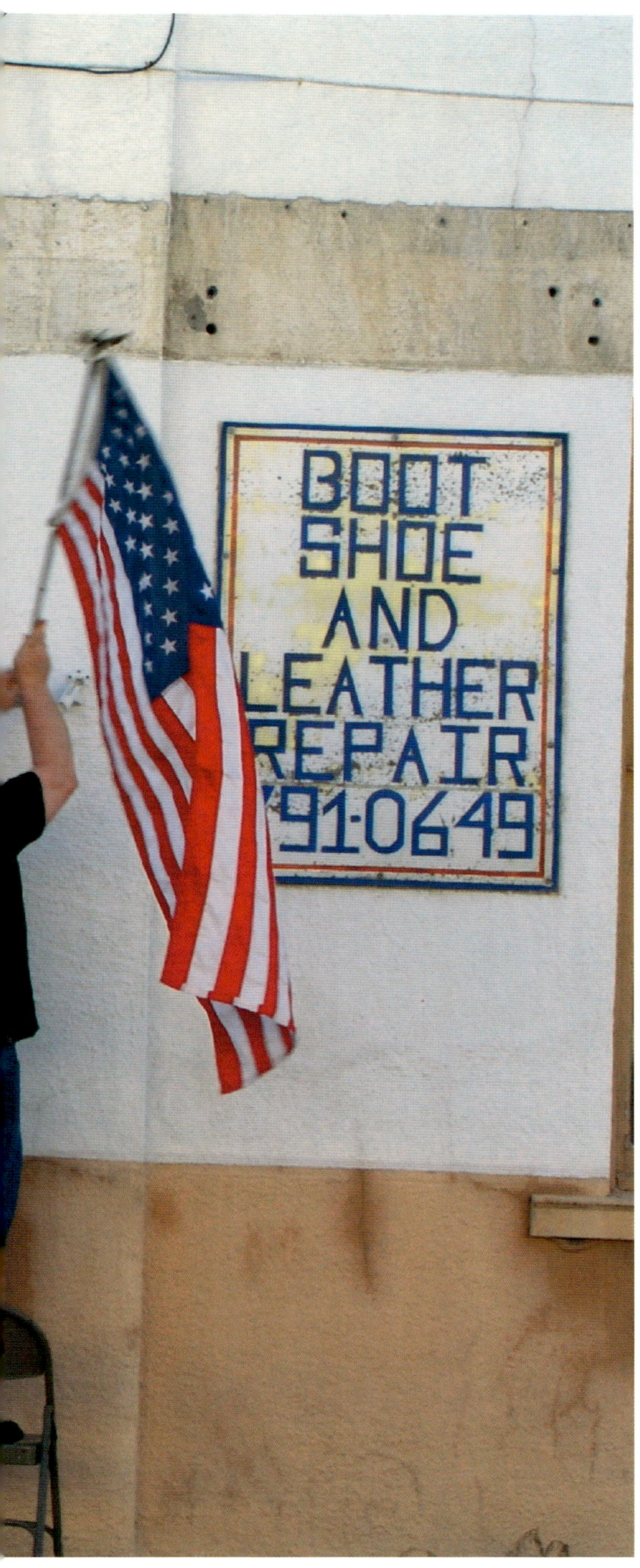

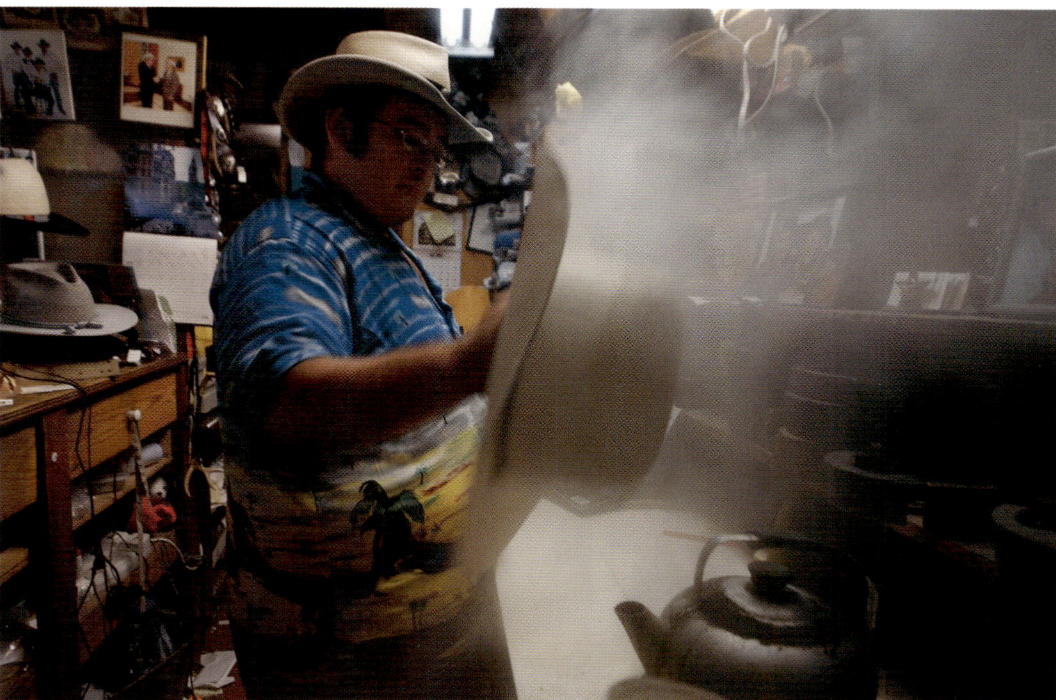

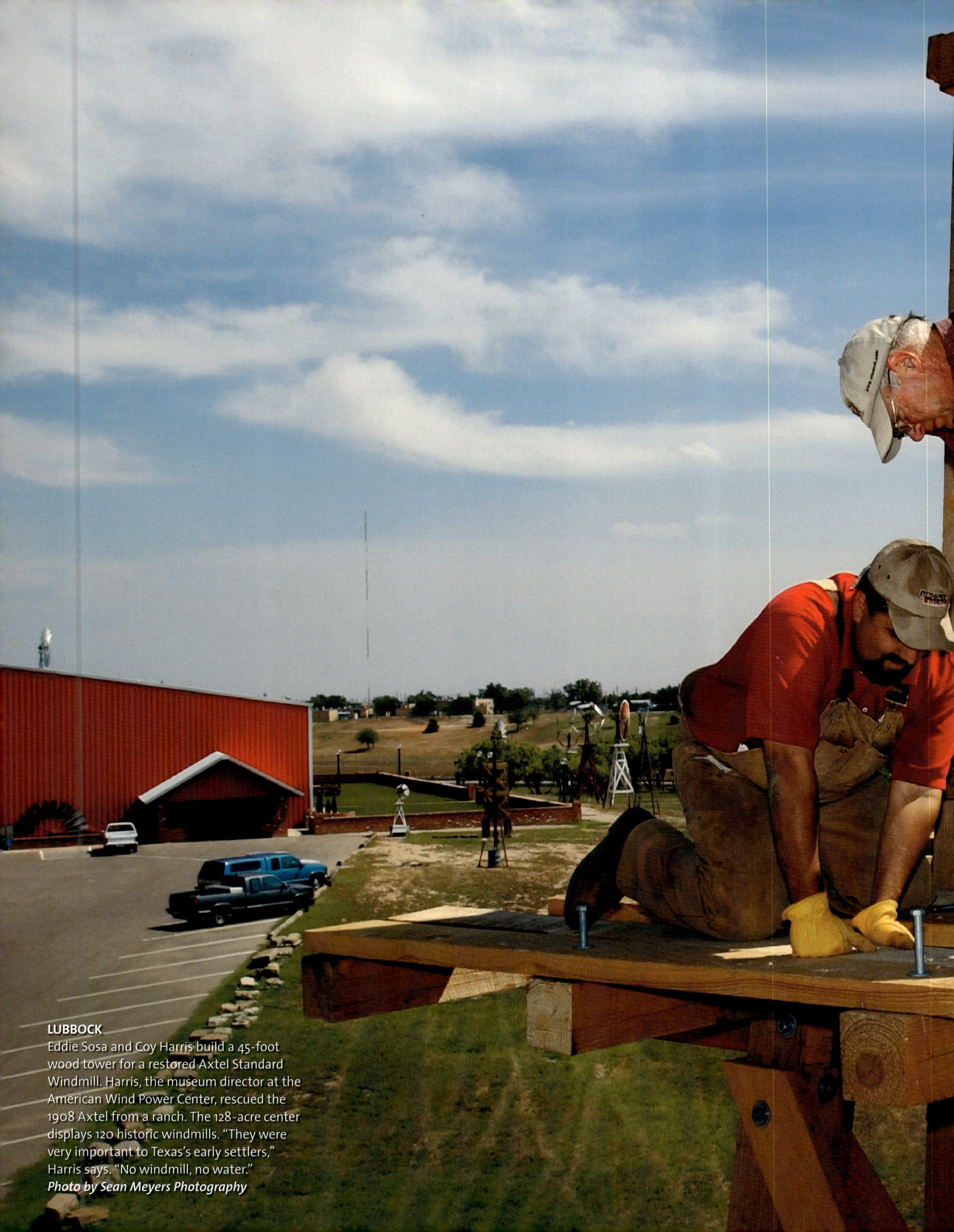

LUBBOCK
Eddie Sosa and Coy Harris build a 45-foot wood tower for a restored Axtel Standard Windmill. Harris, the museum director at the American Wind Power Center, rescued the 1908 Axtel from a ranch. The 128-acre center displays 120 historic windmills. "They were very important to Texas's early settlers," Harris says. "No windmill, no water."
Photo by Sean Meyers Photography

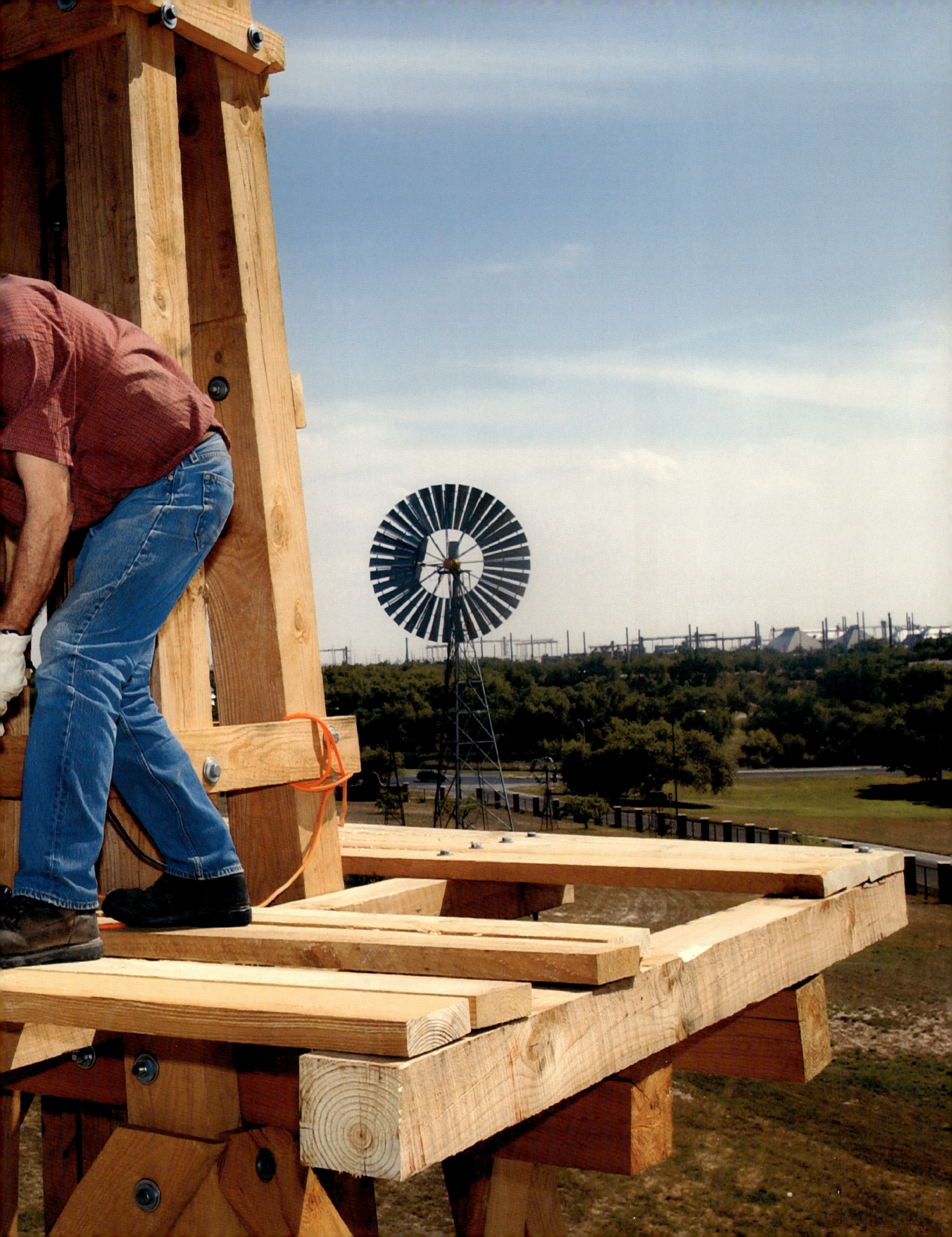

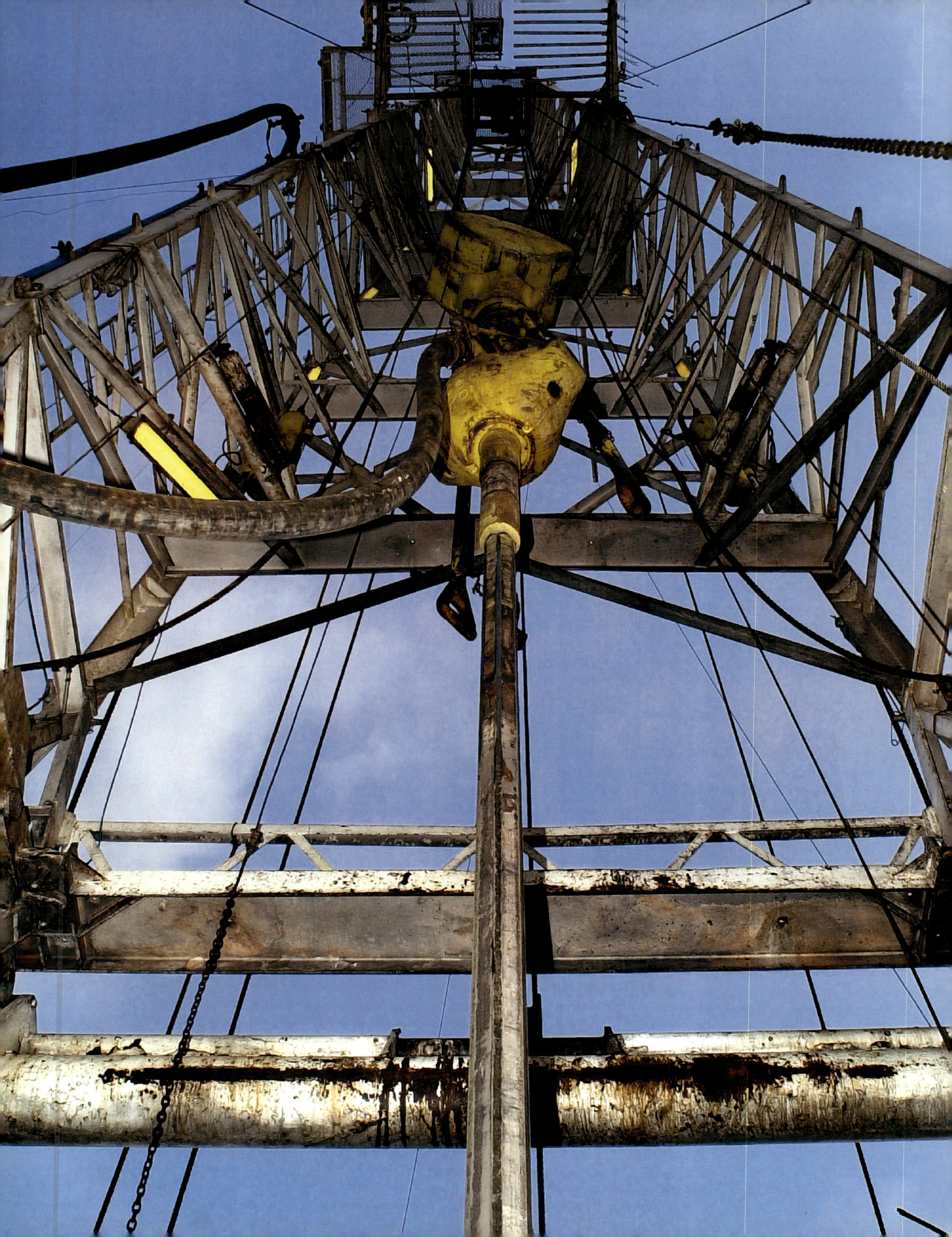

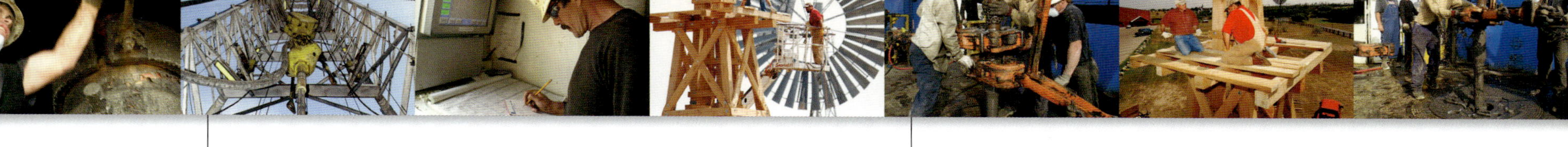

RANKIN
This 100-foot-tall steel drilling rig has come a long way from the small, wooden derricks used after the state had its first oil strike. The Lucas gusher, as it was called, blew on January 10, 1901, in the now famous Spindletop oil fields on the Gulf Coast. Oilmen and promoters swarmed, and the Texas petroleum industry was born.
Photos by Tim Fischer, Midland Reporter-Telegram

RANKIN
Joe Guerra and Scott Johnson brace the pipe clamps as Trine Leal "throws chain." Derrick hand Guerra has worked steadily on rigs in the Rankin area for four years. "It's dangerous," he says. "But you go slow and don't turn a new guy loose out there."

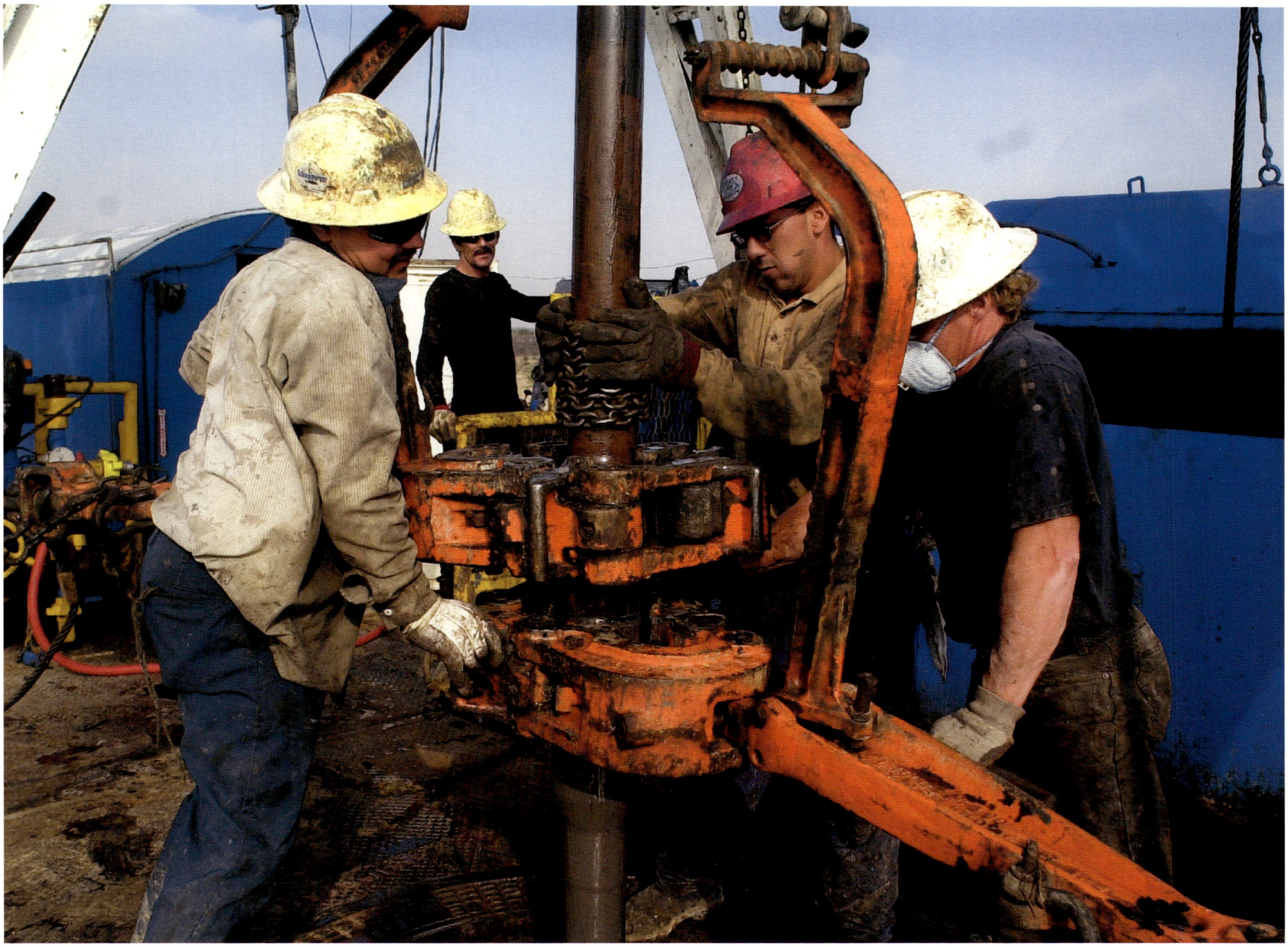

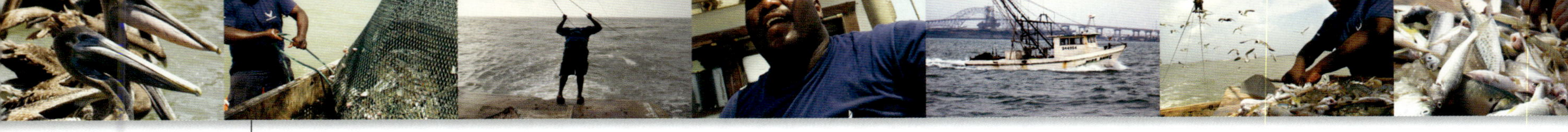

CORPUS CHRISTI
Along with shrimp and blue crabs, Carl "Blue" Bowser catches a tire in his dragnet. Bowser has been fishing around North Padre Island for ten years. During this time, relations between environmentalists and shrimpers have become tense as not just tires but an increasing number of endangered sea turtles have been caught in nets.
Photos by Tim Zielenbach

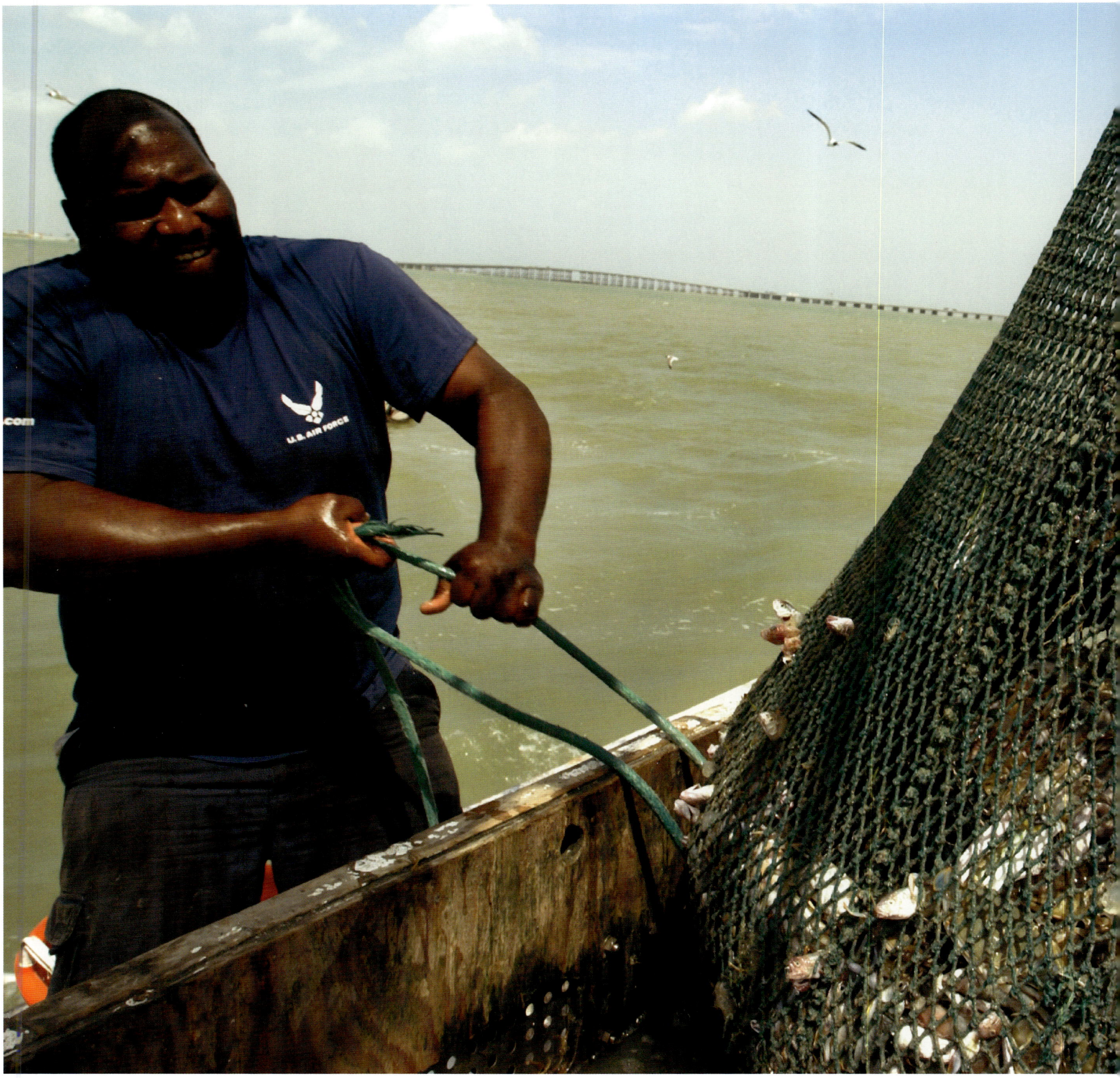

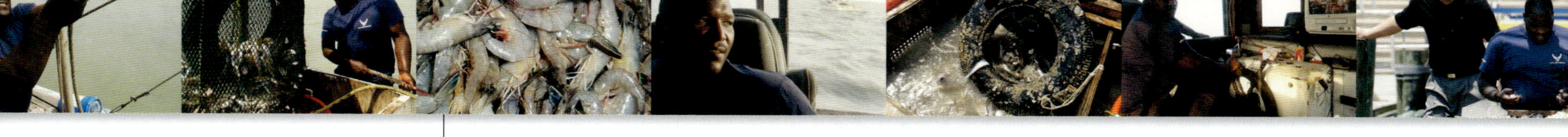

CORPUS CHRISTI
Bowser sells his jumbo shrimp for $8 a pound to customers who wait for him to come ashore every afternoon at the Corpus Christi harbor.

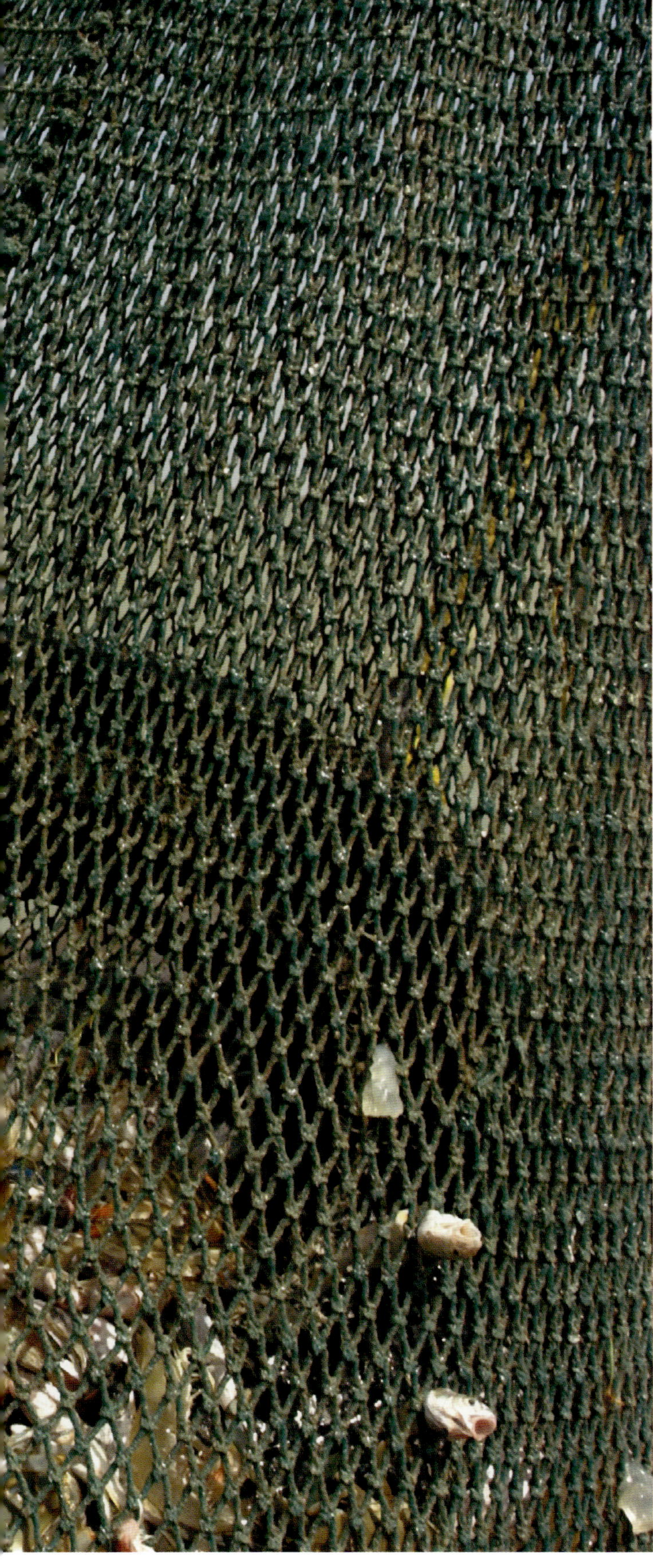

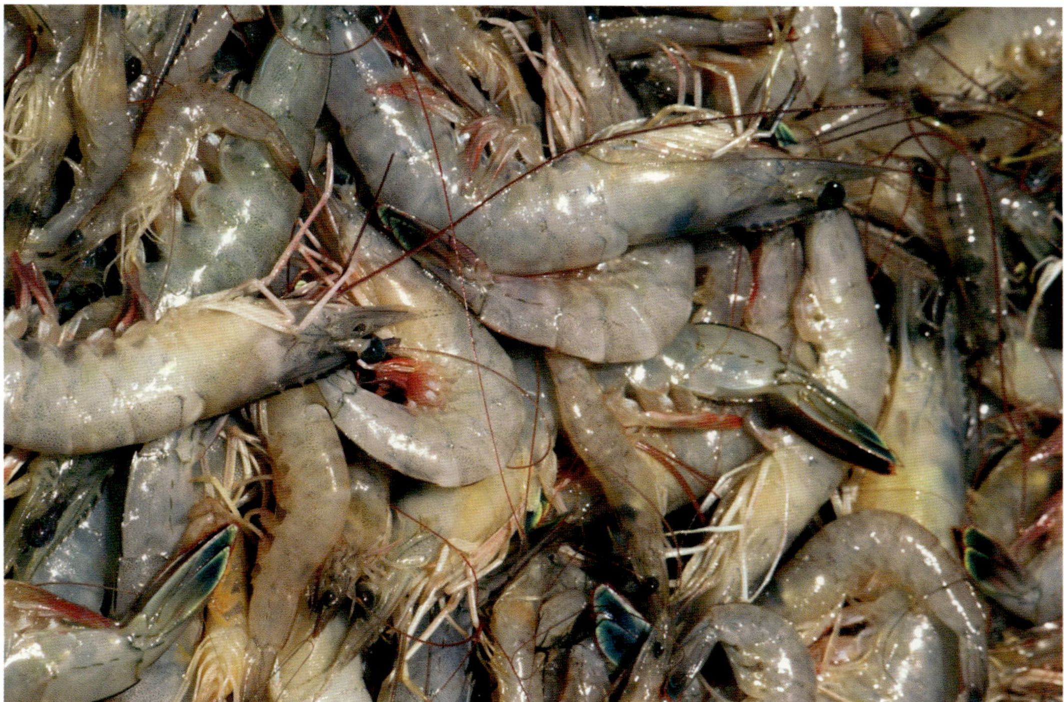

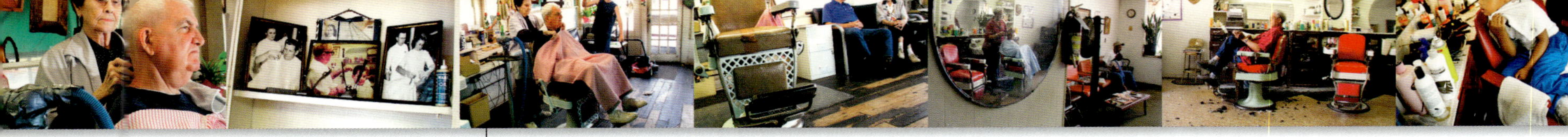

LONGVIEW

Mollie Edmonds, 83, has been cutting hair since she was 12. She got her license from the Texas Barber College at the age of 30—the first woman certified in the state. Though she has outlived three husbands, she still has lots of family nearby, including her 19-year-old grandson Jordan Humphrey, who dropped by to borrow her lawn mower.

Photo by Les Hassell

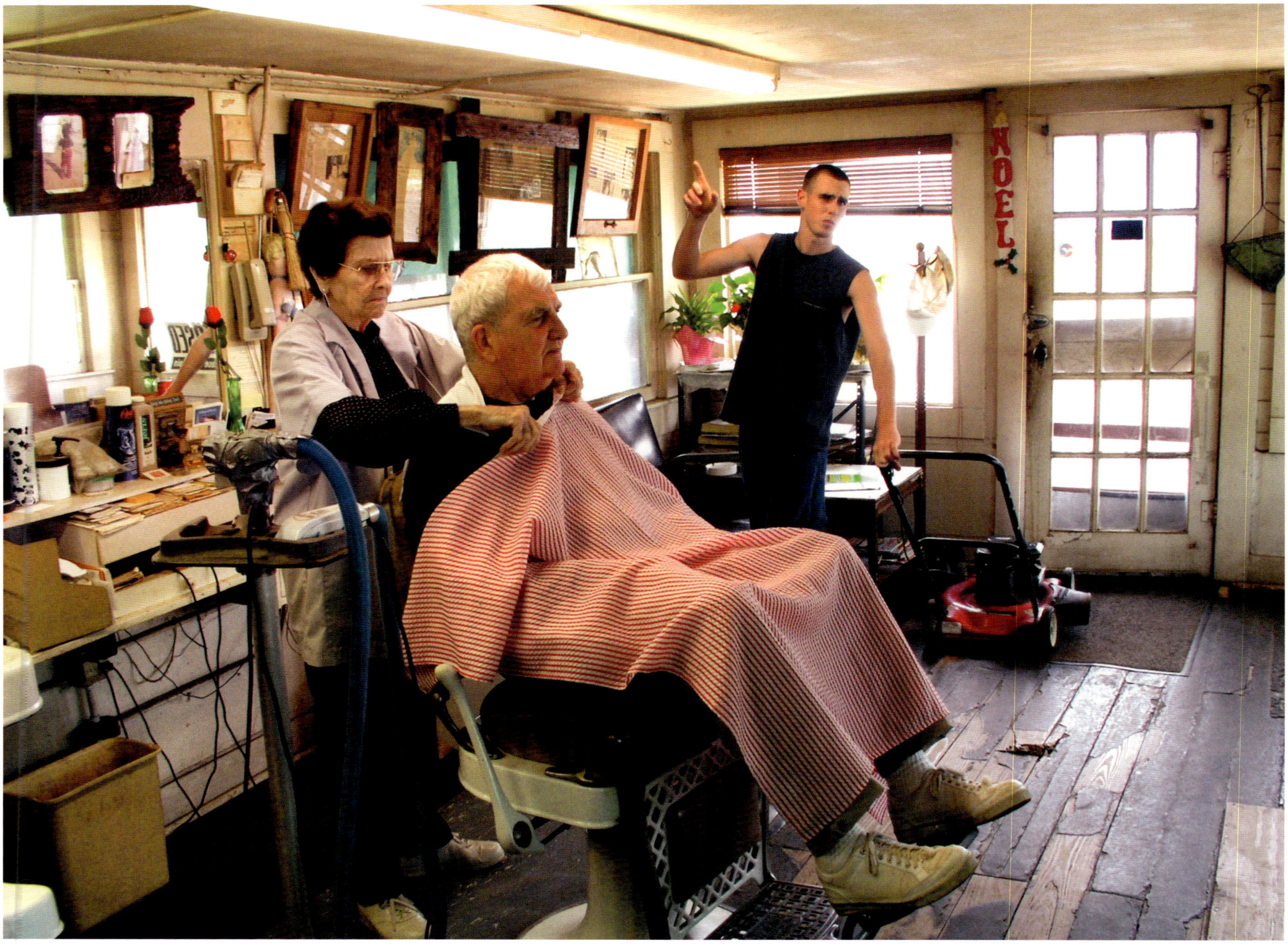

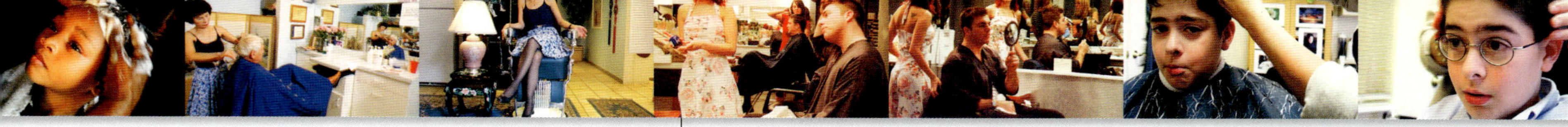

DALLAS
At the Avalon Salon in Snyder Plaza, opposite the SMU campus, Typhany Nevarez awaits a verdict from Kip Collins on her handiwork.
Photo by Danny Hurley

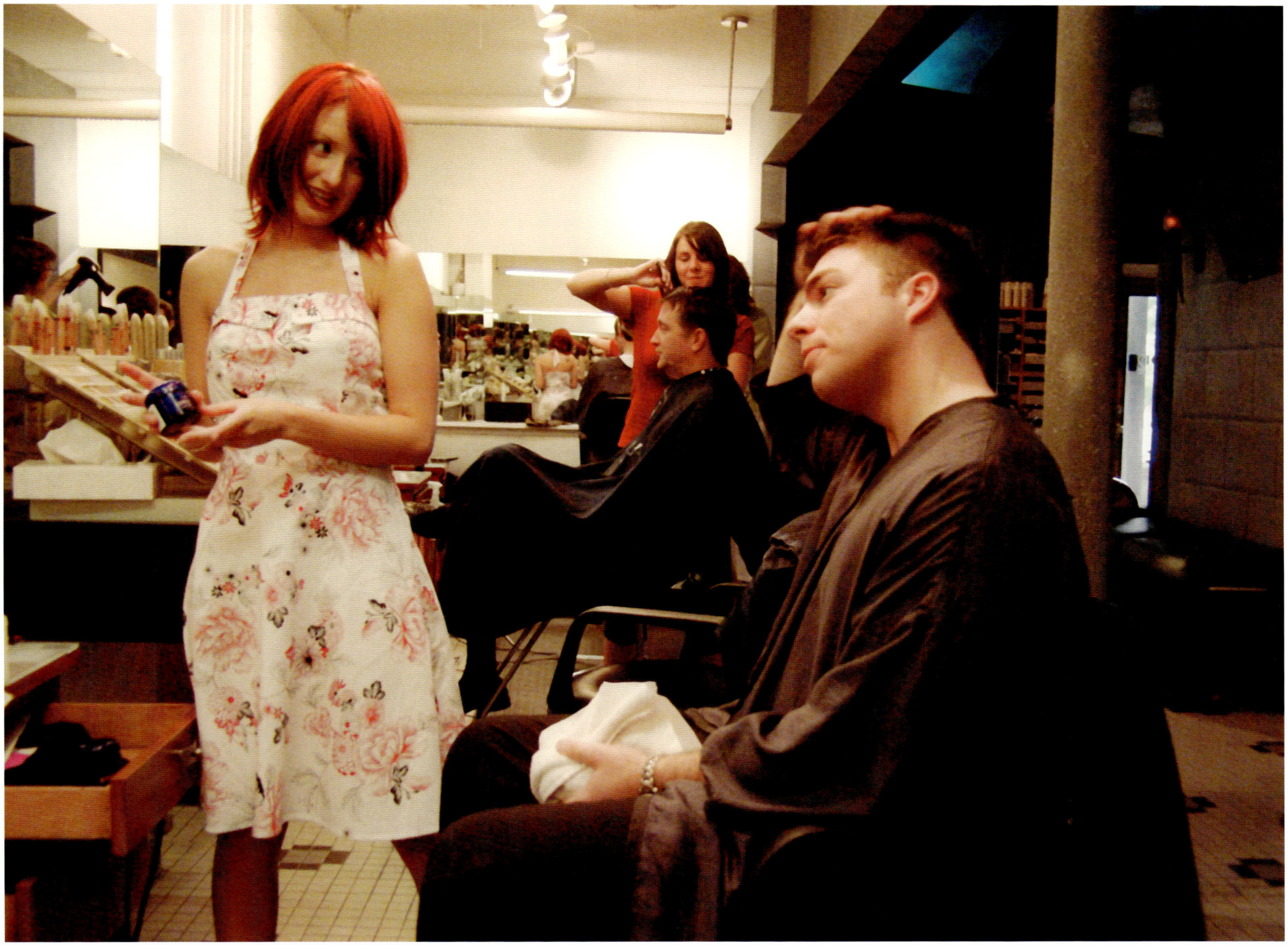

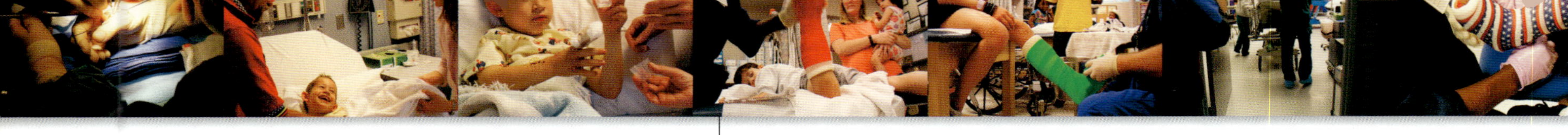

HOUSTON
Melissa Hughlett and her daughter Krystle watch as son Jonathan is fitted with an ankle cast at the Texas Orthopedic Hospital. Jonathan has cerebral palsy and the cast helps stretch his Achilles tendon and calf muscle.
Photos by Cheryl Hatch

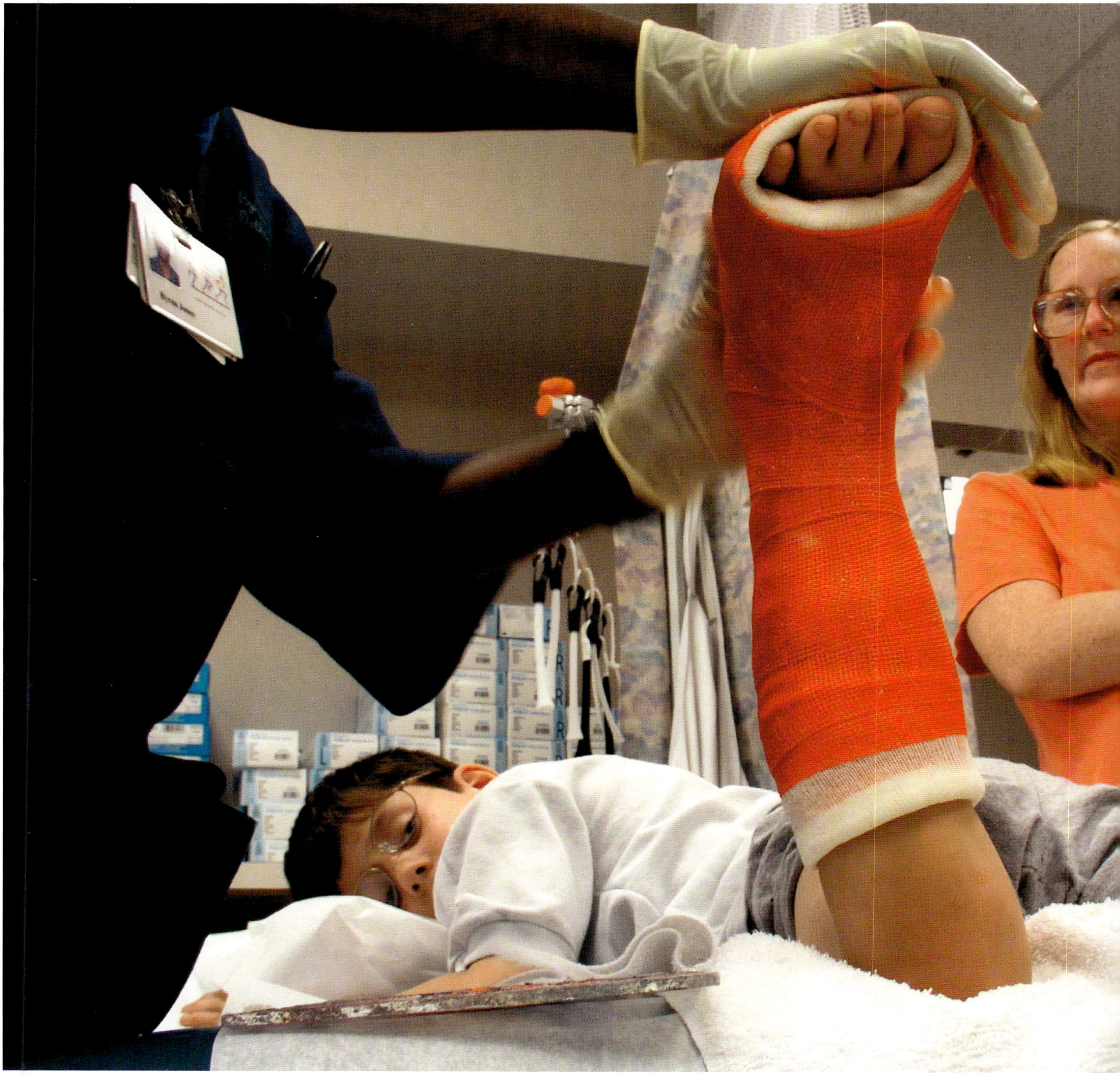

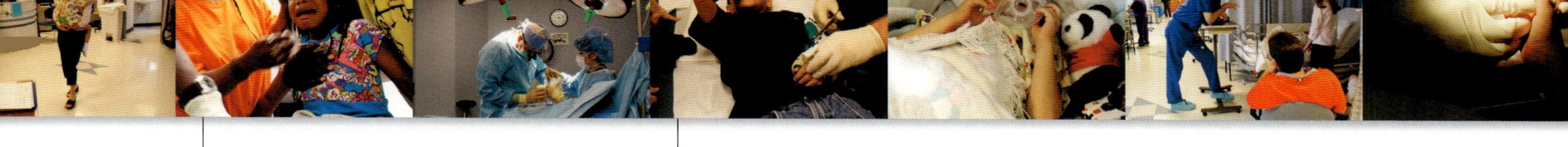

HOUSTON
Being refitted with a cast is no fun for 6-year-old Ghymea Harris, who is comforted by her parents Deborah and David. Ghymea sustained multiple broken bones in her right leg when she was hit by a truck.

HOUSTON
Wake me when it's over: Pasadena resident Ricky Gonzalez broke his arm in a bicyling accident but can't bear to look as his cast is removed.

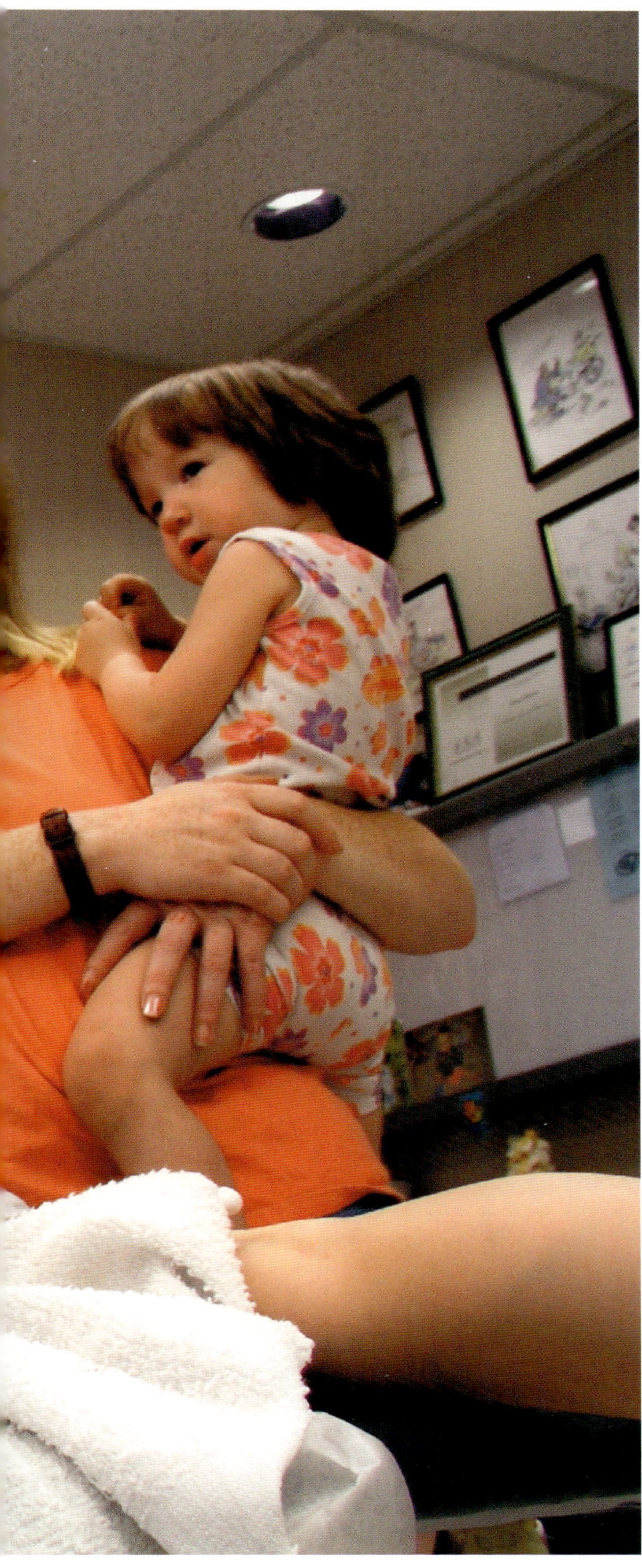

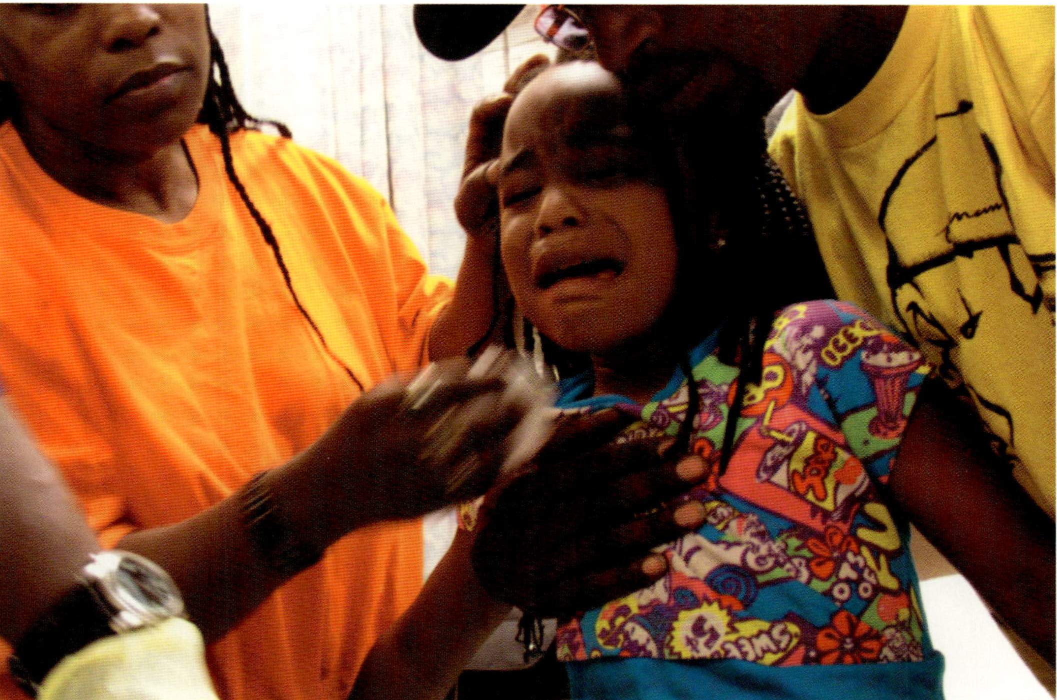

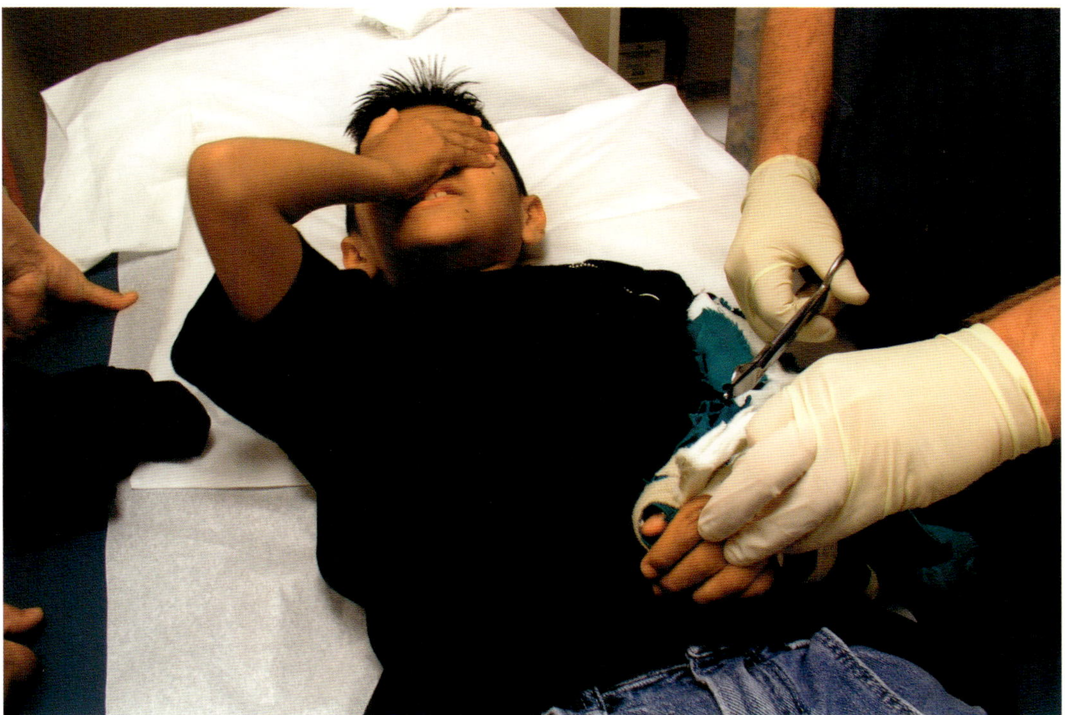

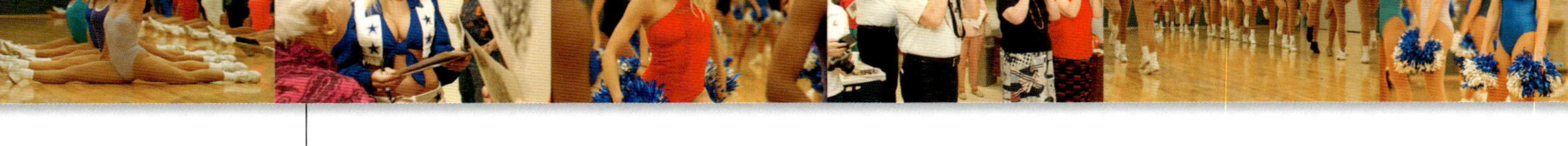

HALTOM CITY
Heather Dunn signs autographs at the Haltom Senior Center, where the Dallas Cowboys Cheerleaders visit every year. The event, which featured the cheerleaders doing the Macarena, was open to the public.
Photos by Shelly Katz Photo

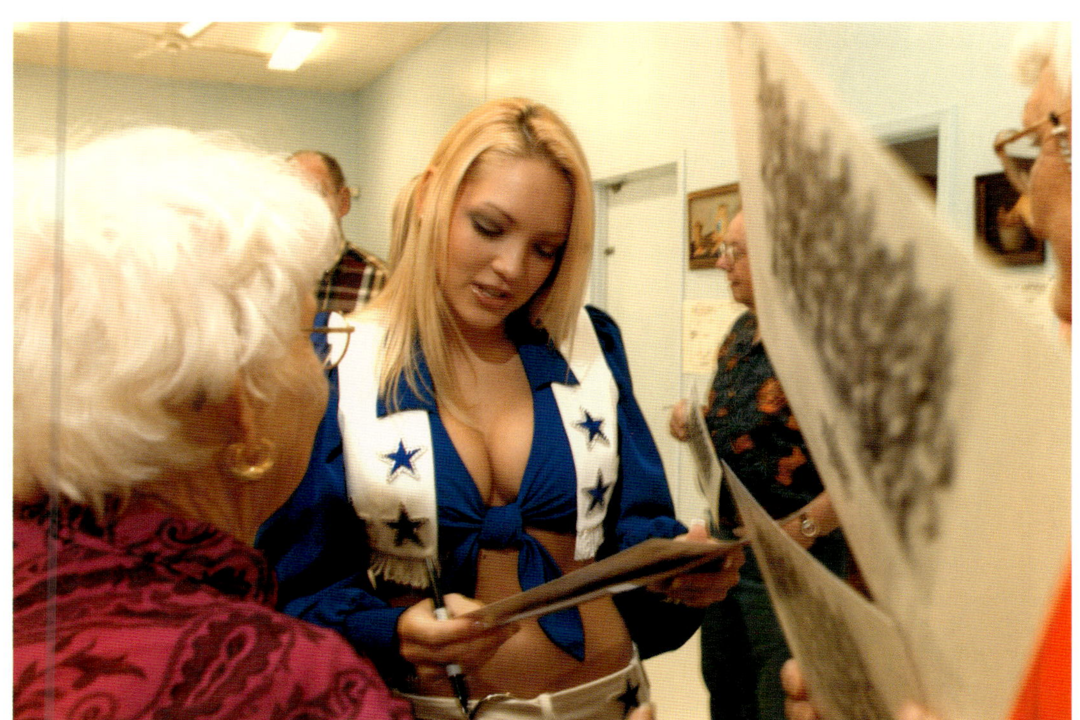

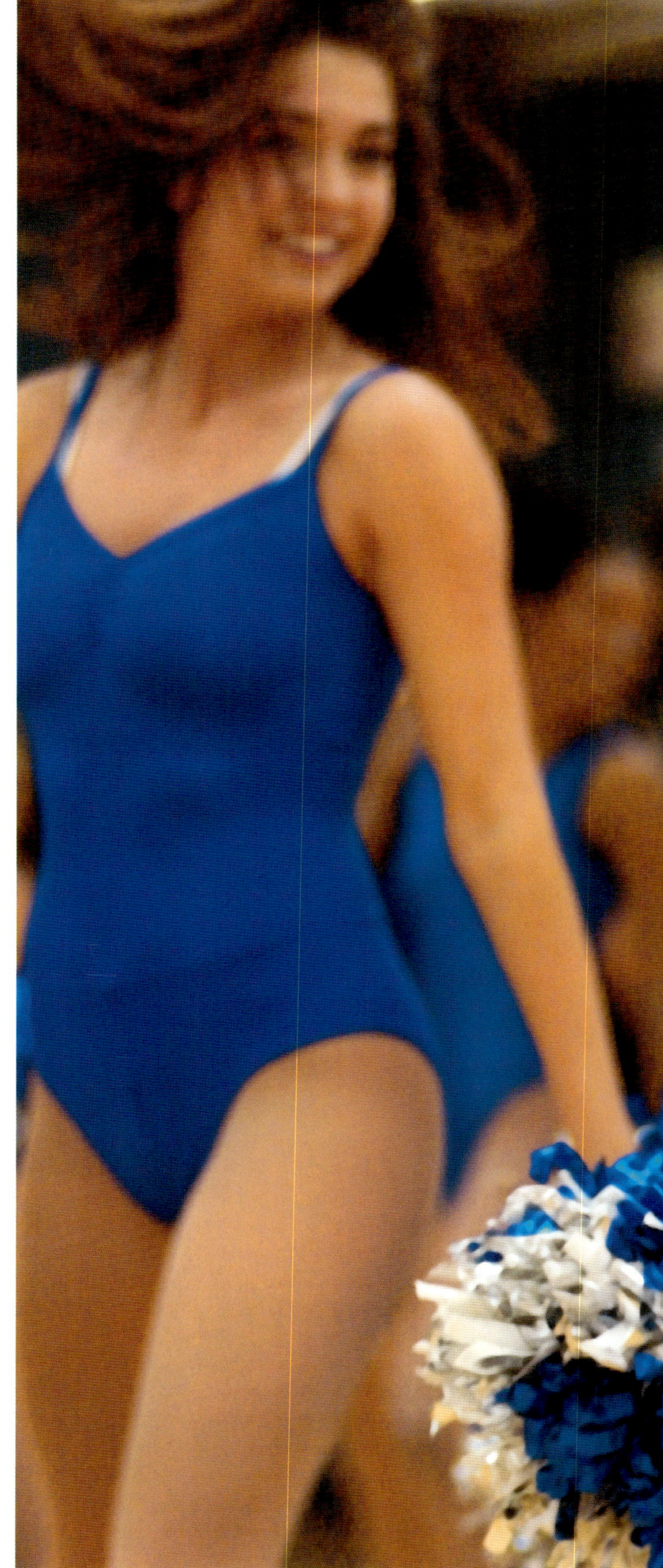

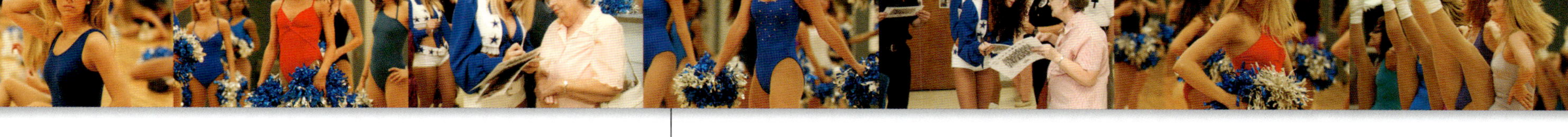

IRVING
Dallas Cowboys Cheerleaders don't stop practicing once the season ends. Heather Pliler and Ashley Melott, along with the rest of the 36-member squad, keep in shape at their Valley Ranch headquarters.

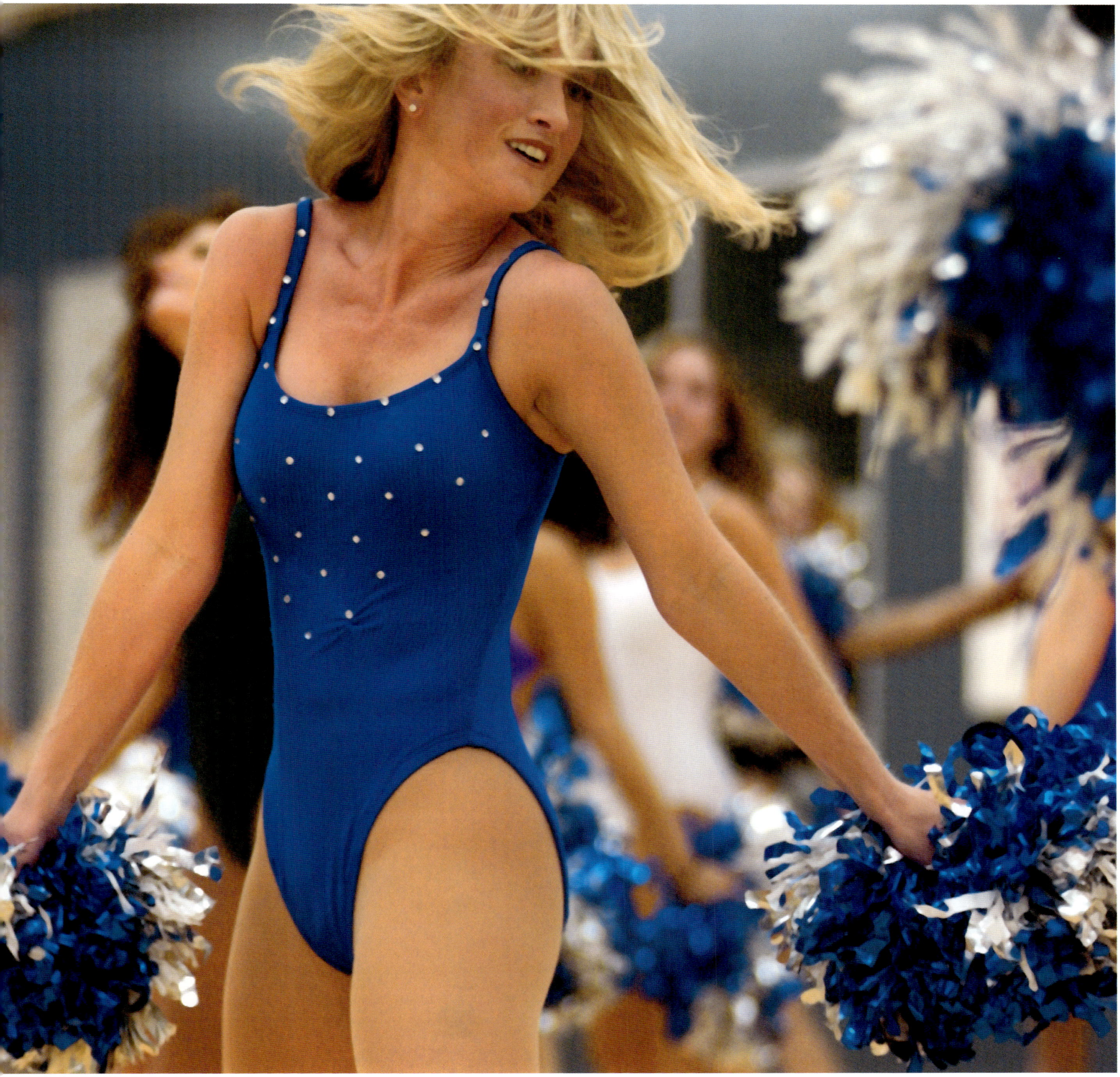

WINTERS

"Bicycle Lee" Colbath rides down Main Street on his Schwinn Beach Cruiser, delivering copies of the *Winters Enterprise*. Customers gave him the bike two years ago as a gift for his 69th birthday. According to his friend, Irma Blackshear, his other bicycle was "asking for mercy."

Photos by Ronald W. Erdrich, Abilene Reporter-News

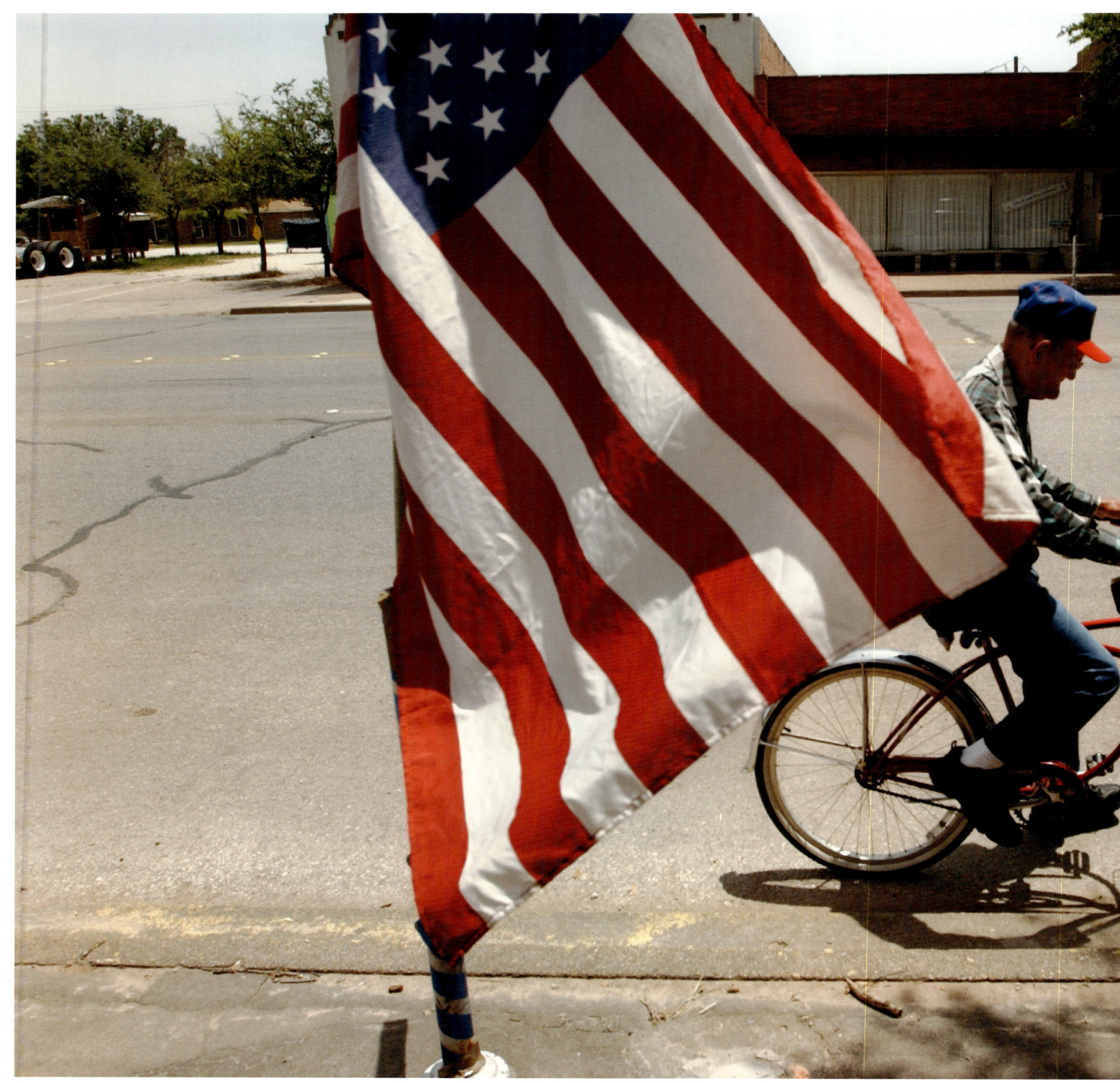

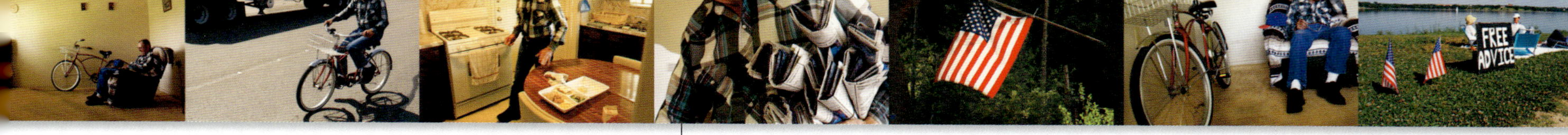

WINTERS

Colbath loads up copies of the paper as he starts out on his daily route. He's been delivering the news to the good citizens of Winters for more than a decade.

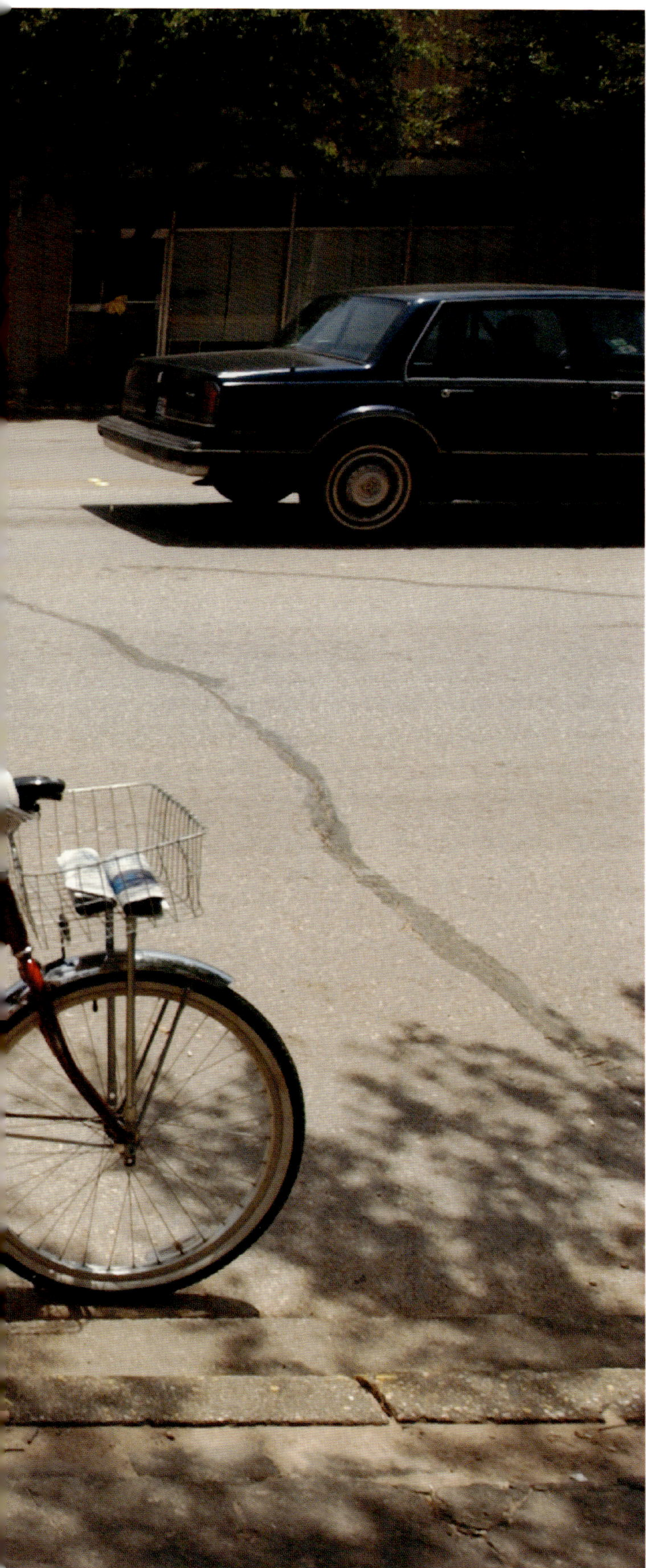

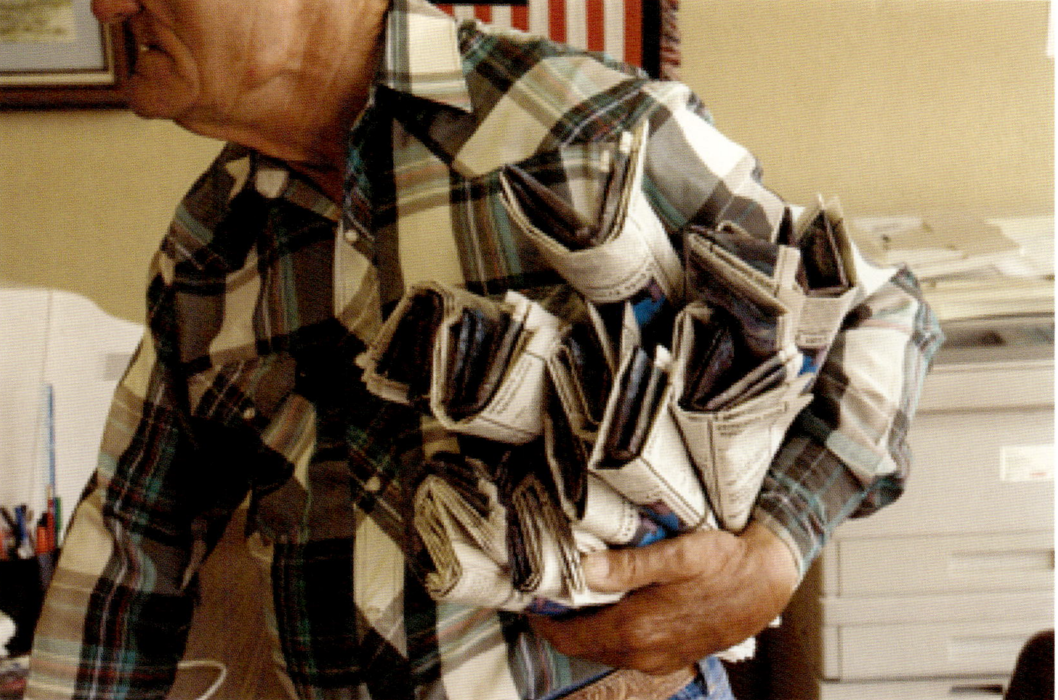

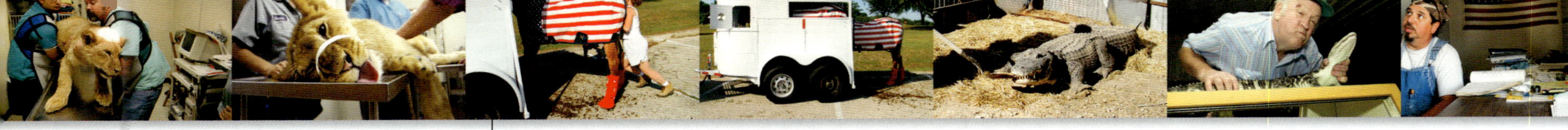

DALLAS
Horse power: An afternoon ride around White Rock Lake ends with the not-so-pleasant task of trying to get a horse back into the trailer. Suzanne Moore finds out the hard way that horses can be led but rarely pushed.
Photo by Scogin Mayo

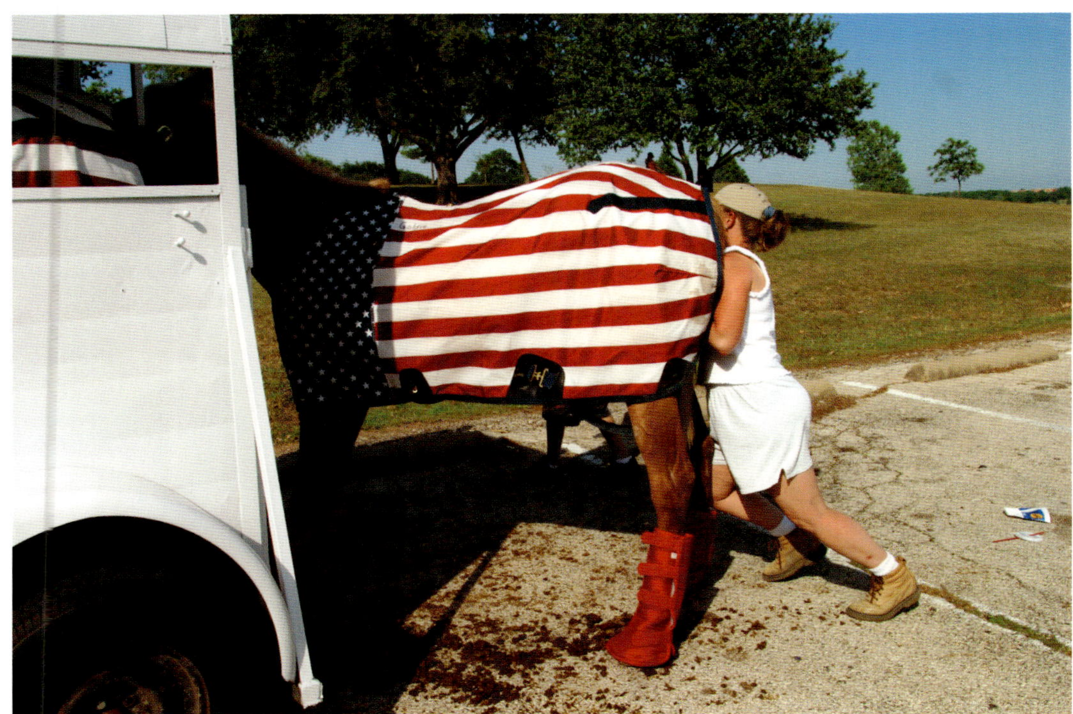

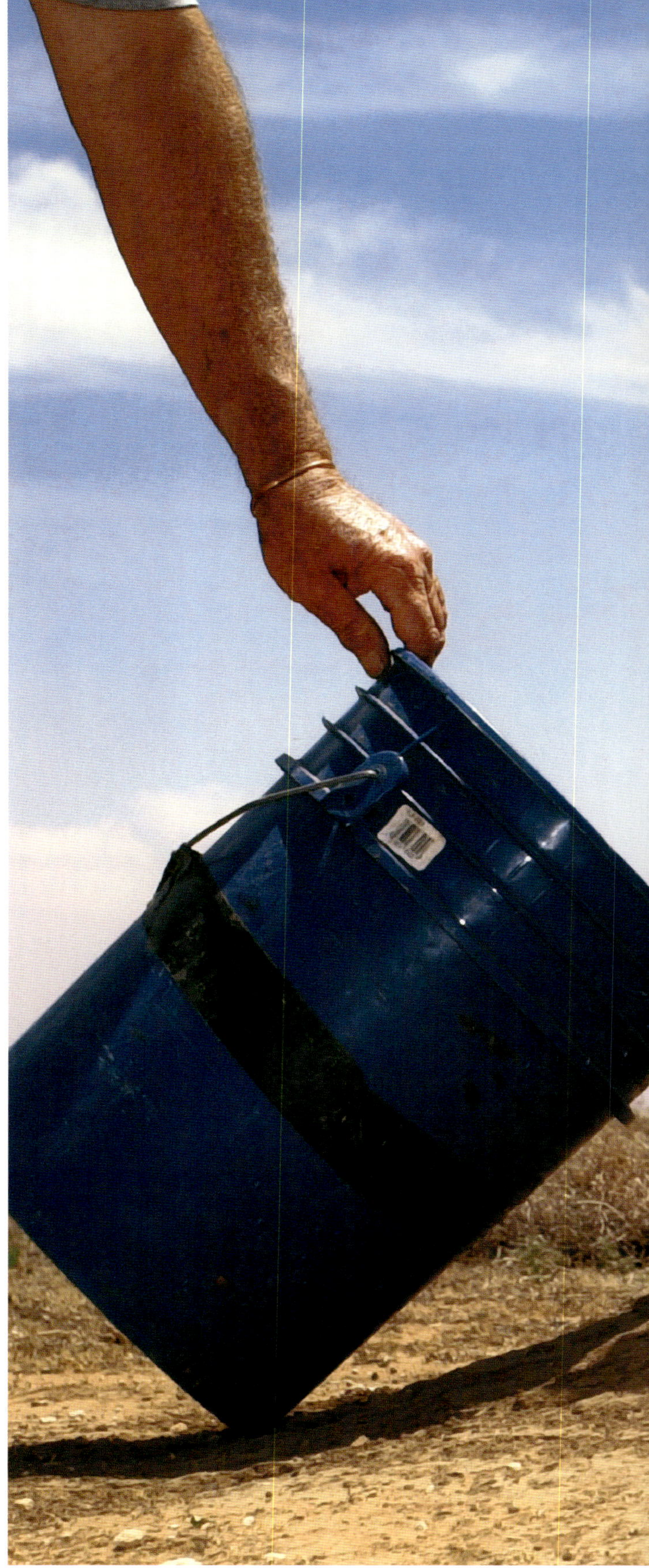

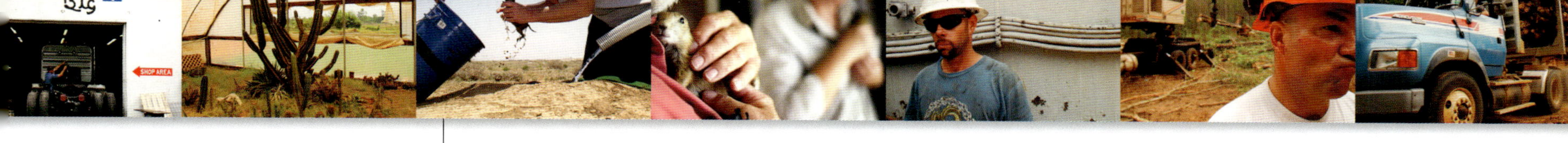

LUBBOCK

When small towns and ranchers have a problem with prairie dogs (actually rodents), they call Lynda Watson. An advocate for these flatland creatures, she removes them from their burrows with bare hands and a water hose. The mature animals are relocated, and the young ones domesticated and sold as pets. A certified Lynda Watson prairie dog can fetch $300 in Japan.
Photo by Sean Meyers Photography

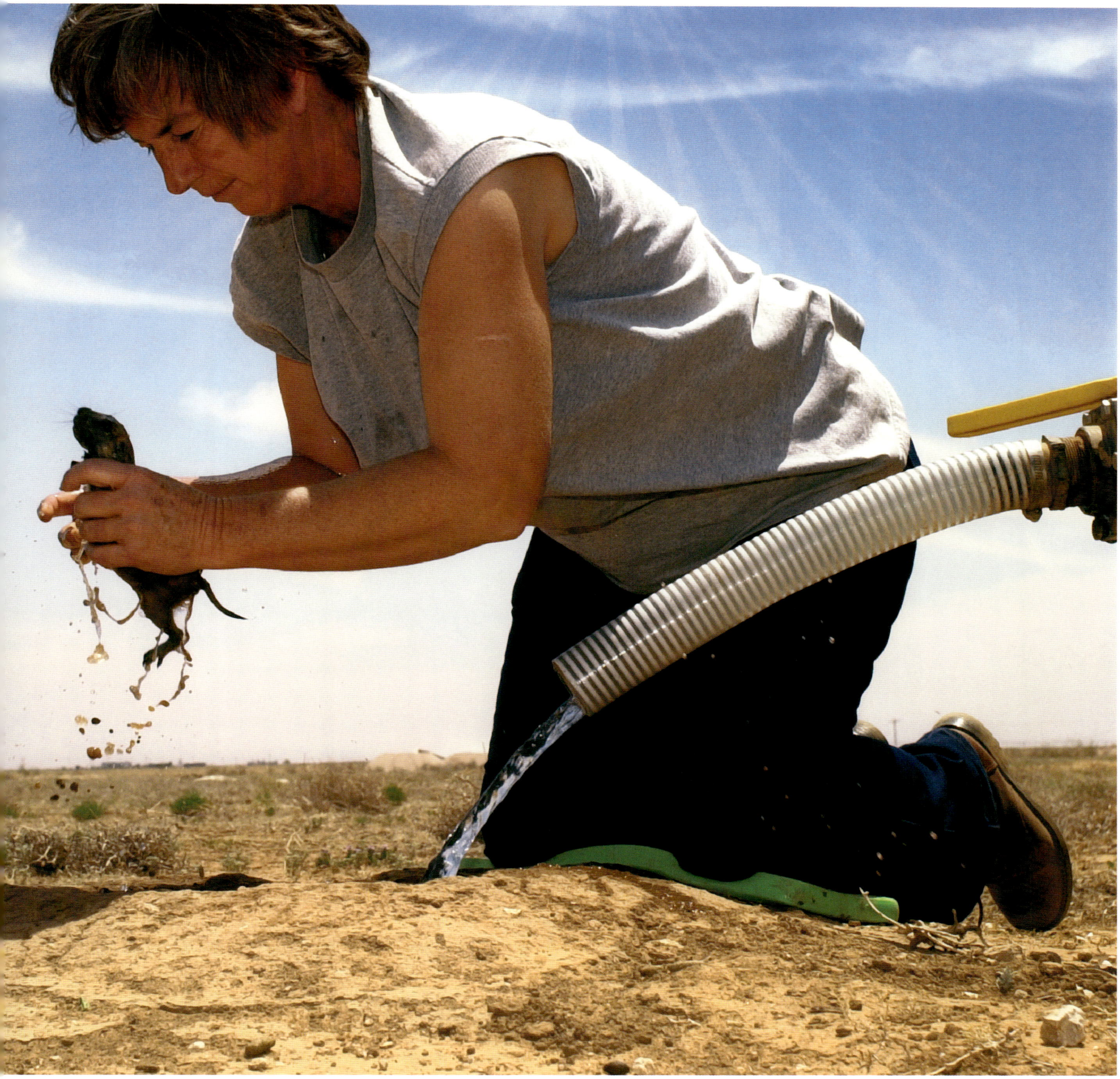

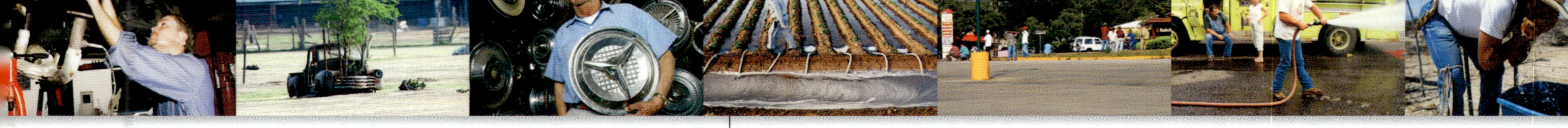

PLAINVIEW
Officer Carl Baird of the Texas Department of Criminal Justice checks a potato field owned by Formby State Correctional Facility. Low-risk prisoners are allowed to work the fields as part of rehabilitation, and the fruits of their labor are consumed by the prison's 931 inmates.
Photo by Sean Meyers Photography

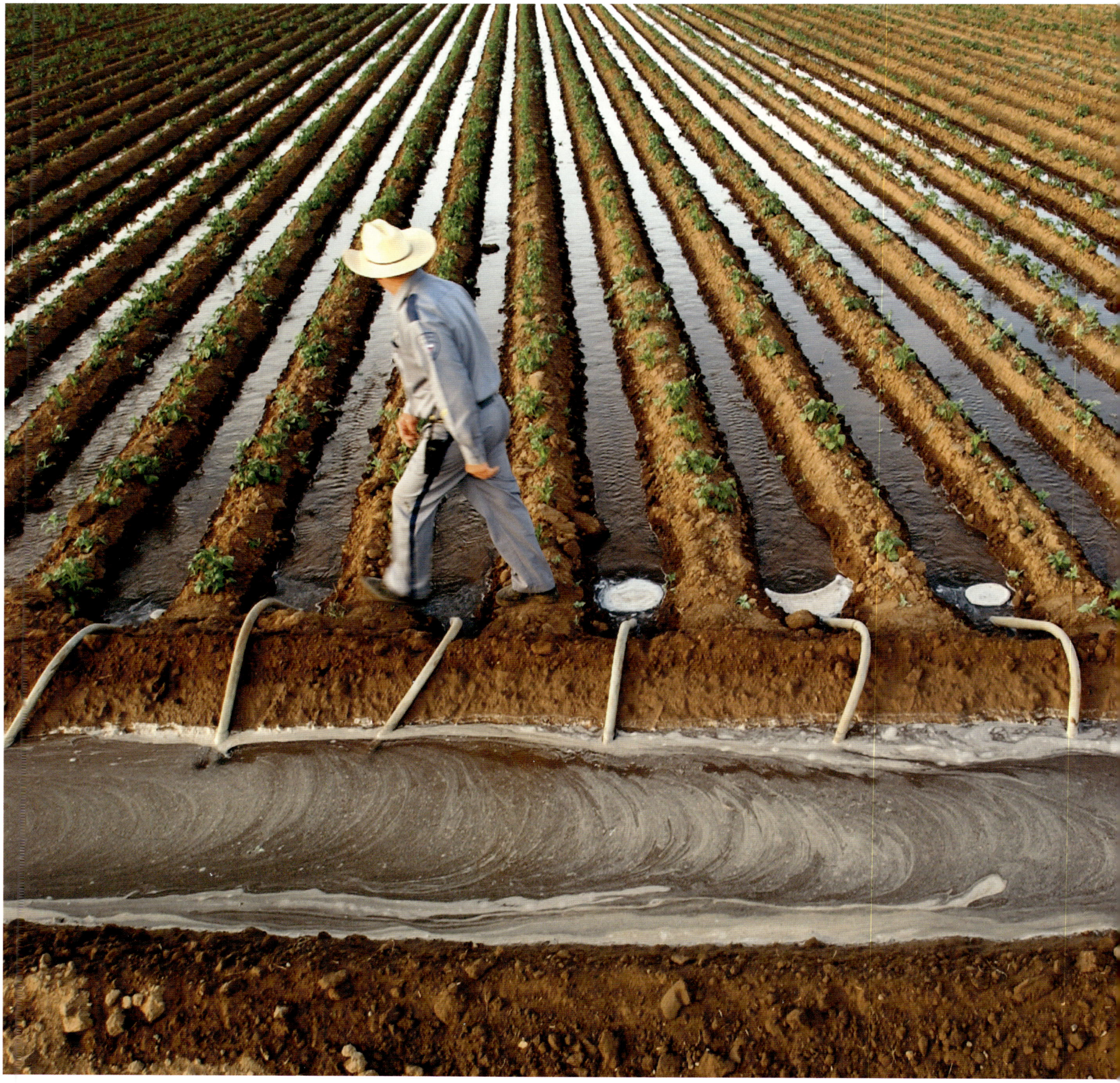

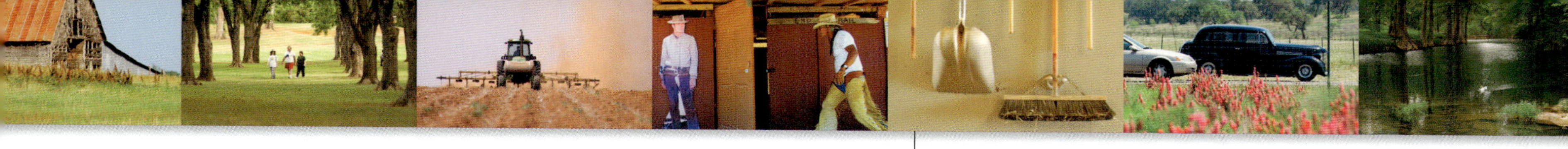

PLANO
Every horse barn has its arsenal for the battle against manure. At Timber Creek Stables, the weapons of choice are two barn forks, a muck rake, a shovel, and a broom. The stalls have to be cleaned daily for equine health.
Photo by Tim Quiring

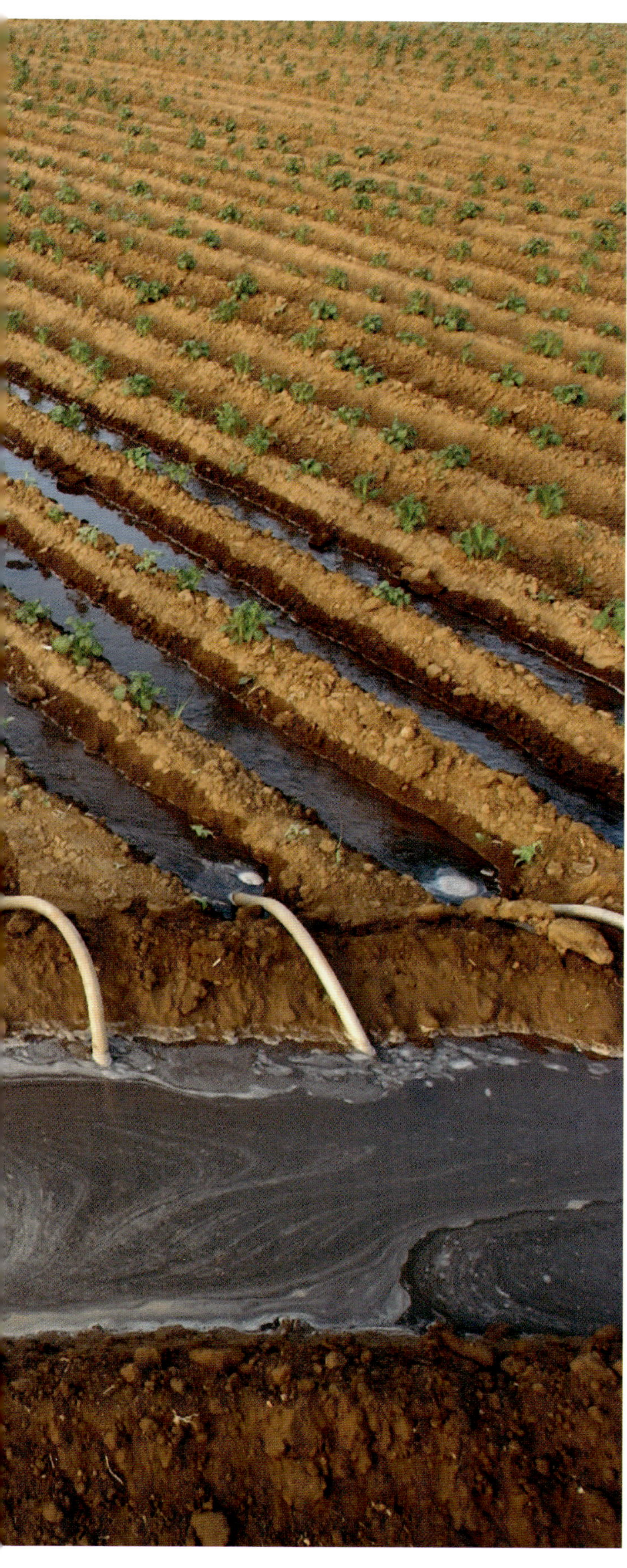

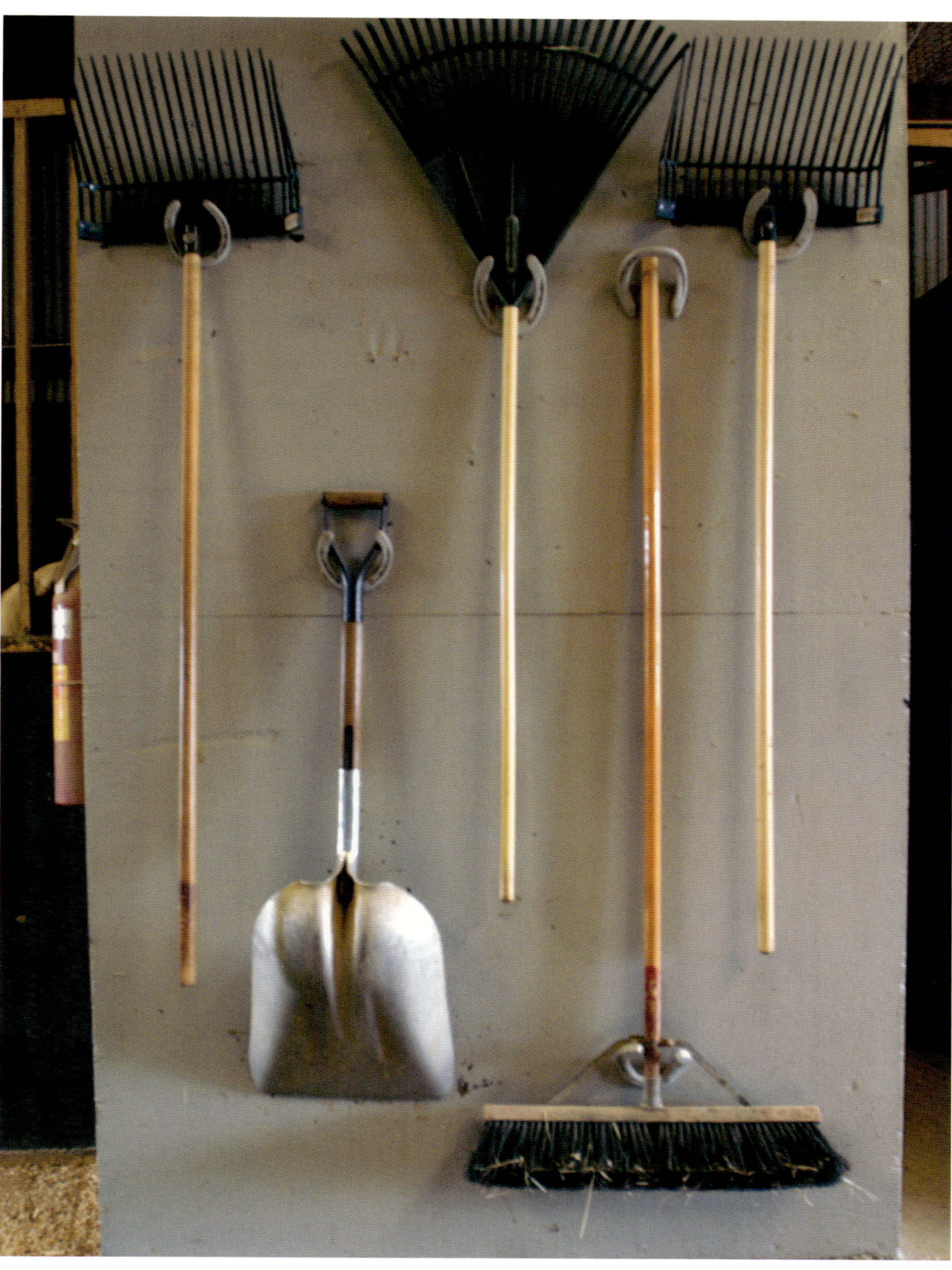

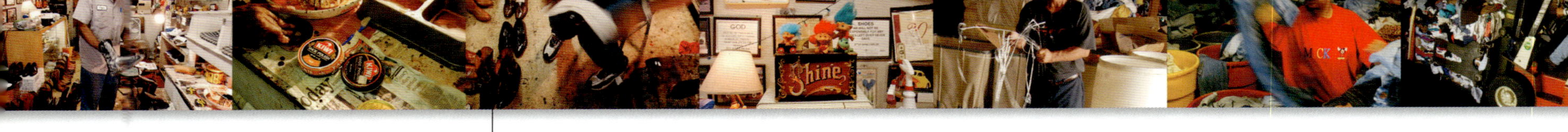

WICHITA FALLS
Formerly a two-man operation, the 8th Street Shine Parlor is now run solely by Ulyss Johnson. On an average day, Johnson, who's been in the business for 30 years, buffs up two dozen pairs of shoes and boots.
Photo by Gary Lawson

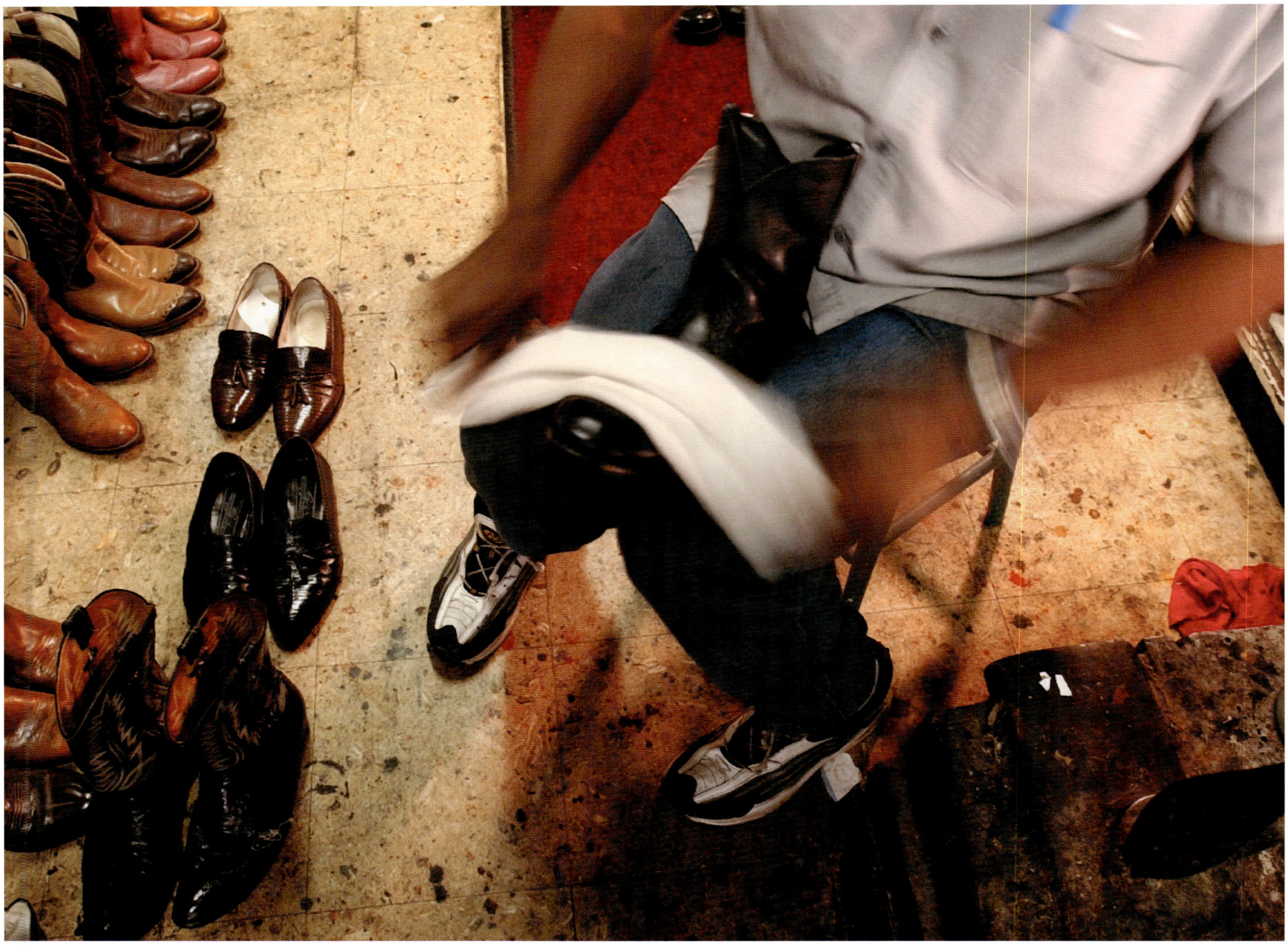

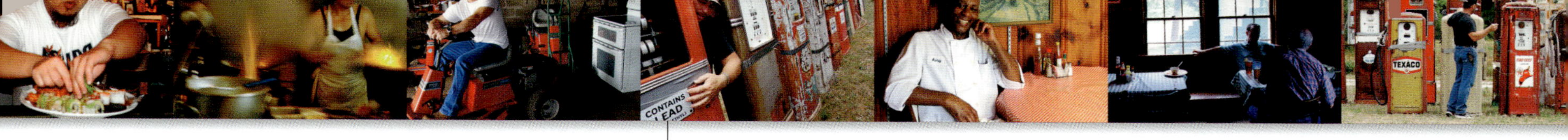

ABBOTT
Larry's Unique Collectibles sits on Highway 135 where passersby see dozens of old gas pumps waiting their turn to get gussied up. Larry Wingate takes the junkers, replaces the wiring so they'll light up, paints them, and installs shelves inside for storage. Customers pay up to $3,000 for the refurbished relics.
Photo by John Davenport, San Antonio Express-News

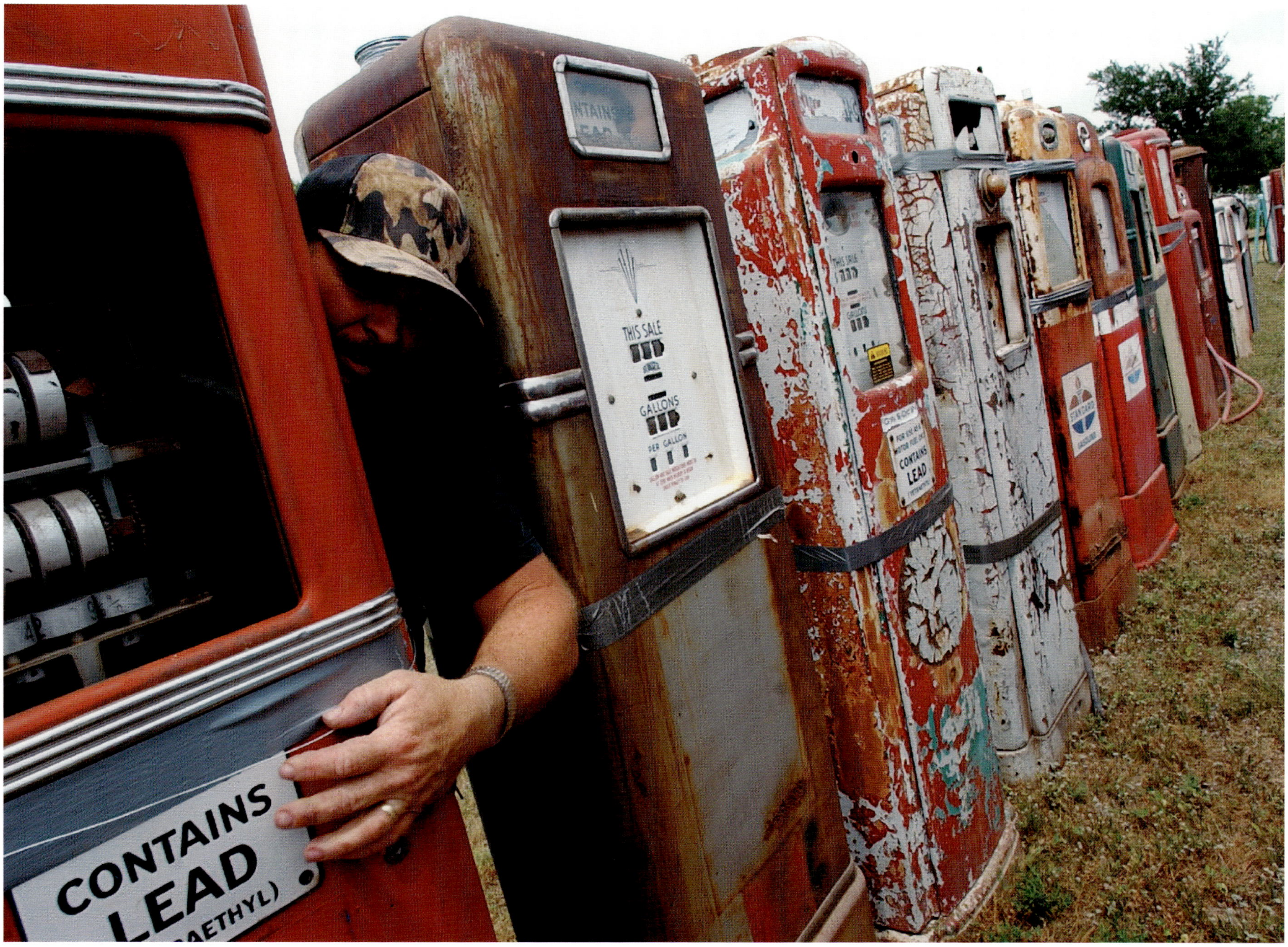

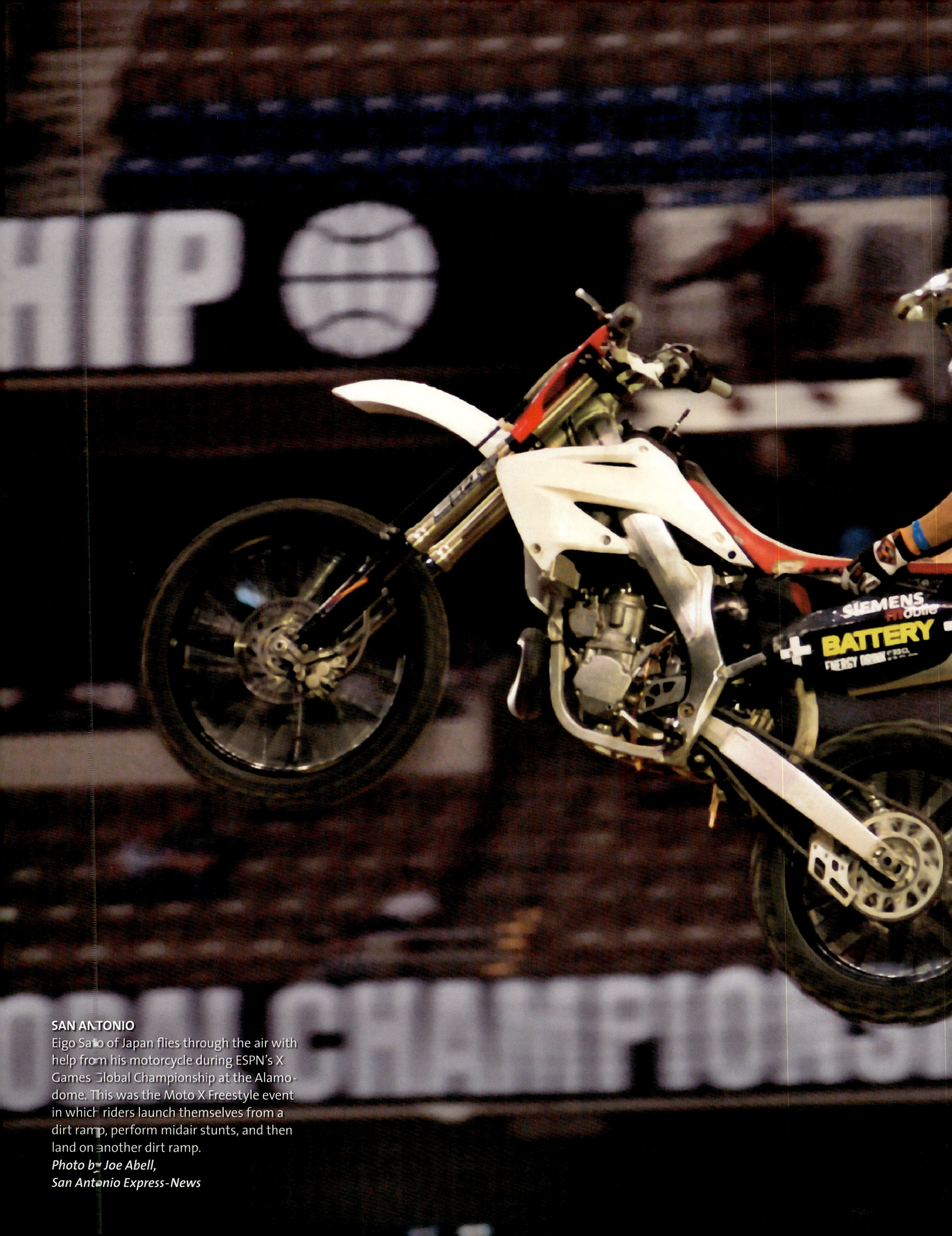

SAN ANTONIO
Eigo Sato of Japan flies through the air with help from his motorcycle during ESPN's X Games Global Championship at the Alamodome. This was the Moto X Freestyle event in which riders launch themselves from a dirt ramp, perform midair stunts, and then land on another dirt ramp.
Photo by Joe Abell, San Antonio Express-News

Texas At Play

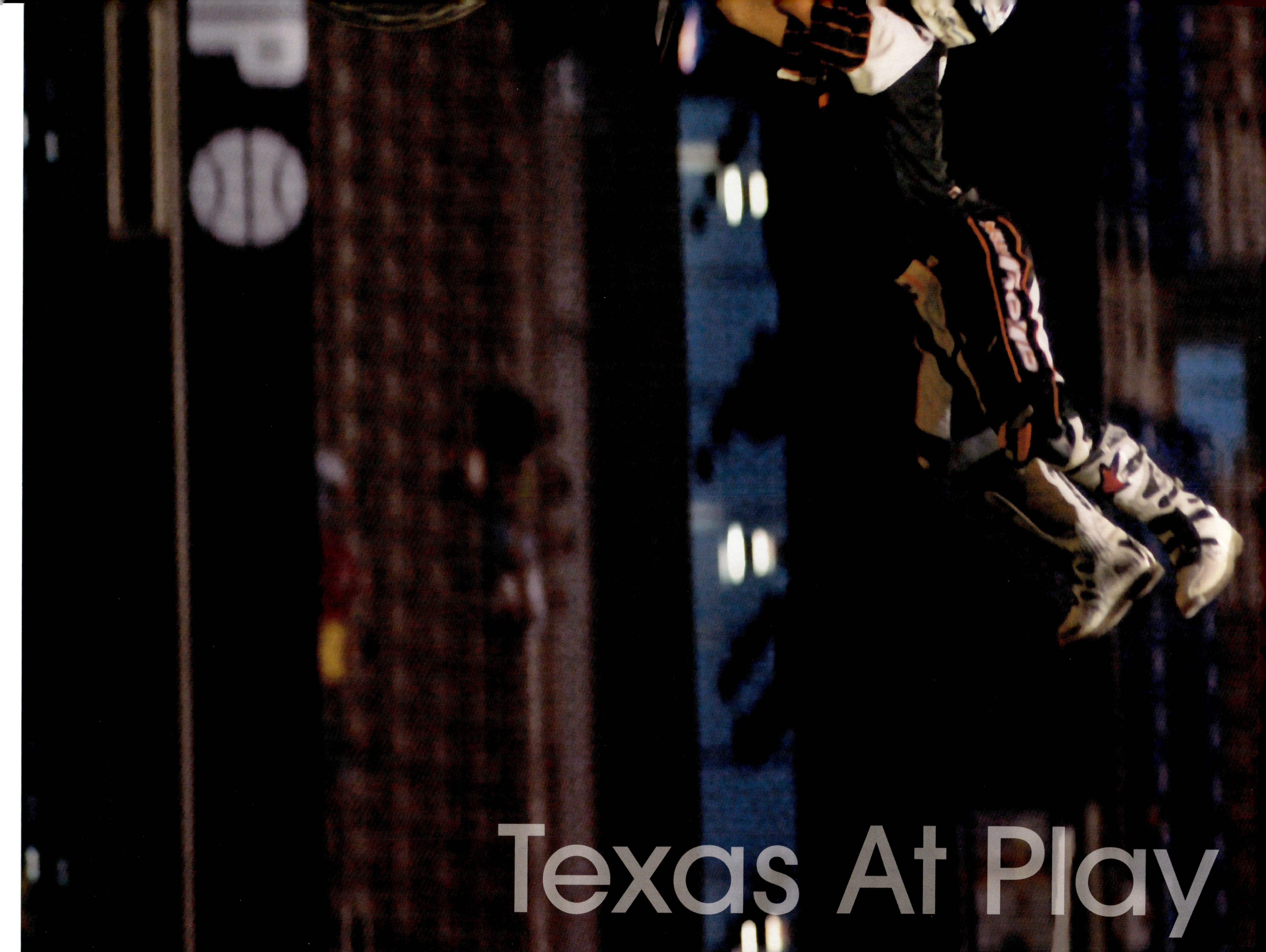

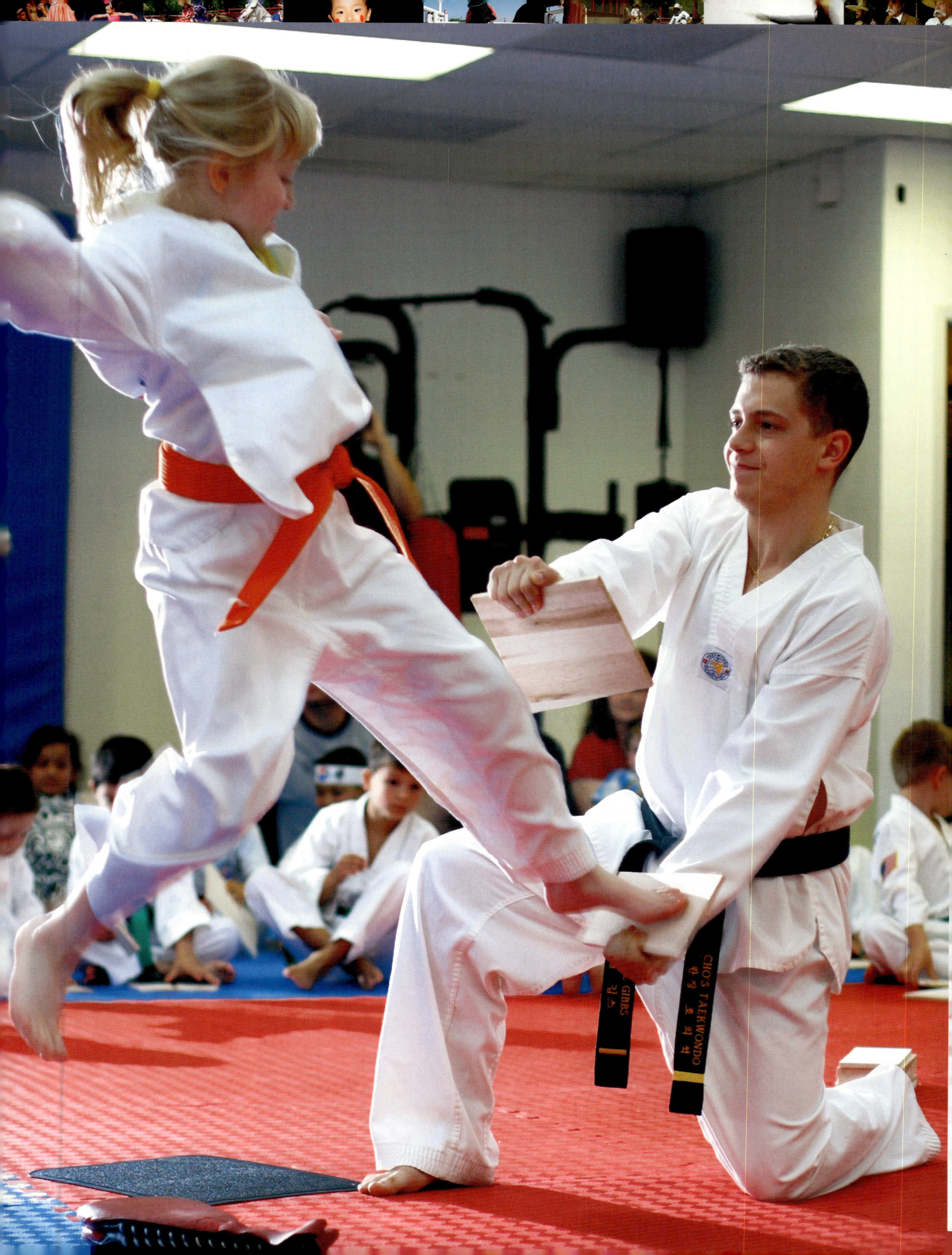
GIBBS
CHO'S TAEKWONDO

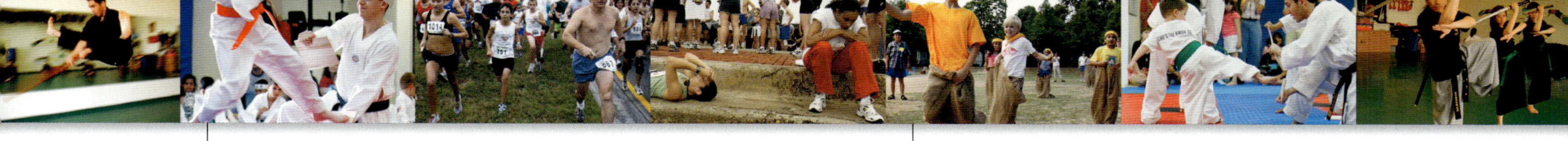

OAK RIDGE
The word karate is a combination of two Japanese characters: *kara* (empty) and *te* (hand). Kaitlyn Pace, 8, may have an empty hand but her foot is full of power as instructor Bill Gibbs of Cho's Tae Kwon Do can confirm.
Photo by Beverly R. Schulz

HOUSTON
Connor Hicks celebrates his victory in a sack race at Travis Elementary School's annual field games. His secret? Pull up very hard on the sack with both hands and take really big leaps.
Photo by F. Carter Smith, Polaris Images

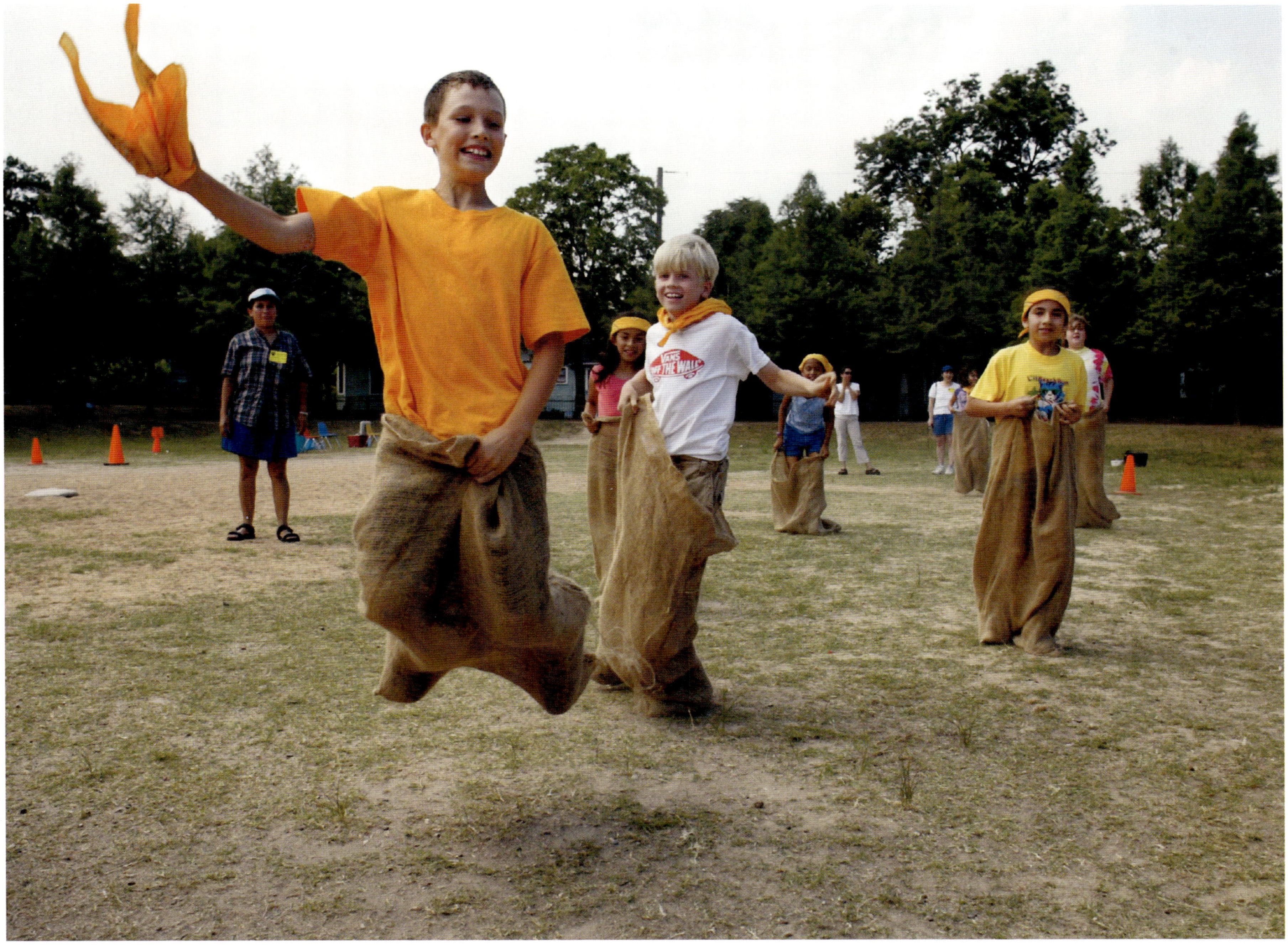

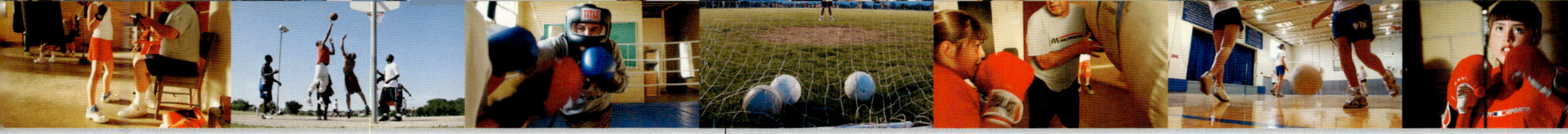

LAKE JACKSON
During an early morning scrimmage at MacLean Park, Scorpions assistant coach Lonnie Rathbun plays goalie. The Scorpions are a 17-and-under club team.
Photo by Todd Yates

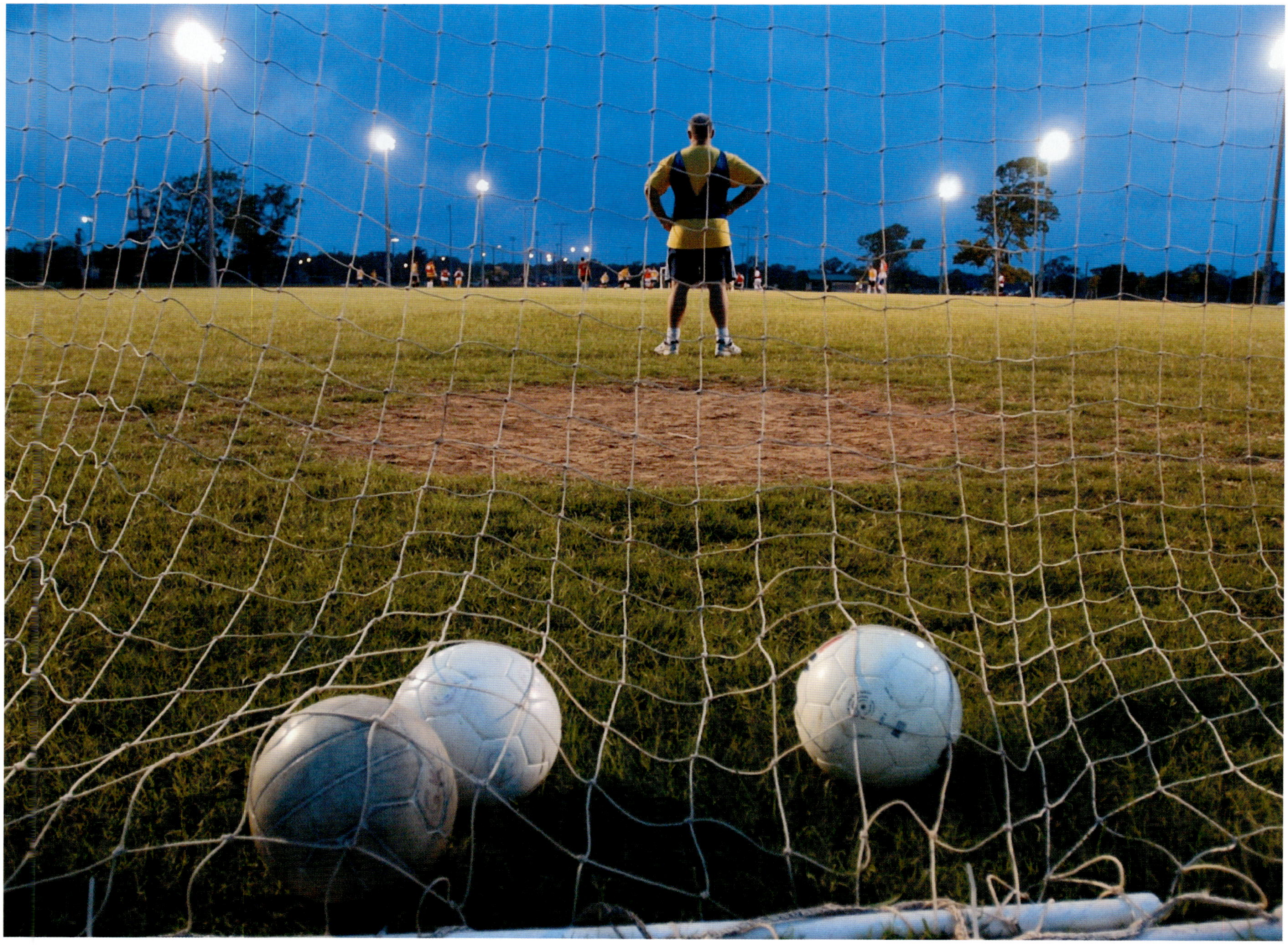

ROUND ROCK
Take that! Sierra Villarreal, a forward on the Austin Capitals girls' soccer team, practices her headers before the team's Division I state soccer tournament against the Houston Challenge.
Photo by Rodolfo Gonzalez

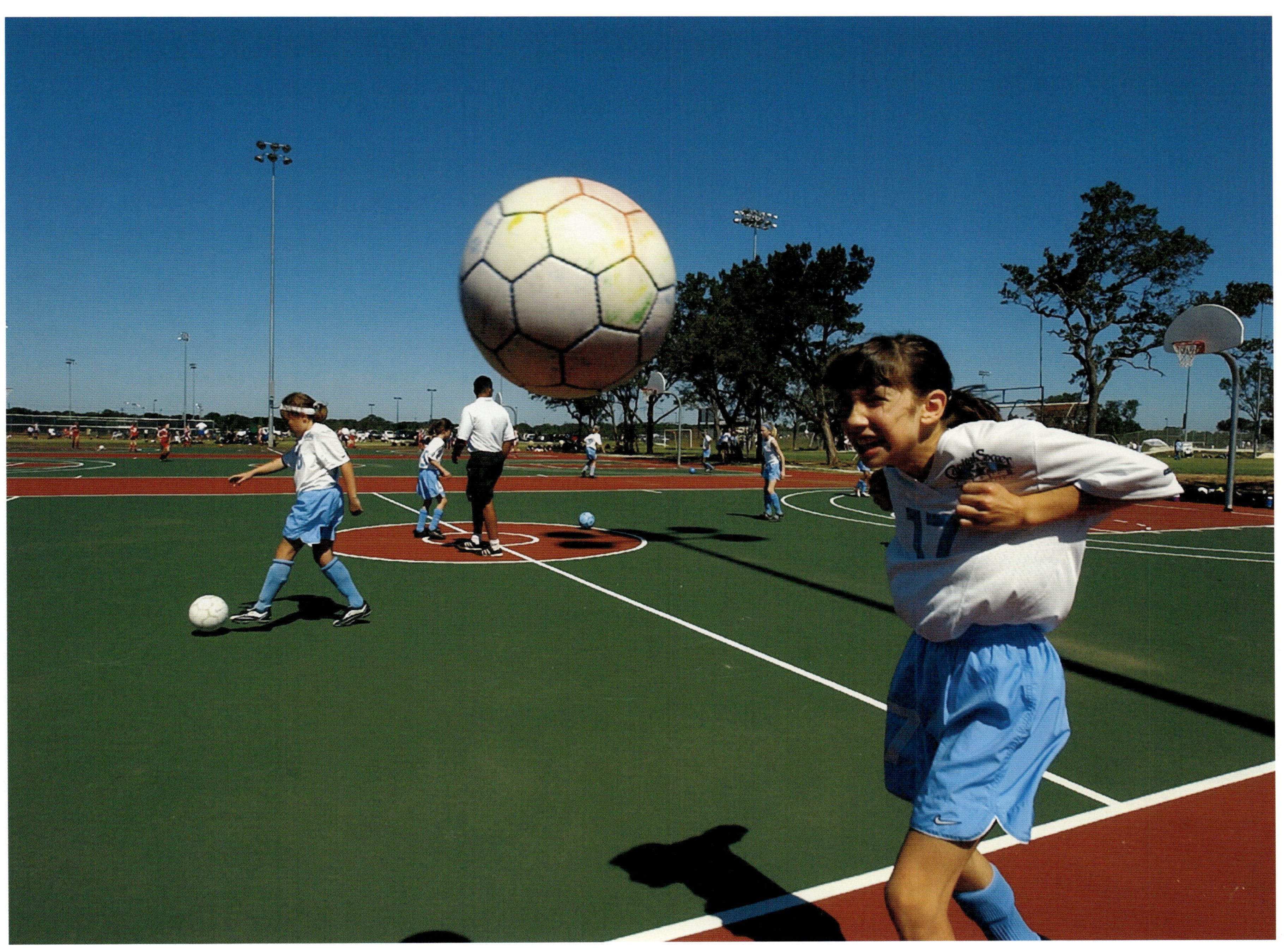

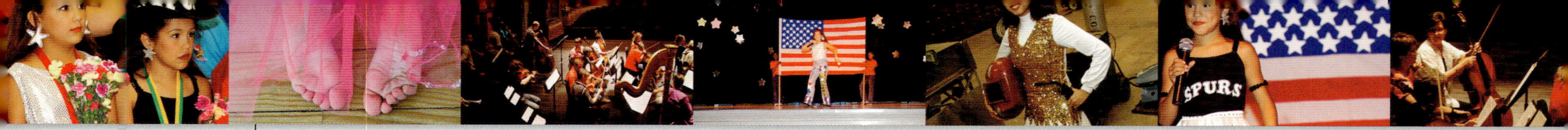

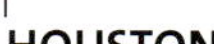

HOUSTON
Twinkle toes: A young ballerina rests her feet before the Claire School of Dance spring recital.
Photos by Cheryl Hatch

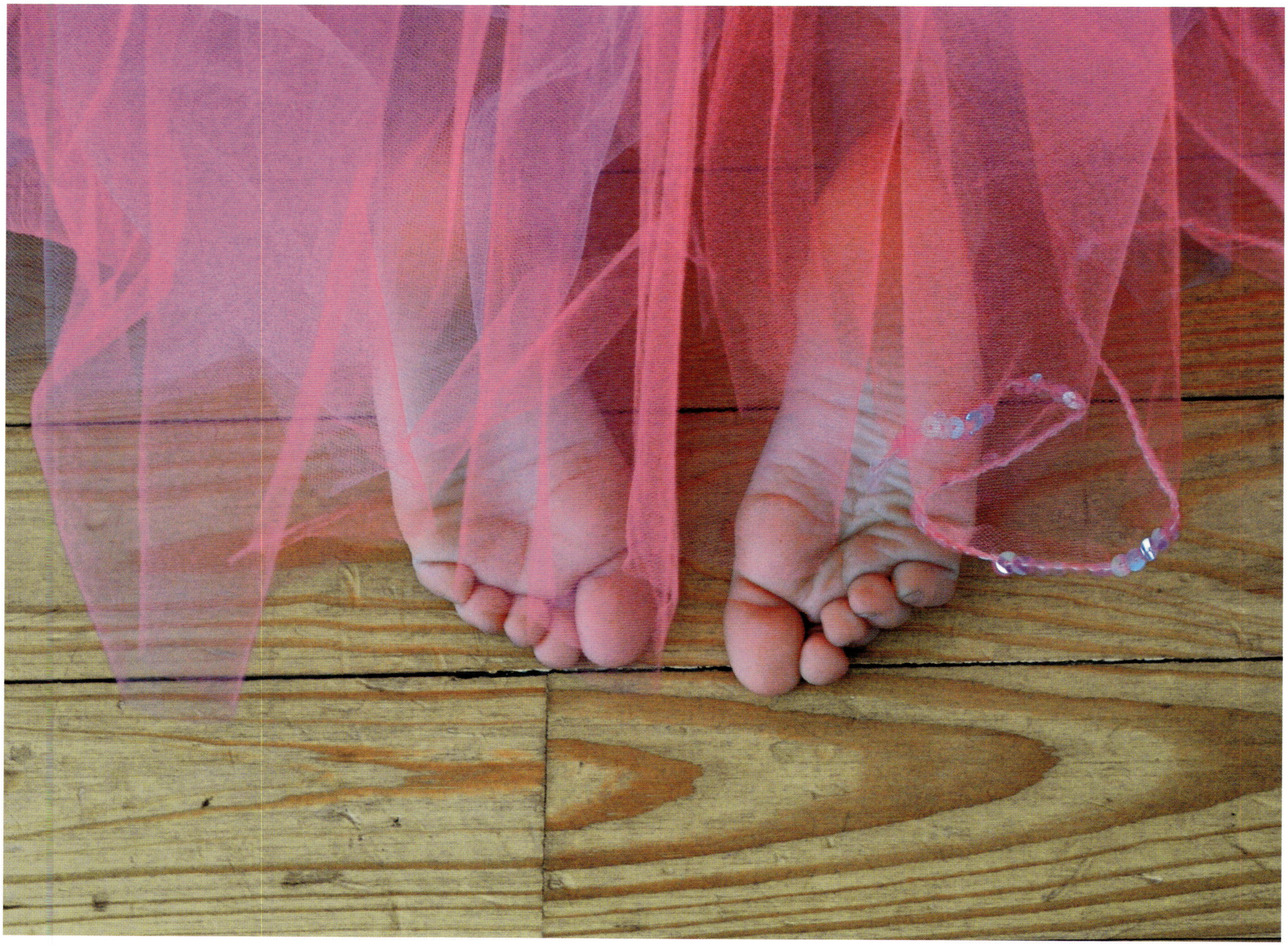

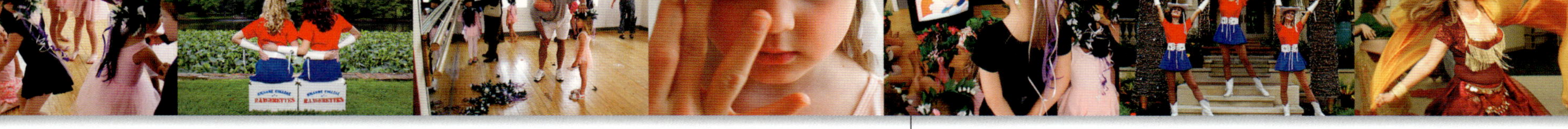

HOUSTON

The performers in the Claire School of Dance spring recital can wear different costumes, but each sports a fairy crown. To keep them entertained (not to mention calm) before they go on, the kids are treated to a video. *The Little Mermaid* appears to do the trick.

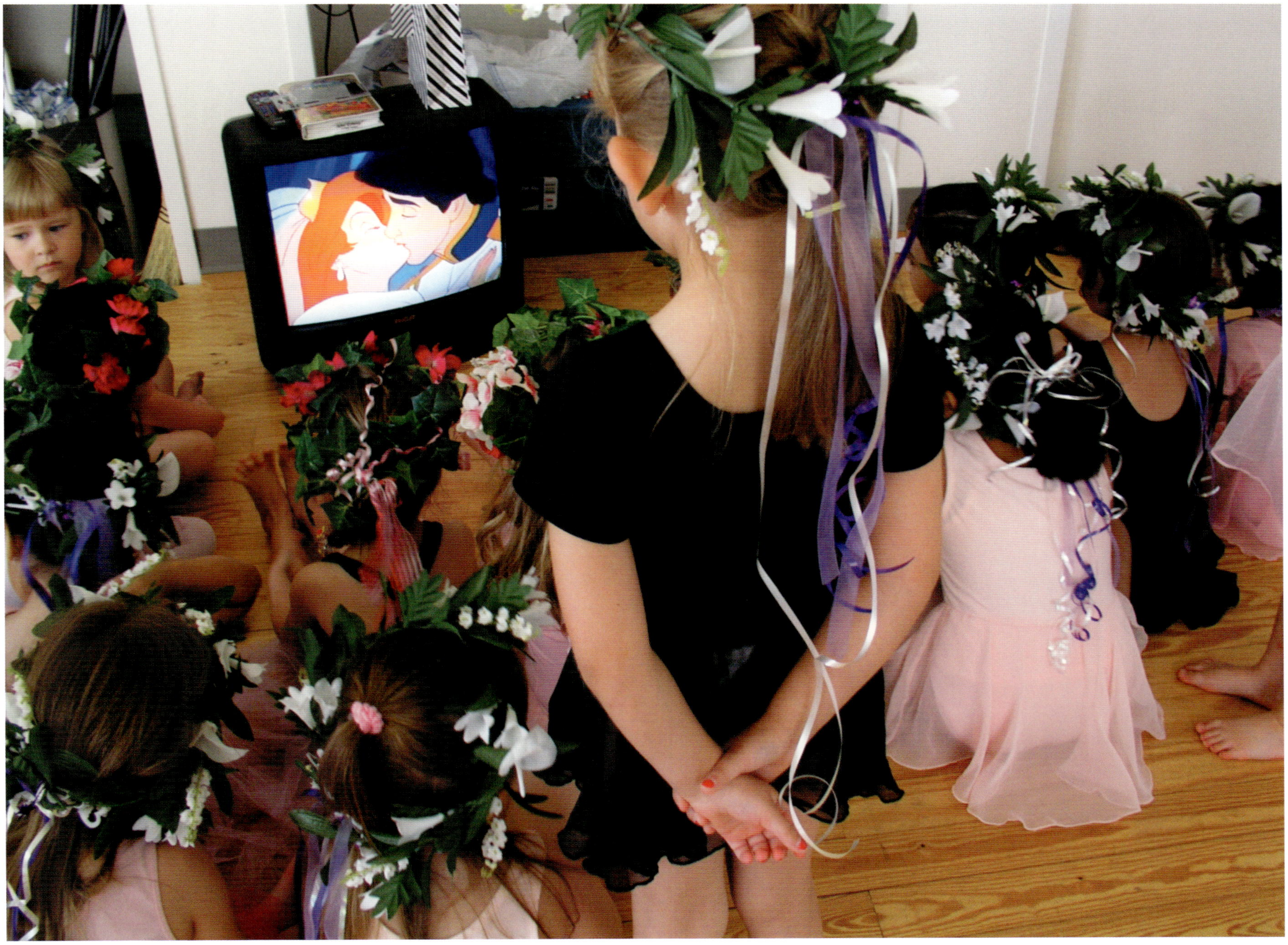

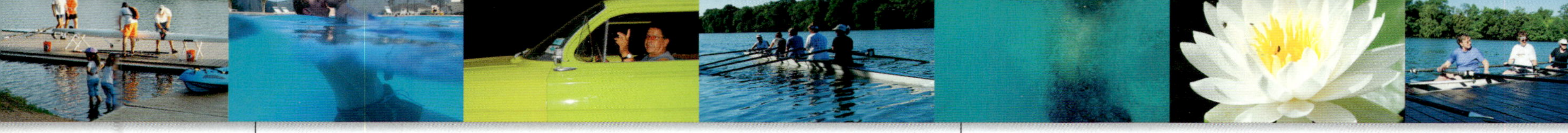

KYLE

Doug McCormick and his son Ethan go for a dunk in the Plum Creek subdivision's swimming pool. In the Austin suburb of Kyle, where summer temperatures reach well above 100 with 100 percent humidity, the pool is the community focal point.
Photo by Rodolfo Gonzalez

KYLE

Bombs away! Luke Terry sinks in a sea of bubbles after executing a cannonball into the Plum Creek pool.
Photo by Rodolfo Gonzalez

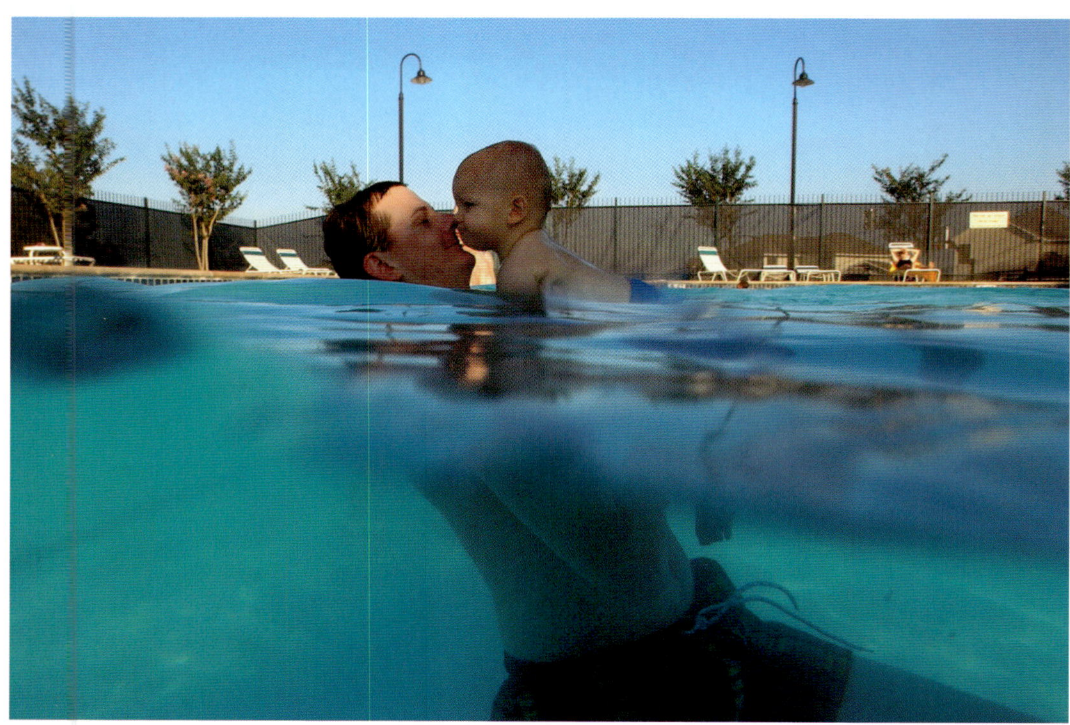

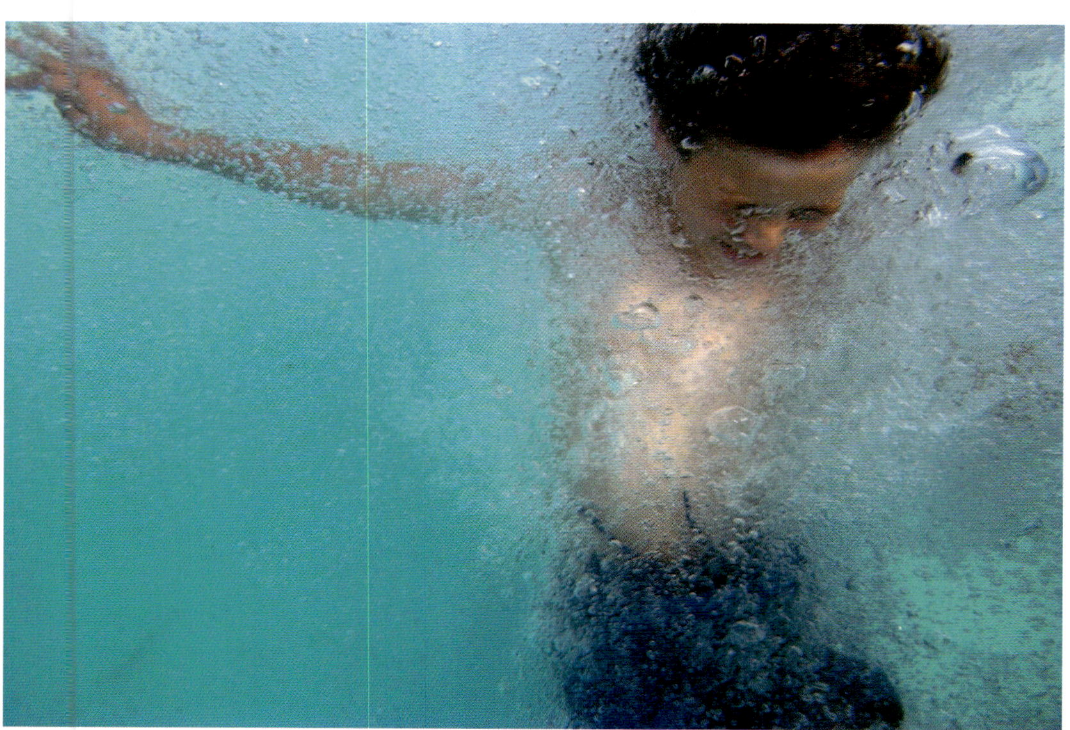

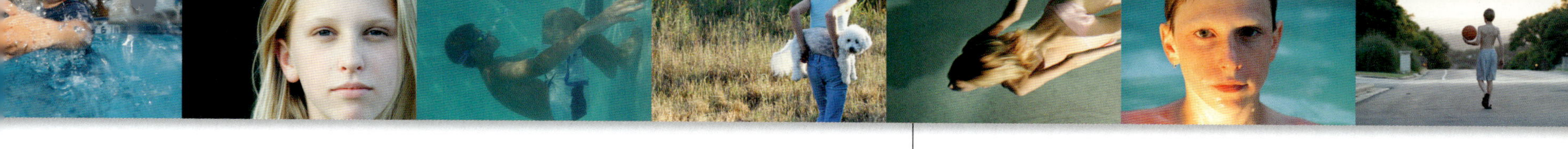

AUSTIN
Gods and monsters drift away as 15-year-old Owen O'Brien glides through the night, alone with her thoughts, in her backyard pool.
Photo by Michael O'Brien

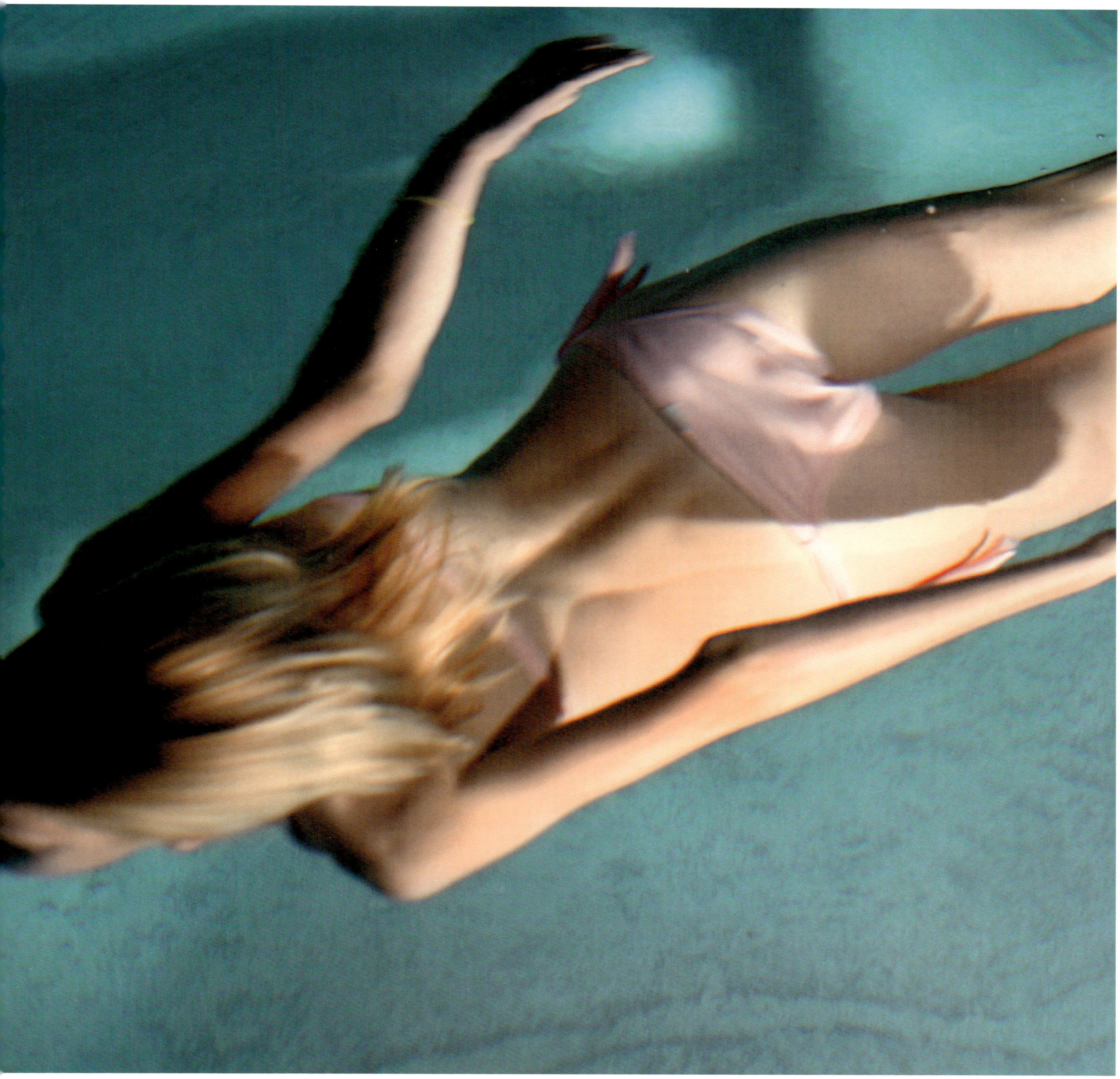

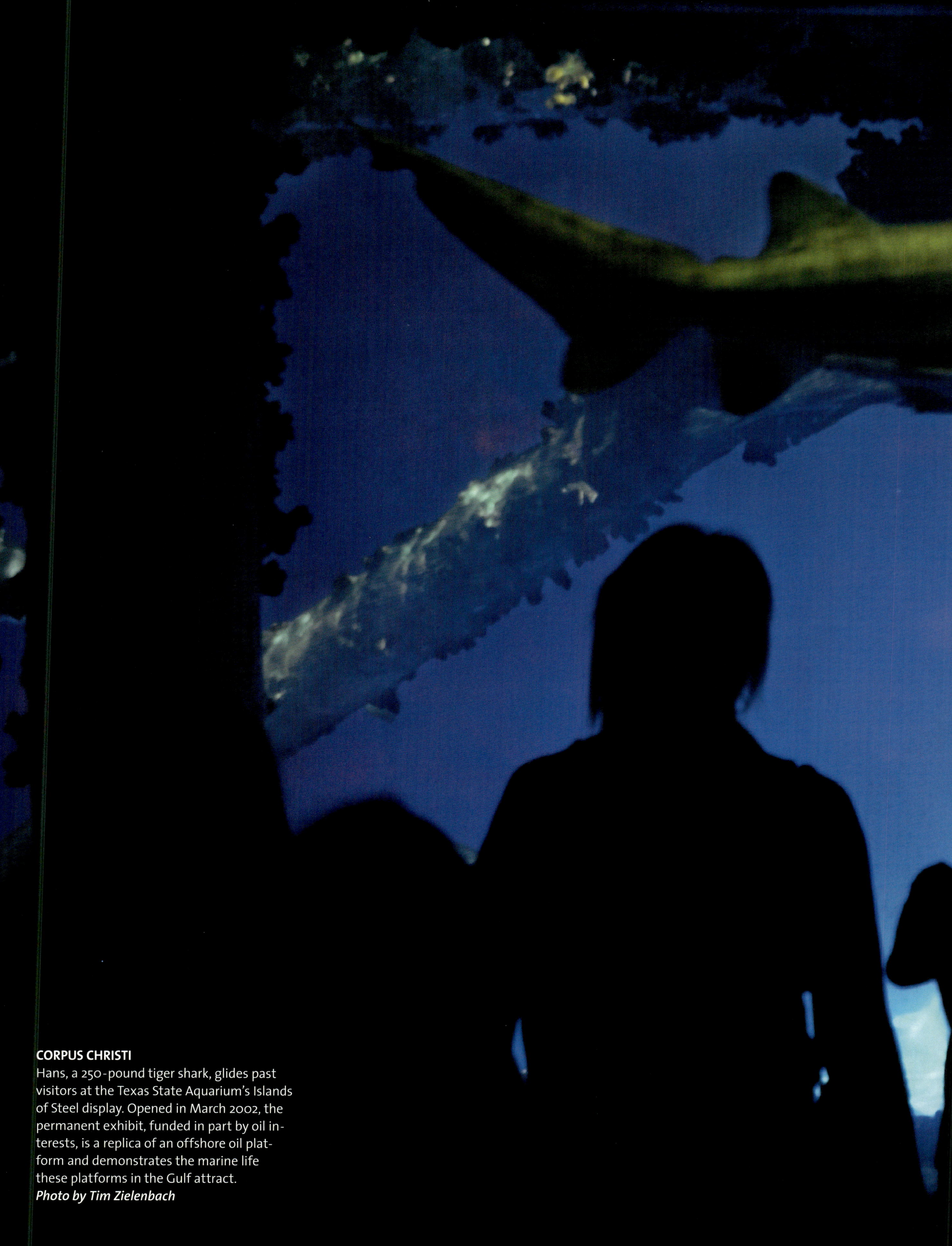

CORPUS CHRISTI
Hans, a 250-pound tiger shark, glides past visitors at the Texas State Aquarium's Islands of Steel display. Opened in March 2002, the permanent exhibit, funded in part by oil interests, is a replica of an offshore oil platform and demonstrates the marine life these platforms in the Gulf attract.
Photo by Tim Zielenbach

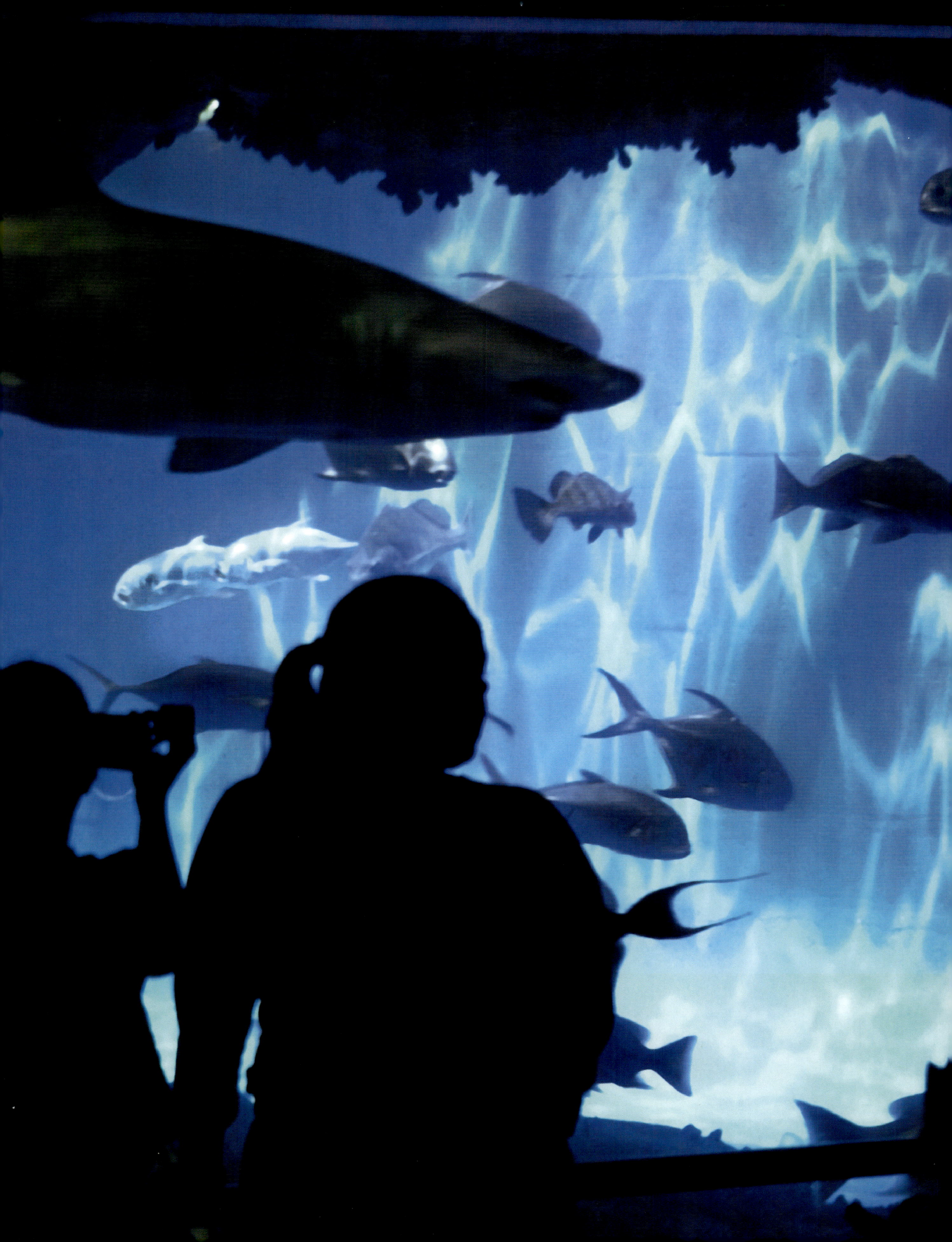

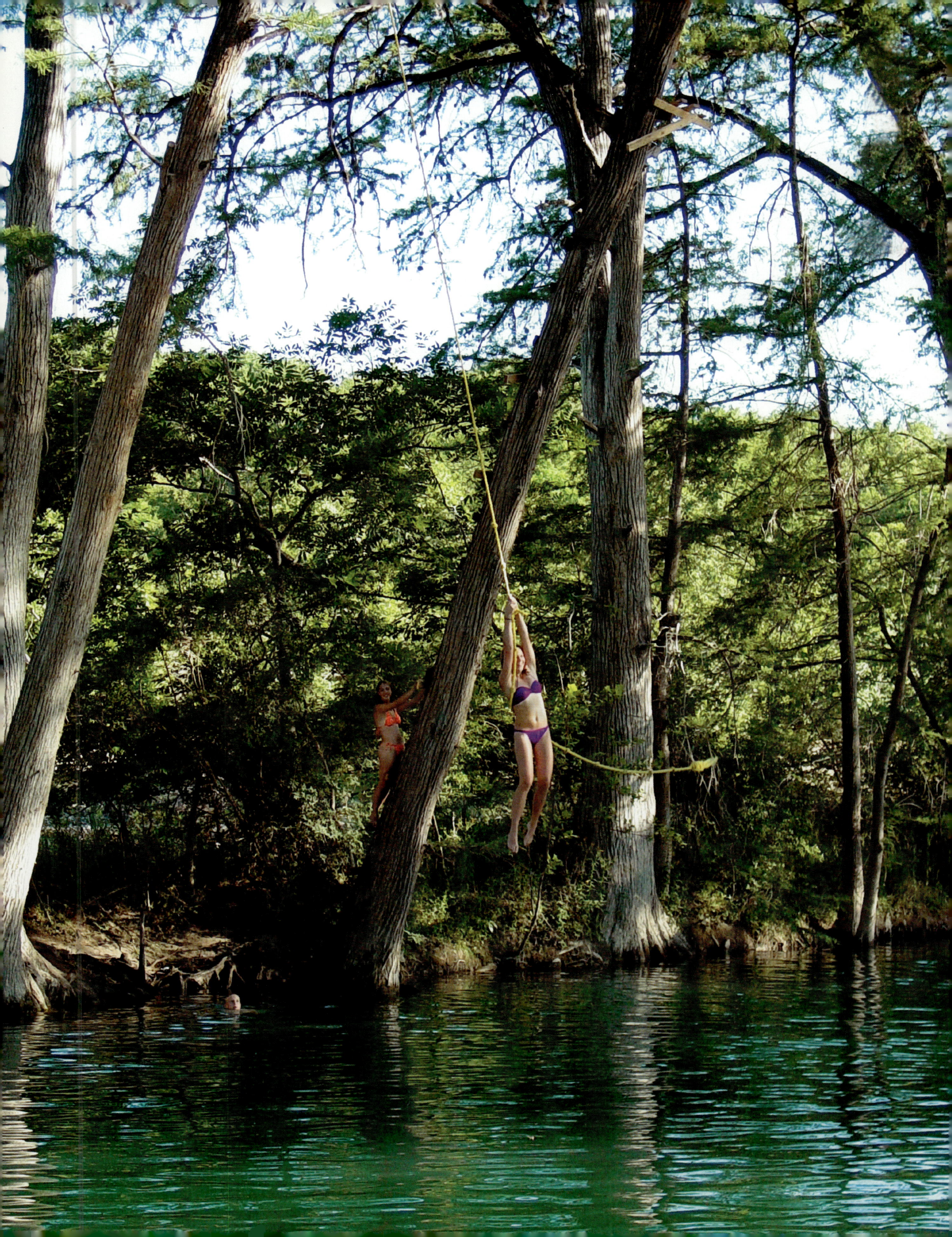

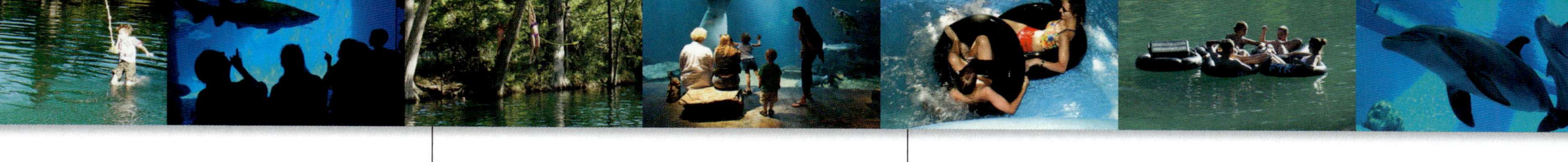

BANDERA
Me Jane, not Tarzan: Candace Robles launches from a Cypress tree into the Medina River.
Photo by Jim Johnston, Sundance Photographic Arts

NEW BRAUNFELS
Schlitterbahn Waterpark Resort's 39 attractions run the gamut from low speed to high thrill. The names are as wild as the rides: Master Blaster Uphill Water Coaster, Wolfpack Raft Slide, Banzai Pipeline Tube Slides, and Boogie Bahn Surfing Ride.
Photo by Joe Abell, San Antonio Express-News

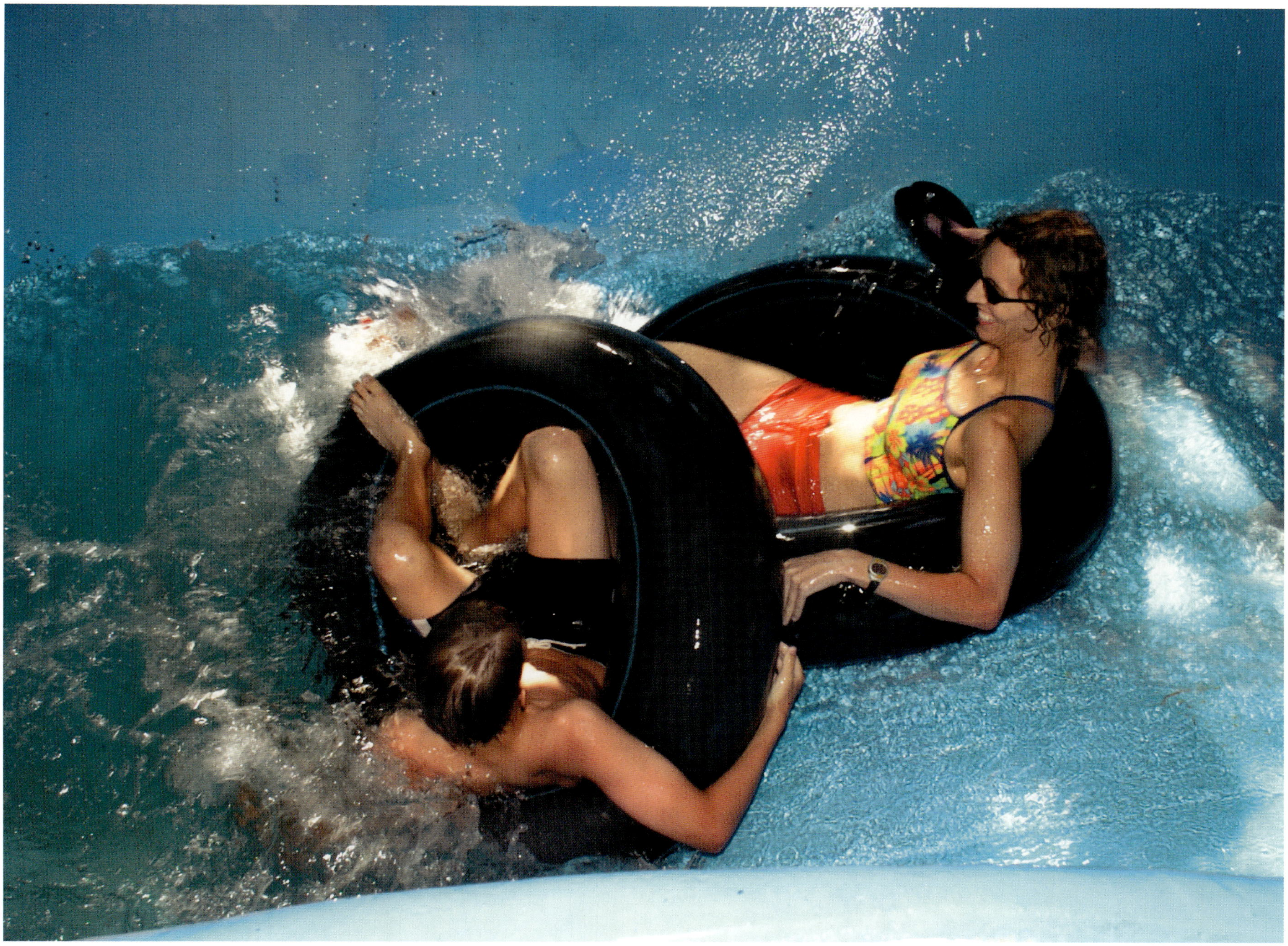

FRISCO

The Frisco RoughRiders mascots Dusty (aka Kevin Bode) and his horse Storm take a pregame gallop in Dr. Pepper/Seven Up Ballpark. The RoughRiders are the new Double-A affiliate of the Texas Rangers.

Photos by Louis DeLuca

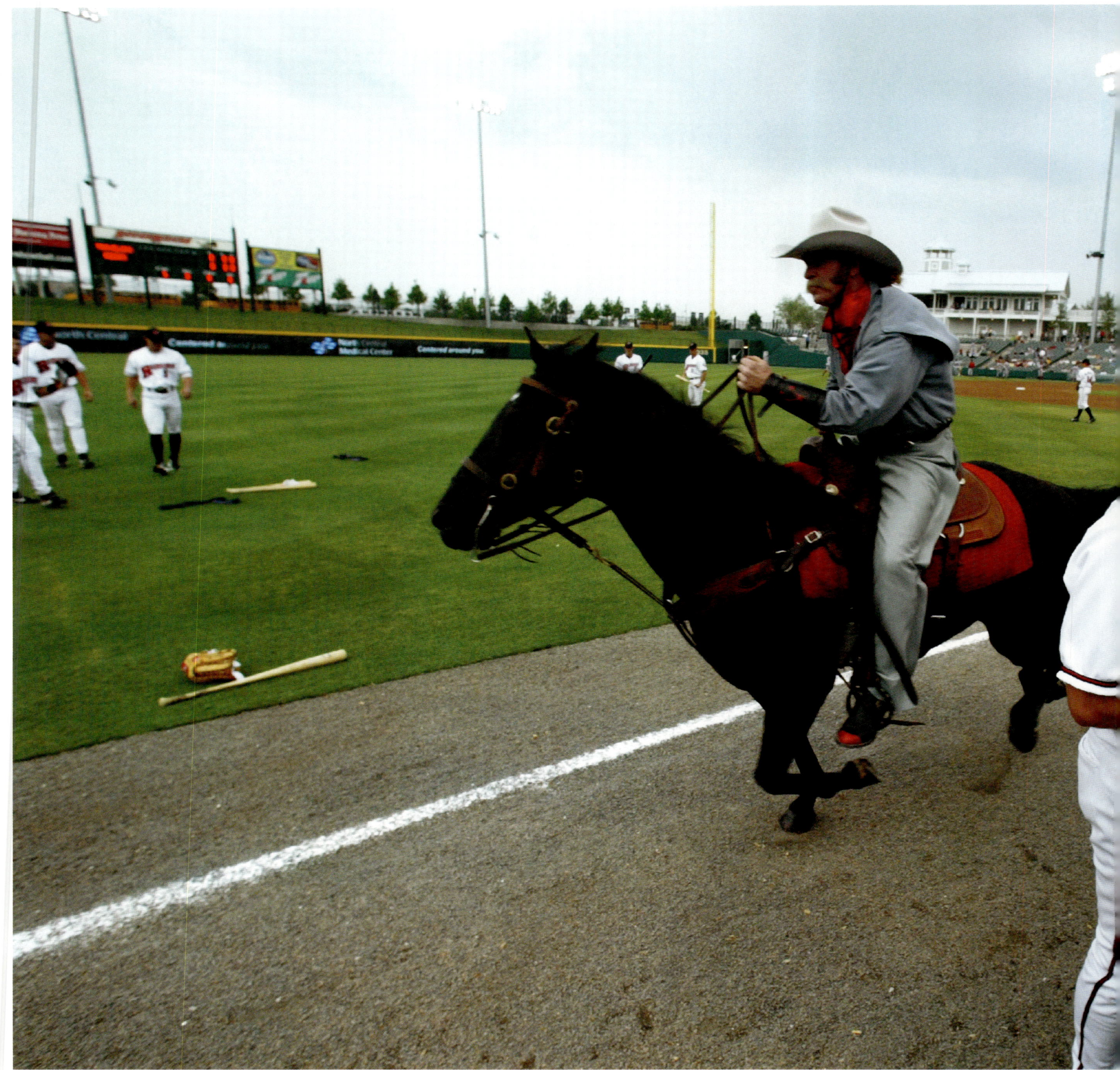

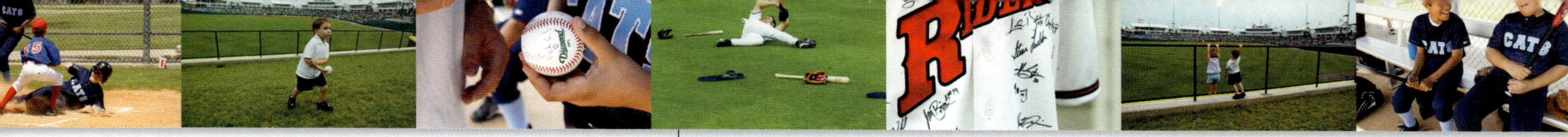

FRISCO

If players want to stretch a single into a double without injuring themselves, they need to stretch their legs first. Kurt Airoso of the RoughRiders does just that prior to a game against the Arkansas Travelers.

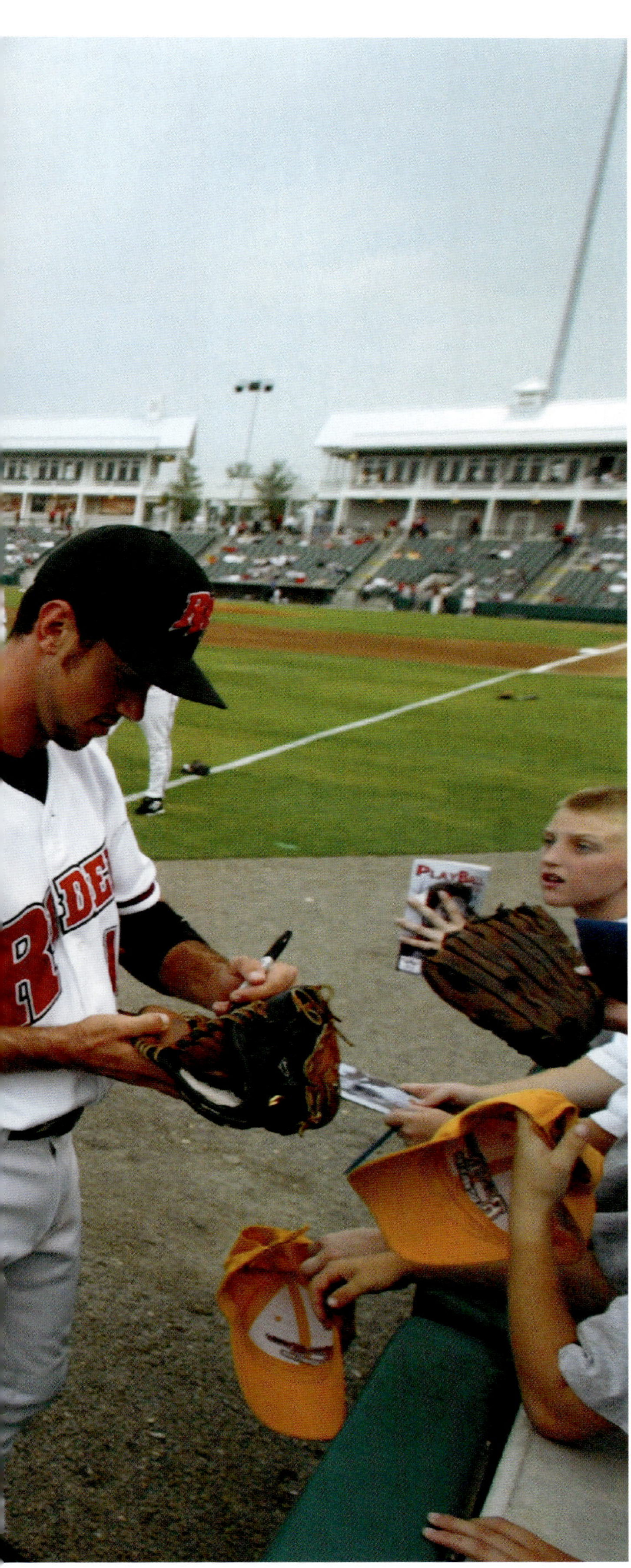

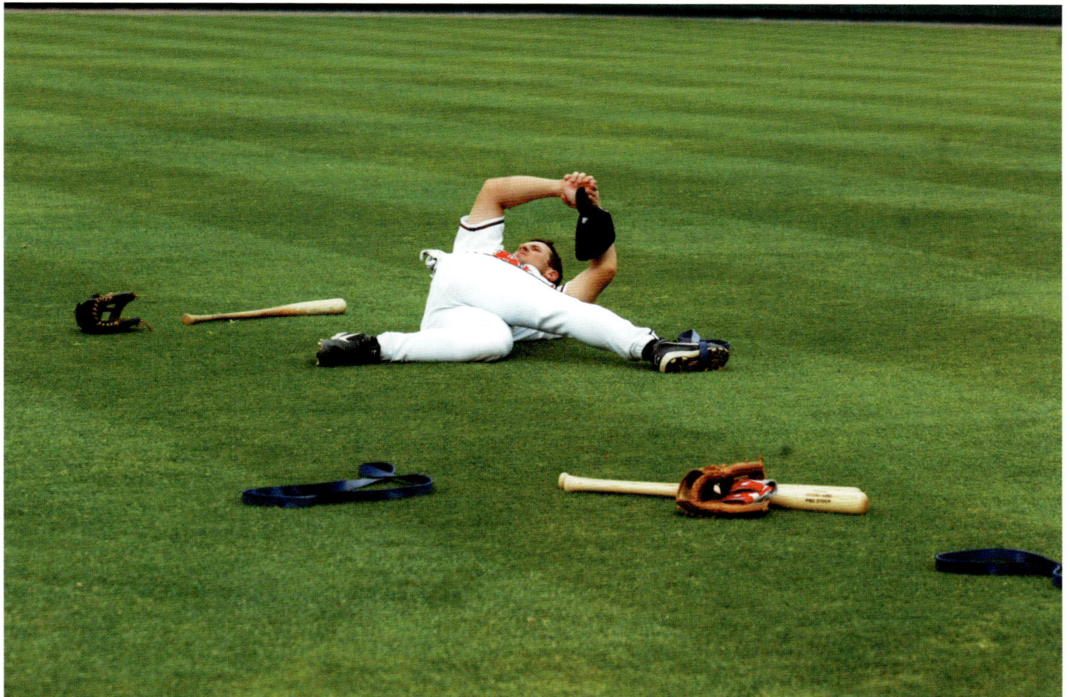

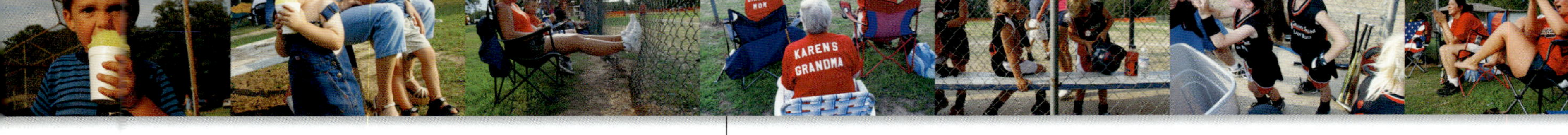

FRUITVALE

Friends and relatives cheer on the Fruitvale Bad Girls T-ball team. Despite the well-wishers, the score at the end of the third inning was 18 to zero, in favor of the opposing team, the Grand Saline Lady Bugs. To let the girls continue playing, both coaches agreed to stop keeping score.

Photos by Scogin Mayo

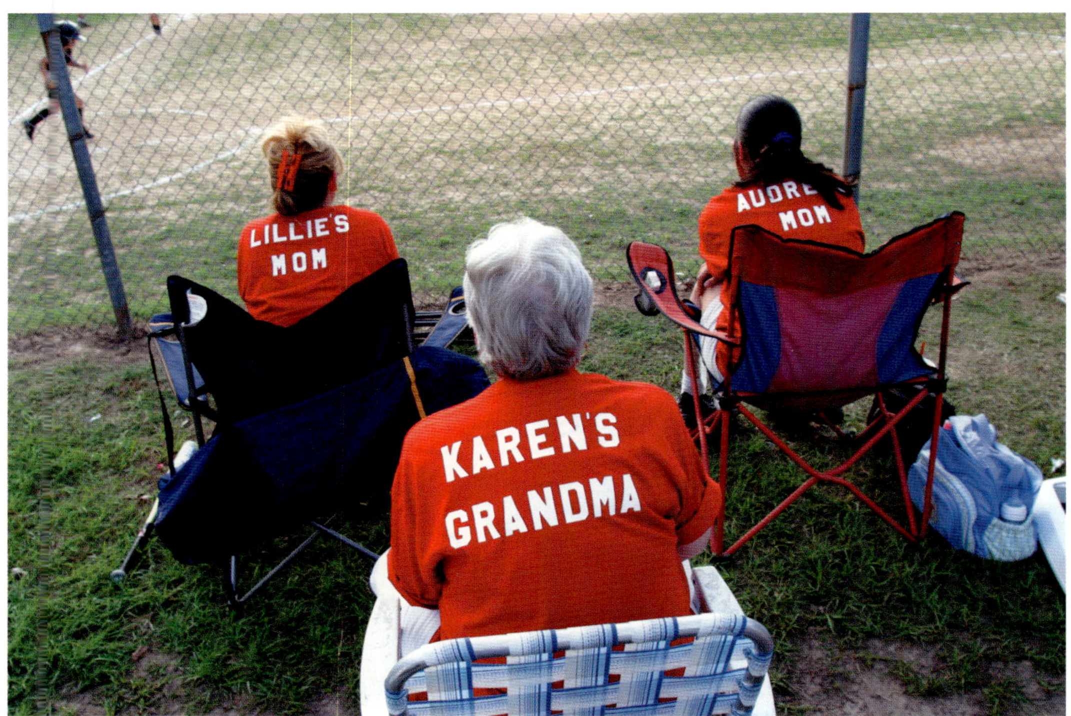

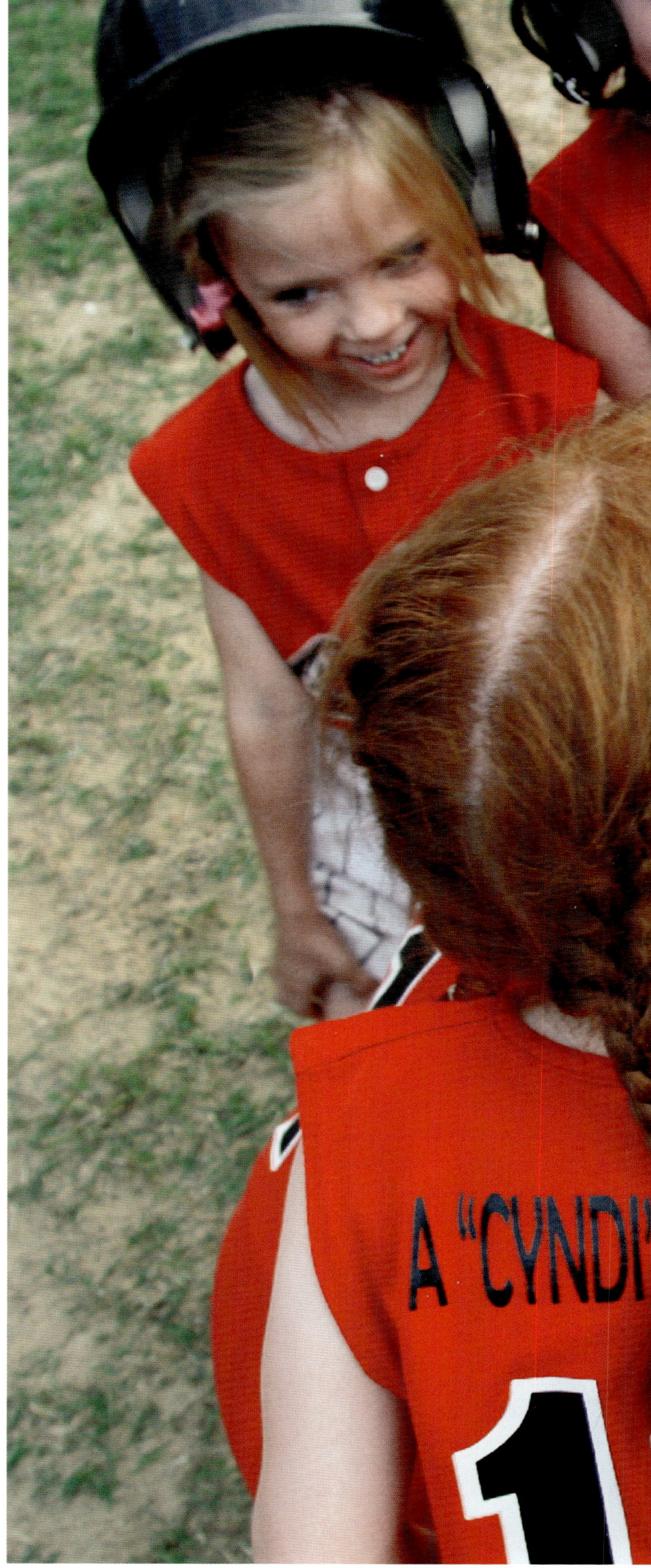

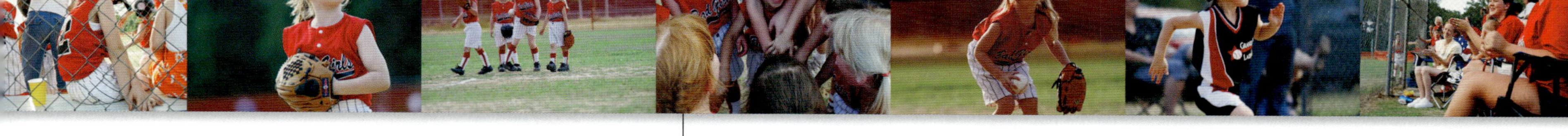

FRUITVALE

The Bad Girls huddle for the "team scream" to get pumped up for a T-ball game. Girls start playing T-ball at the age of 4. Once they turn 7, they can move up to "coach-pitch" games.

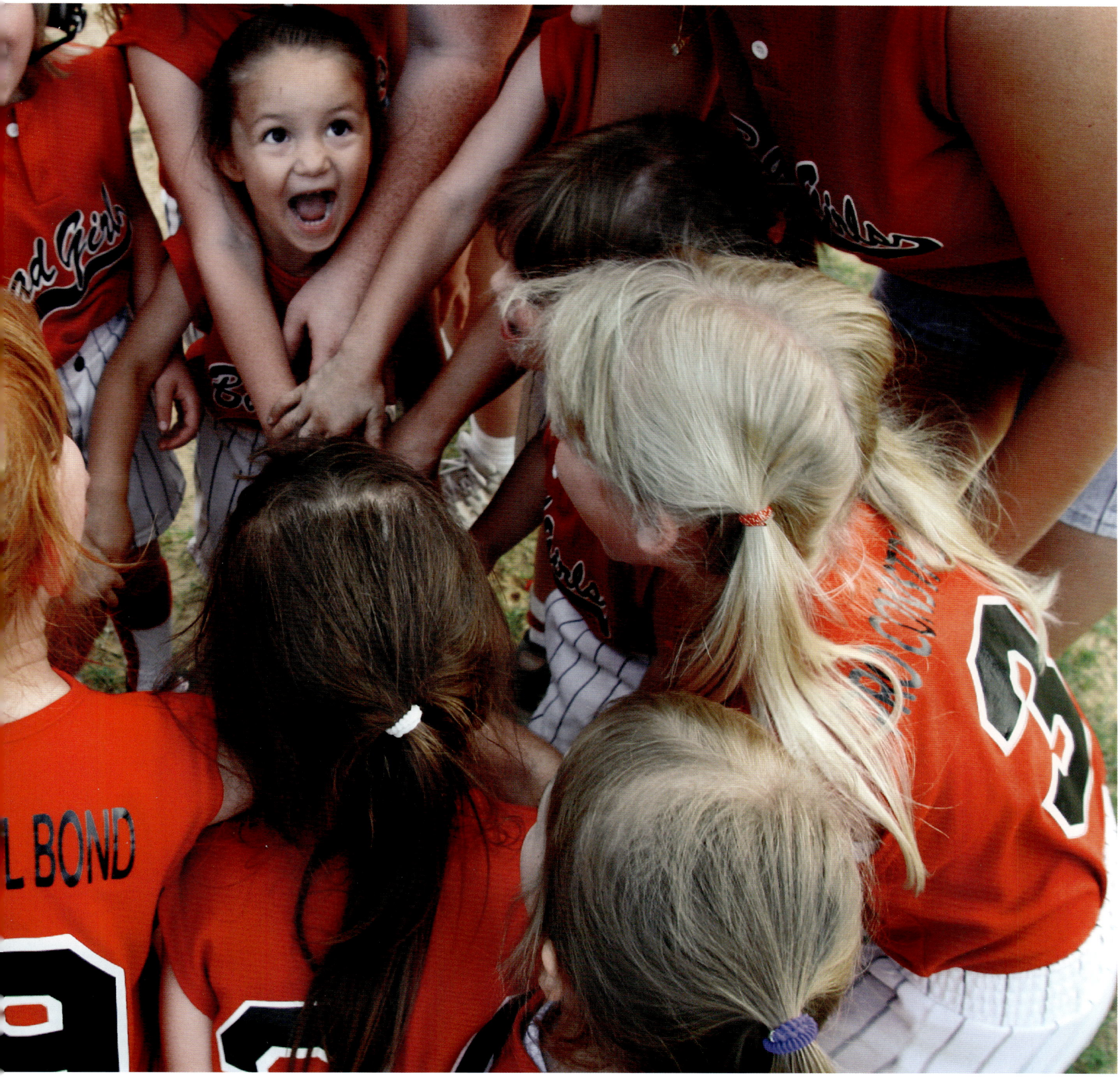

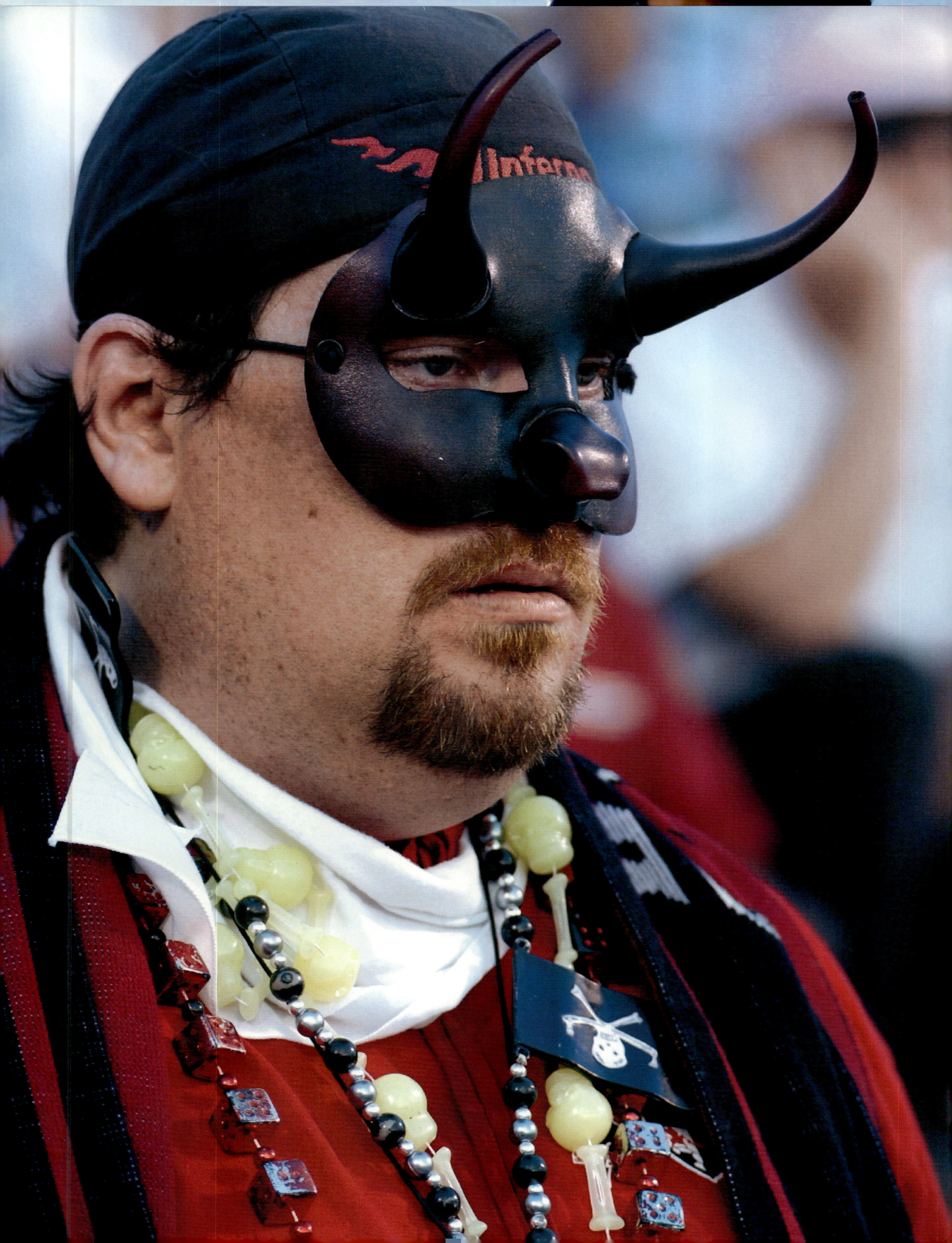

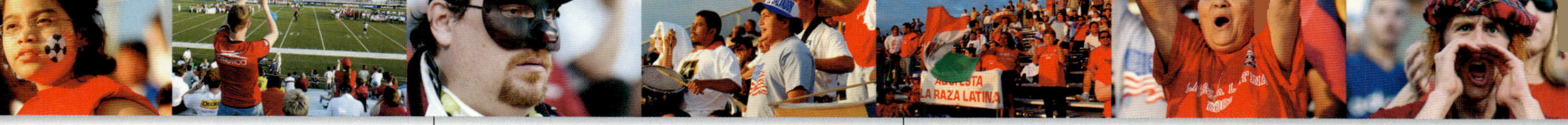

SOUTHLAKE
Who is that masked man? He's a member of the Inferno, a club of Dallas Burn fans. It's one of three groups that sit in the same section and root for the Major League Soccer team, now in its eighth season.
Photos by Shelly Katz Photo

SOUTHLAKE
The La Raza Latina fan club rallies for the Dallas Burn as they battle the Los Angeles Galaxy at Southlake Carroll High School's Dragon Stadium. The team, whose home field had been the Cotton Bowl, is playing here while a new stadium is being built.

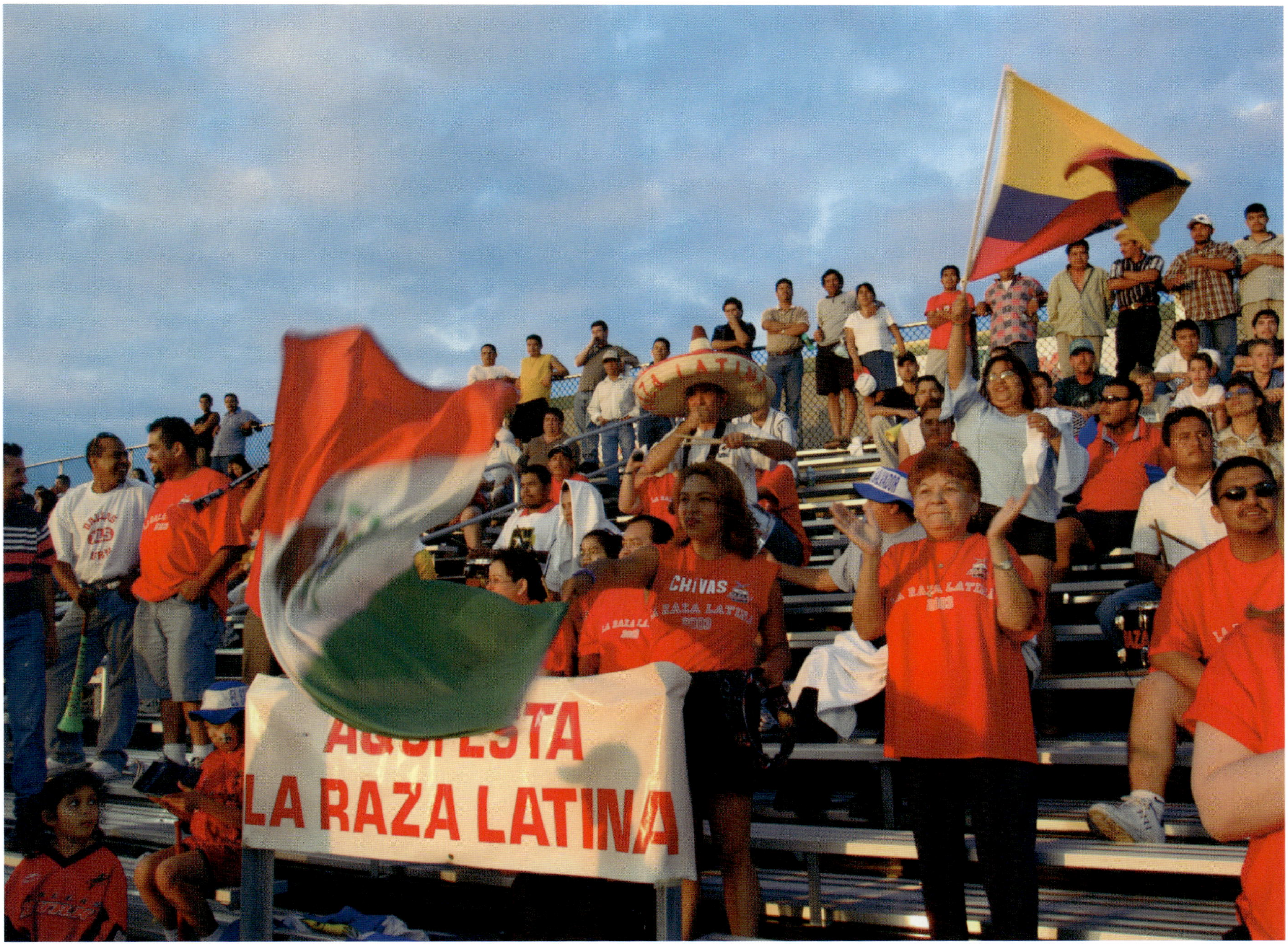

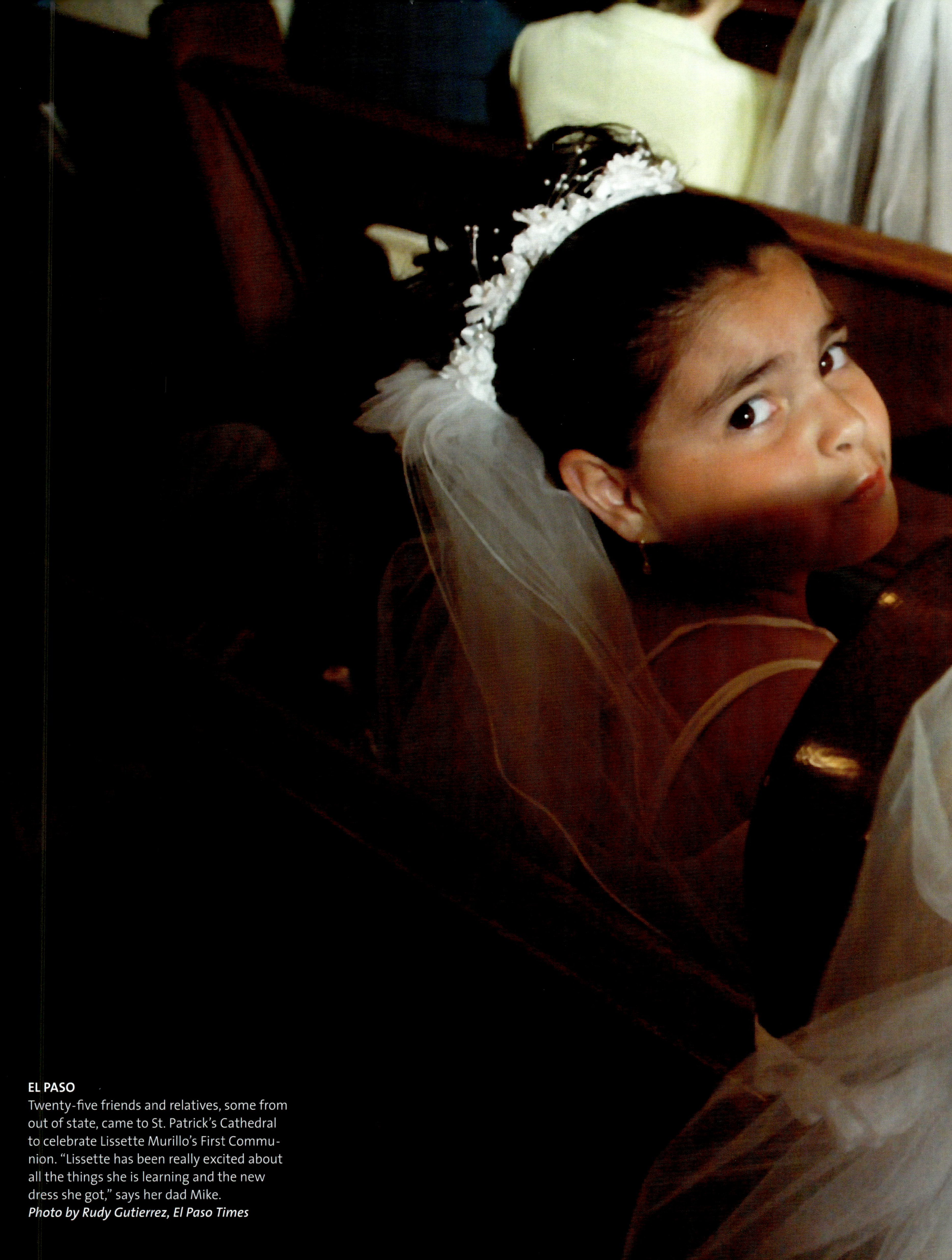

EL PASO
Twenty-five friends and relatives, some from out of state, came to St. Patrick's Cathedral to celebrate Lissette Murillo's First Communion. "Lissette has been really excited about all the things she is learning and the new dress she got," says her dad Mike.
Photo by Rudy Gutierrez, El Paso Times

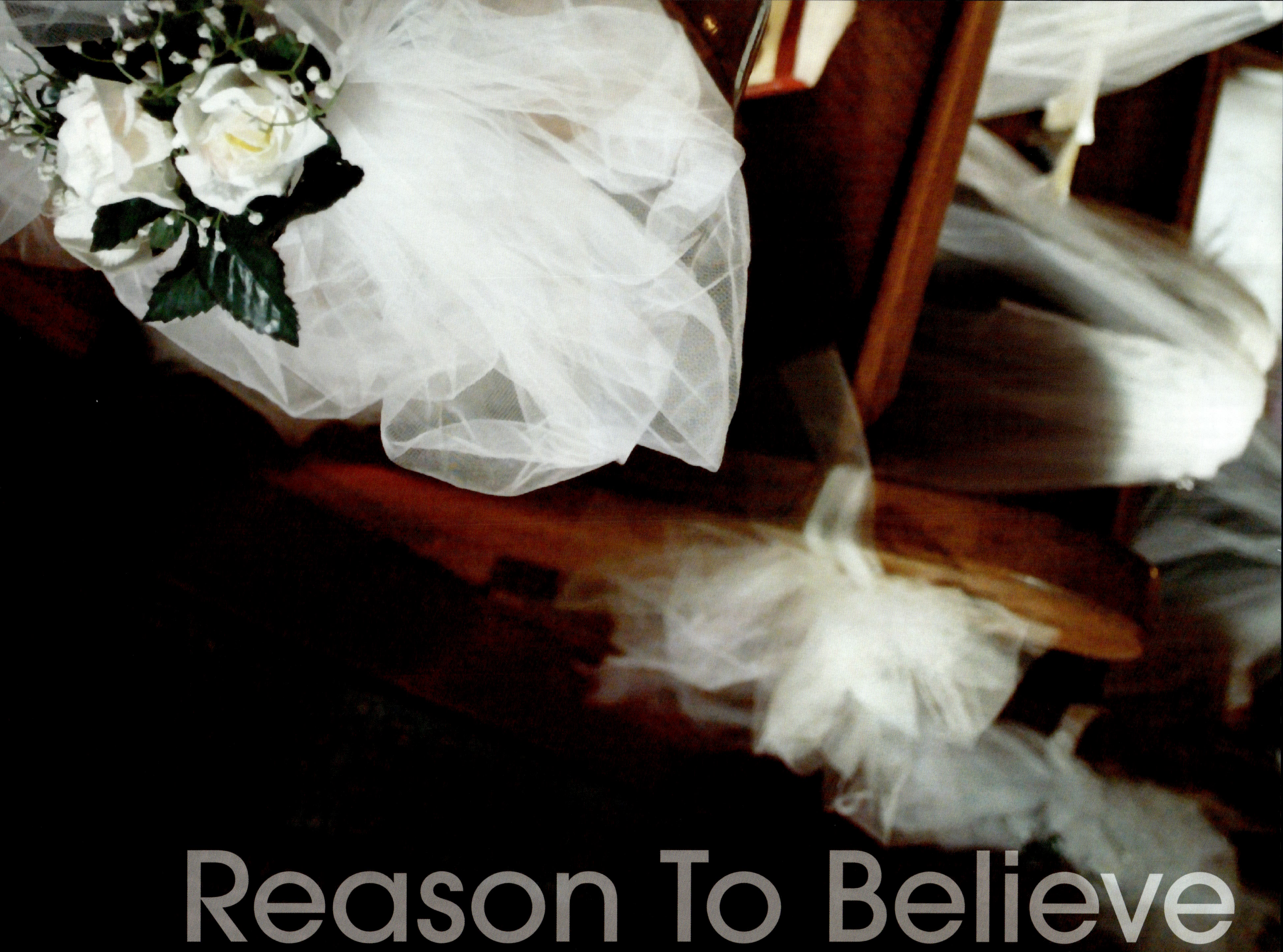

Reason To Believe

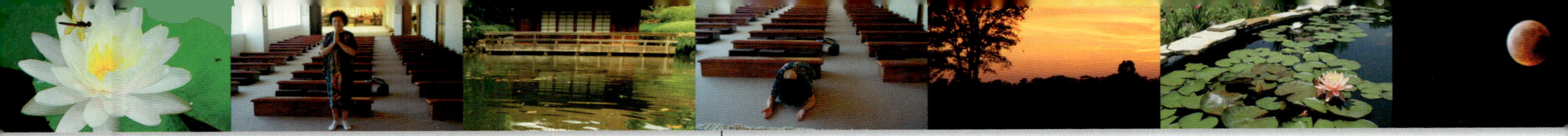

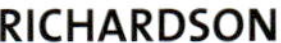

RICHARDSON
Taiwan native Weng-Mai Chiu prays for her husband's health every Sunday at the International Buddhist Progress Society, one of 14 Buddhist temples in the Dallas area. Chiu, a 62-year-old health care worker, supports herself and her husband, who has been bedridden for ten years.
Photo by B'Lan Kao

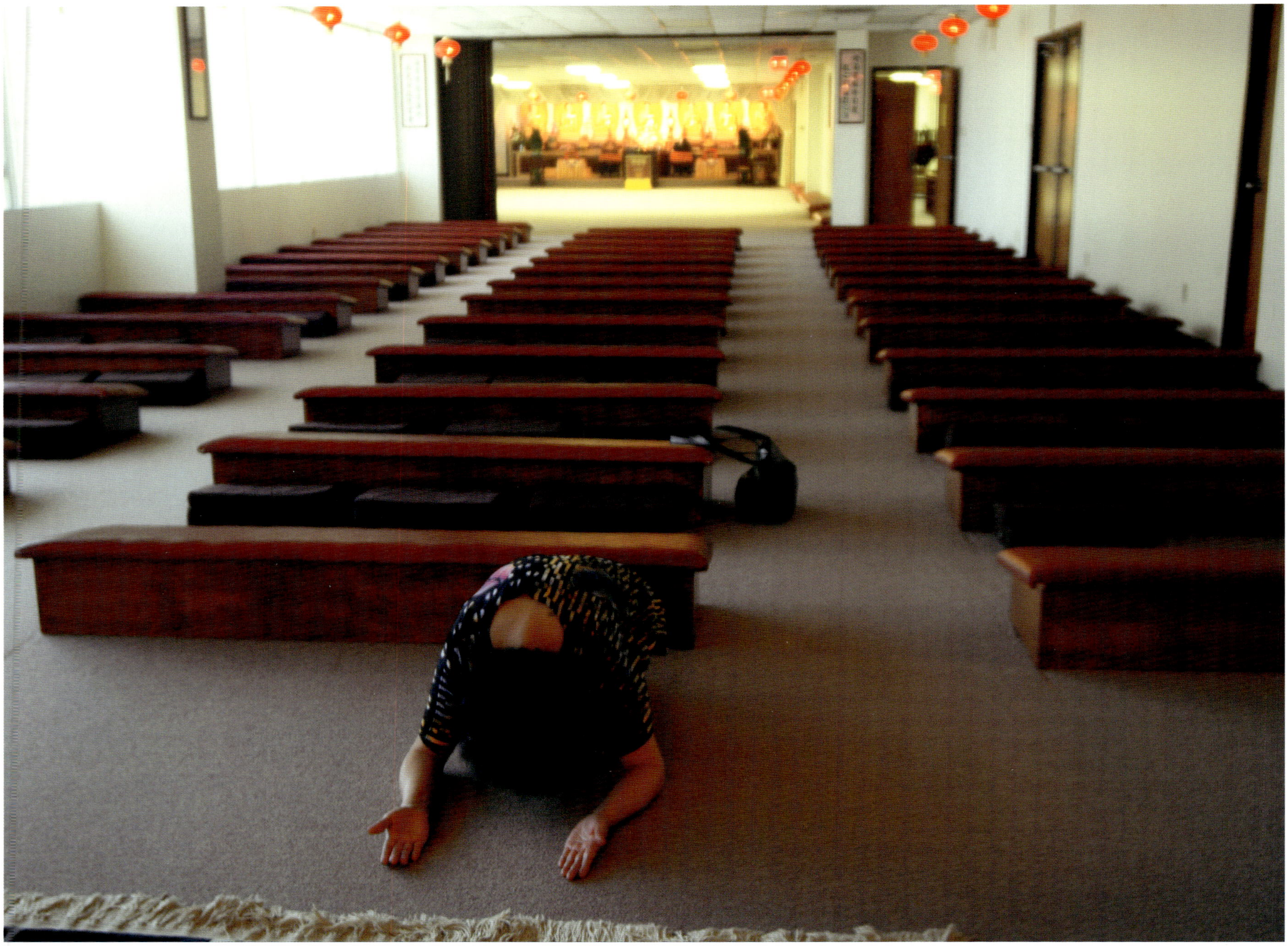

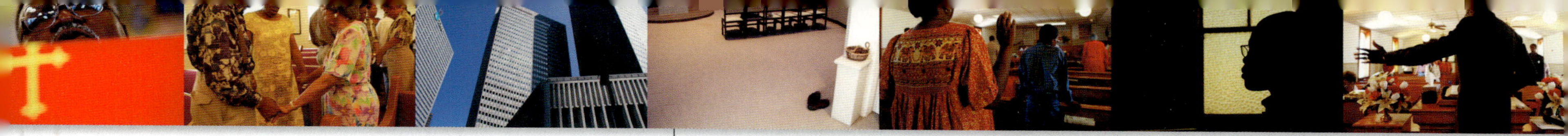

DALLAS
After praying, a Muslim worshipper sits near the 7,000-pound Carrera marble altar at the interfaith Chapel of Thanksgiving, where people can attend services or meditate alone. The chapel is part of Thanks-Giving Square, an institute for the cross-cultural study of gratitude and prayer. In 1988, the nonprofit's research led President Ronald Reagan to declare May 5th a "National Day of Prayer."
Photo by Peter A. Calvin

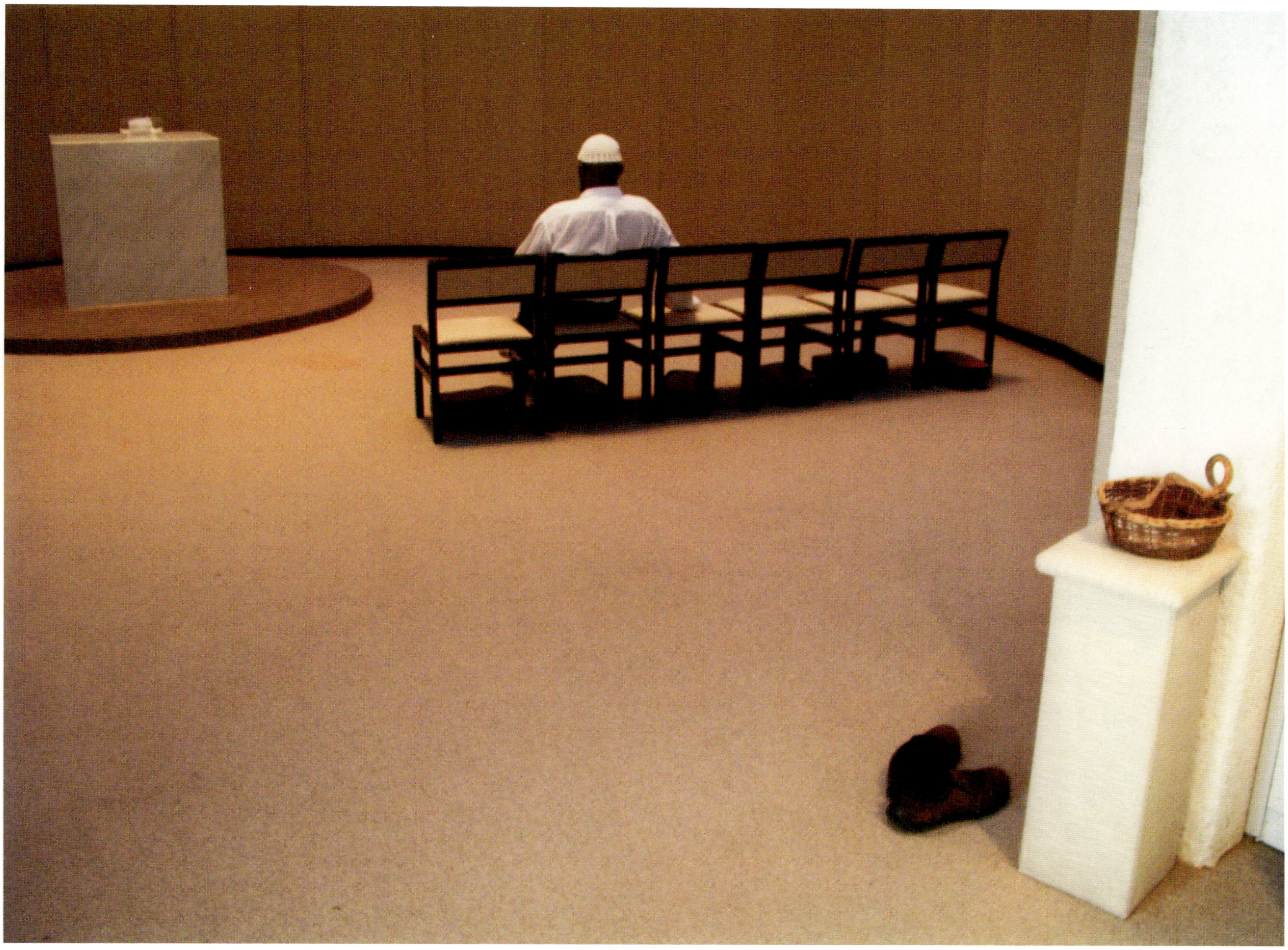

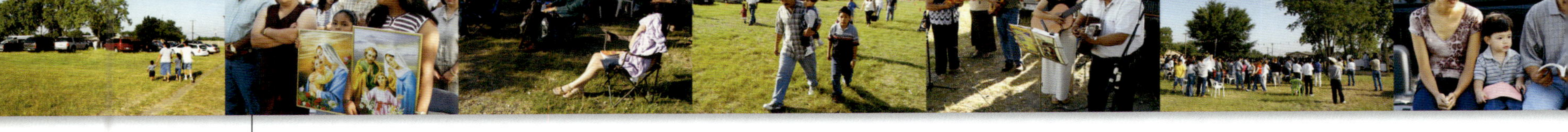

DALLAS

At an outdoor mass on a 3-acre plot of land near the Calvary Cemetery, San Juan Diego parishioners await a blessing from Father Anibal Adorno. With 1,100 members, the congregation has outgrown its home at nearby Saint Monica Church and is now fundraising for a new chapel on this North Dallas plot, which is owned by the Catholic Diocese.

Photos by Peter A. Calvin

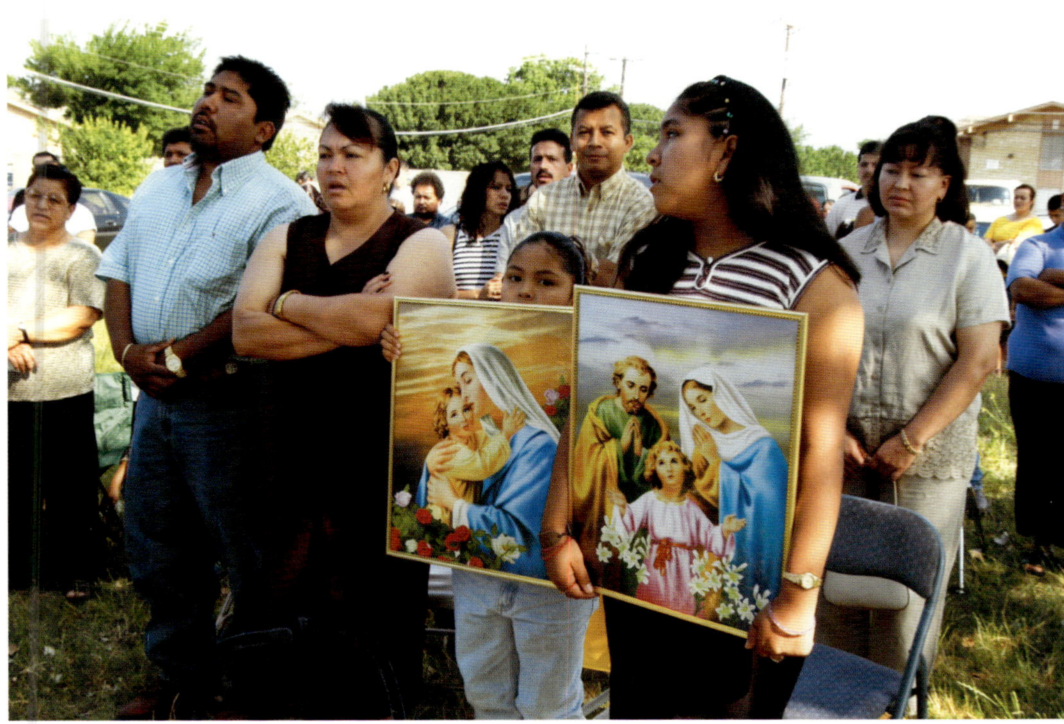

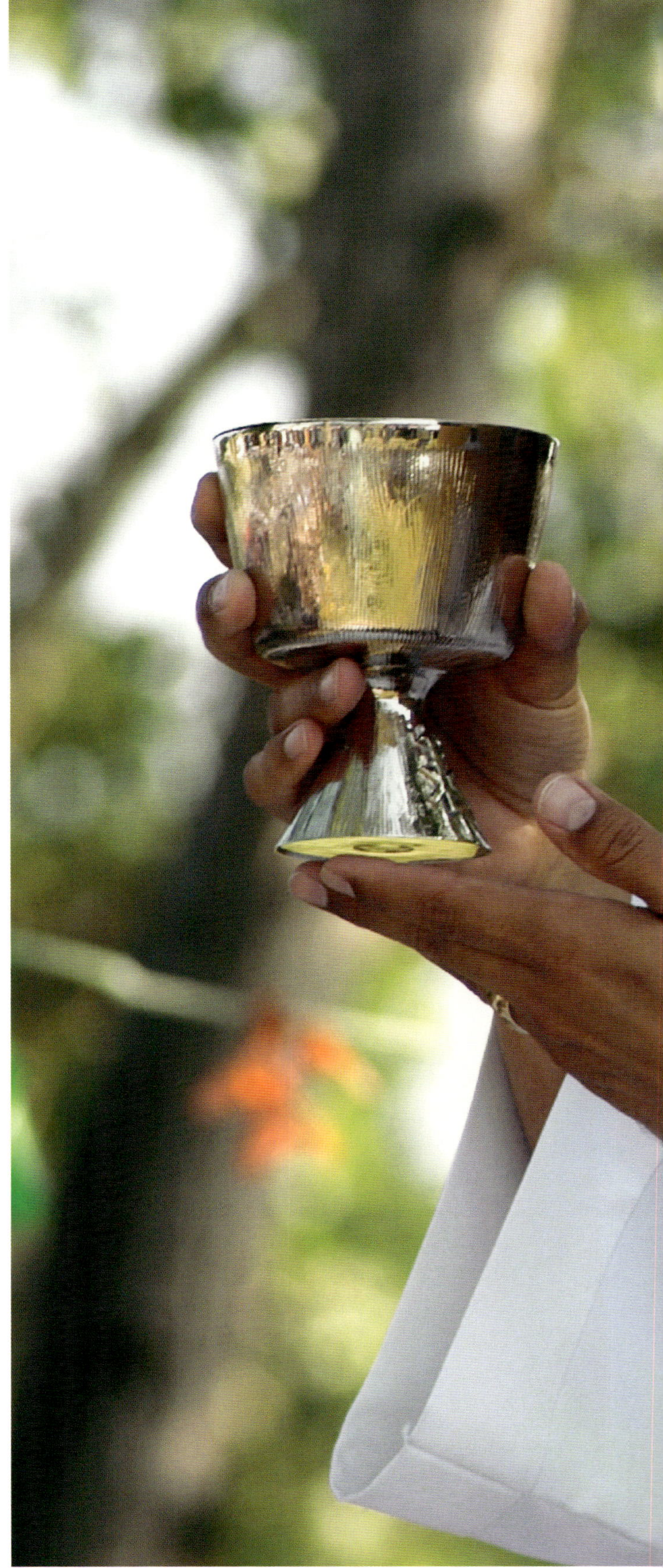

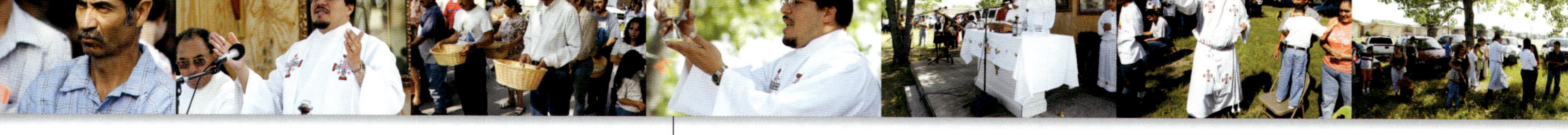

DALLAS
Father Adorno prepares to serve communion. Congregants come in any weather, including low temperatures and rain, to hear the Puerto Rican priest preach in Spanish.

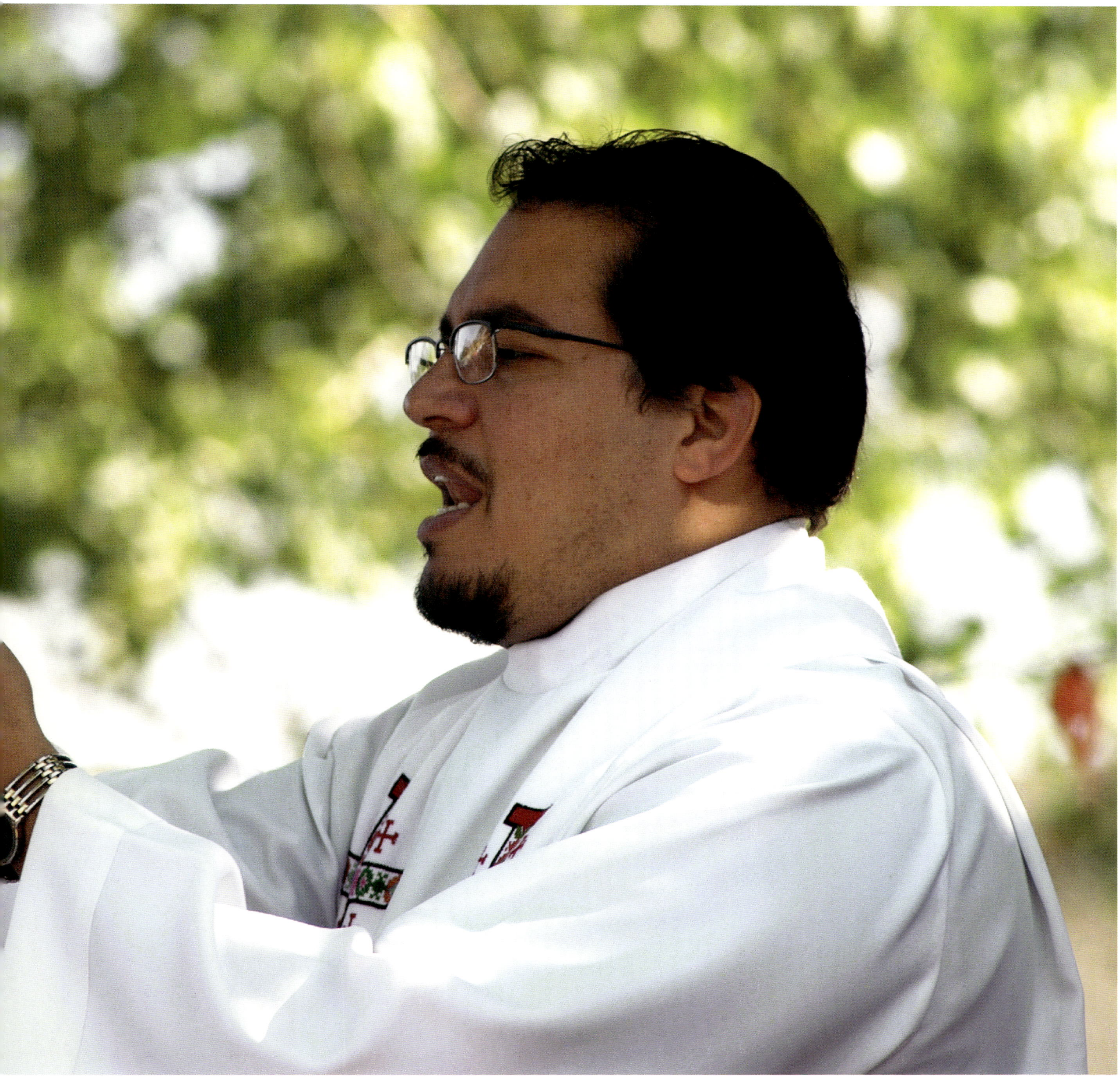

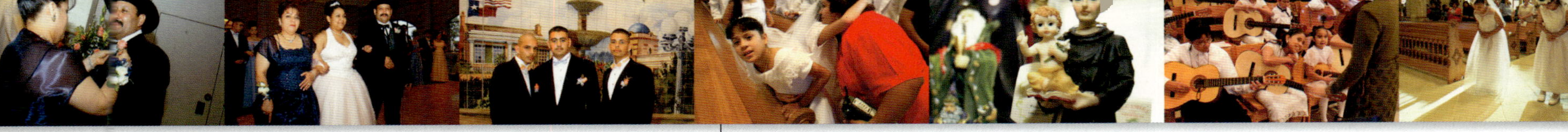

SAN ANTONIO
Elvira Quiñonez looks for a friend while her twin Steffanie gets a hug from their mom Juana as a "sign of peace" during the First Communion mass at San Fernando Cathedral. As part of mass, the priest invites everyone to give another person either a verbal or physical sign of peace.
Photo by Joe Abell, San Antonio Express-News

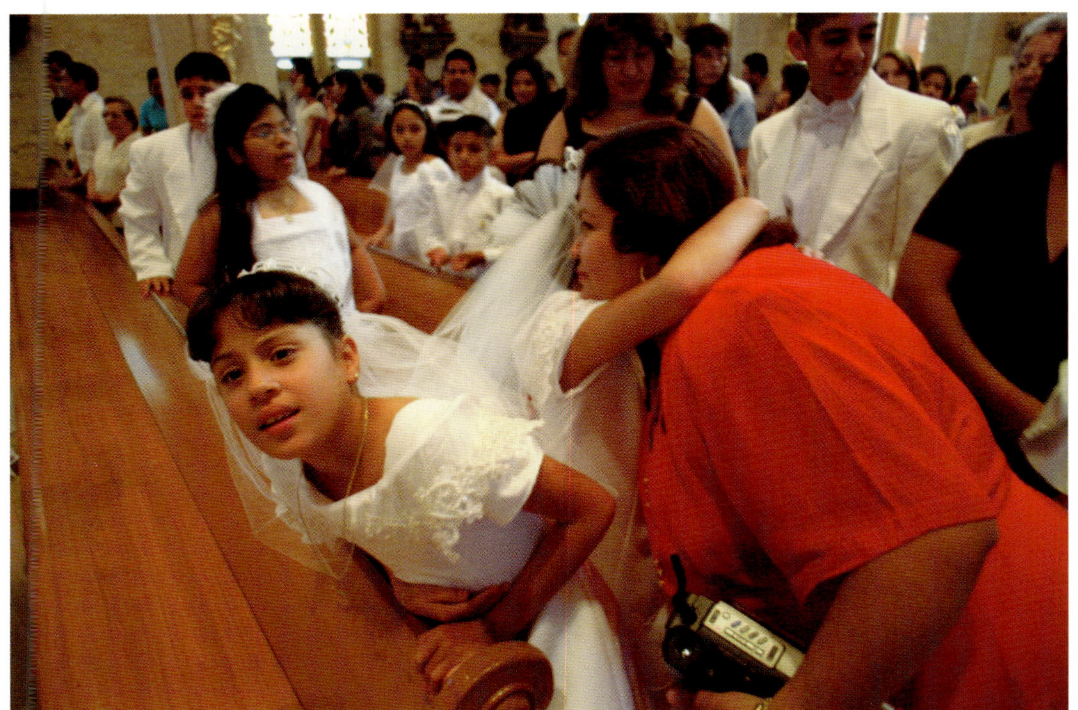

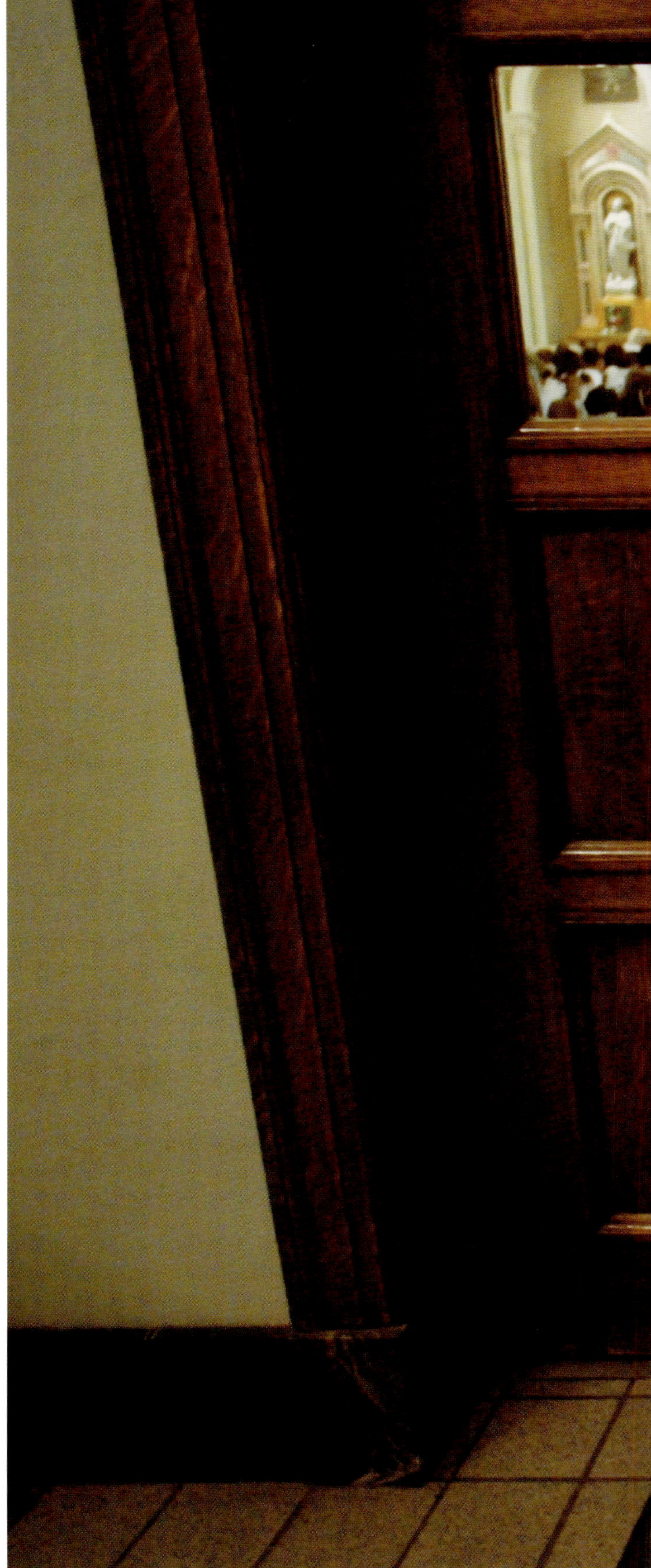

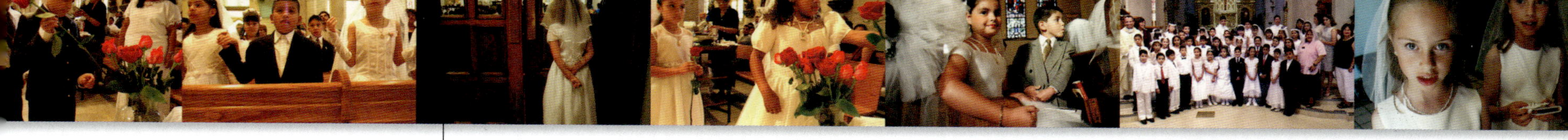

EL PASO
Breeanna Veilleux, 8, peers through the doors at St. Patrick's Cathedral, waiting for her First Communion mass to start. The ceremony culminates two years of classes.
Photo by Rudy Gutierrez, El Paso Times

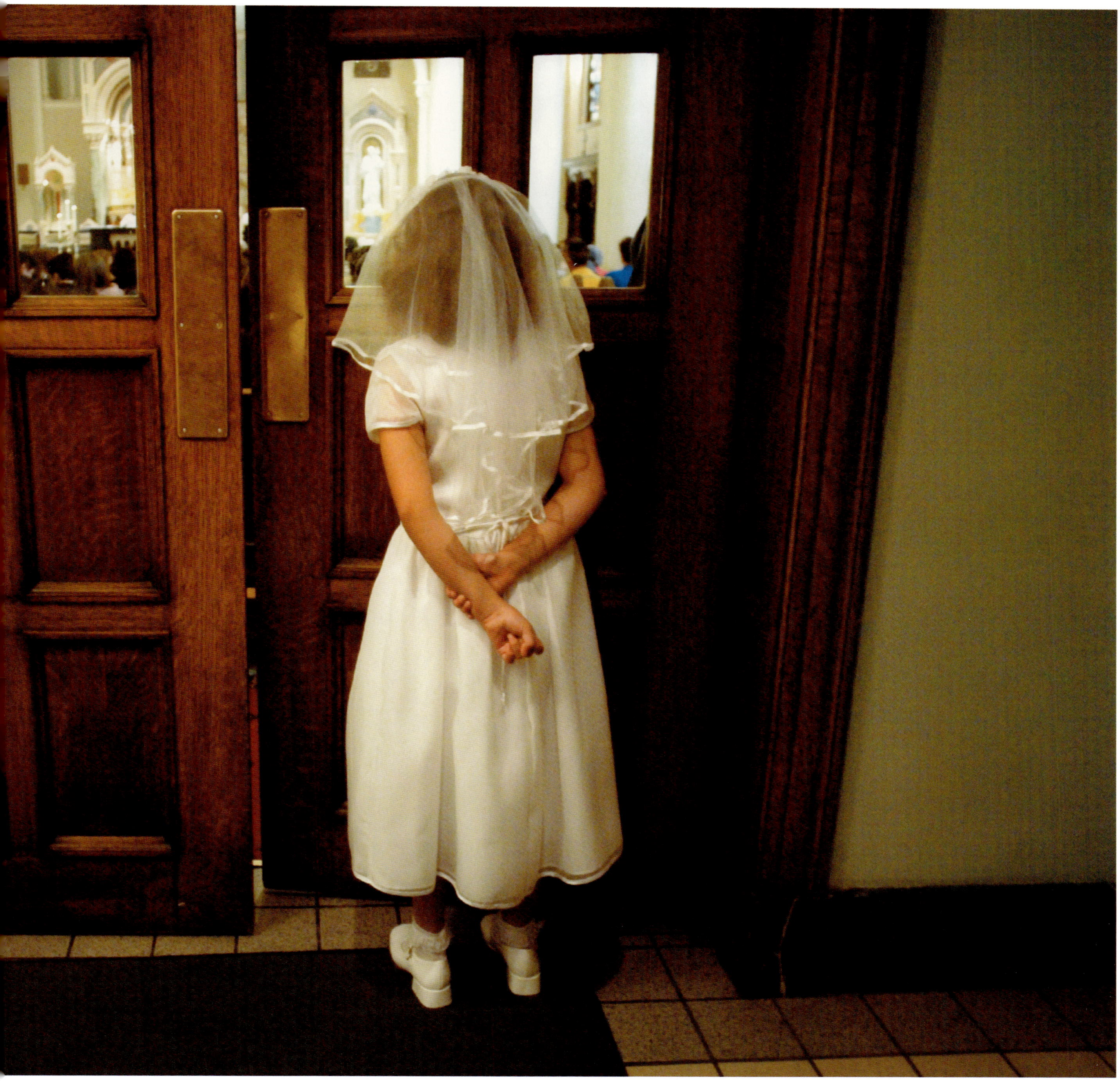

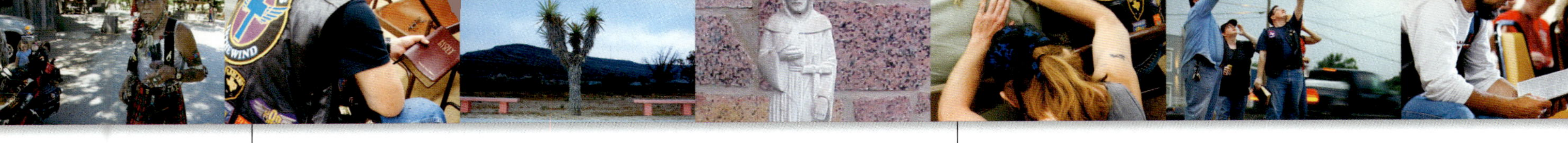

LONGVIEW
Chris Hughes hadn't been to church in 20 years when a biker friend recommended Church in the Wind. The church welcomes "anyone who feels out of place in conventional worship settings," says Pastor CC Gower. Hughes, a welder at Vessel Technology, says the church has brought him closer to his wife and four kids.
Photos by Les Hassell

LONGVIEW
Jeff Pearman lays hands on Patty Hughes during a worship service. Many of the church's 55 members take motorcycle trips on Sundays, so evening prayer sessions are held on Wednesdays and Fridays.

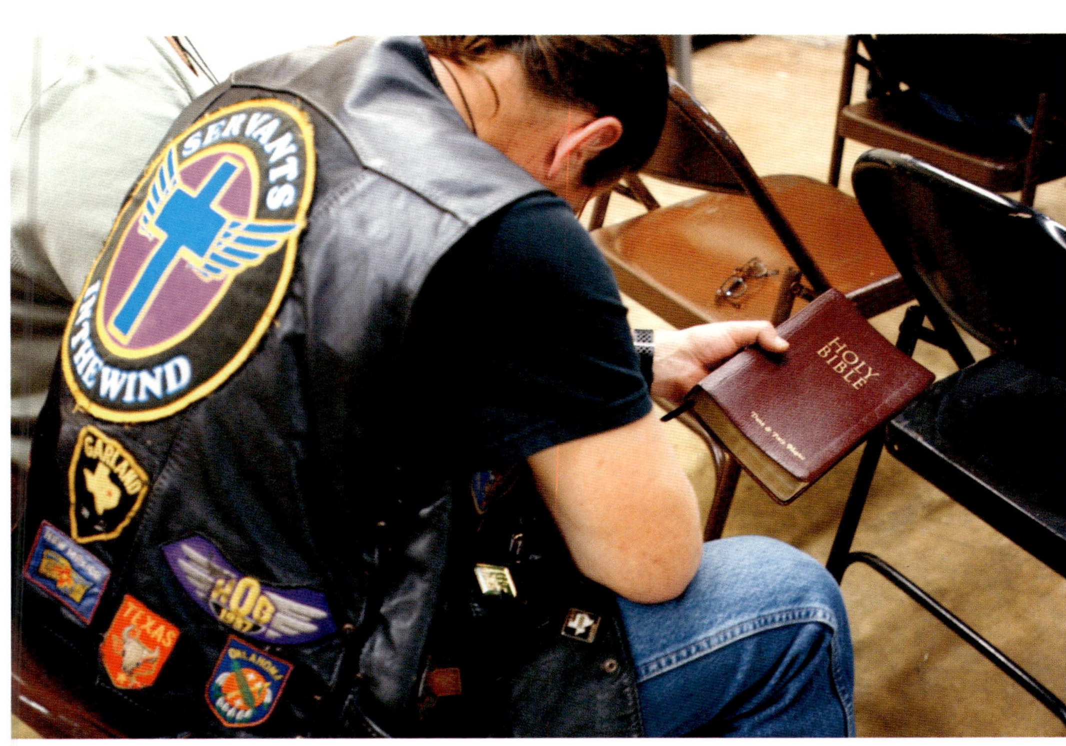

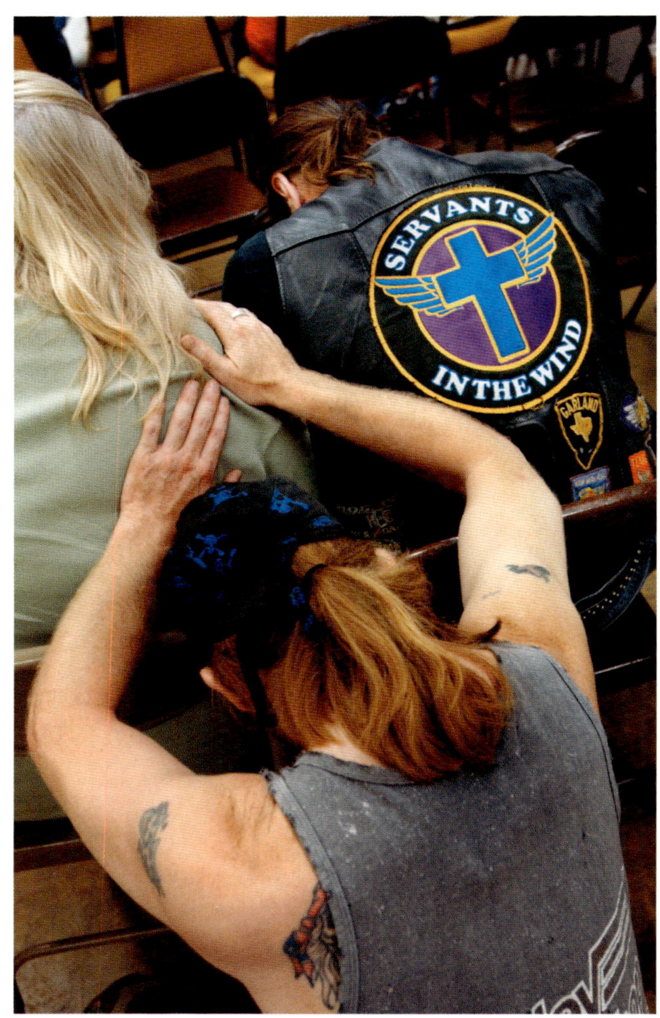

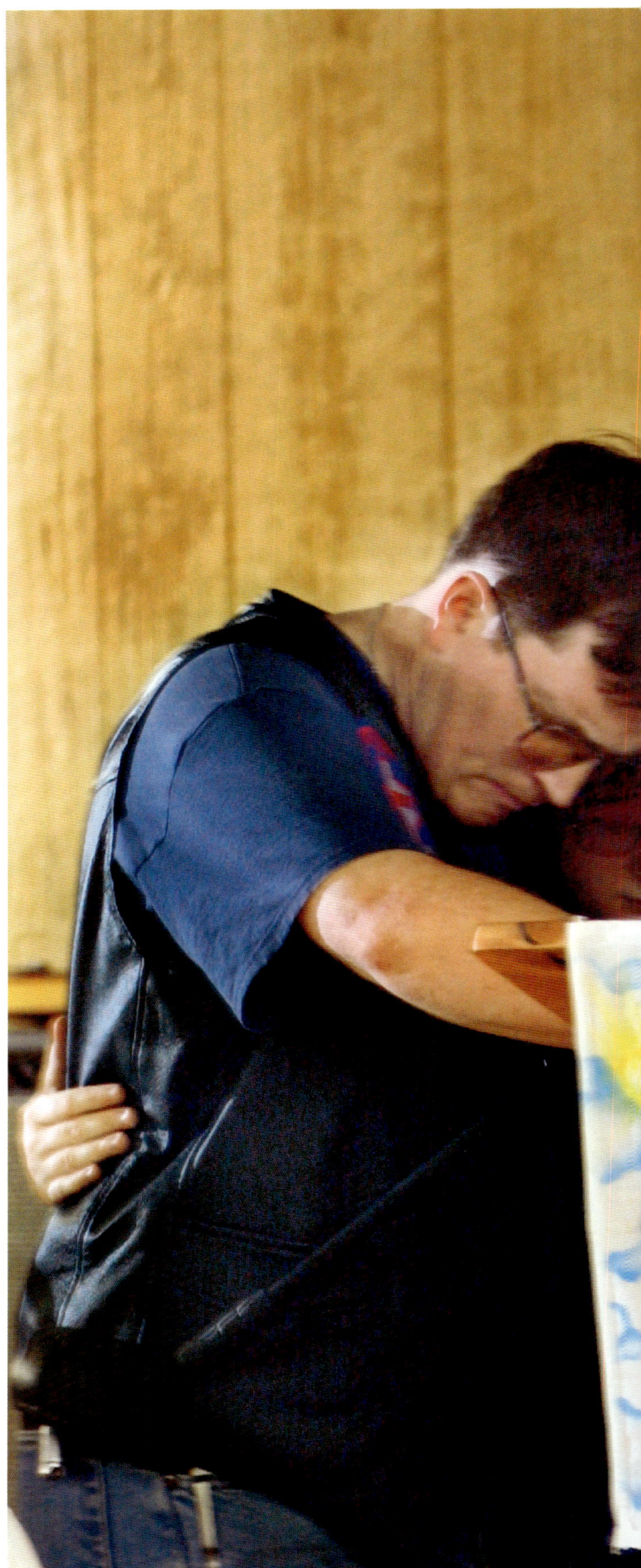

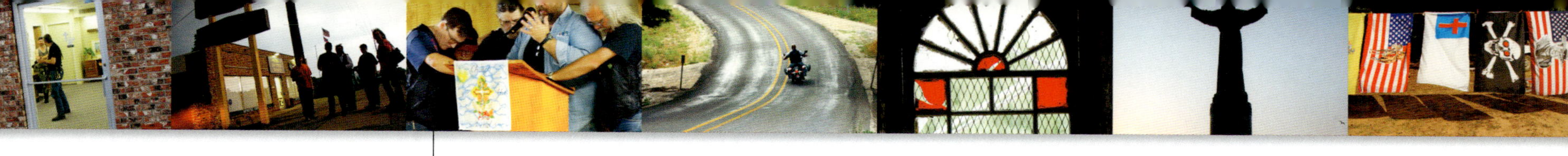

LONGVIEW

The Church in the Wind regularly invites members to offer praise reports and requests. Charles and Buffy Sullivan (left), Pastor CC Gower, Glenn French (at microphone), and George Pliler gather around the pulpit to provide encouragement to the congregation. Pastor Gower, a self-described "old biker," started the church in June 2000, after receiving his Christian ministry degree from East Texas Baptist University.

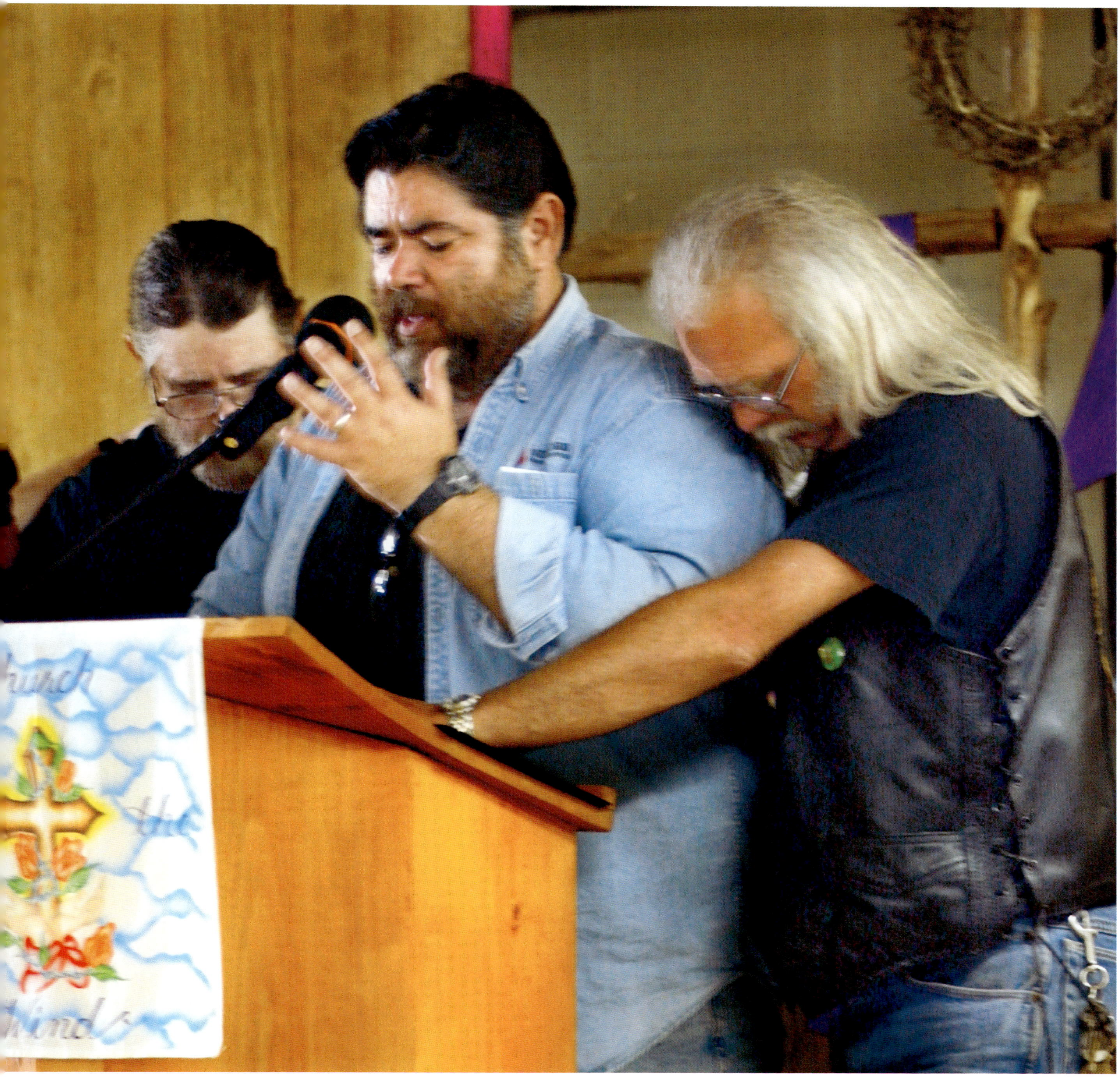

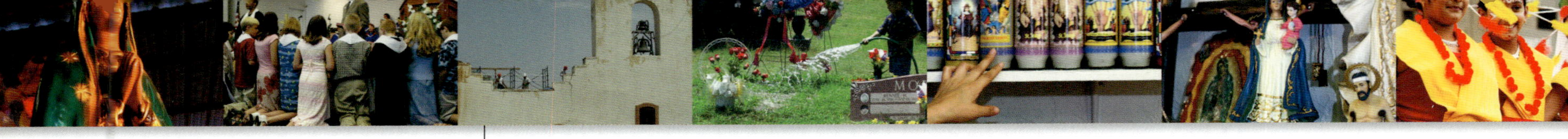

SOCORRO

The first Socorro Mission, ancestral home of the Piro Indians, was built in 1692. Damaged twice by the flooding of the Rio Grande River, it was rebuilt in 1843. Cement (rather than mud and lime) used in the reconstruction, however, led to extensive deterioration. A major restoration is again underway, fueled by $1.3 million in federal, state, and private funds.

Photos by Rudy Gutierrez, El Paso Times

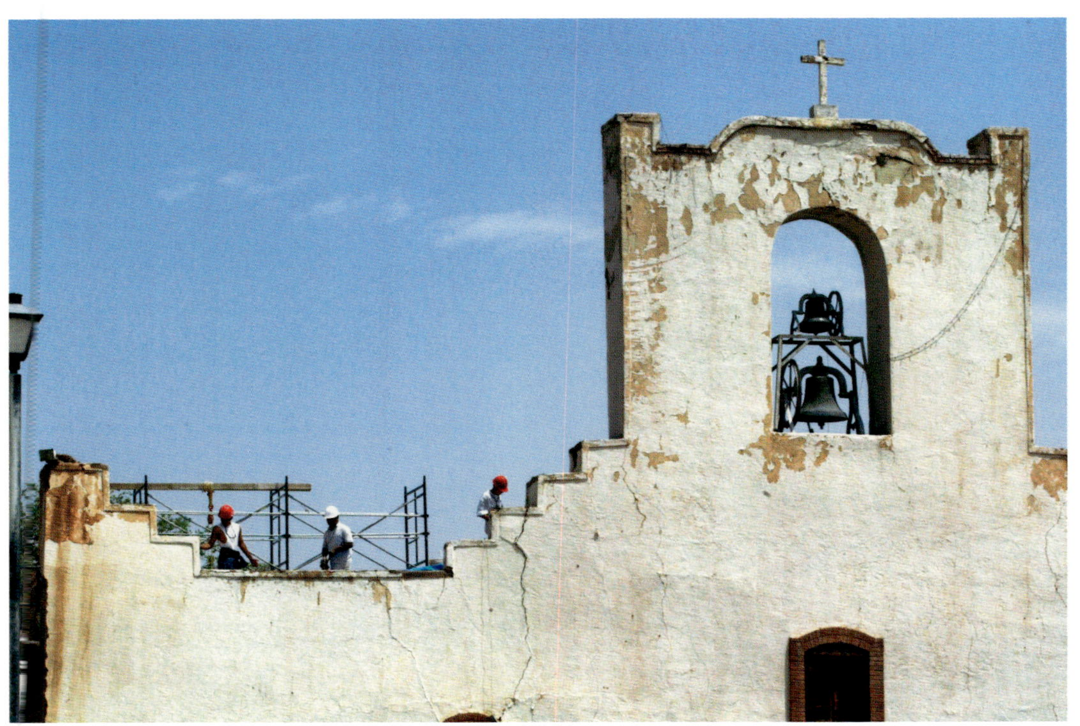

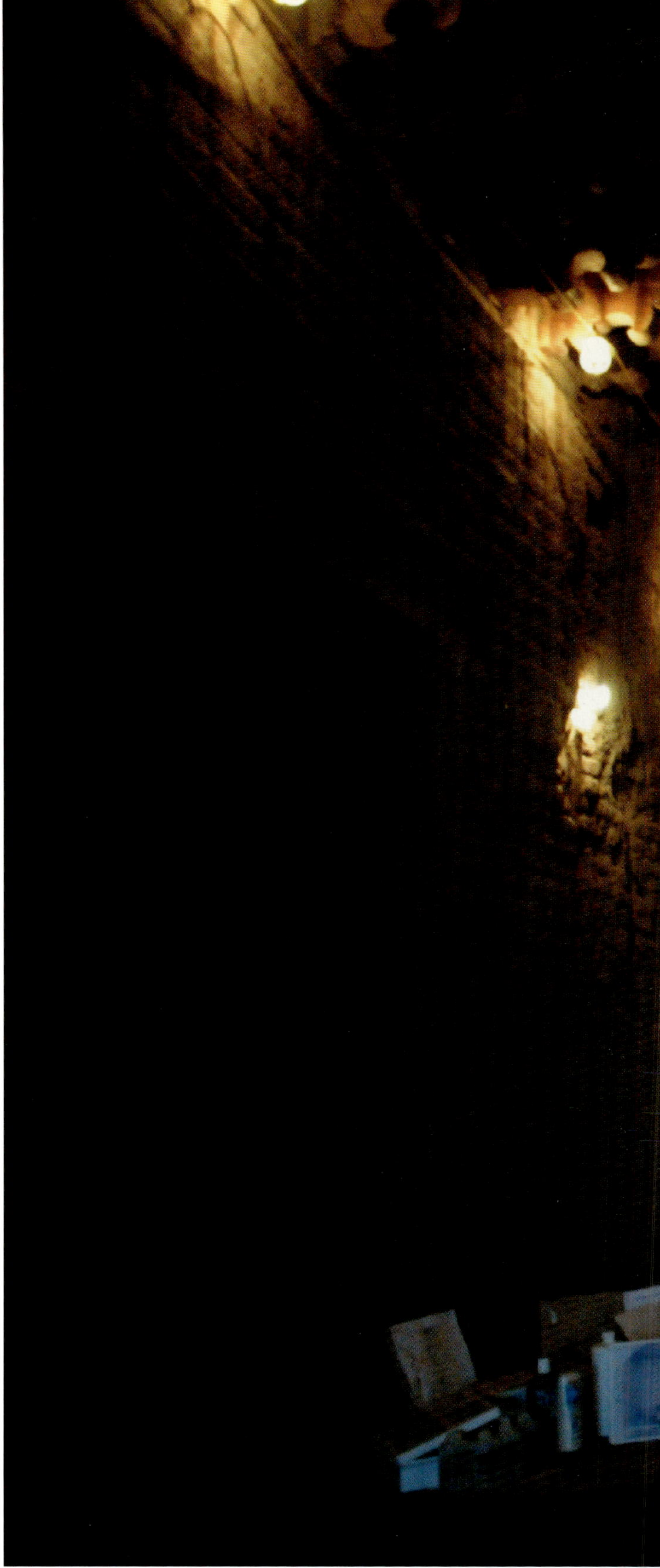

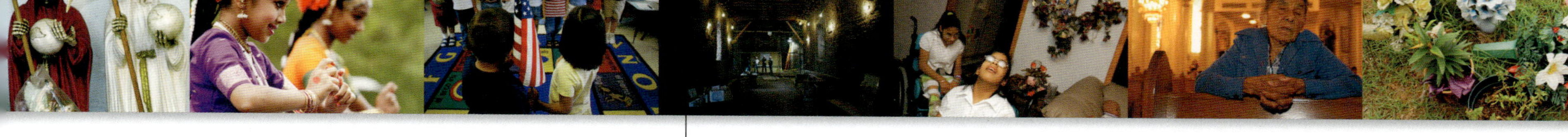

SOCORRO
The nave of the Socorro Mission Church has adobe walls that are 5-feet-thick, so the interior stays cool and dark. Some of the original vigas (hand-carved beams painted with plant material) have survived intact and are being used during the reconstruction.

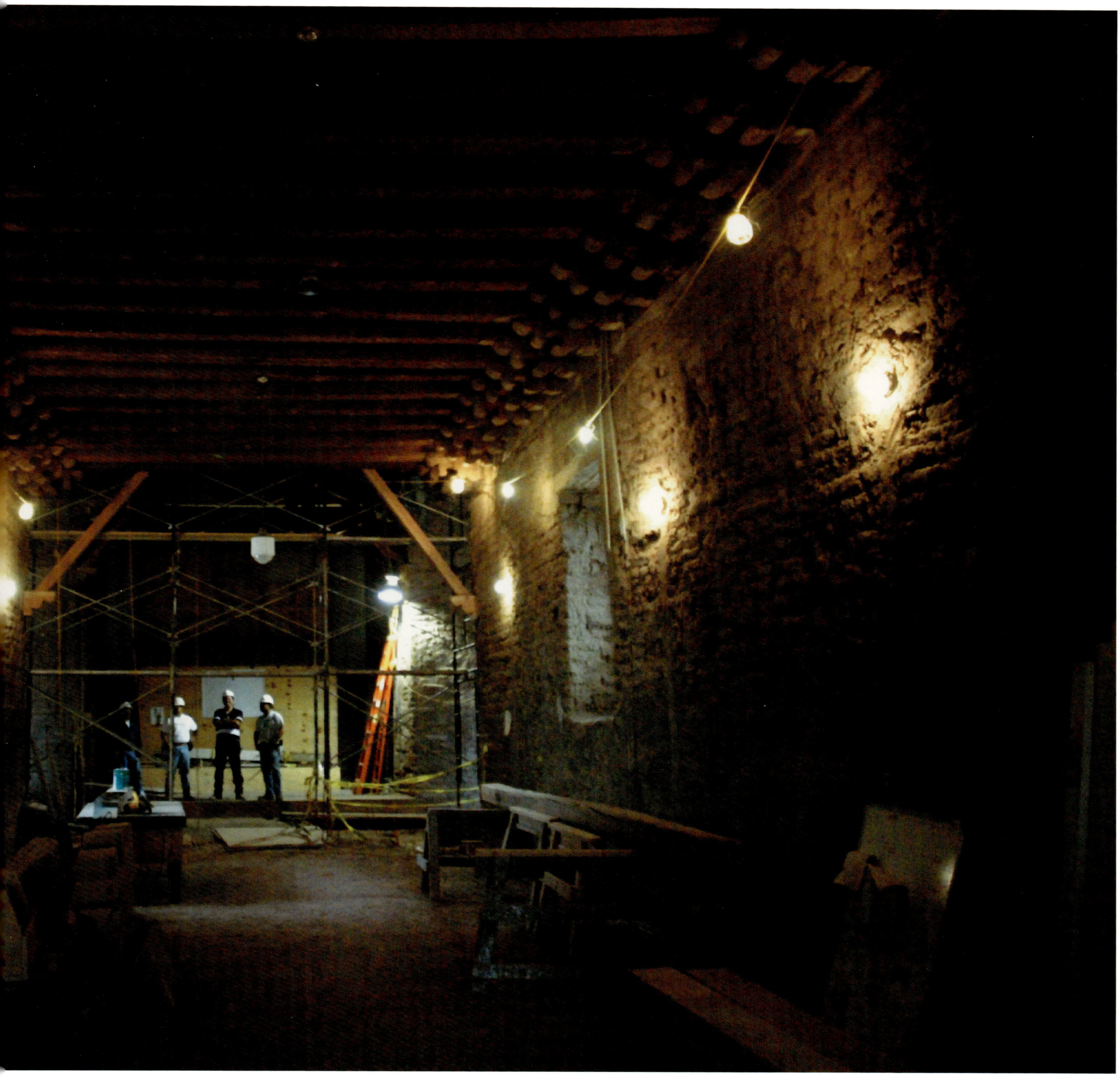

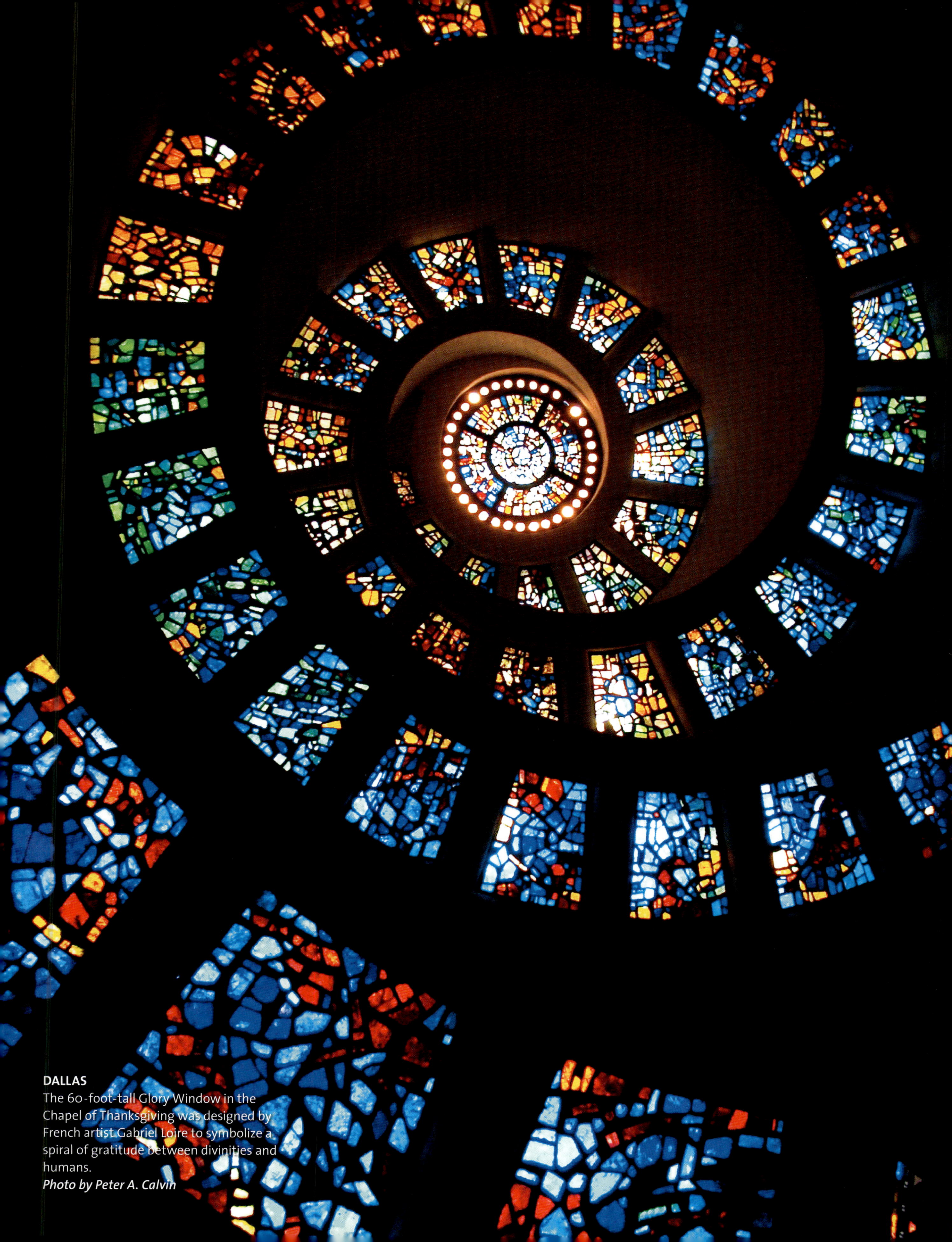

DALLAS
The 60-foot-tall Glory Window in the Chapel of Thanksgiving was designed by French artist Gabriel Loire to symbolize a spiral of gratitude between divinities and humans.
Photo by Peter A. Calvin

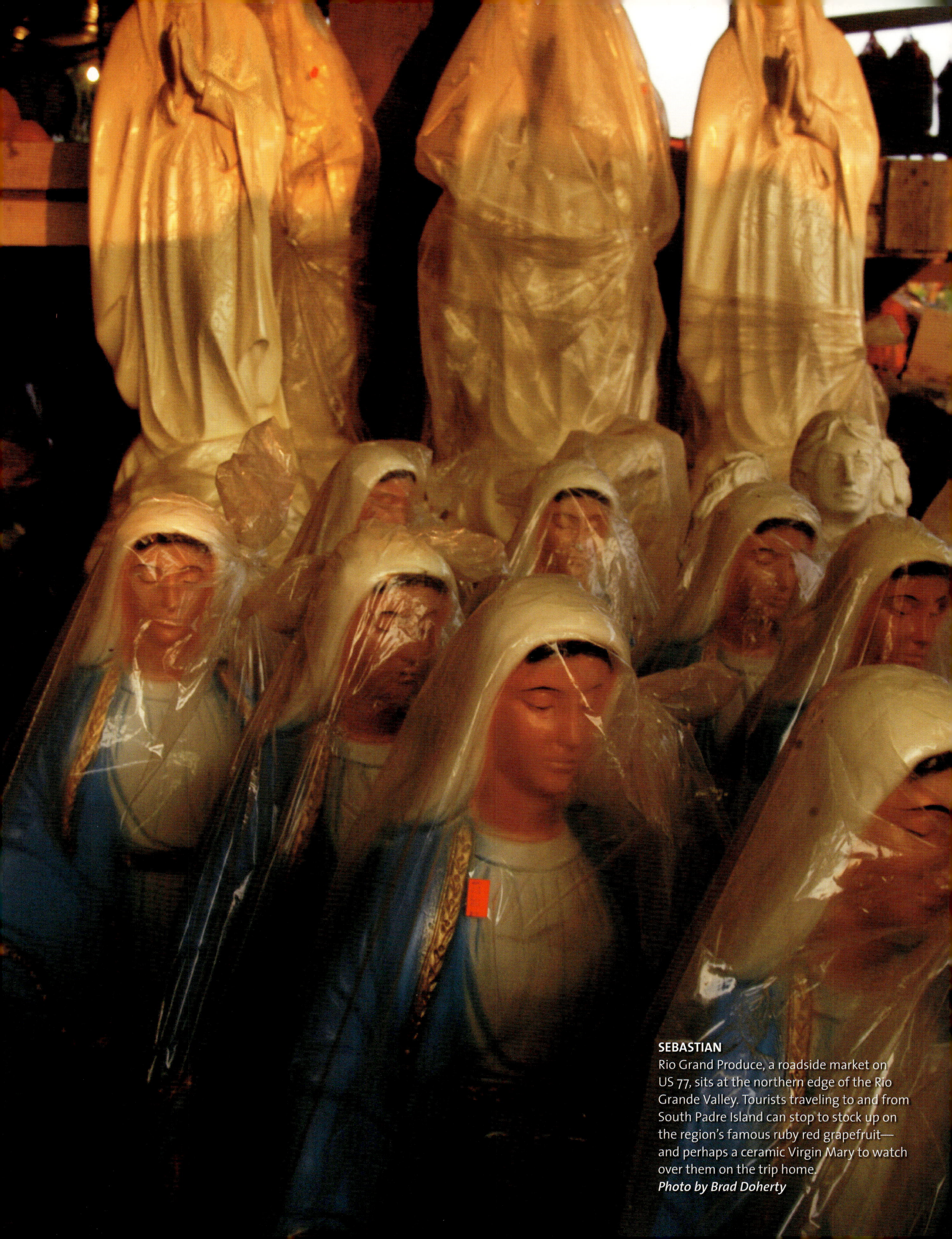

SEBASTIAN
Rio Grand Produce, a roadside market on US 77, sits at the northern edge of the Rio Grande Valley. Tourists traveling to and from South Padre Island can stop to stock up on the region's famous ruby red grapefruit—and perhaps a ceramic Virgin Mary to watch over them on the trip home.
Photo by Brad Doherty

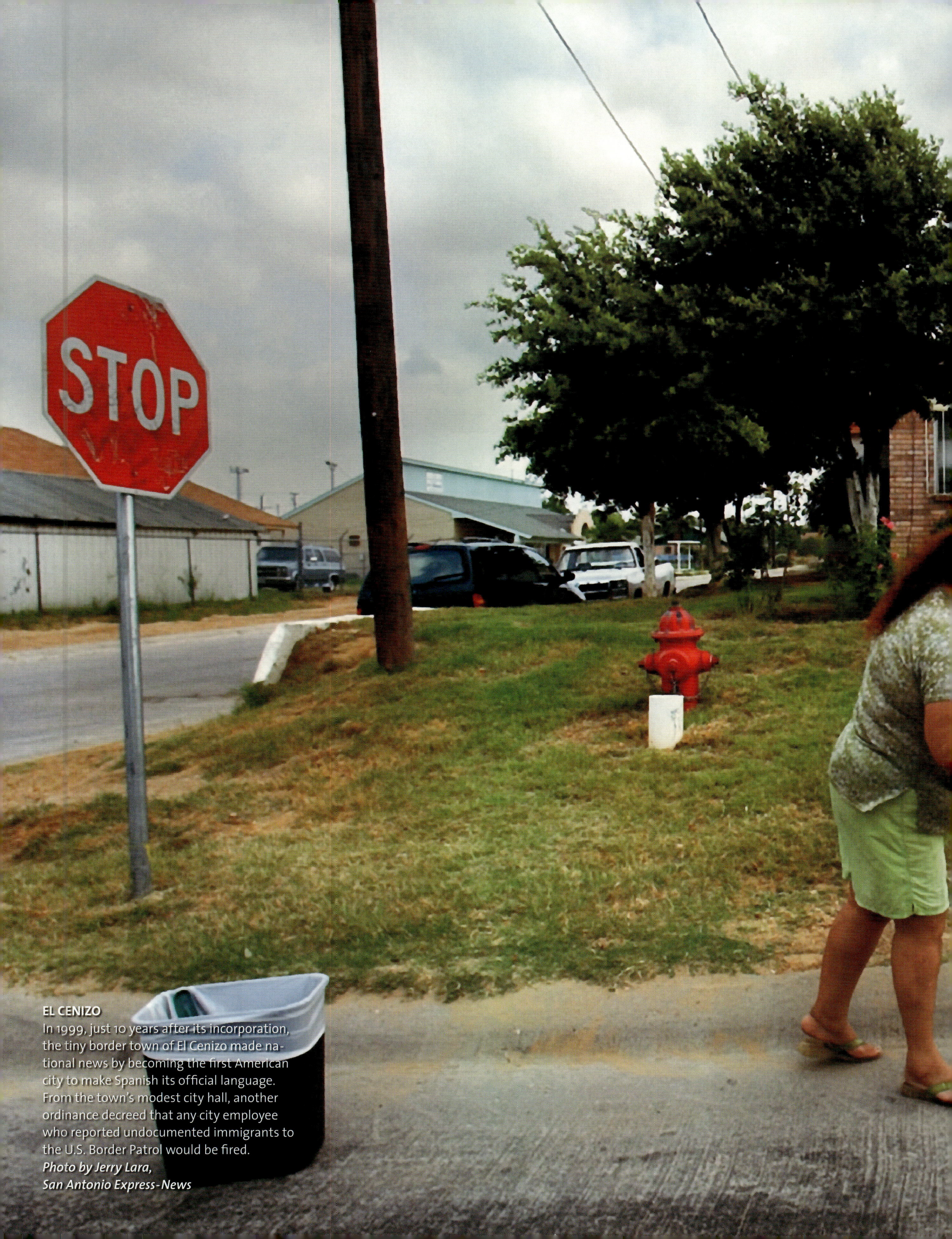

EL CENIZO
In 1999, just 10 years after its incorporation, the tiny border town of El Cenizo made national news by becoming the first American city to make Spanish its official language. From the town's modest city hall, another ordinance decreed that any city employee who reported undocumented immigrants to the U.S. Border Patrol would be fired.
Photo by Jerry Lara, San Antonio Express-News

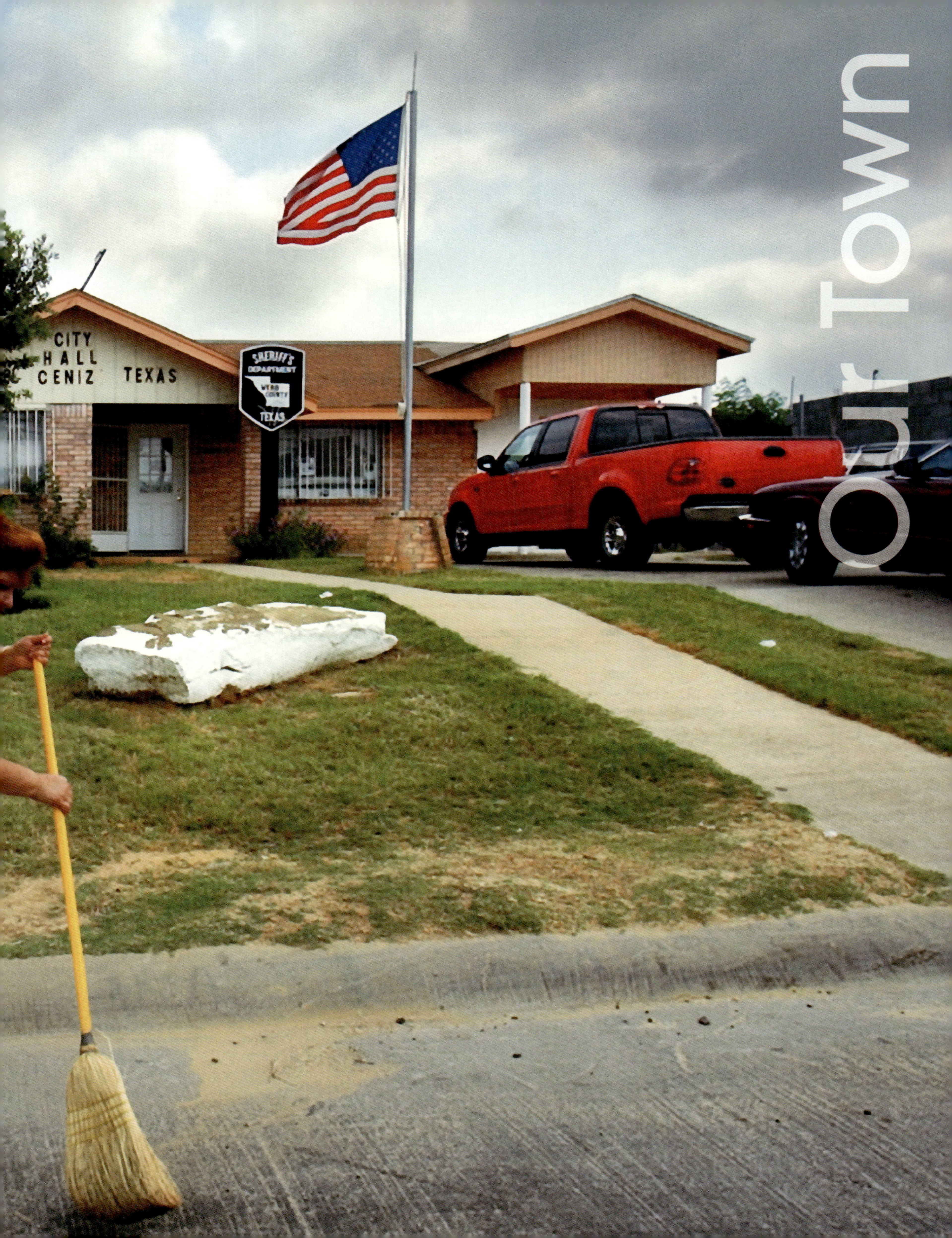

Our Town

DALLAS
The Texas School Book Depository plaque reads: "On November 22, the building gained national notoriety when Lee Harvey Oswald allegedly shot and killed President John F. Kennedy from a sixth floor window…" According to a 2003 Gallup Poll, 75 percent of Americans believe that more than one person was involved in the assassination. Visitors reinforce that sentiment by underscoring the word "allegedly."
Photos by Peter A. Calvin

DALLAS
Scott Dew is one of several people making a living selling souvenirs at Dealey Plaza, the site of President Kennedy's assassination. Dew's "The JFK Newspaper" includes area maps, the route of the presidential motorcade, and articles about the conspiracy theories.

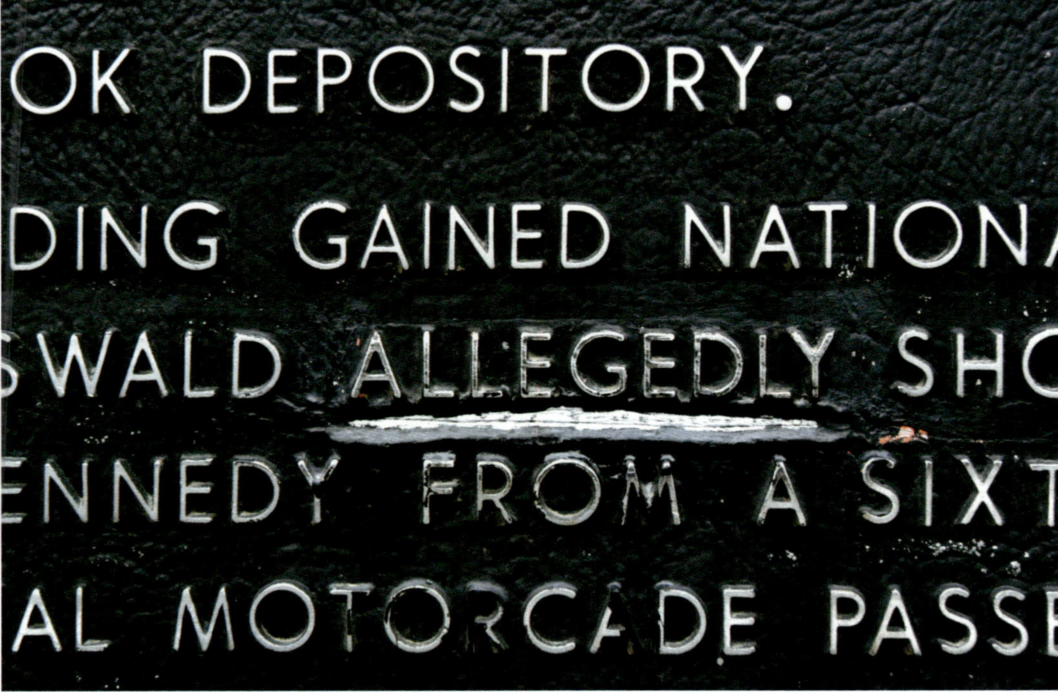

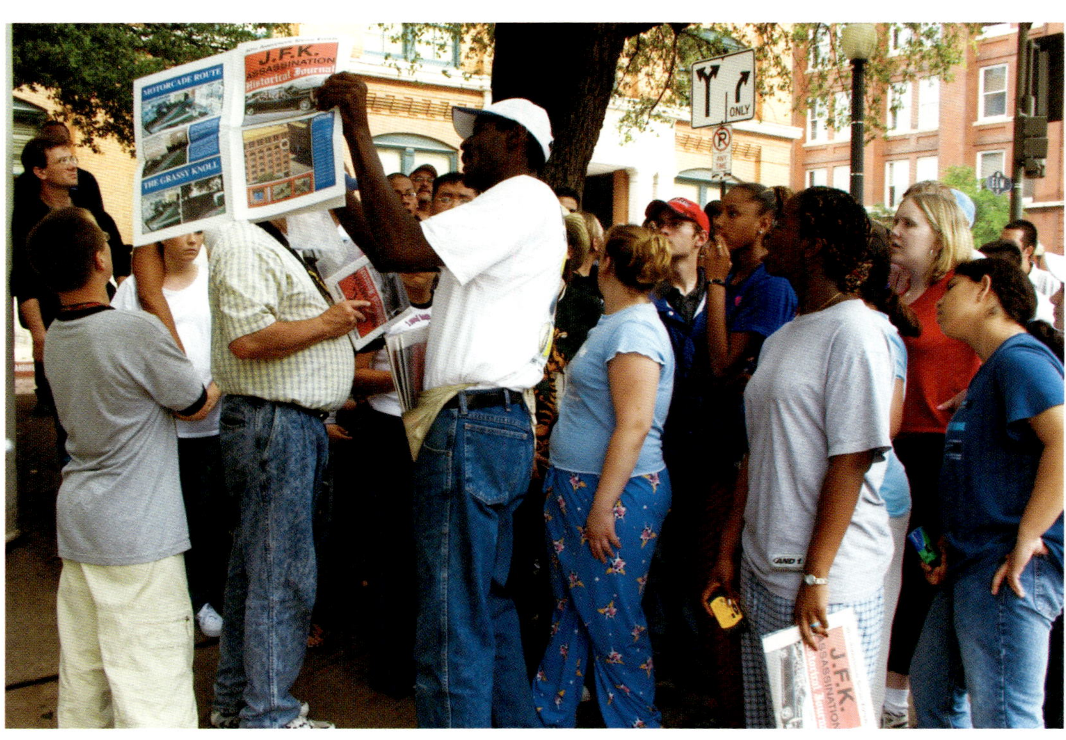

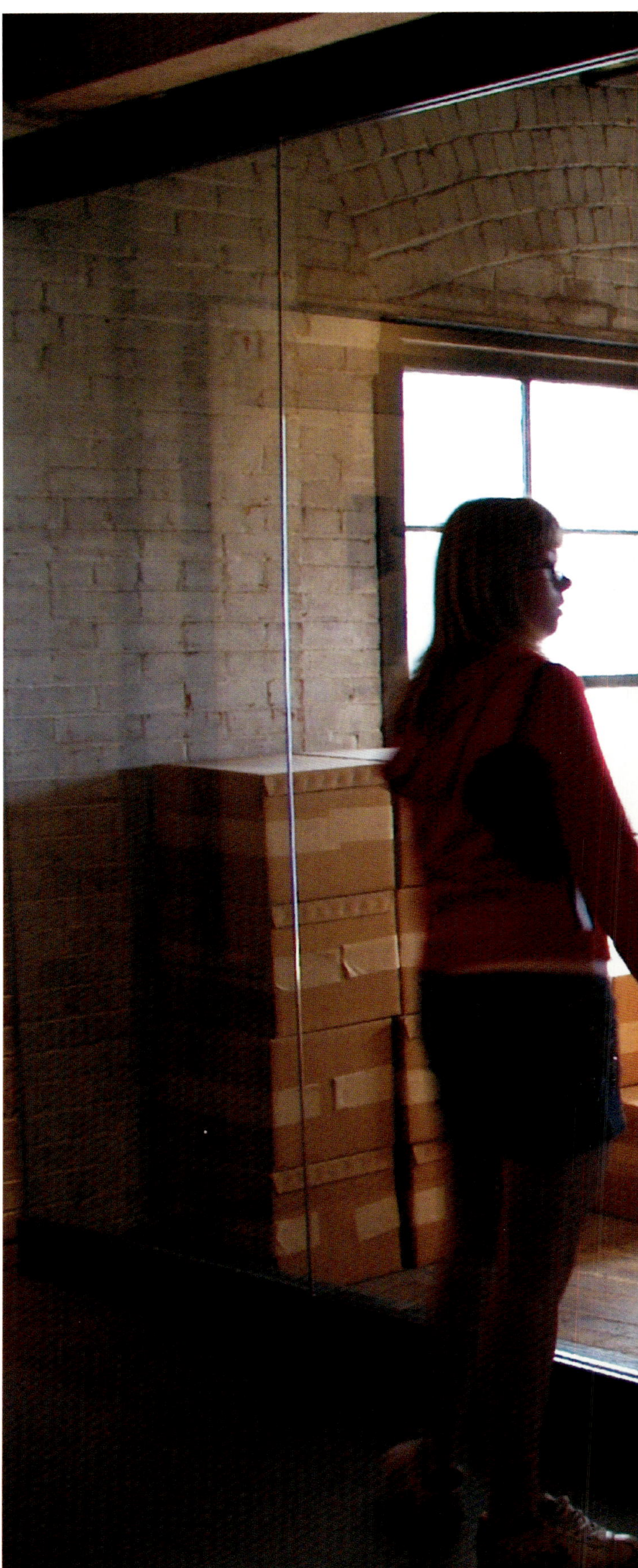

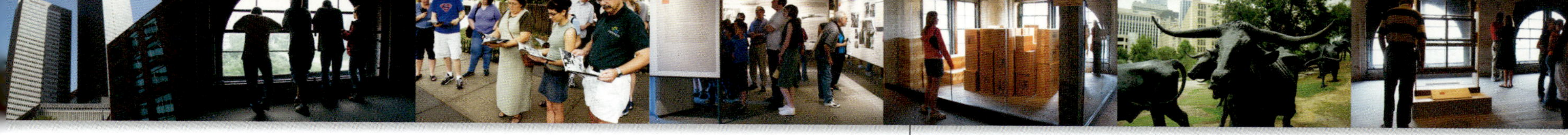

DALLAS

The sixth floor of the Texas School Book Depository has become a museum where tourists can view the "sniper's nest" (the original boxes are in the National Archives). Another corner shows where Lee Harvey Oswald's rifle was found. More items are displayed on the seventh floor, and the rest of the building is used for Dallas County government offices.

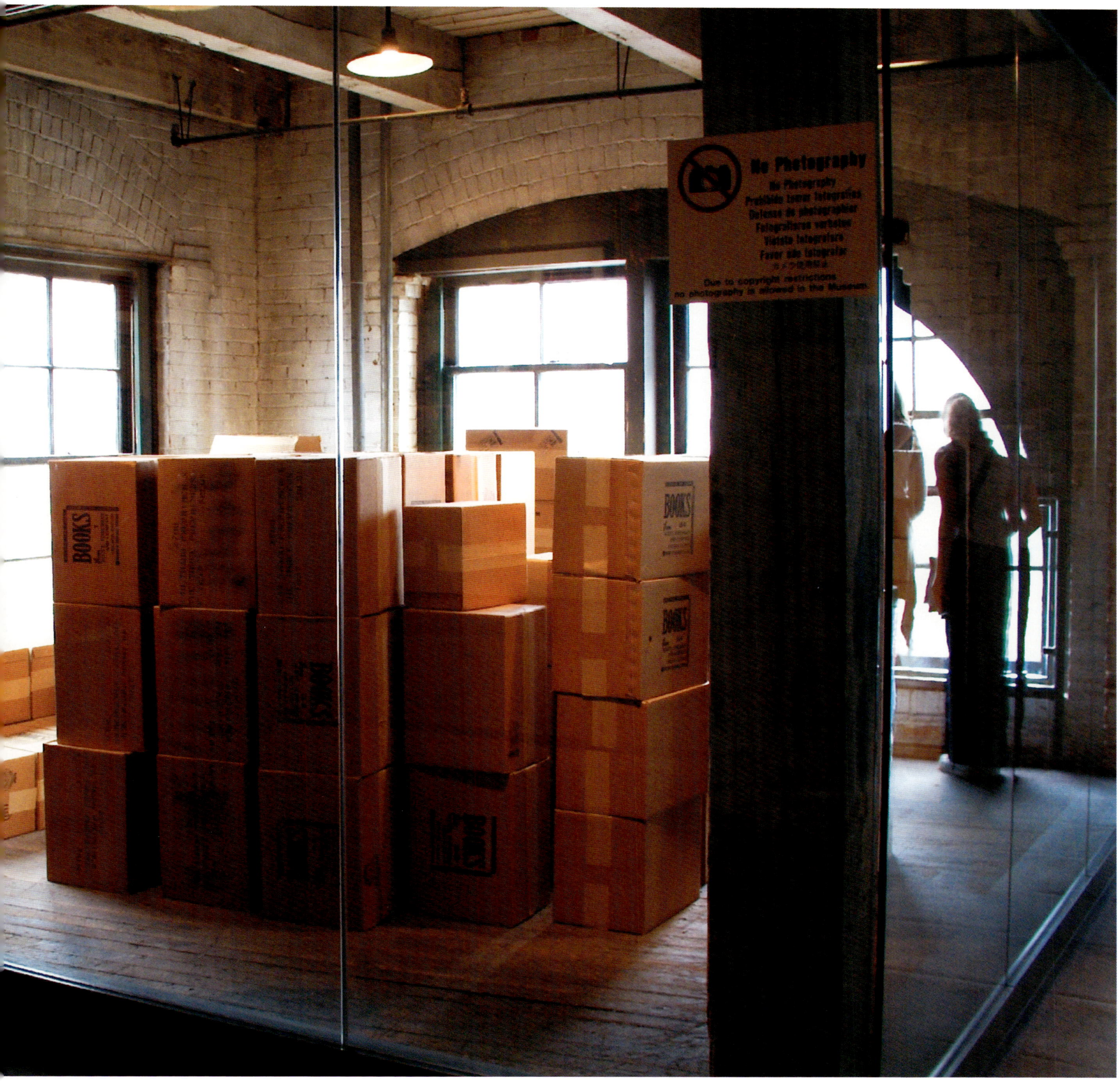

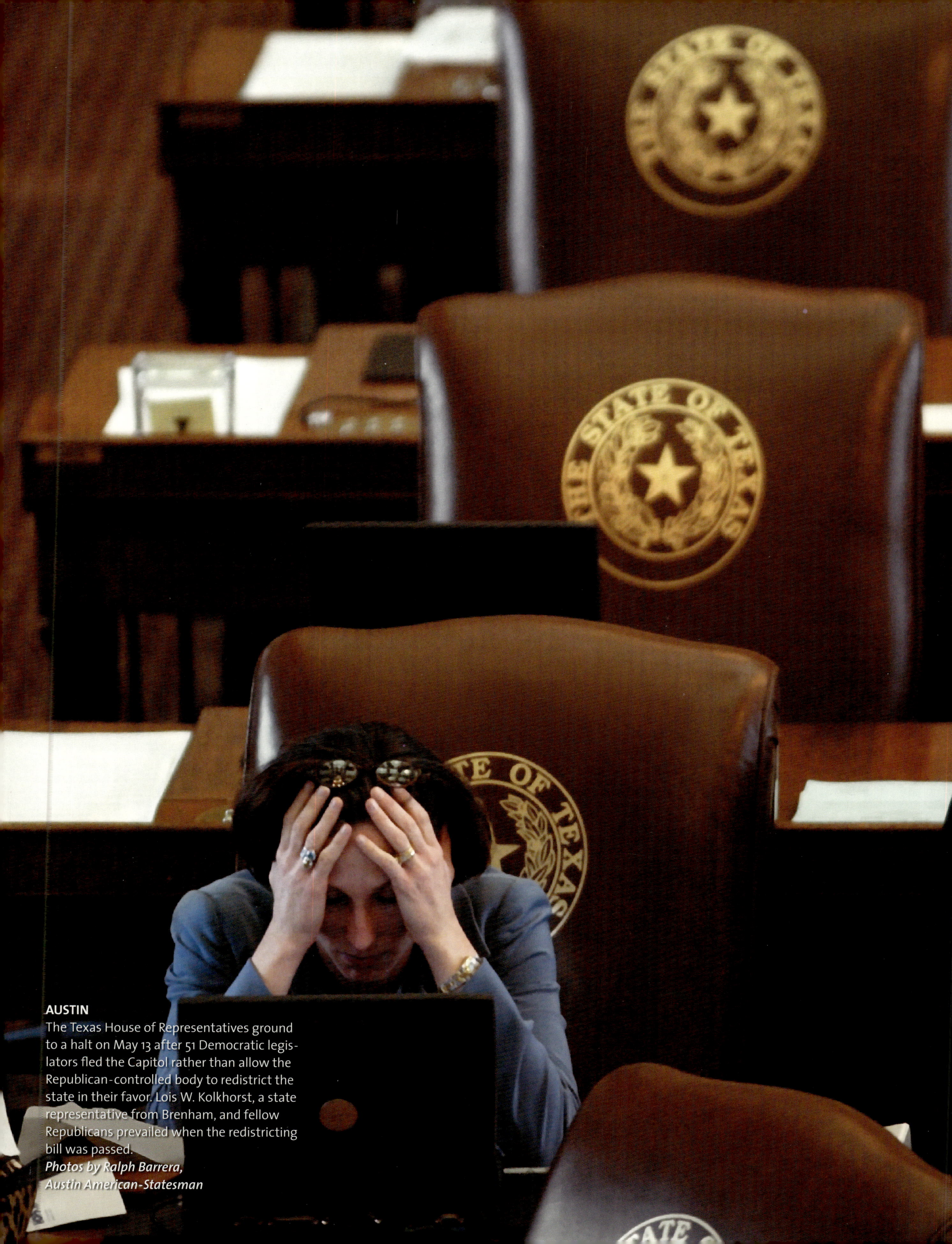

AUSTIN

The Texas House of Representatives ground to a halt on May 13 after 51 Democratic legislators fled the Capitol rather than allow the Republican-controlled body to redistrict the state in their favor. Lois W. Kolkhorst, a state representative from Brenham, and fellow Republicans prevailed when the redistricting bill was passed.

Photos by Ralph Barrera, Austin American-Statesman

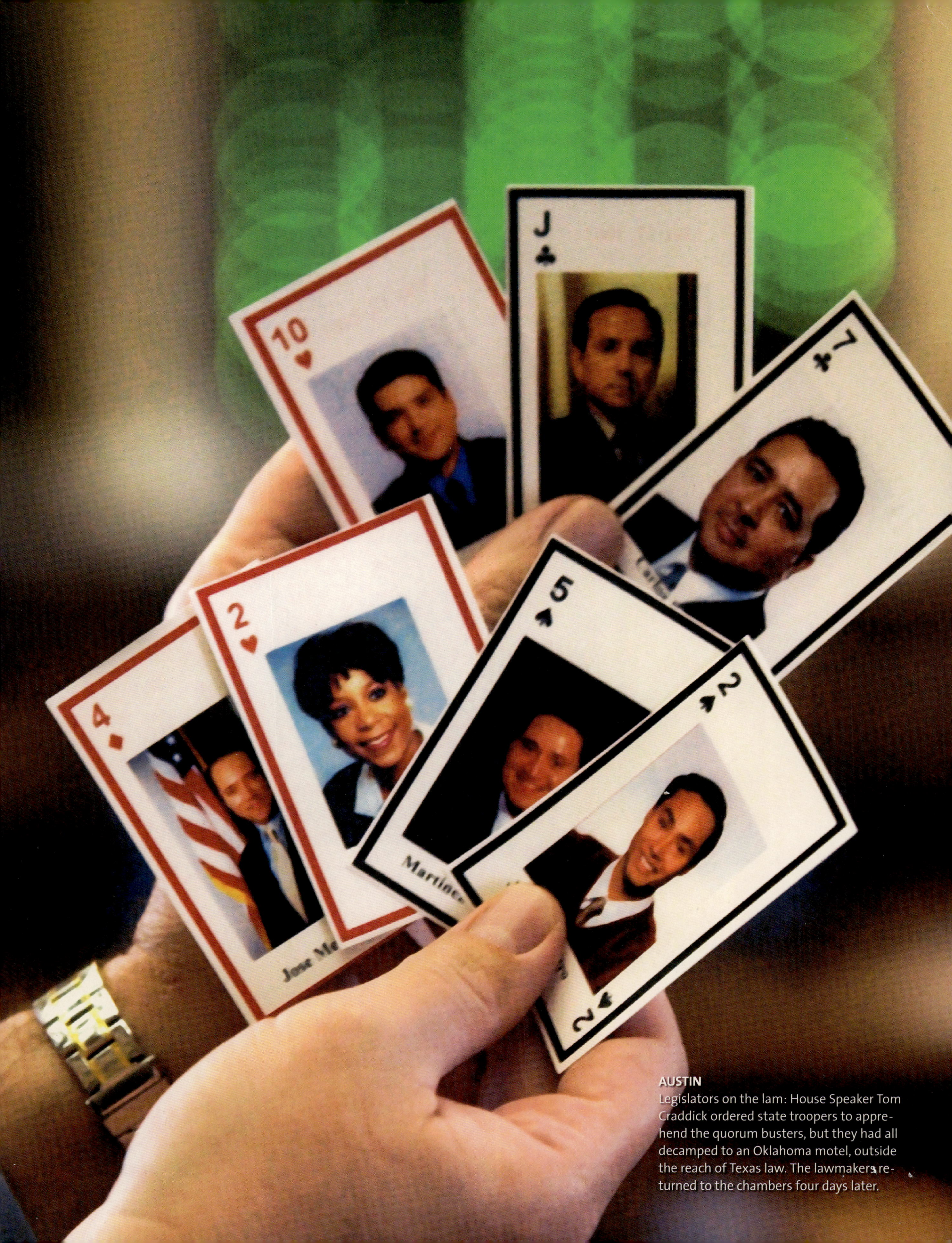

AUSTIN
Legislators on the lam: House Speaker Tom Craddick ordered state troopers to apprehend the quorum busters, but they had all decamped to an Oklahoma motel, outside the reach of Texas law. The lawmakers returned to the chambers four days later.

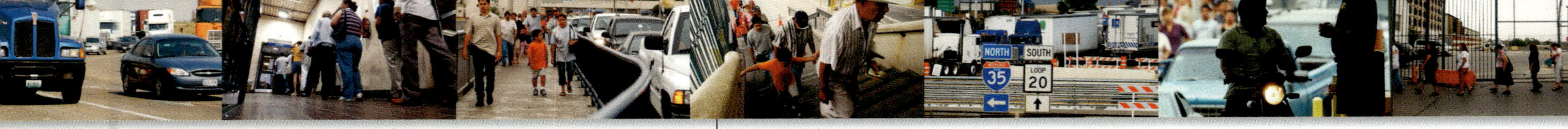

LAREDO

Each week, nearly 94,000 Mexicans cross International Bridge 1 from Nuevo Laredo, Mexico, into Laredo, the busiest crossing in south Texas. Using a laser visa (a border-passing card imbedded with the carrier's fingerprints), Mexicans can shop and visit in the U.S. for up to 72 hours, traveling up to 25 miles inside the border. The $100 visa is good for ten years.

Photo by Jerry Lara, San Antonio Express-News

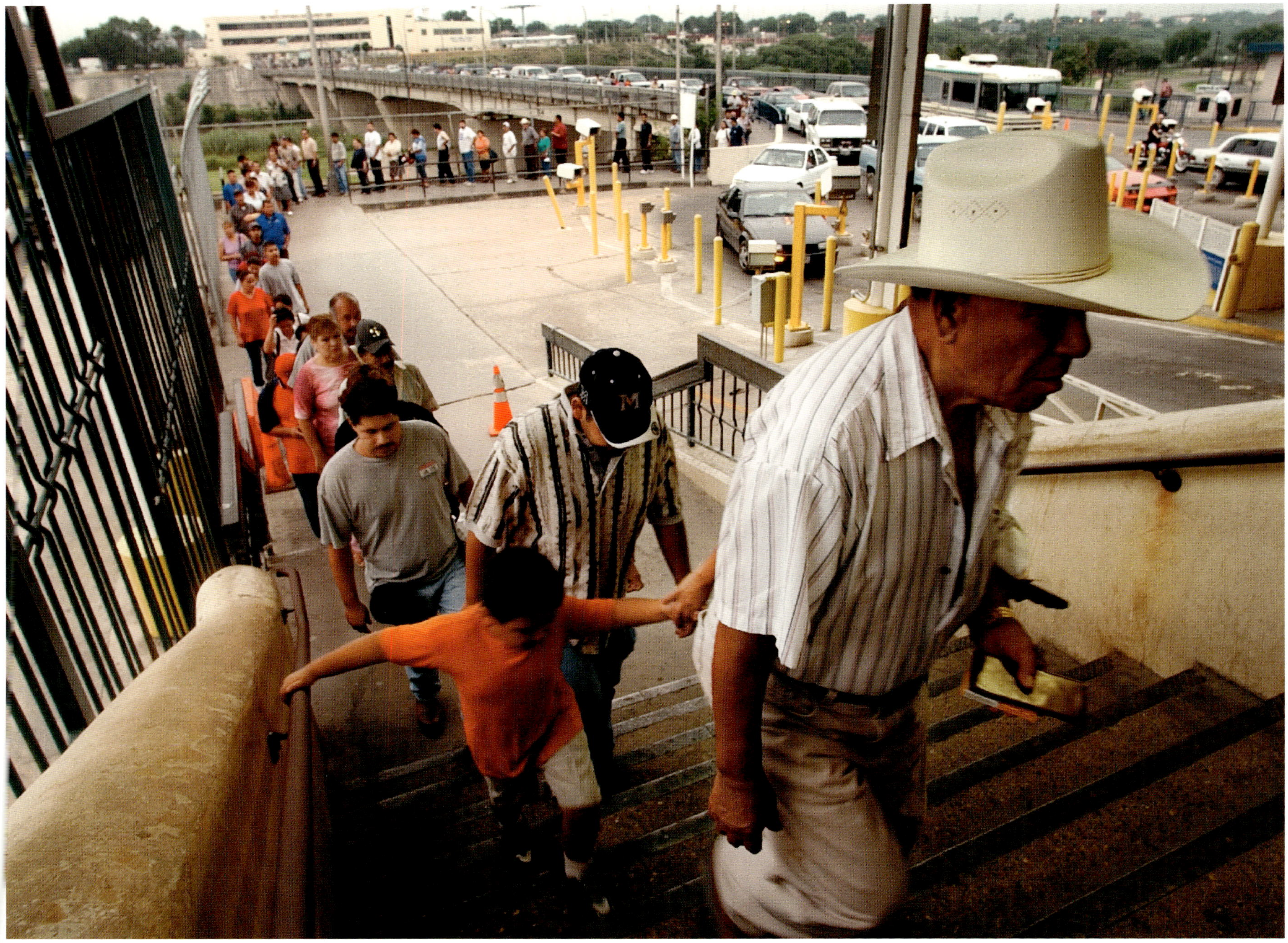

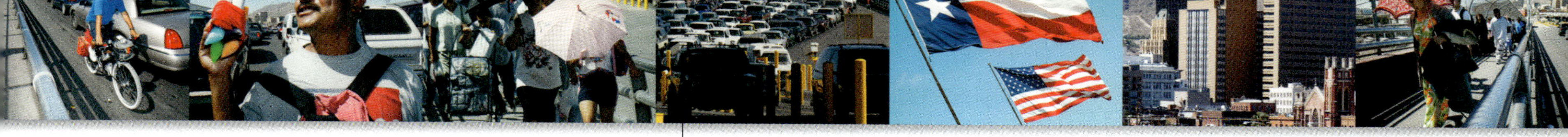

EL PASO

The Paso del Norte bridge links downtown Juarez with downtown El Paso. Of the four official border crossings in El Paso, this bridge logs the most pedestrians. On May 16, 2003, 19,700 walkers and 12,100 cars (it allows only northbound vehicle traffic) came into the U.S. via the bridge. Commercial trucks cross at another location.

Photo by Rudy Gutierrez, El Paso Times

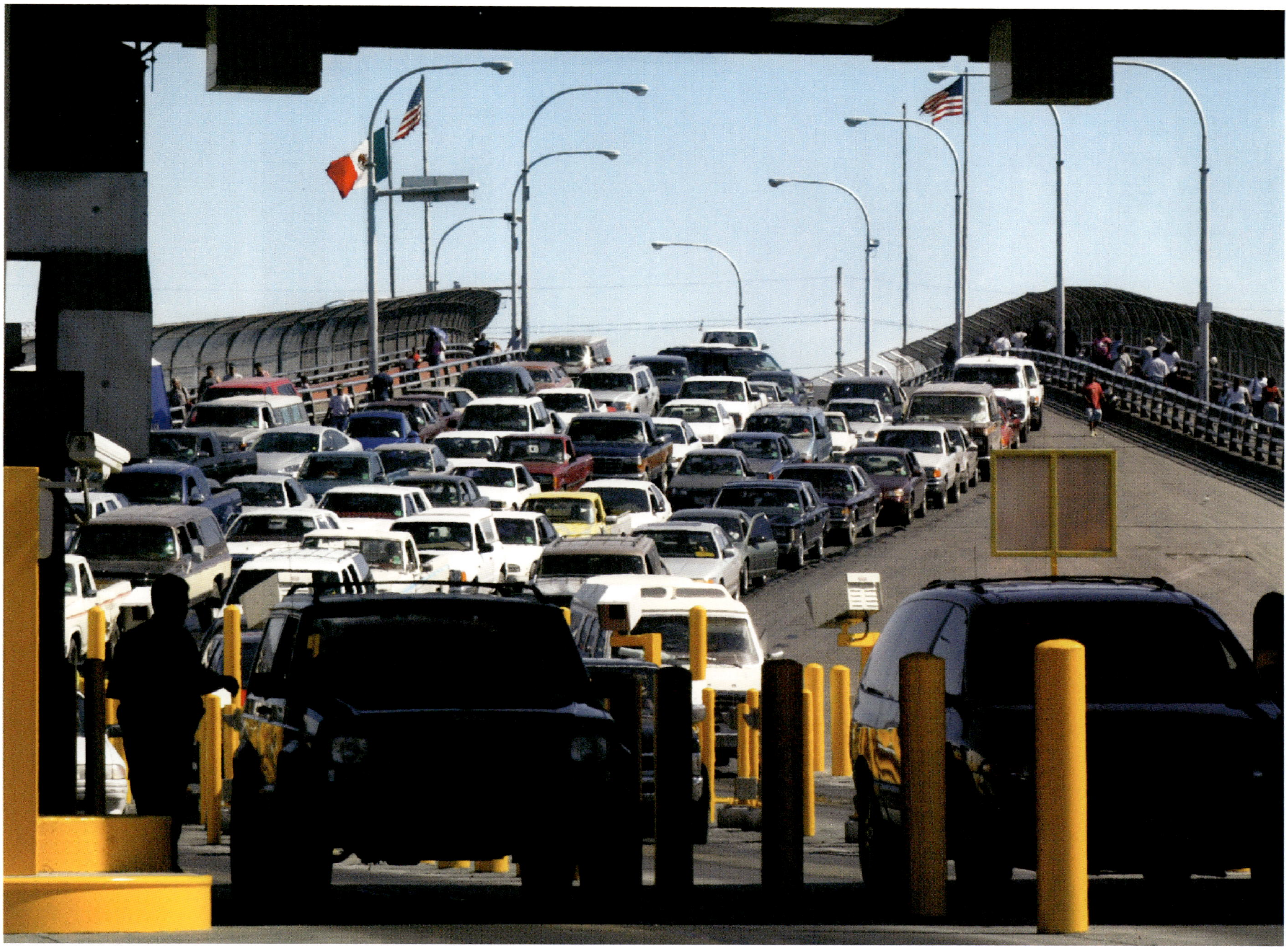

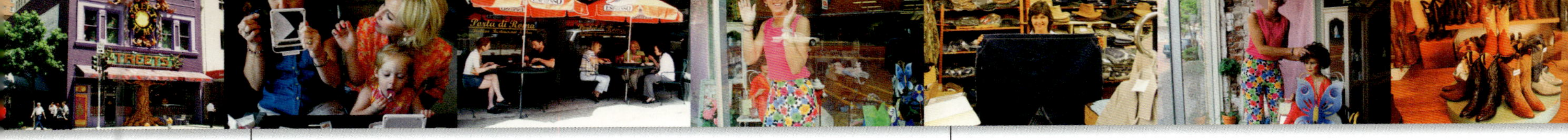

LEWISVILLE

At her friend Kelly Lawrence's house, Pamela Strickland gets makeup advice from Brenda Fenner (right), a senior Mary Kay sales director. Lawrence's 2-year-old daughter Caroline needs no instruction on how to paint her tongue with eye shadow.

Photo by Barbara Davidson, The Dallas Morning News

NACOGDOCHES

Everything's bigger in Texas: Shaws Department Store meets the needs of every customer. These size 74 denim overalls (displayed with their tops folded down by employee Regina Randall) are kept in stock for three regular patrons.

Photo by Scogin Mayo

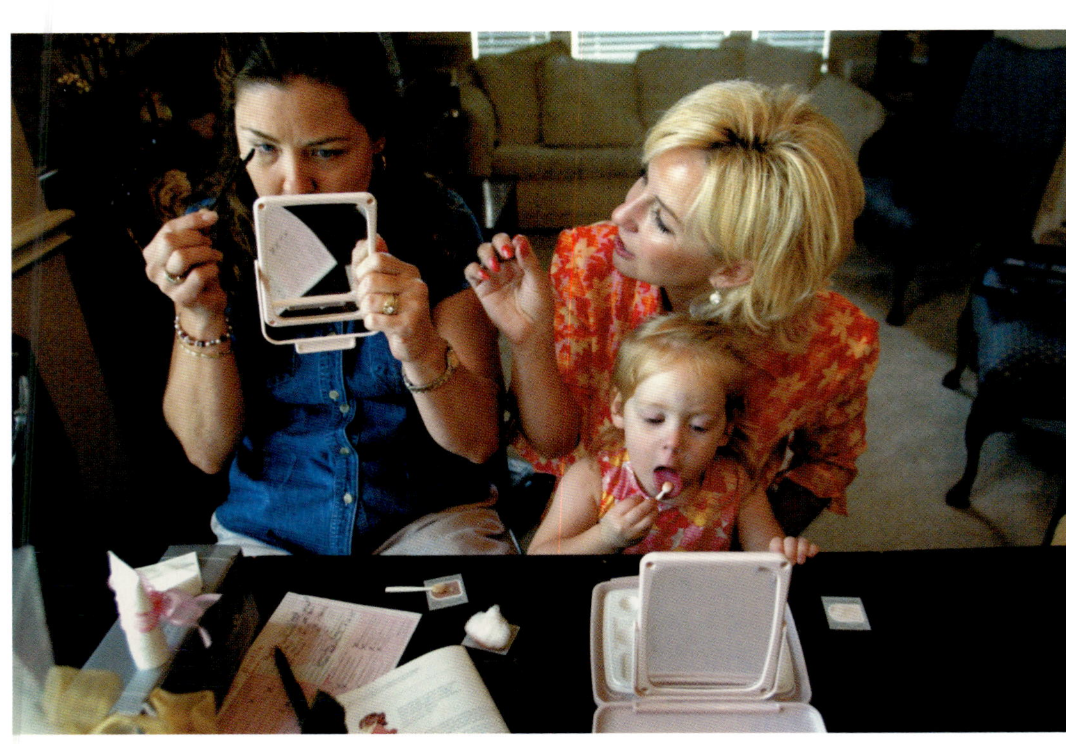

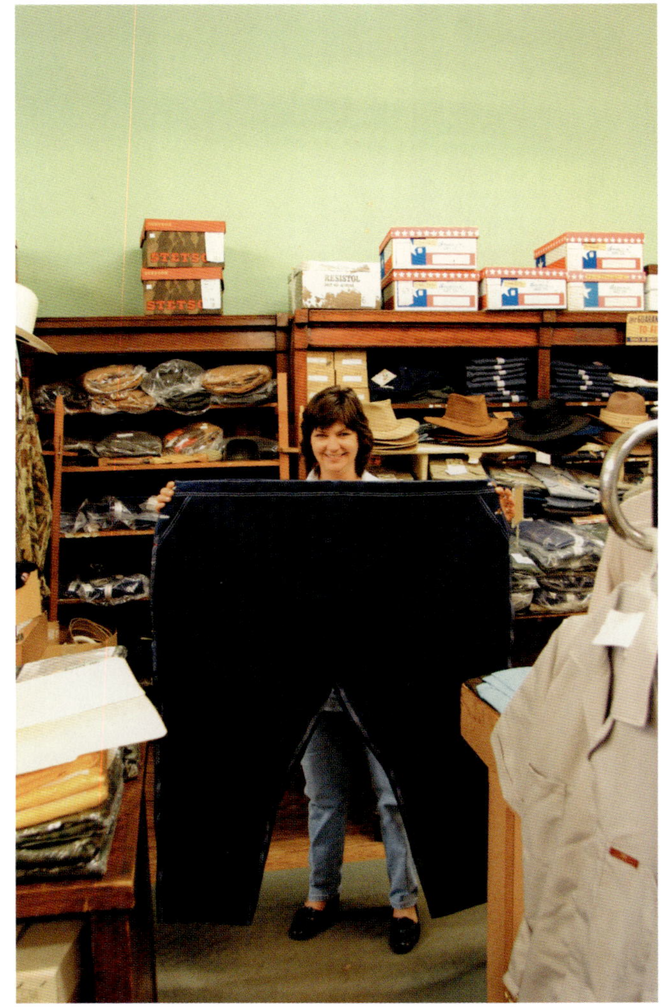

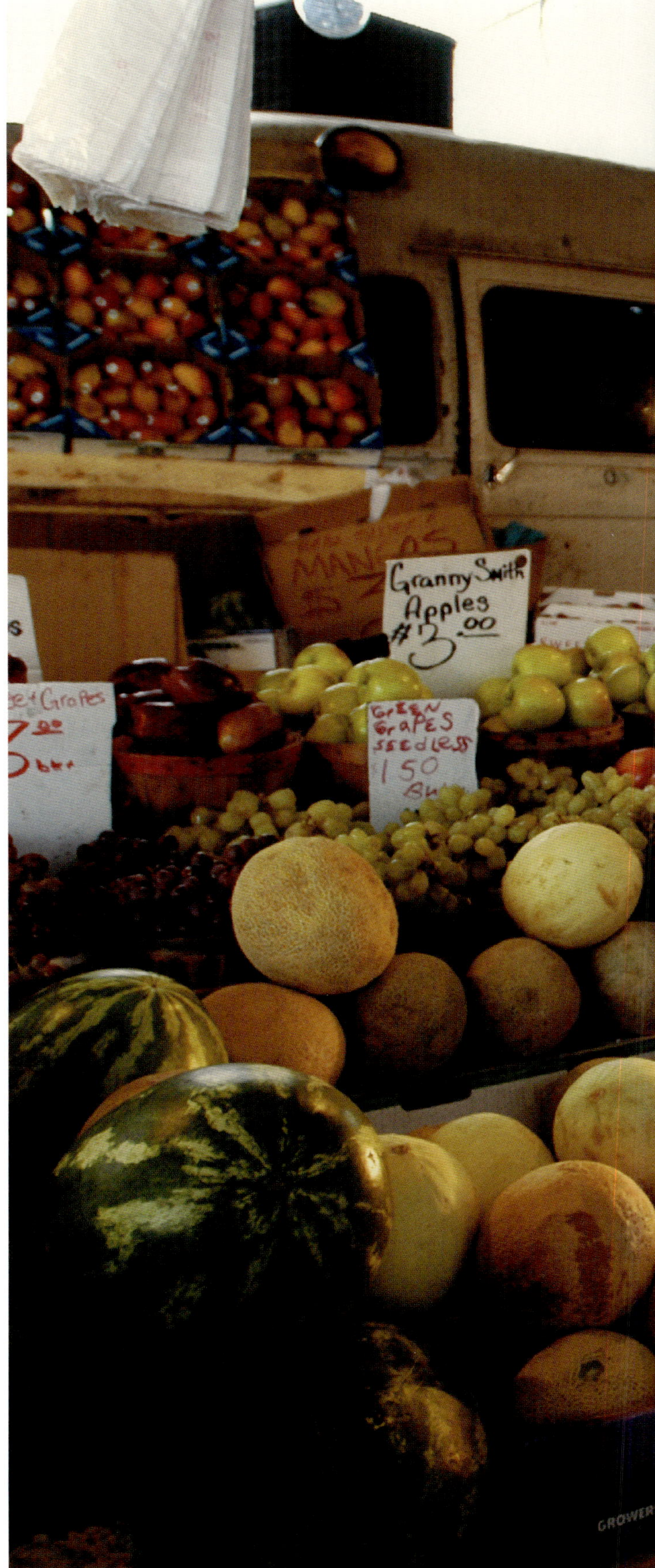

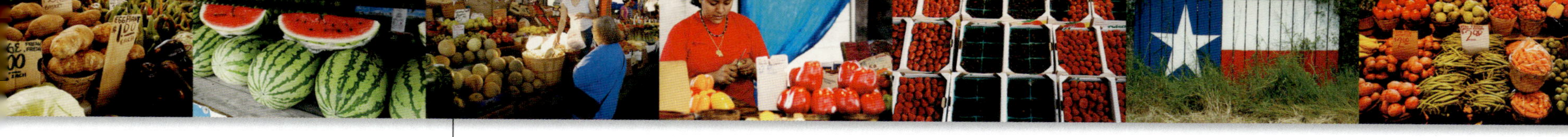

DALLAS

In the last ten years, people have rediscovered the city center, moving into lofts in refurbished buildings. Because there are no large grocery stores downtown, the city dweller's de facto supermarket is the Dallas Farmers Market. Begun in the late 1800s, it's a cornucopia of fresh produce, flowers, and gourmet foods.

Photo by Peter A. Calvin

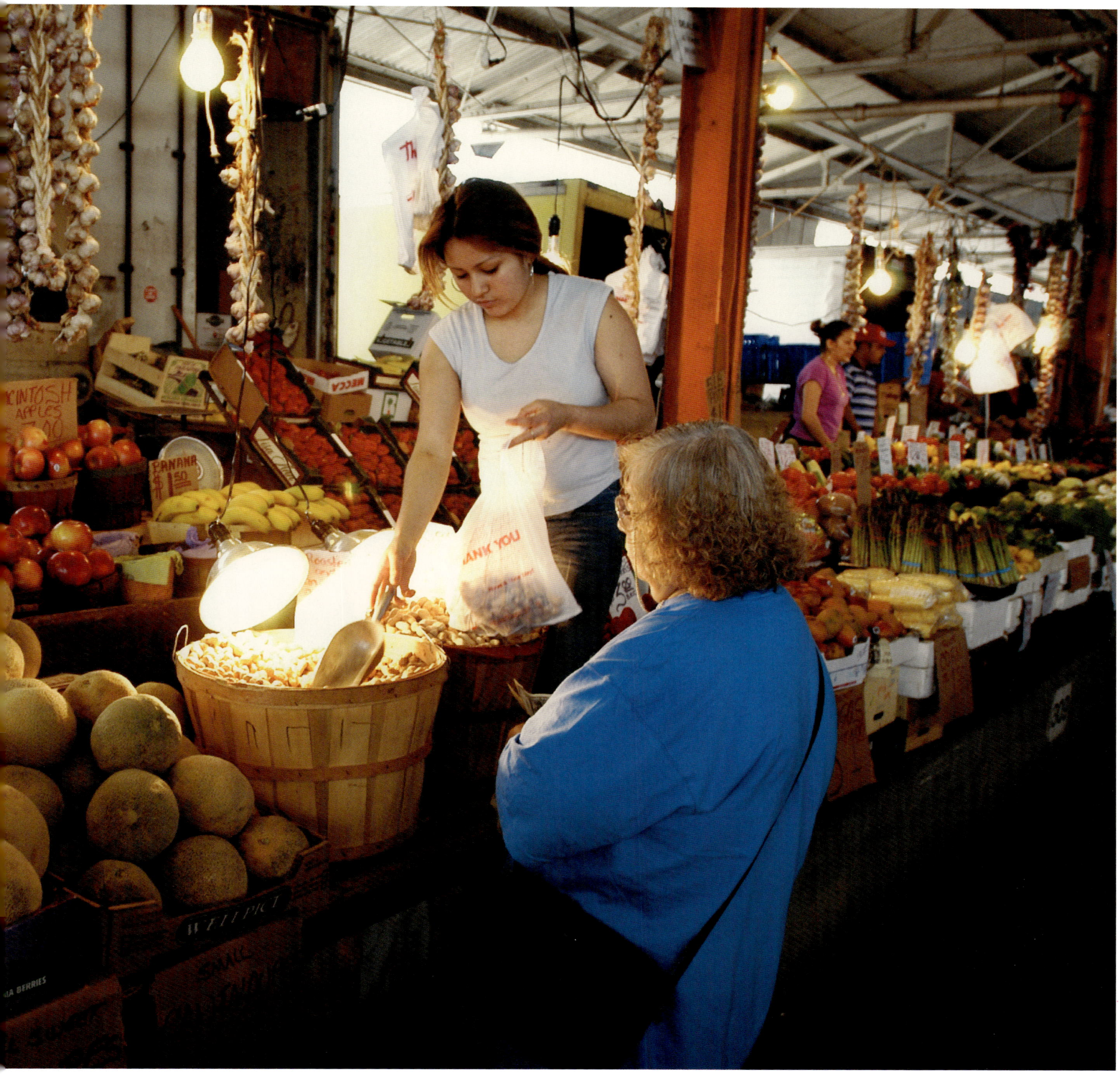

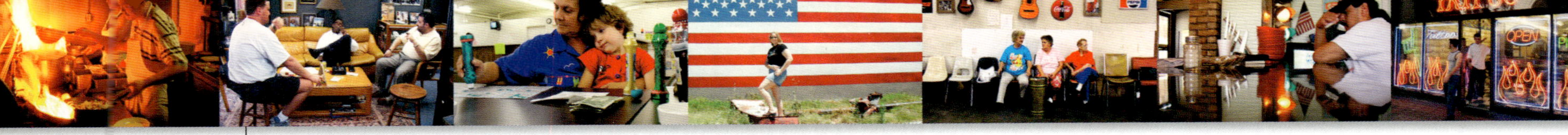

DALLAS

At The Smoker's Shoppe cigar lounge, owner Jeff Smith (right) puffs on a stogie with customers. Downtown Dallas's oldest independent tobacco store opened in 1960 and recently underwent a major expansion that included moving the lounge to the front of the store. "It's an important traffic builder," Smith says.

Photos by Peter A. Calvin

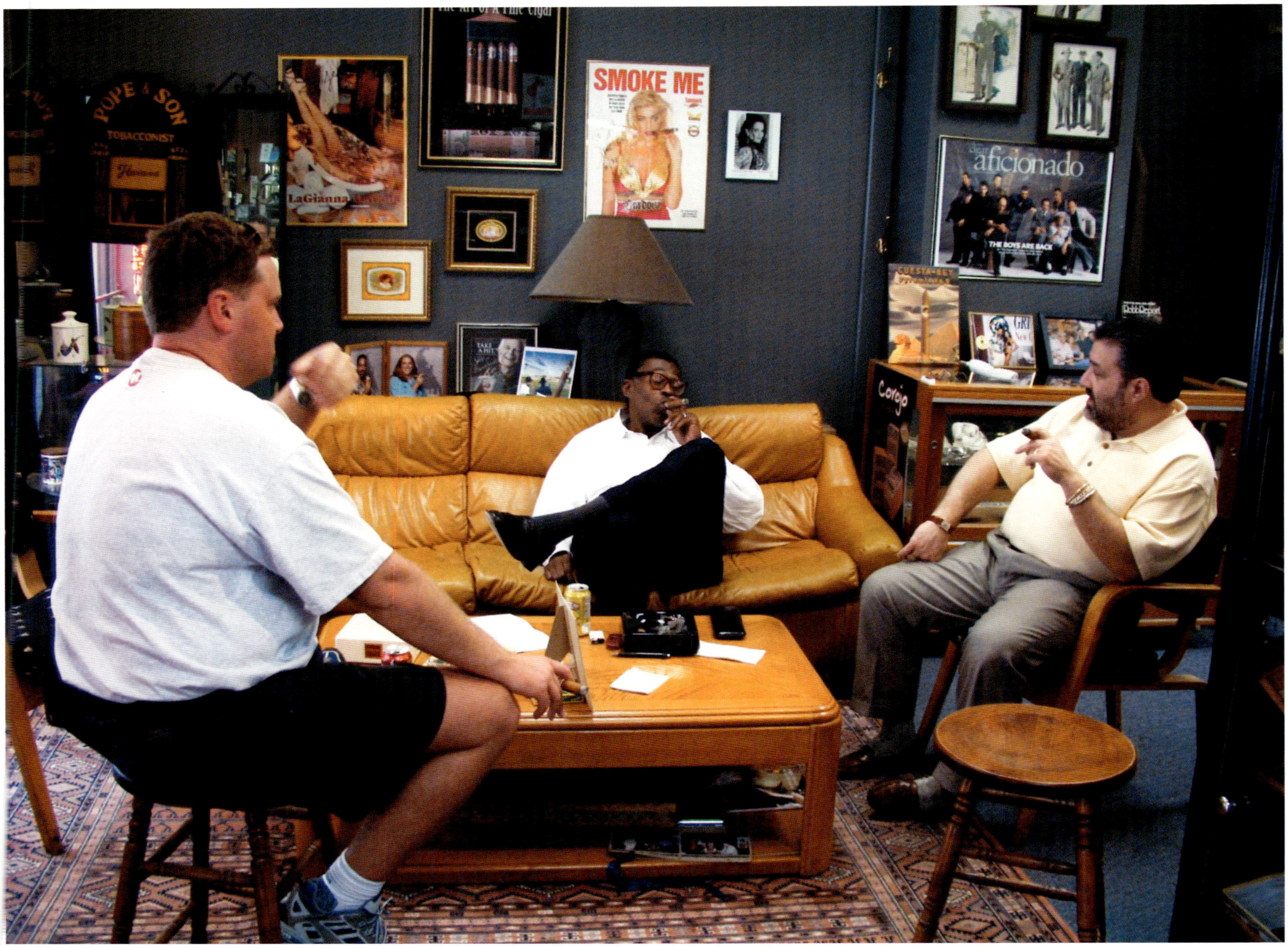

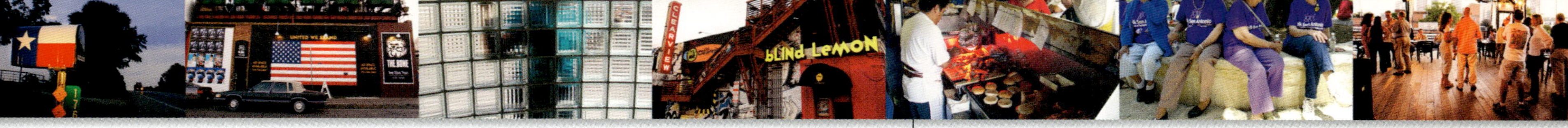

DALLAS

The late Sonny Bryan grew up with barbecue in his veins—both his dad and grandfather owned barbecue joints. In 1958, he opened Sonny Bryan's Smokehouse, and soon his brisket and ribs had a national following. Although the business expanded to 20 national locations after Sonny's death in 1989, the original restaurant on Inwood Road remains unchanged.

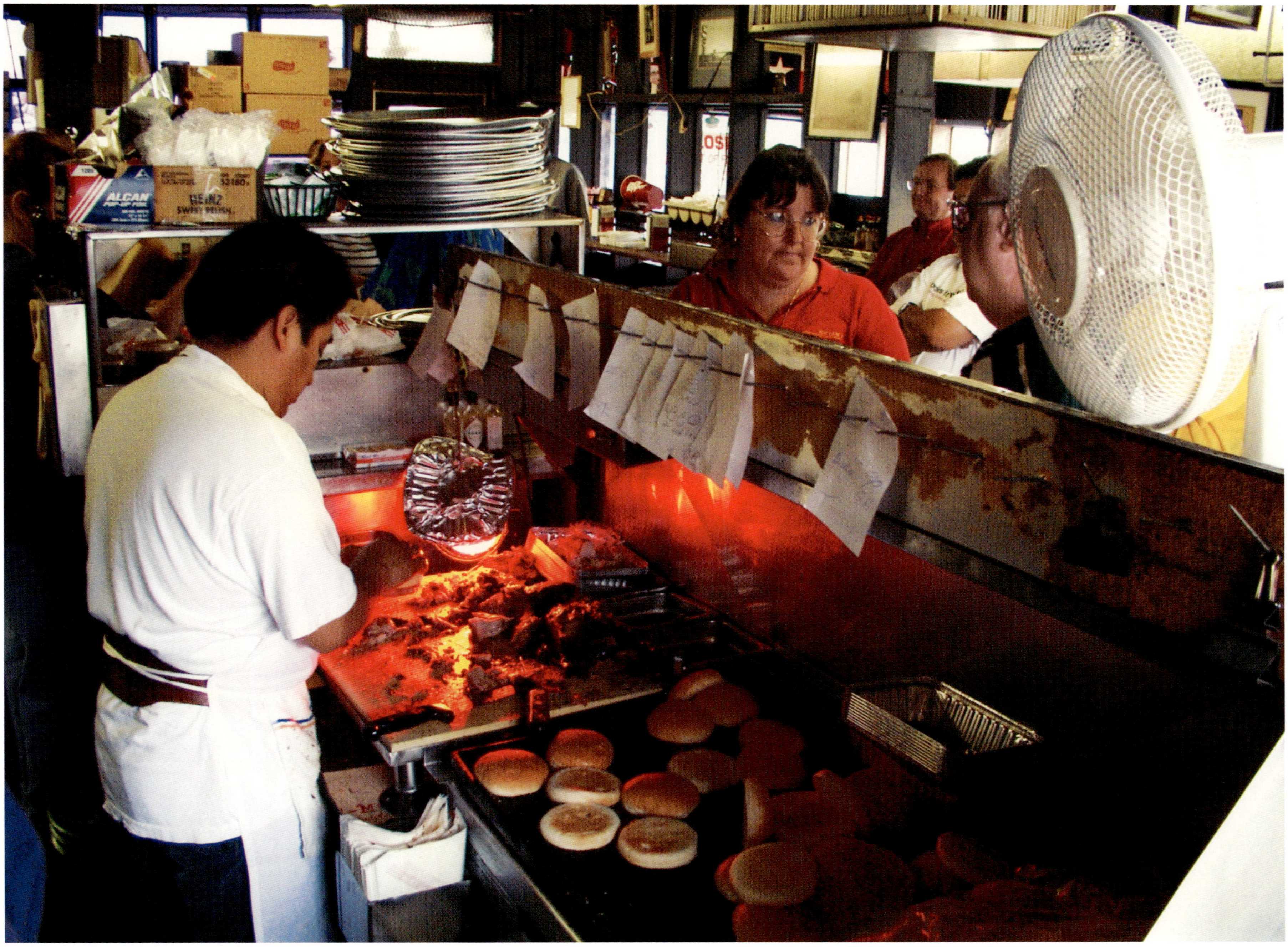

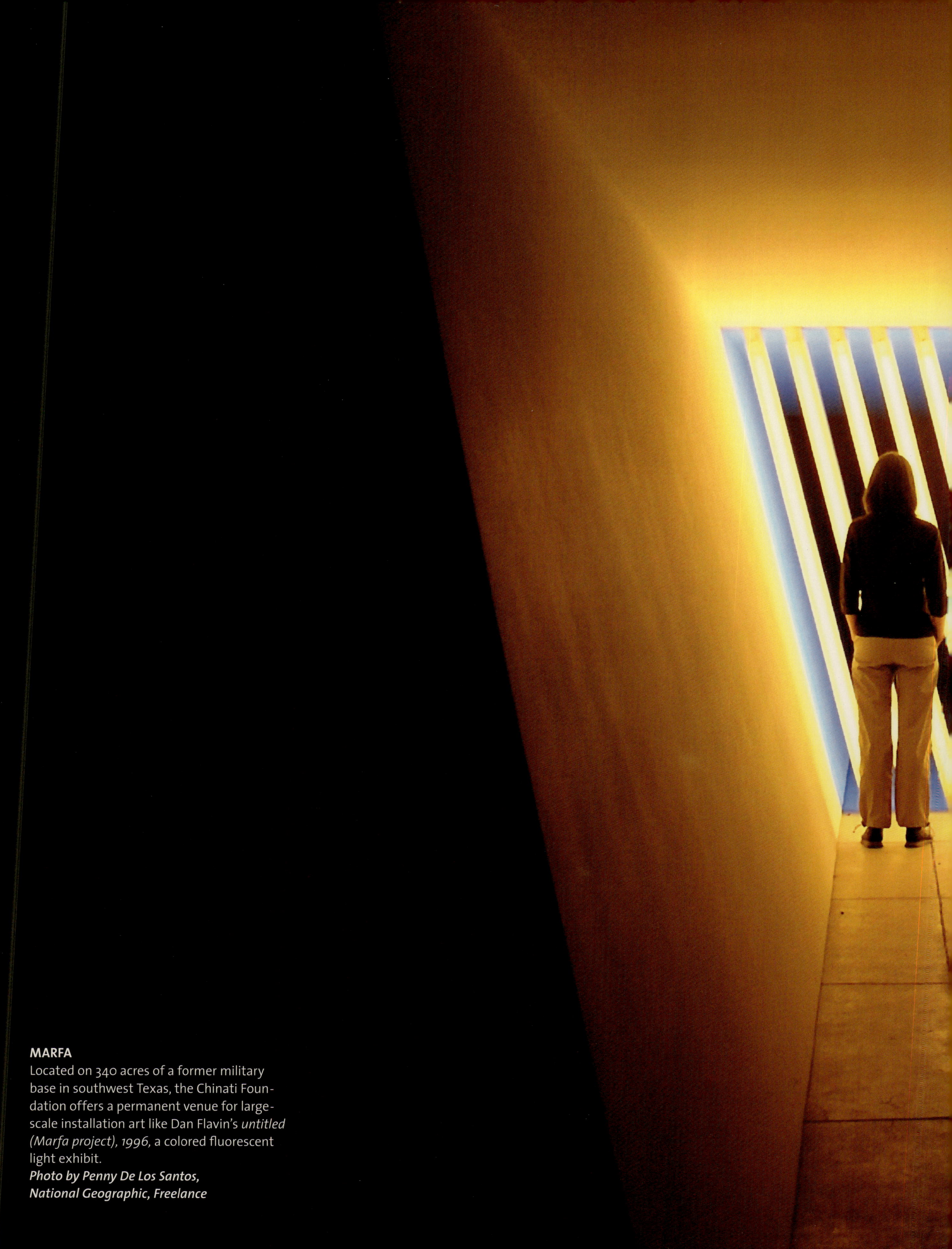

MARFA
Located on 340 acres of a former military base in southwest Texas, the Chinati Foundation offers a permanent venue for large-scale installation art like Dan Flavin's *untitled (Marfa project), 1996,* a colored fluorescent light exhibit.
Photo by Penny De Los Santos, National Geographic, Freelance

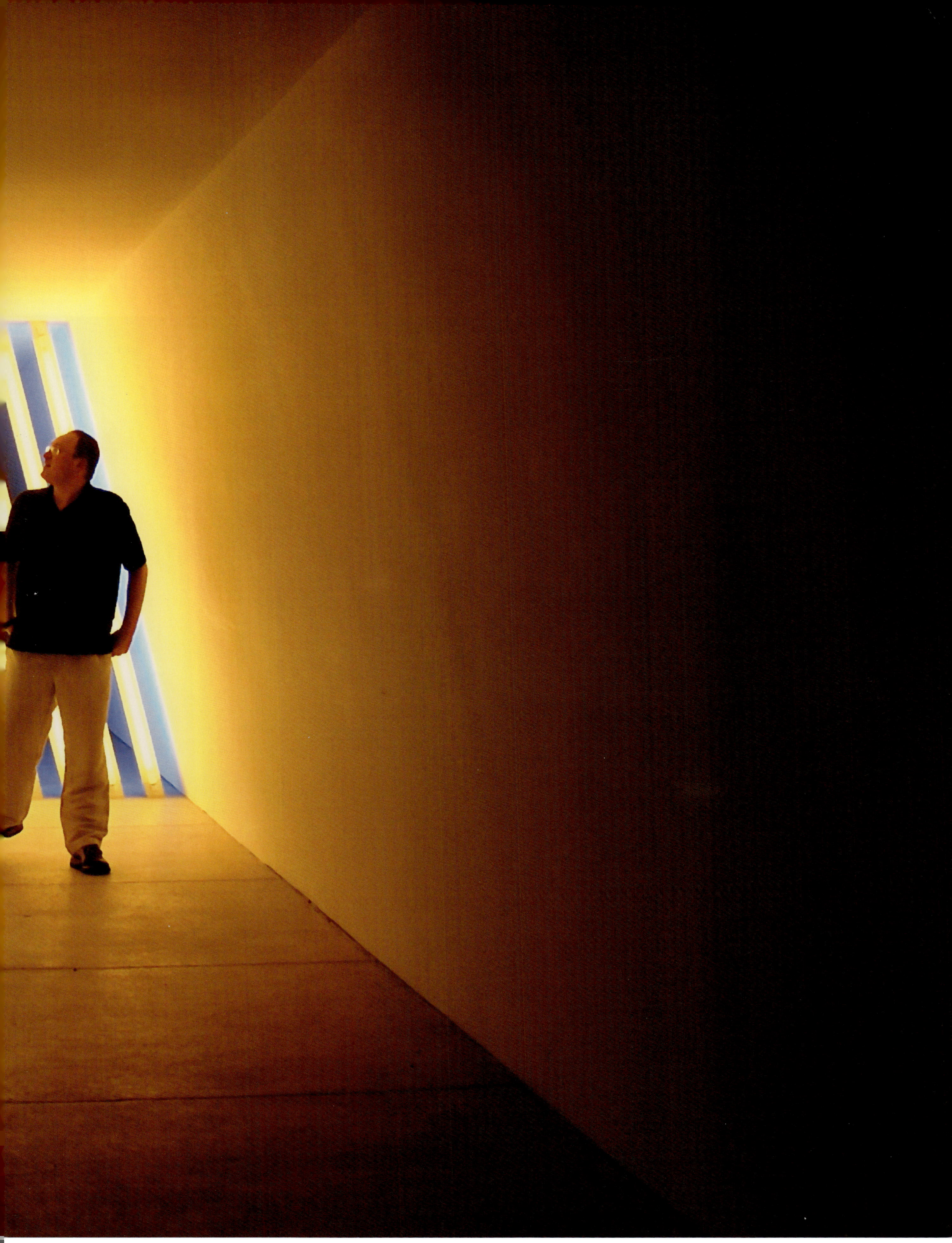

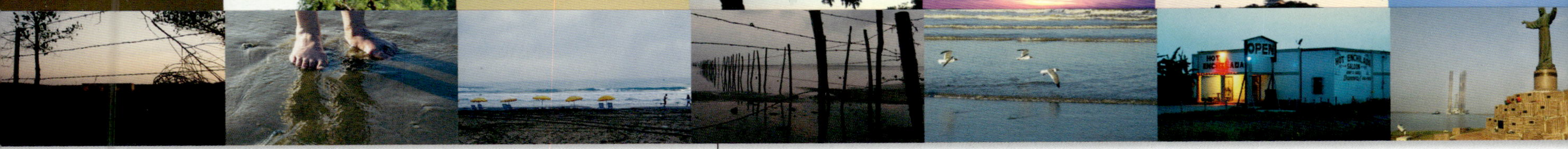

PORT ISABEL
Before the construction of Highway 48 between Port Isabel and Brownsville in the 1930s, 6,000-acre Bahia Grand was home to shrimp, crabs, and finfish. After the construction, the drained bay became a barren flat, producing great clouds of salty dust. The U.S. Fish & Wildlife Service recently acquired the forlorn expanse, and is in the process of restoring it to its wetland glory.
Photos by Brad Doherty

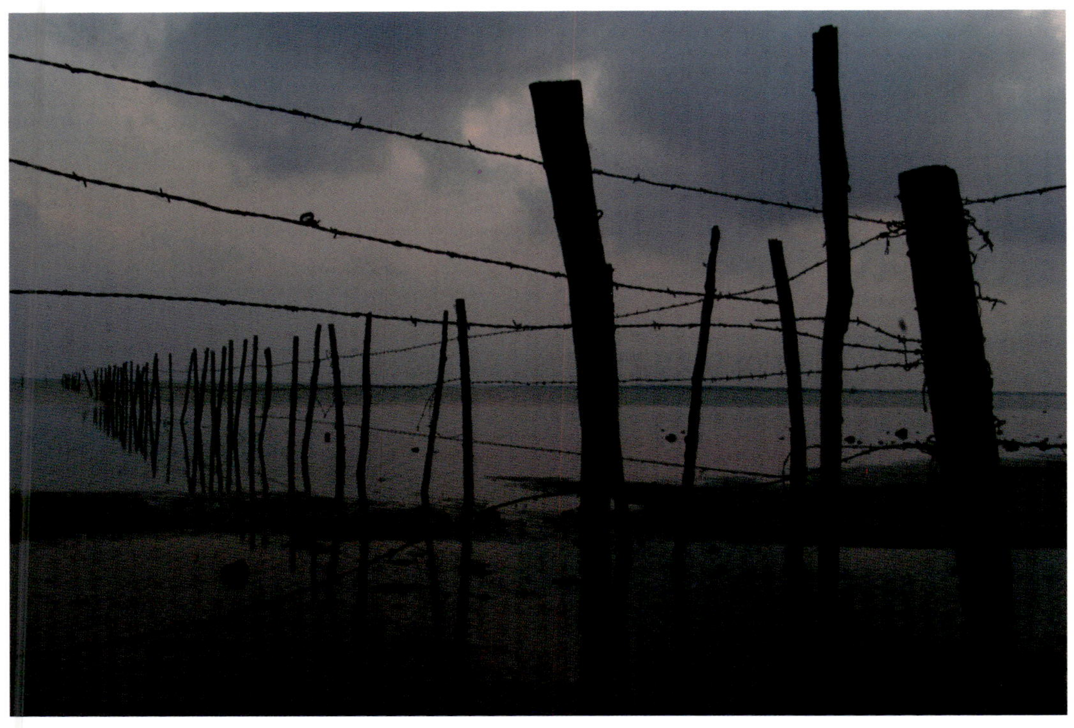

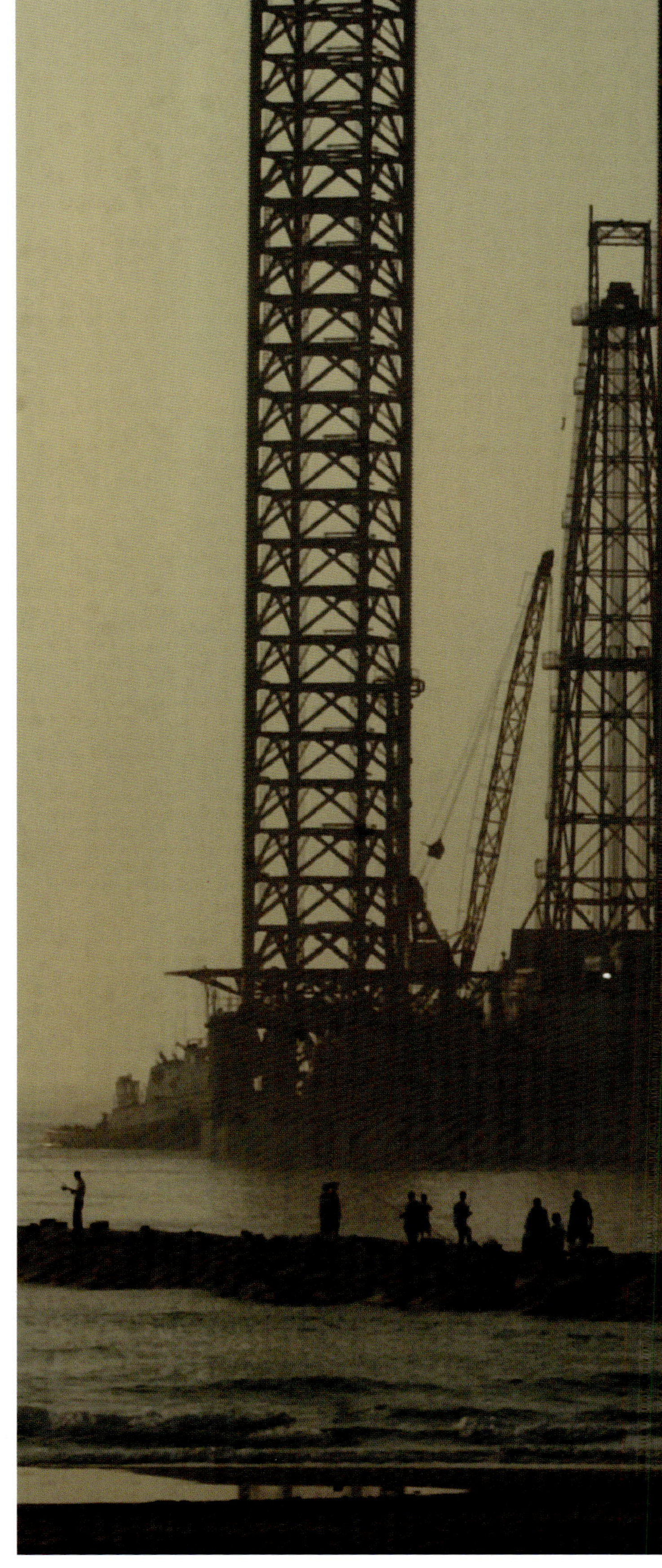

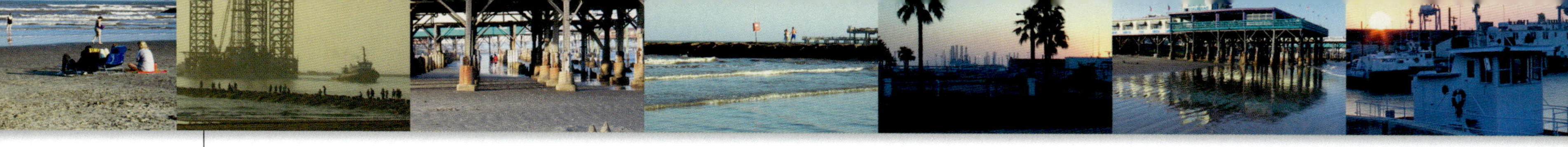

PORT ISABEL

A jack-up oil rig is towed into the Brownsville Ship Channel for repairs at an AMFELS Inc. shipyard. The company builds and repairs jack-up or self-elevating drilling platforms. Some of the structures are 50 stories high and able to drill in waters 375 feet deep.

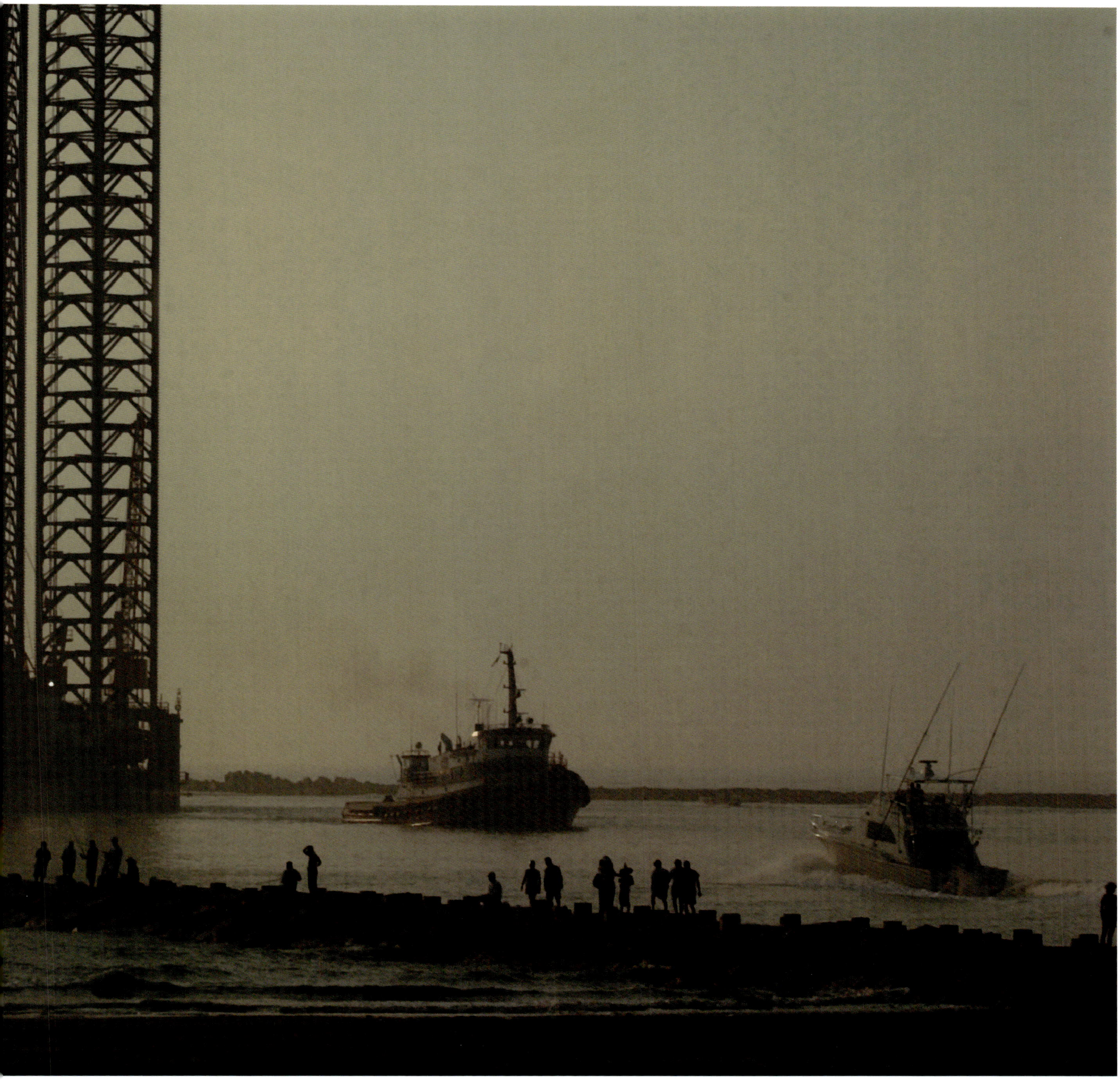

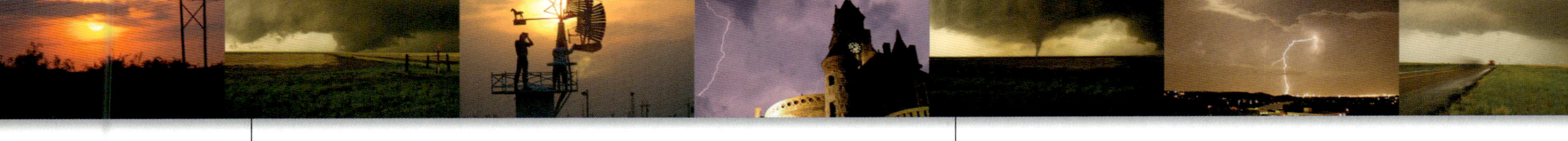

CONLEN
An F1 tornado roars across the Texas panhandle, one of 28 that day. The northern plains of Texas are part of the infamous Tornado Alley that includes Oklahoma and Kansas.
Photos by Kyle Gerstner

CONLEN
The town was lucky today; this tornado hit open country and caused only $50,000 in damage. The same complex of storms later produced tornadoes that hit Liberal, Kansas, causing $16 million in damage.

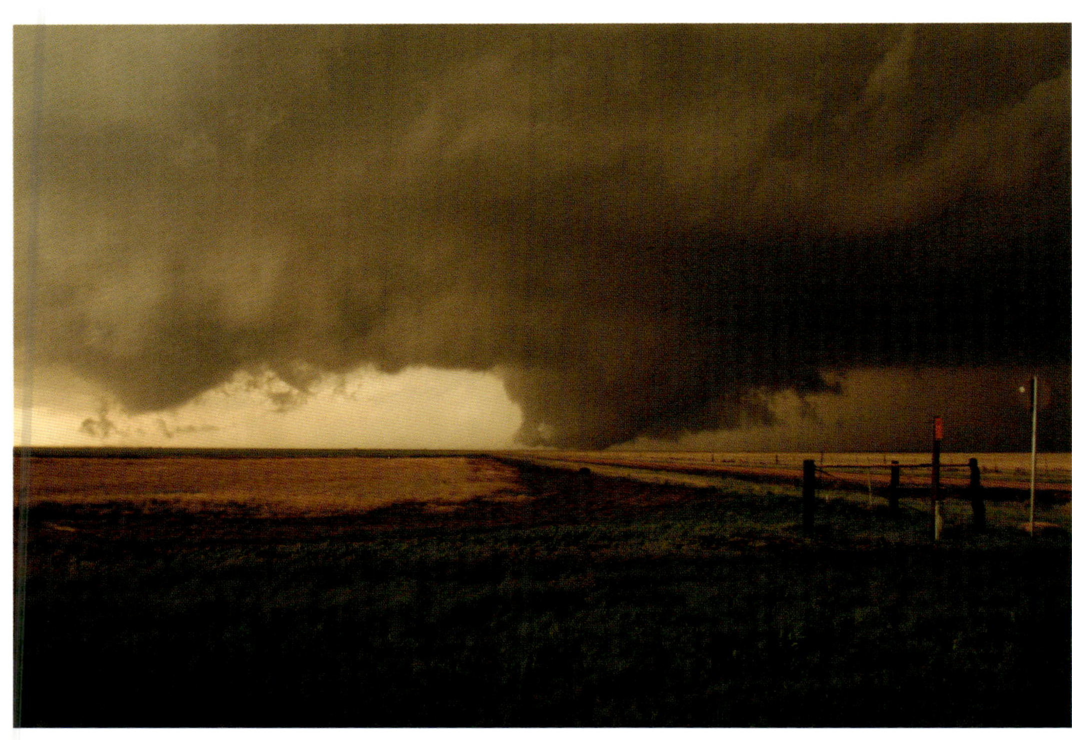

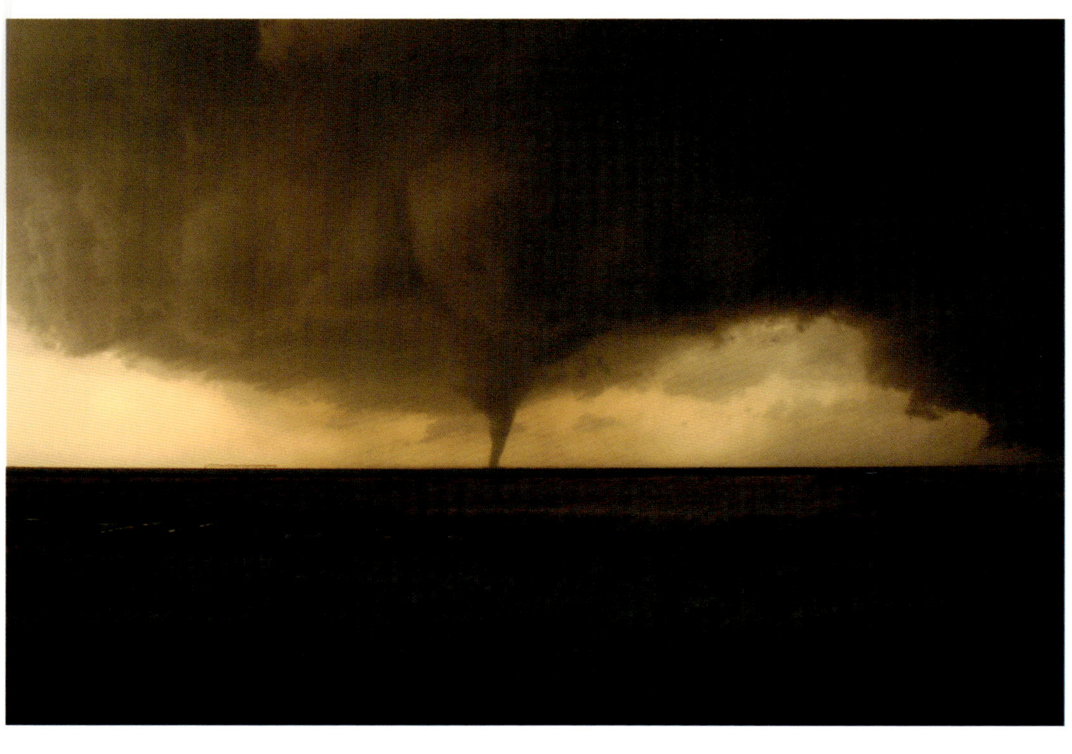

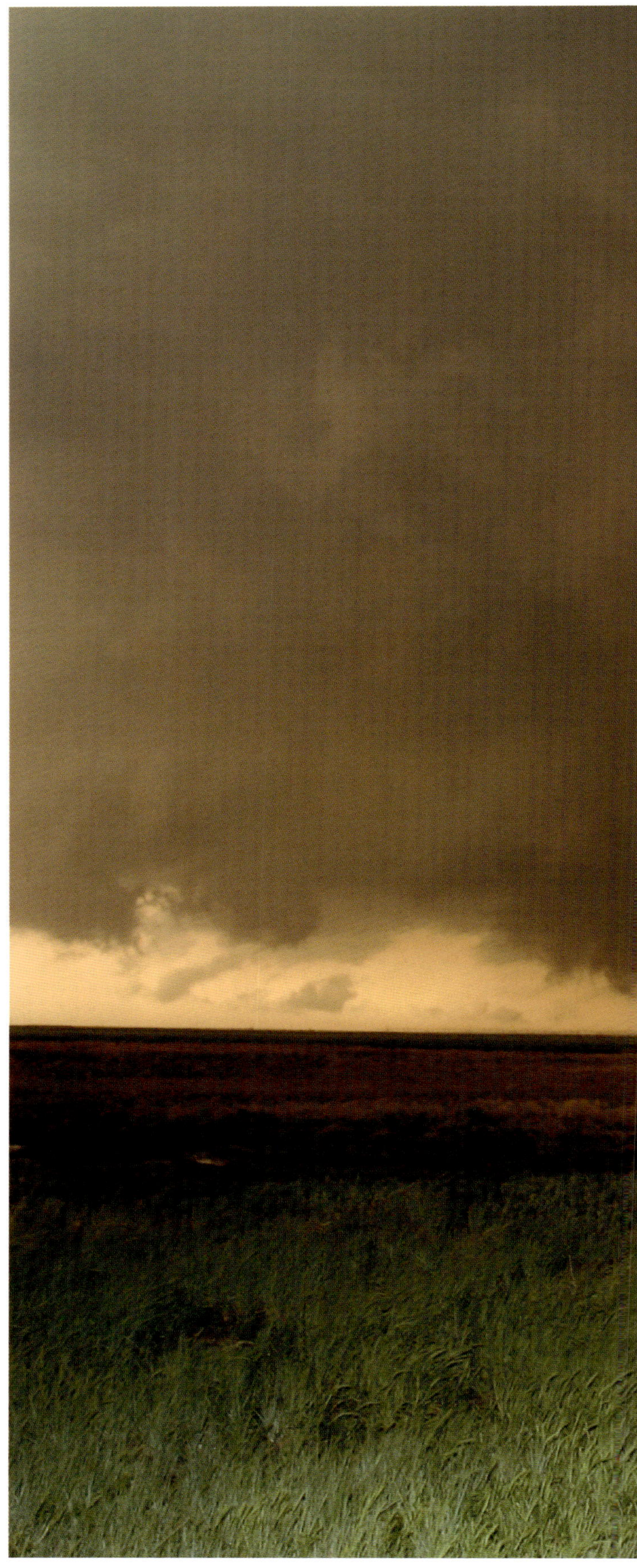

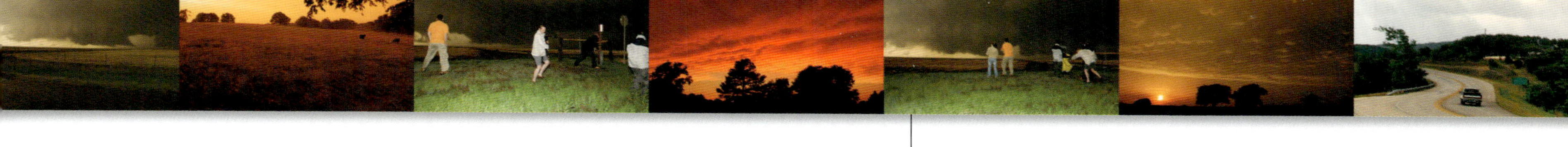

CONLEN

Storm chasers risk their lives to get within a half-mile of the tornado system sweeping through the area. Within minutes of this shot, they, along with the photographer, were forced to flee.

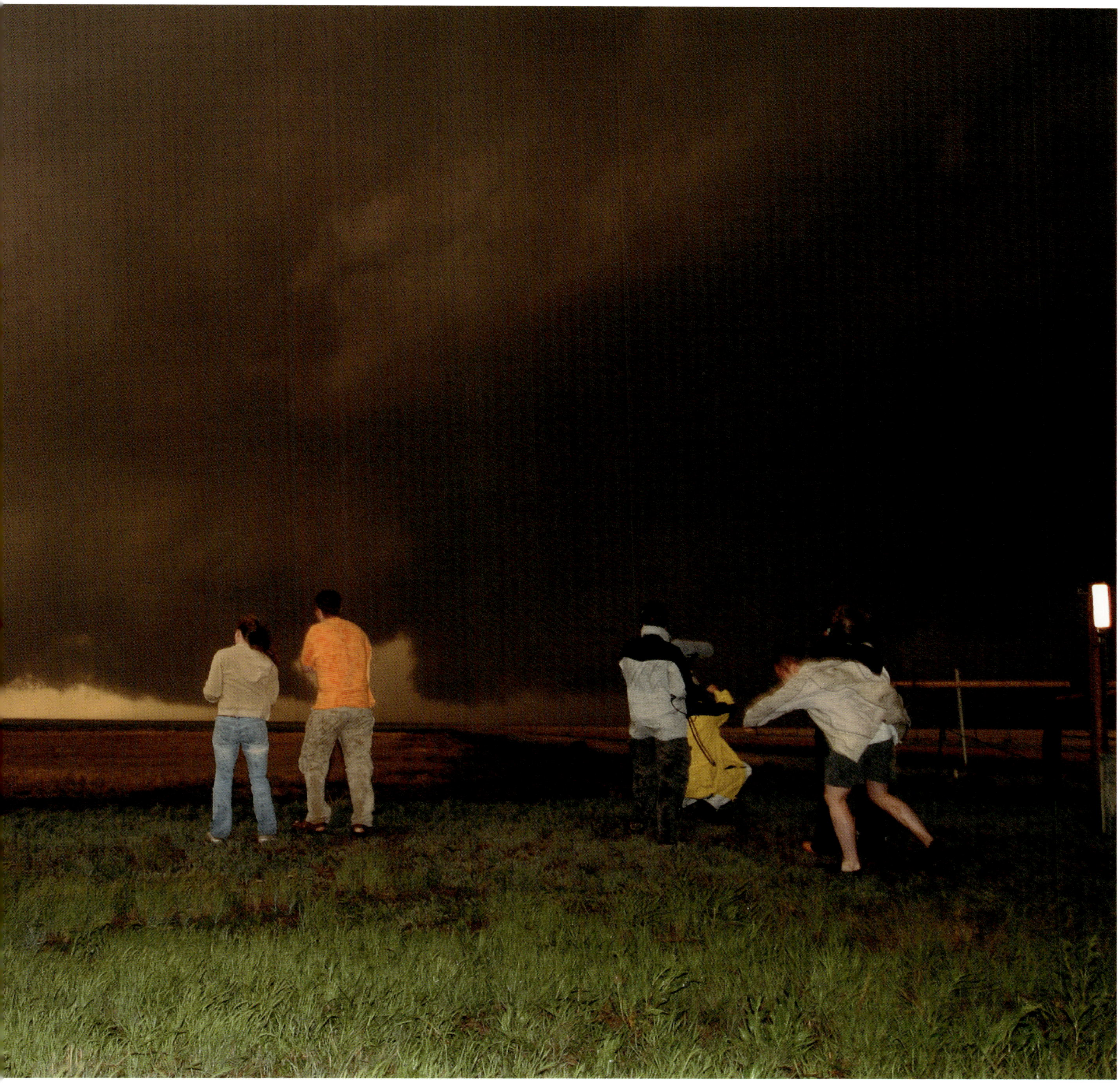

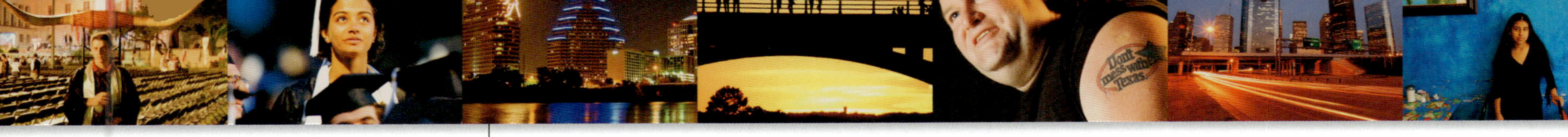

AUSTIN

The downtown skyline of the "Live Music Capital of the World" shimmers in Town Lake. According to the city's music commission, Austin has more live venues per capita than Nashville, Memphis, or New York City. Most of the city's music clubs are concentrated in a mile-and-a-half stretch along 6th Street.

Photo by Randy Smith

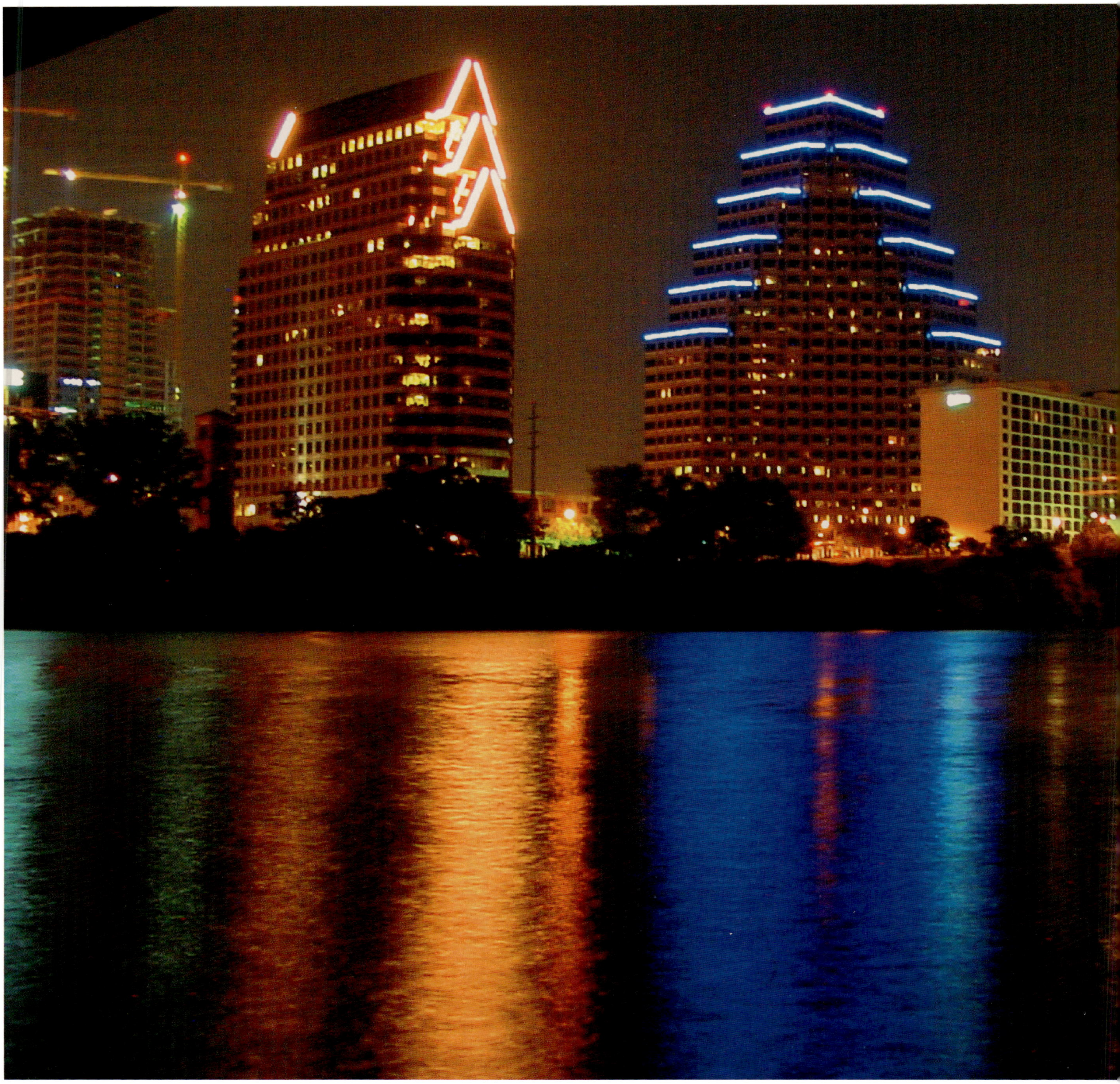

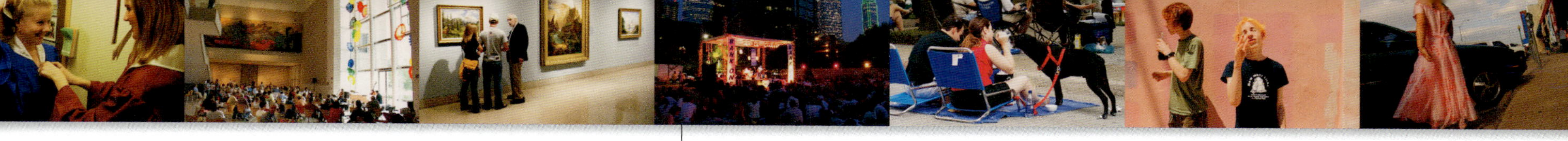

DALLAS

The Arlington Jones Trio fills downtown with music during the Dallas Museum of Art's Jazz Under the Stars free concert series. Every Thursday from May through June, jazz artists perform on the museum's Ross Street lawn.

Photo by Peter A. Calvin

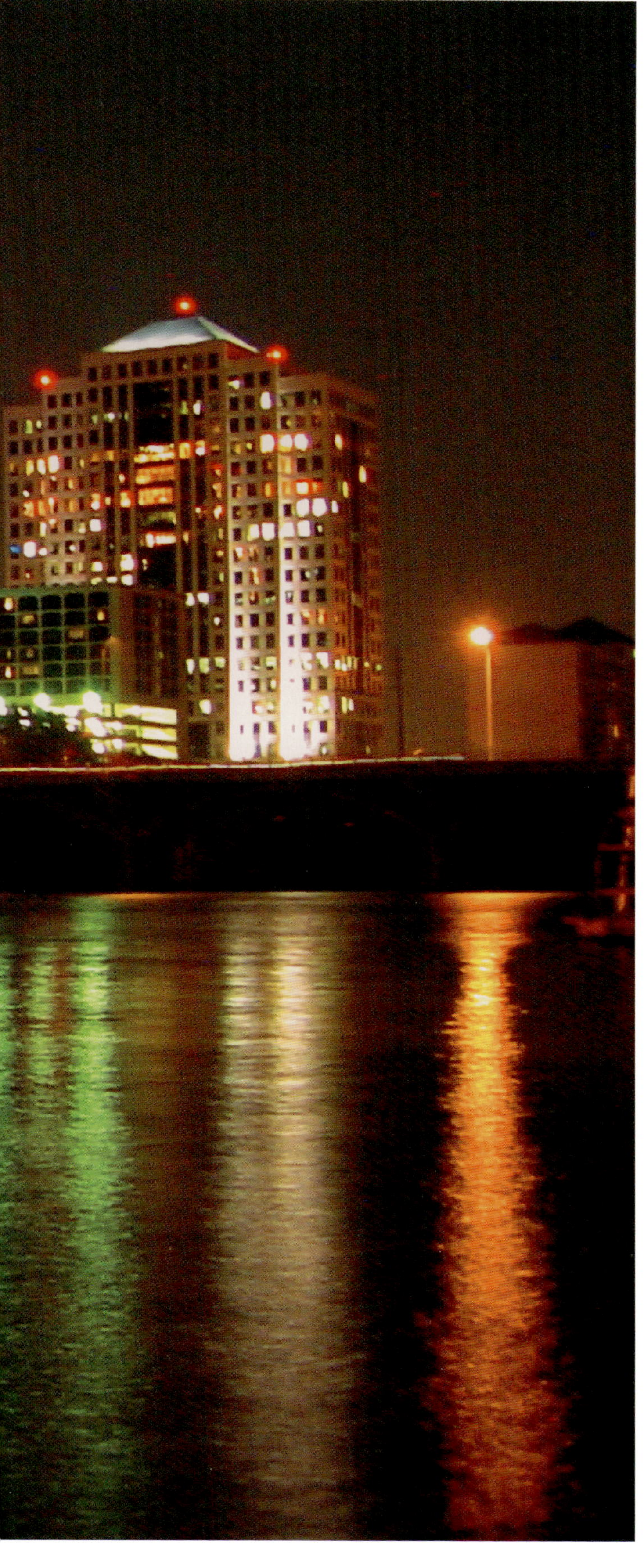

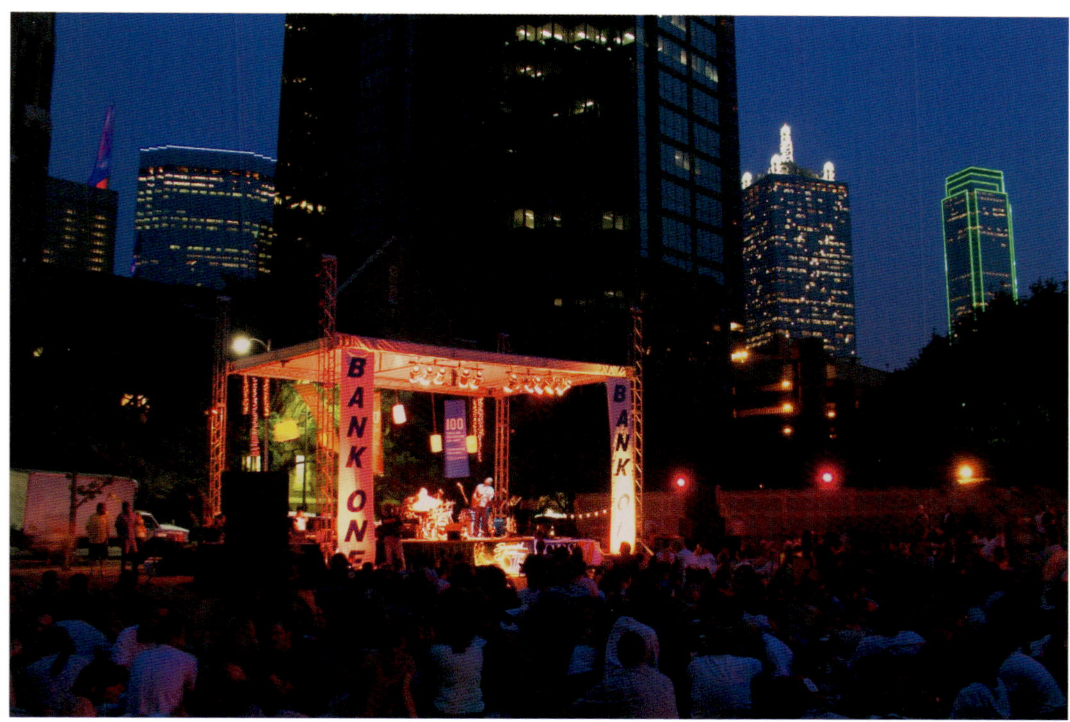

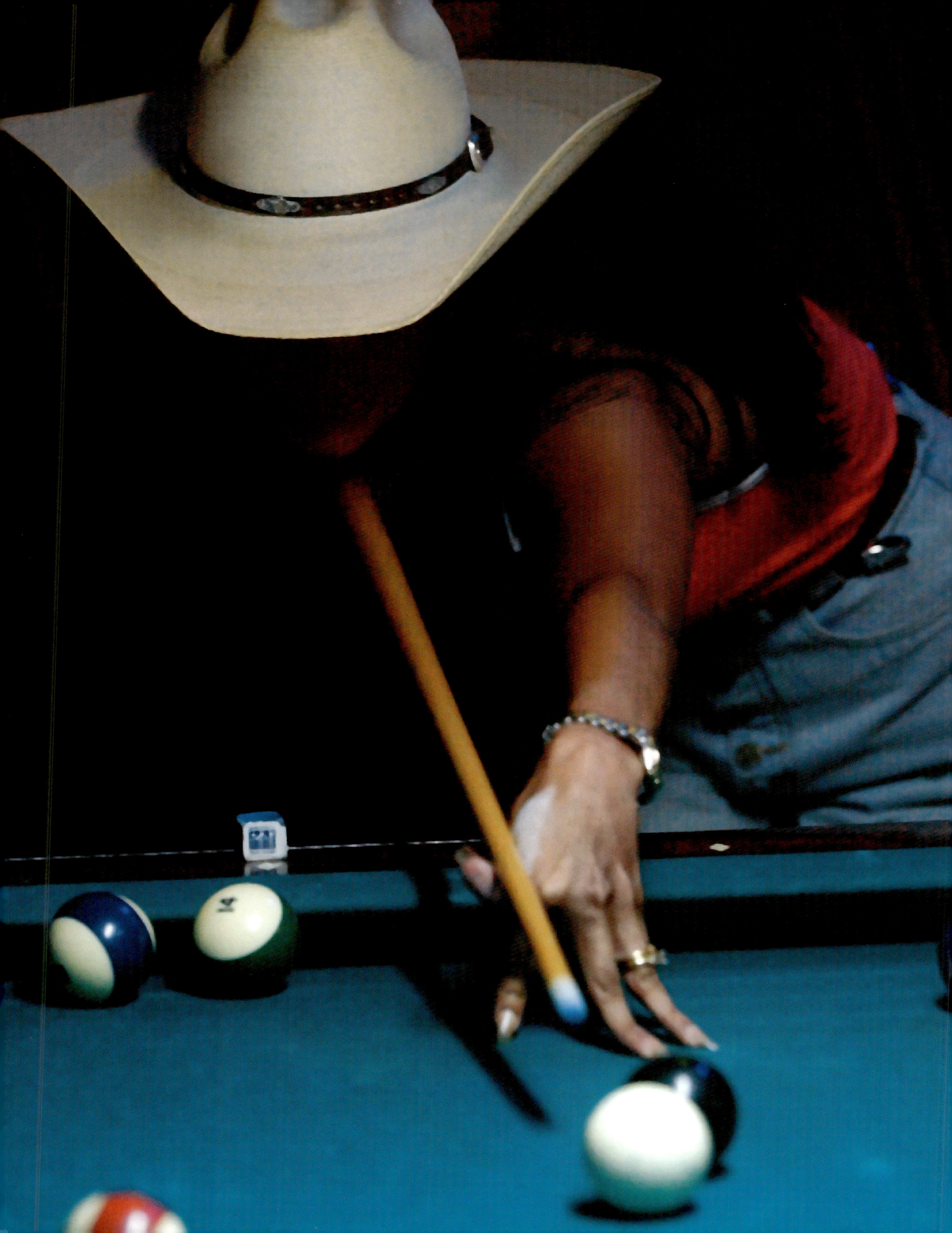
14

ANGLETON
Showing fine form, Tera Loyacano lines up a shot at Kick's Club, a country-western bar in dry Brazoria County. To get around the antialcohol laws, Kick's charges an annual $1 membership fee, thus qualifying it as a private club.
Photo by Todd Yates

AUSTIN
At the Carousel Lounge, Alissa Moran listens to her boyfriend Tad Catalano sing along with the country-jazz-swing-surf-a-billy group, Jim Stringer & the AM Band. The 40-year-old Carousel Lounge, popular with old-timers and young folks alike, has a wall-to-wall circus motif and a dilapidated carousel behind the bar.
Photo by Rodolfo Gonzalez

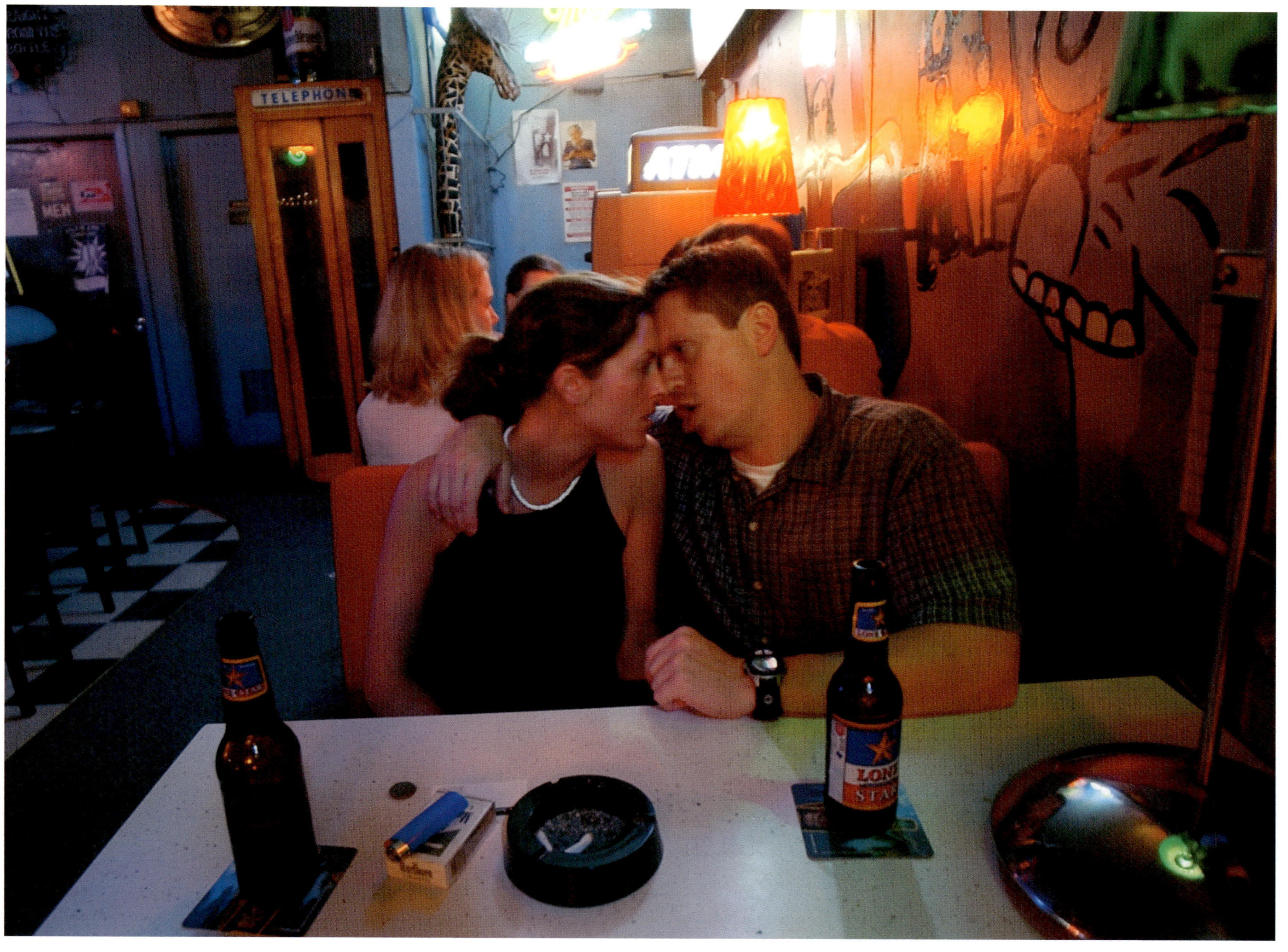

FORT WORTH

Bunkbed Incident lead singer Gabe Bowling regales the crowd at The Door, a Fort Worth club that caters to Christian teens. The band is into the alternative side of Christian music, which wraps its messages in a variety of packages—metal, hip-hop, ska, and reggae.

Photo by Louis DeLuca

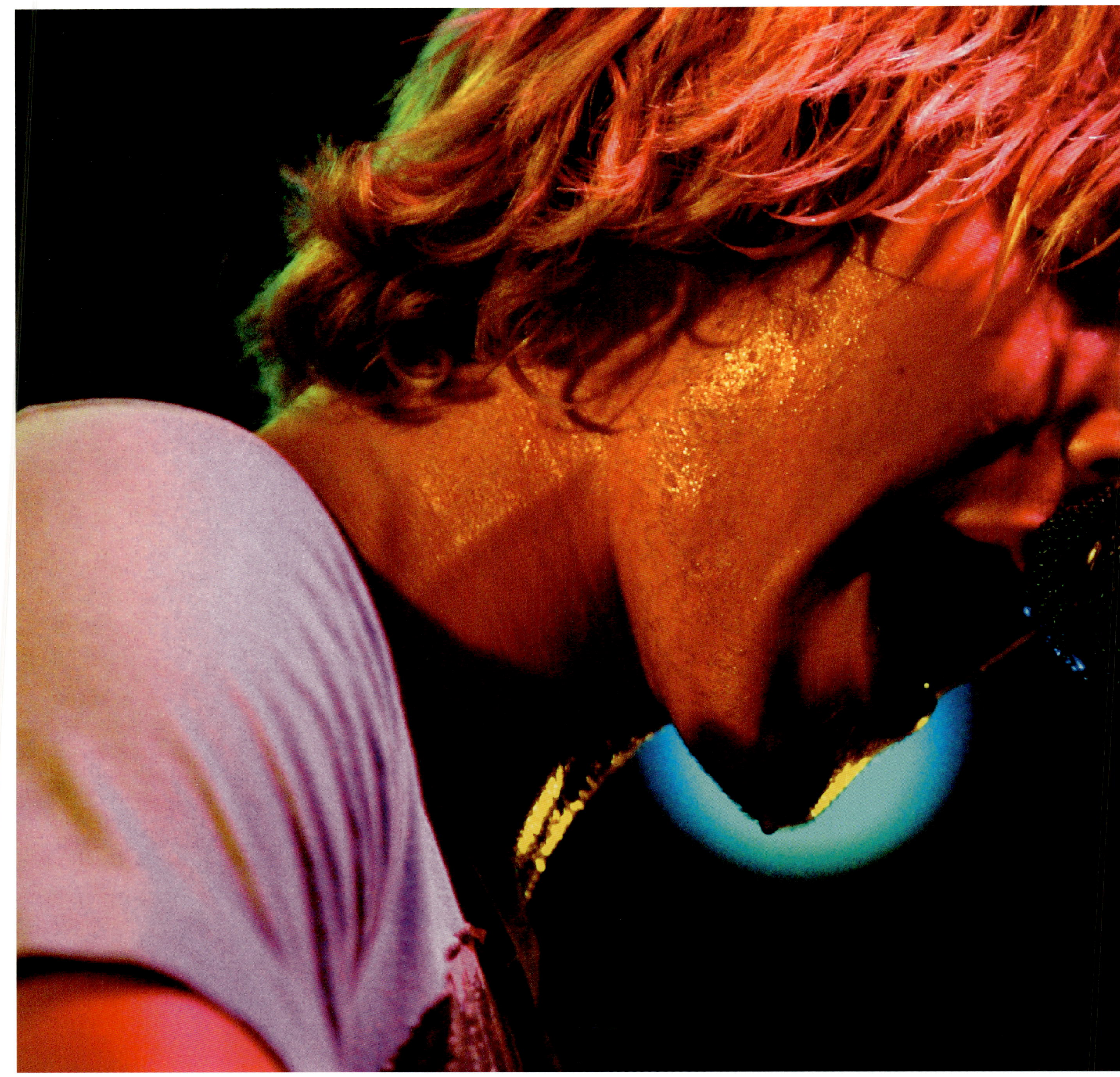

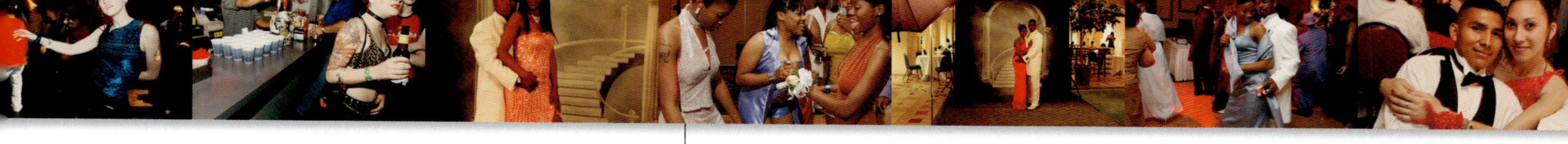

DALLAS

All dressed up and somewhere to go: A gaggle of students share a giggle between dances at the Franklin D. Roosevelt High School prom at the Crowne Plaza off I-35.

Photo by Shelly Katz Photo

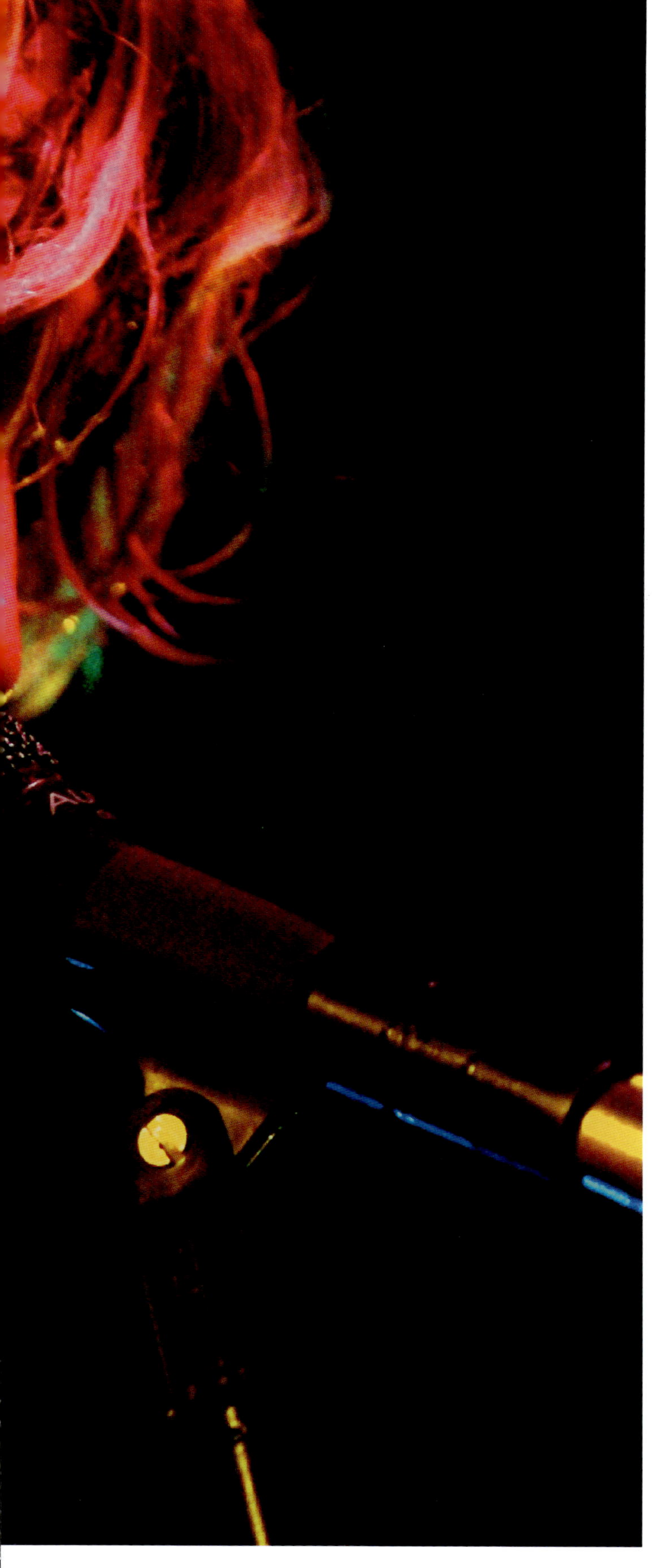

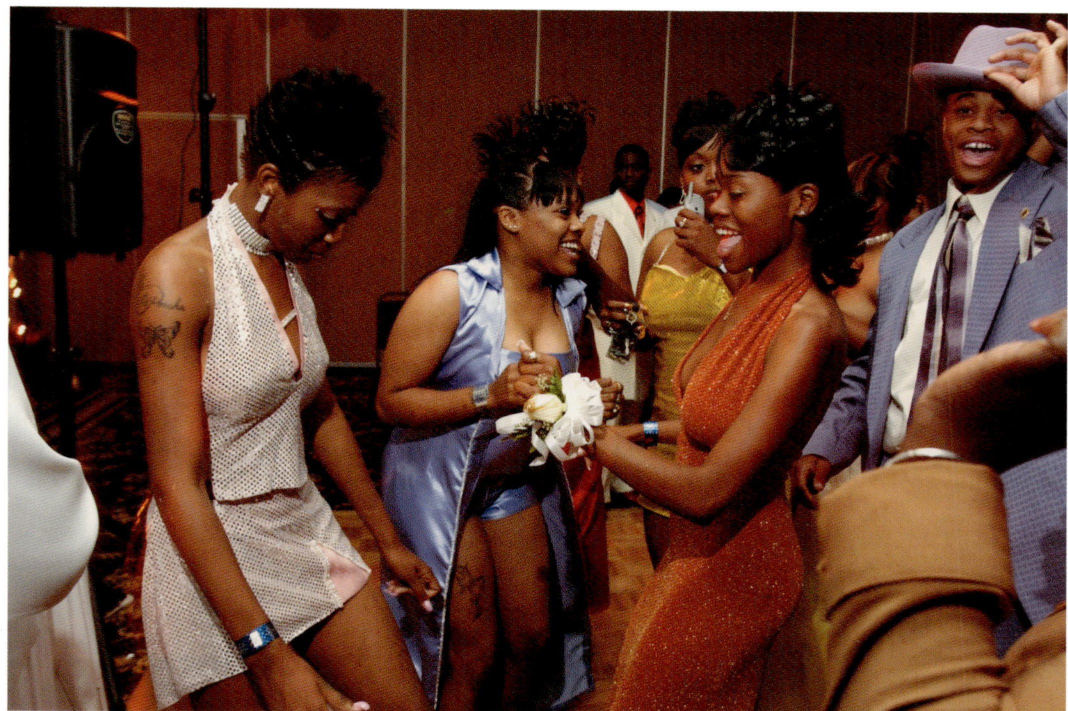

MARATHON

On a Friday night in the sleepy west Texas town of Marathon, a local watches *Austin Powers: The Spy Who Shagged Me*, projected in the parking lot of the Marathon Motel. Built in 1940 and renovated in 1987, the motel serves as a stopover for motorists heading to or from Big Bend National Park.

Photo by Penny De Los Santos, National Geographic, Freelance

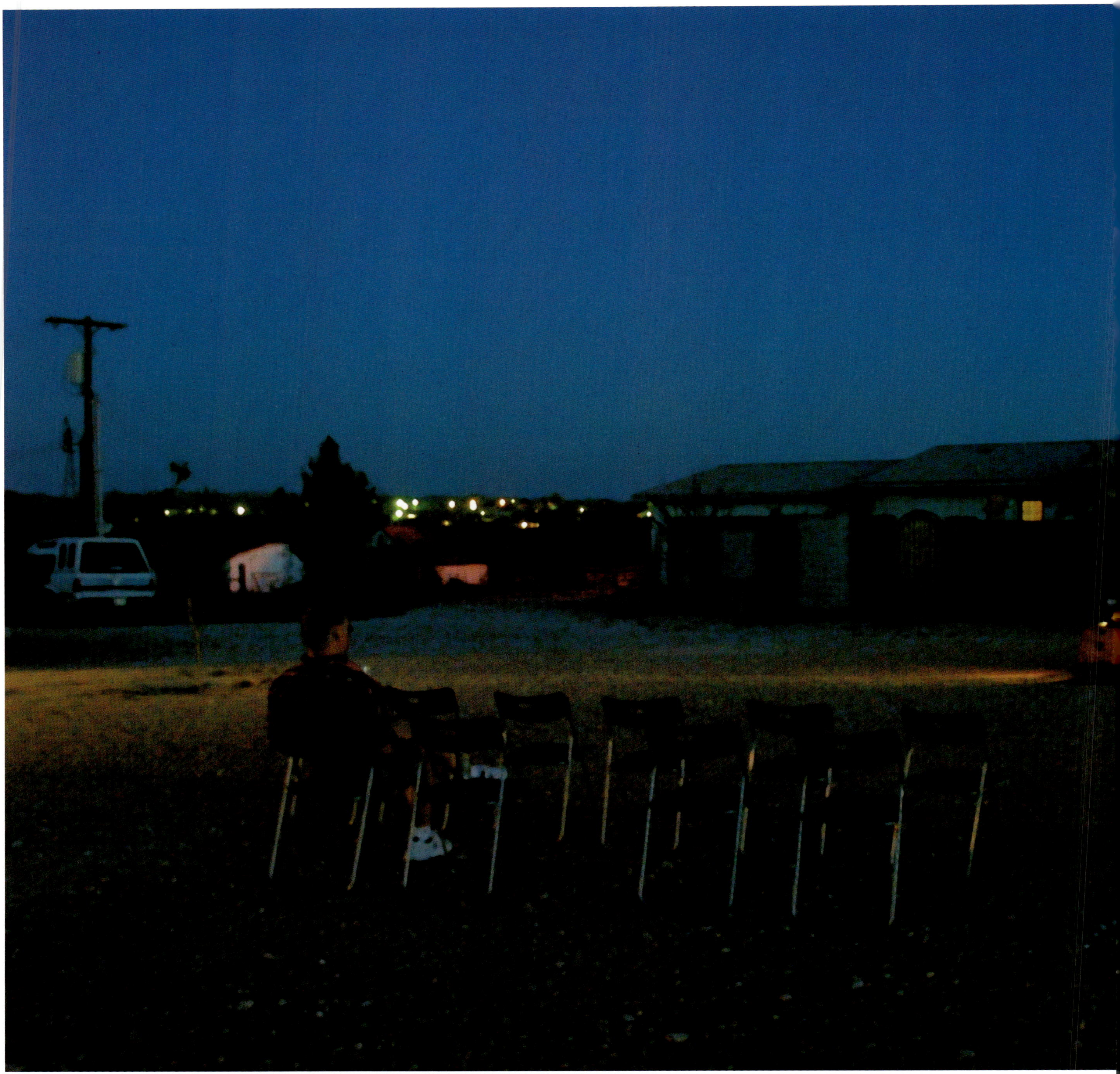

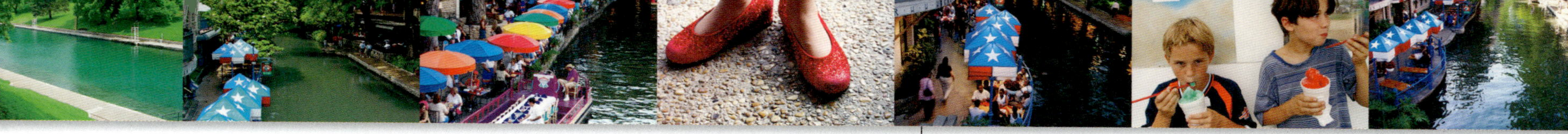

SAN ANTONIO

After a disastrous flood in 1921, some local groups wanted to cover the San Antonio River with concrete. Architect Robert Hugman had a different idea—deepen the channel, open cafes and shops, add extensive landscaping, and offer gondola rides. His Riverwalk project broke ground in 1939, was enhanced for the 1968 World's Fair, and is now one of the city's most popular attractions.
Photo by Alicia Wagner Calzada

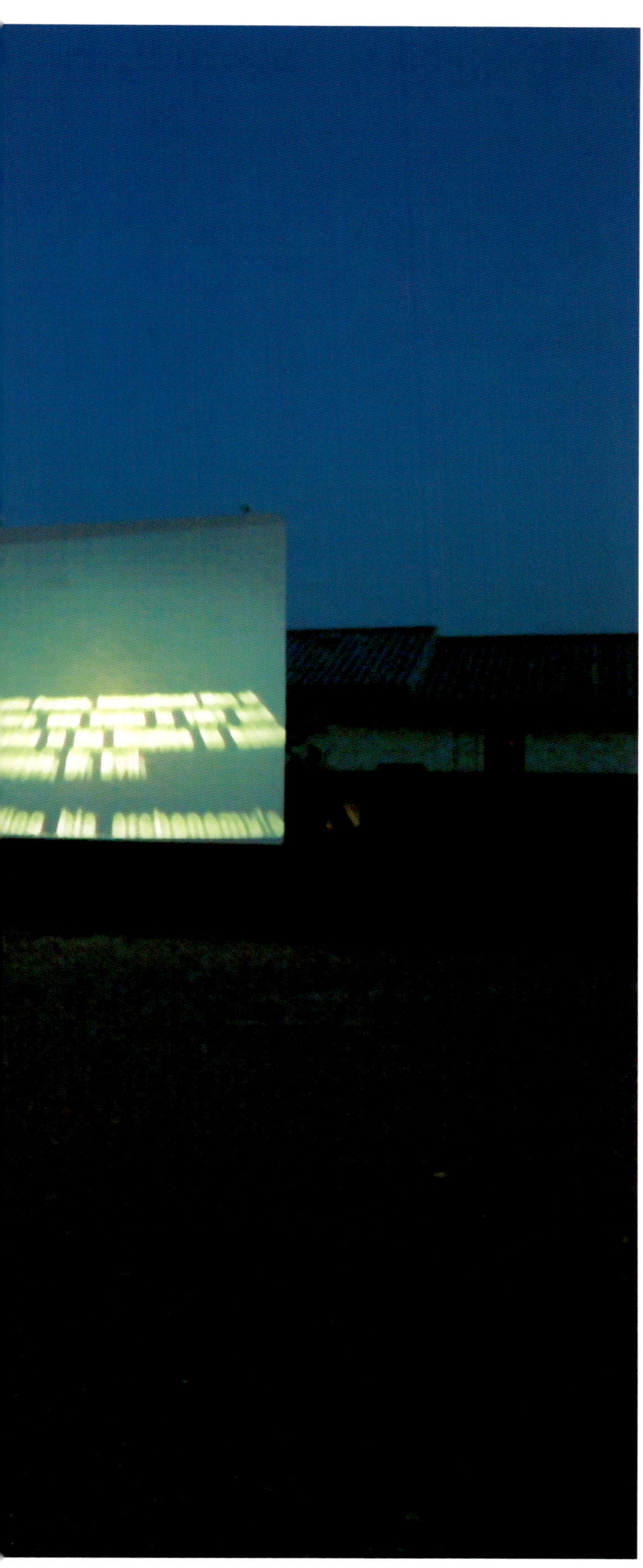

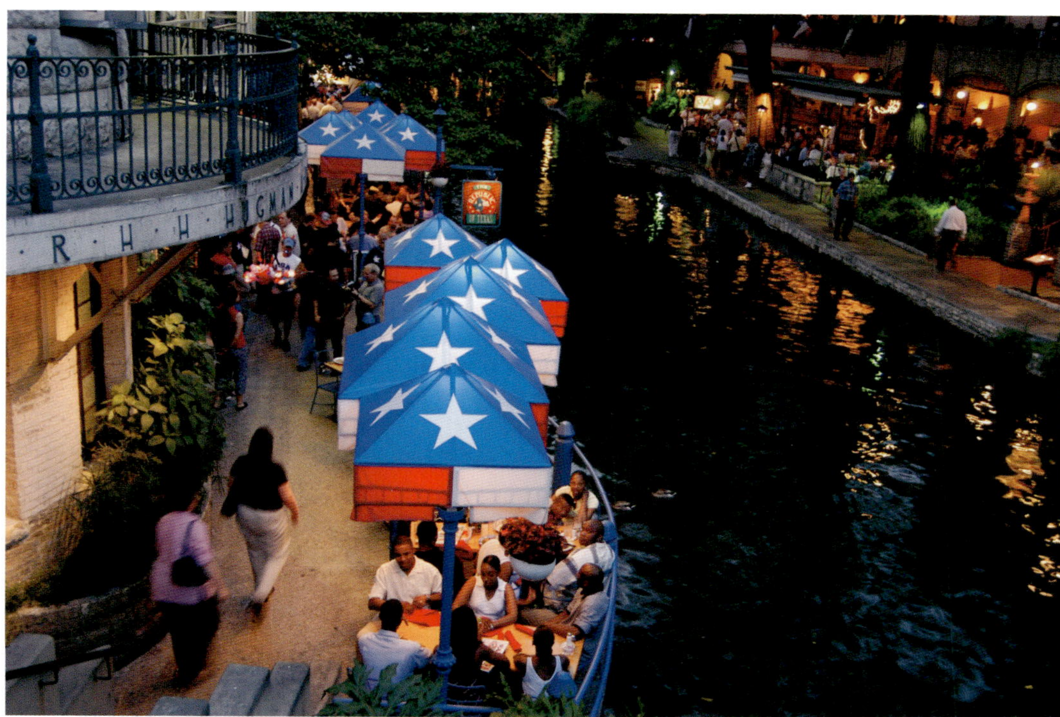

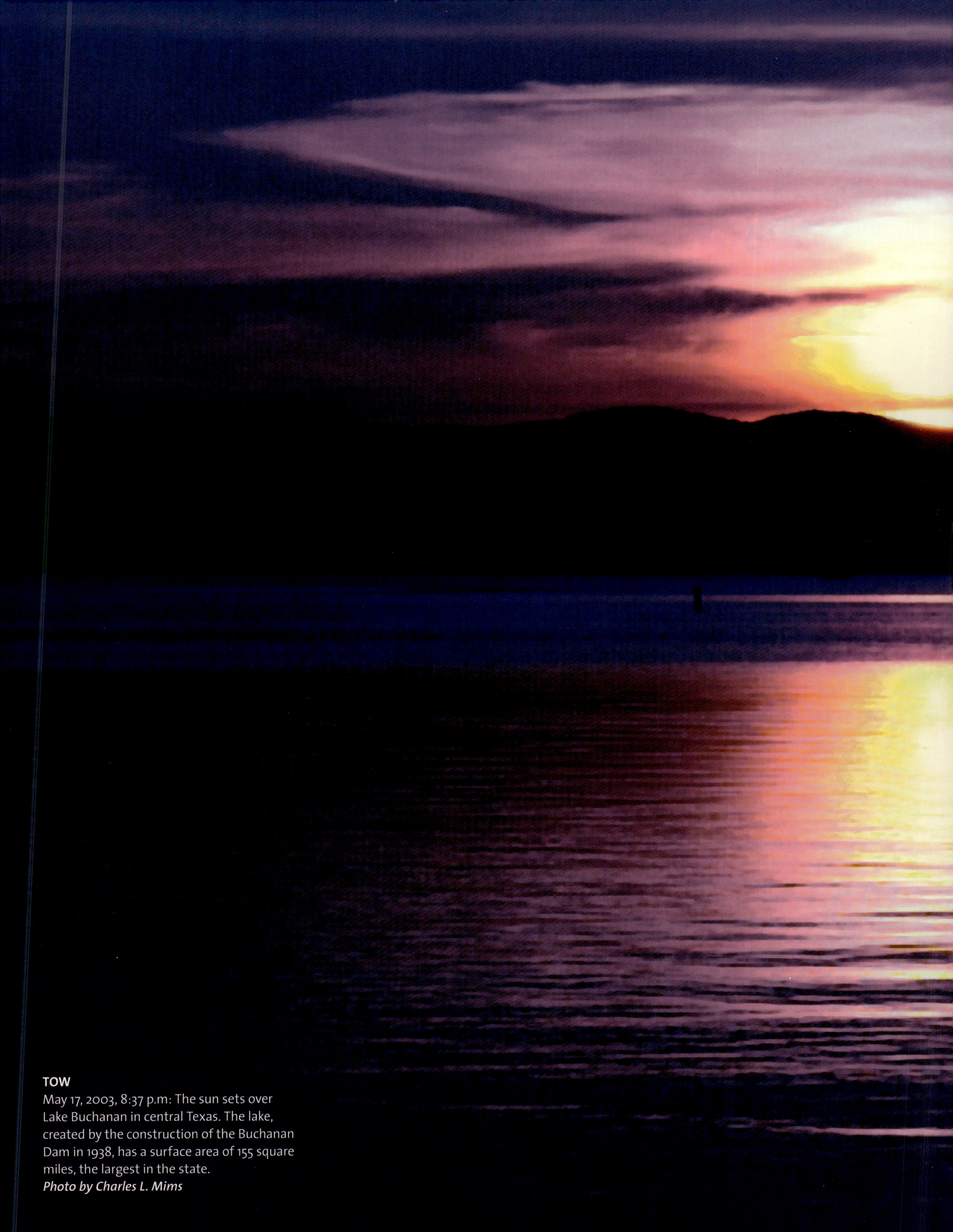

TOW
May 17, 2003, 8:37 p.m: The sun sets over Lake Buchanan in central Texas. The lake, created by the construction of the Buchanan Dam in 1938, has a surface area of 155 square miles, the largest in the state.
Photo by Charles L. Mims

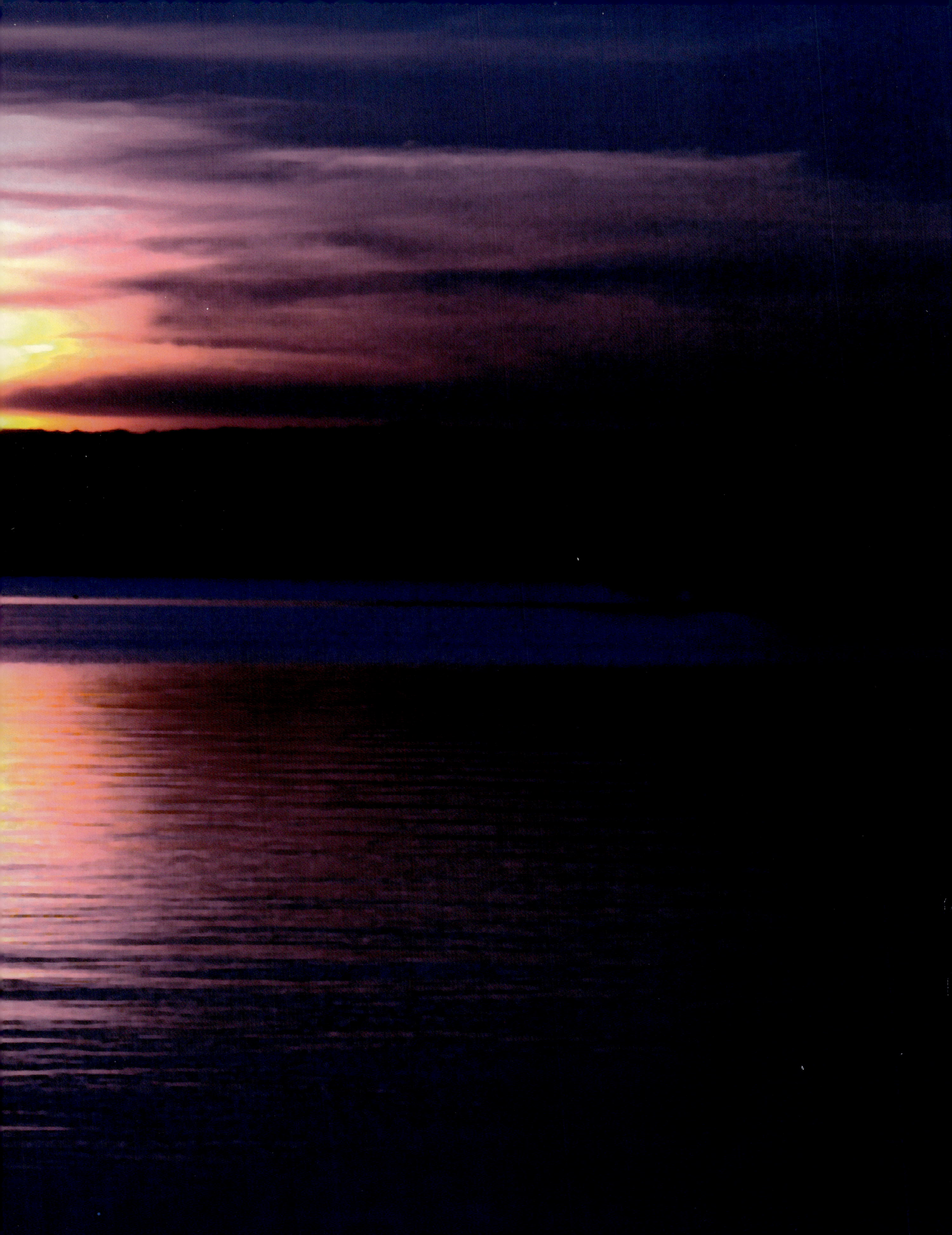

How It Worked

The week of May 12-18, 2003, more than 25,000 professional and amateur photographers spread out across the nation to shoot over a million digital photographs with the goal of capturing the essence of daily life in America.

The professional photographers were equipped with Adobe Photoshop and Adobe Album software, Olympus C-5050 digital cameras, and Lexar Media's high-speed compact flash cards.

The 1,000 professional contract photographers plus another 5,000 stringers and students sent their images via FTP (file transfer protocol) directly to the *America 24/7* website. Meanwhile, thousands of amateur photographers uploaded their images to Snapfish's servers.

At *America 24/7*'s Mission Control headquarters, located at CNET in San Francisco, dozens of picture editors from the nation's most prestigious publications culled the images down to 25,000 of the very best, using Photo Mechanic by Camera Bits. These photos were transferred into Webware's ActiveMedia Digital Asset Management (DAM) system, which served as a central image library and enabled the designers to track, search, distribute, and reformat the images for the creation of the 51 books, foreign language editions, web and magazine syndication, posters, and exhibitions.

Once in the DAM, images were optimized (and in some cases resampled to increase image resolution) using Adobe Photoshop. Adobe InDesign and Adobe InCopy were used to design and produce the 51 books, which were edited and reviewed in multiple locations around the world in the form of Adobe Acrobat PDFs. Epson Stylus printers were used for photo proofing and to produce large-format images for exhibitions. The companies providing support for the *America 24/7* project offer many of the essential components for anyone building a digital darkroom. We encourage you to read more on the following pages about their respective roles

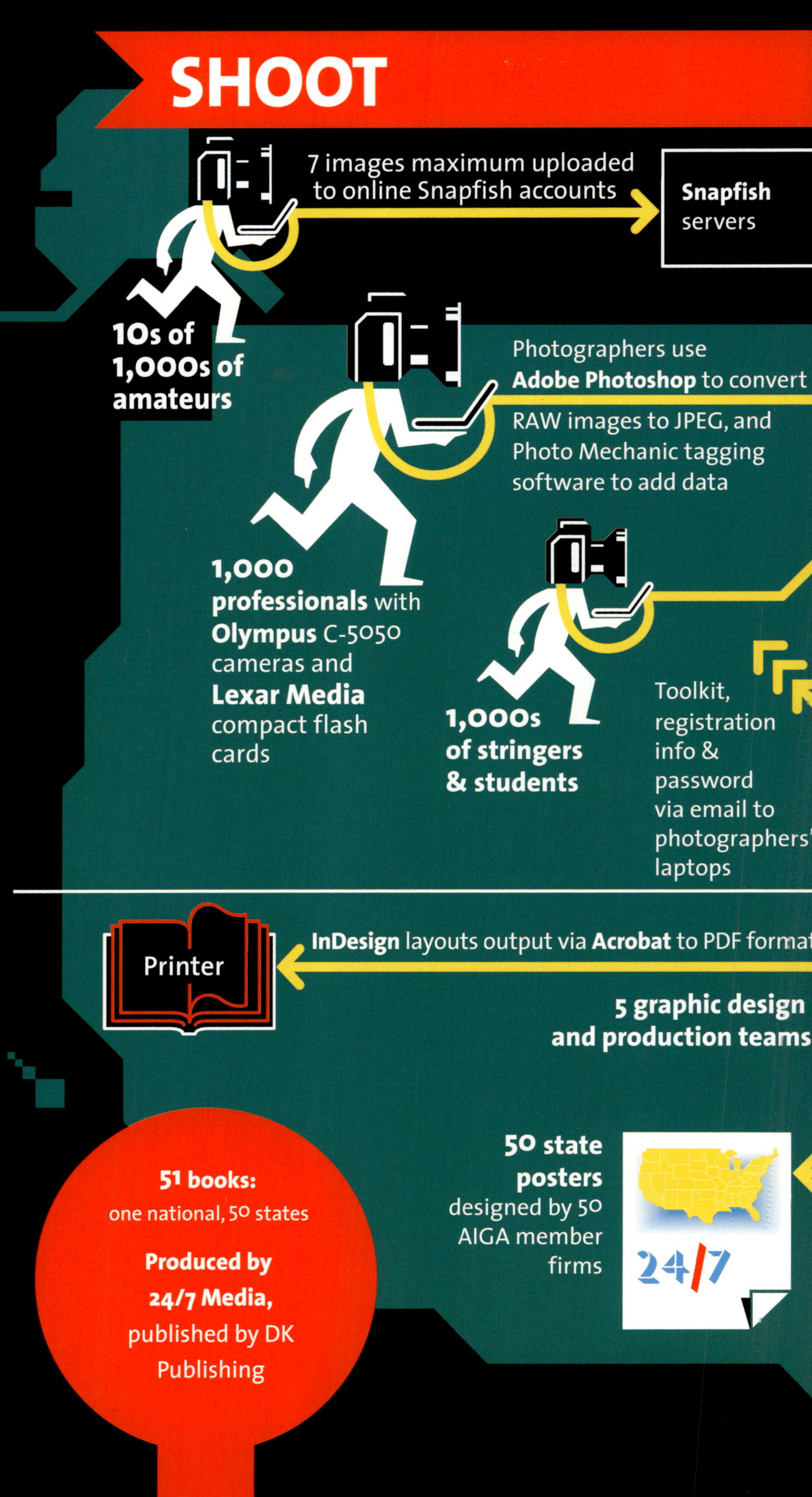

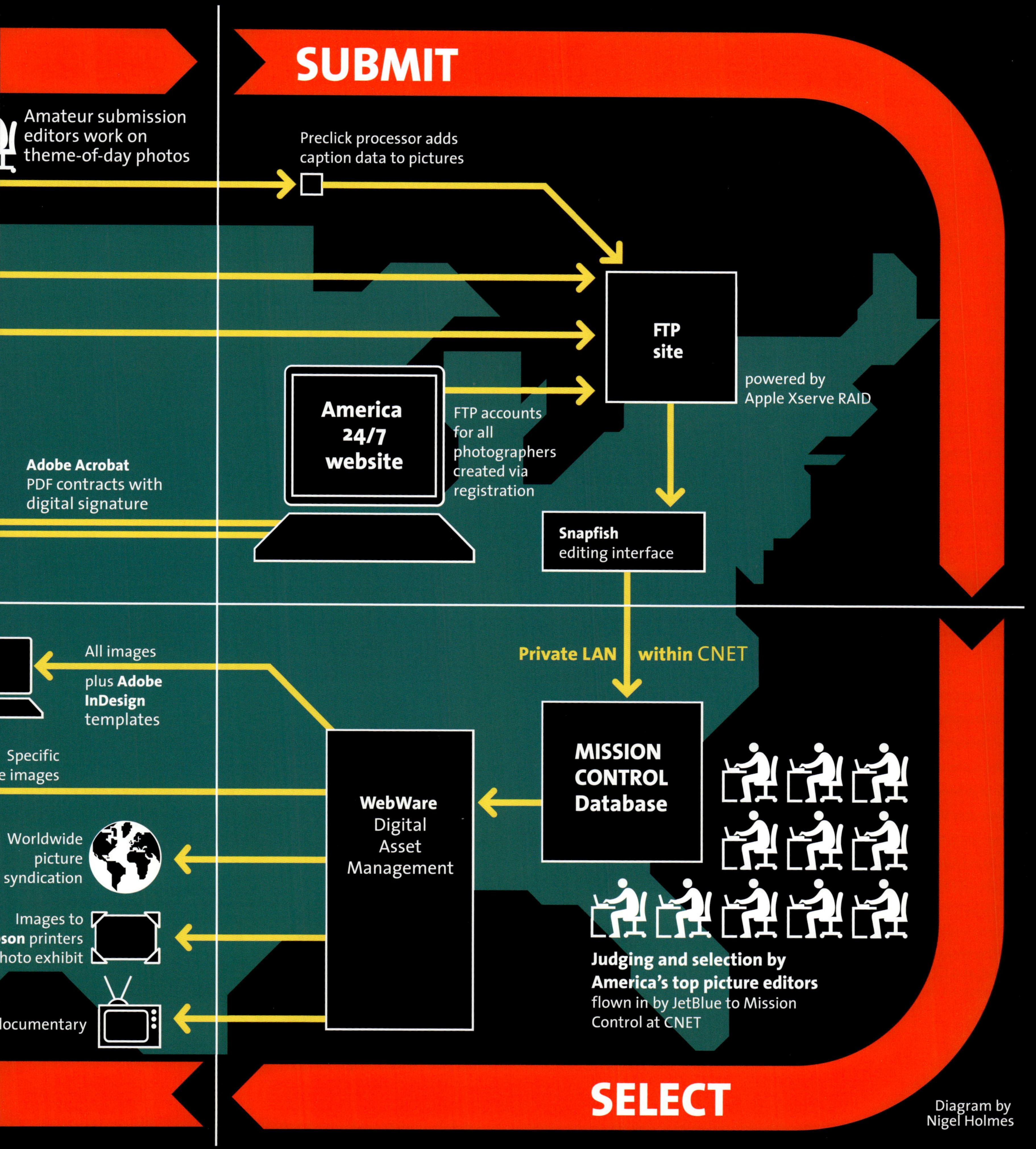

Diagram by Nigel Holmes

Participating Photographers

Texas Coordinator: Joe Abell, Systems Editor, *San Antonio Express-News*

Joe Abell, *San Antonio Express-News*
Lana Morgan Adler
John Ater, www.johnater.com
Henry Bargas, *Amarillo Globe*
Ralph Barrera, *Austin American-Statesman*
James Benton
Peter A. Calvin
Alicia Wagner Calzada
David Cazier
Lance Cheung, *Airman Magazine*
Peter Christensen
Rey Cortez
Dee G. Crawford
John Davenport, *San Antonio Express-News*
Barbara Davidson, *The Dallas Morning News*
Penny De Los Santos, *National Geographic*, Freelance
Chris Dean
Louis DeLuca
Barbara DeMoulin
Brad Doherty
Ronald W. Erdrich, *Abilene Reporter-News*
Tim Fischer, *Midland Reporter-Telegram*
Kyle Gerstner
Rodolfo Gonzalez*
Rudy Gutierrez, *El Paso Times*
Dirck Halstead
Ronald Harmon
Les Hassell
Cheryl Hatch
Danny Hurley
David Johnson
Jim Johnston, Sundance Photographic Arts
B'Lan Kao
Shelly Katz Photo
Jerry Lara, *San Antonio Express-News*
Gary Lawson
Scogin Mayo
Sean Meyers Photography
Charles L. Mims
Steven Noreyko
Michael O'Brien
Sarah Orr
Gary W. Porter
Tim Quiring
Craig Robinson
Beverly R. Schulz
F. Carter Smith, Polaris Images
James D. Smith
Randy Smith
Steve Soza-Gorham
Rae Lynn Tipping
Joshua Trujillo
Todd Yates
Tim Zielenbach

***Pulitzer Prize winner**

Thumbnail Picture Credits

Credits for thumbnail photographs are listed by the page number and are in order from left to right.

22 Gary Lawson
Joe Abell
Alicia Wagner Calzada
George Fargo
Alicia Wagner Calzada
Joe Abell
Patrick Nugent

23 Todd Yates
Todd Yates
Sarah Orr
Ronald W. Erdrich, *Abilene Reporter-News*
Sarah Orr
Ronald W. Erdrich, *Abilene Reporter-News*
Sarah Orr

25 Penny De Los Santos, *National Geographic*, Freelance
Scogin Mayo
F. Carter Smith, Polaris Images
Tim Quiring
Scogin Mayo
Scogin Mayo
Scogin Mayo

26 Steven Noreyko
Steven Noreyko
Steven Noreyko
Steven Noreyko
Annalisa Rodriguez Barroso
Annalisa Rodriguez Barroso
Annalisa Rodriguez Barroso

27 Brad Doherty
Brad Doherty
Penny De Los Santos, *National Geographic*, Freelance
Brad Doherty
Penny De Los Santos, *National Geographic*, Freelance
Brad Doherty
Brad Doherty

28 F. Carter Smith, Polaris Images
B'Lan Kao
F. Carter Smith, Polaris Images
James D. Smith
James D. Smith
Kate Stewart
Craig Robinson

29 Mary Stone
Patrick Nugent
Ralph Barrera, *Austin American-Statesman*
Sean Meyers Photography
Danny Hurley
Peter A. Calvin
Lana Morgan Adler

30 Annalisa Rodriguez Barroso
Annalisa Rodriguez Barroso
B'Lan Kao
Rodolfo Gonzalez
Ralph Barrera, *Austin American-Statesman*
F. Carter Smith, Polaris Images
Davis Smith

31 Tim Zielenbach
Todd Yates
Rodolfo Gonzalez
Sarah Orr
Rodolfo Gonzalez
Sarah Orr
Rodolfo Gonzalez

32 Annalisa Rodriguez Barroso
Annalisa Rodriguez Barroso
John Ater, www.johnater.com
Beverly R. Schulz
James D. Smith
Scogin Mayo
John Ater, www.johnater.com

33 John Ater, www.johnater.com
John Ater, www.johnater.com
Scogin Mayo
Barbara Davidson, *The Dallas Morning News*
Barbara Davidson, *The Dallas Morning News*
Barbara Davidson, *The Dallas Morning News*
Scogin Mayo

34 Lana Morgan Adler
Aaron Francis
Lana Morgan Adler
Gary W. Porter
Tim Quiring
Dee G. Crawford
Scogin Mayo

35 Scogin Mayo
Scogin Mayo
Hubert W. Weldon II
Scogin Mayo
Scogin Mayo
Scogin Mayo
Scogin Mayo

36 Lana Morgan Adler
James D. Smith
Beverly R. Schulz
Dee G. Crawford
Beverly R. Schulz
Beverly R. Schulz
James D. Smith

37 Lana Morgan Adler
Tim Zielenbach
Les Hassell
Anthony Ku
Lana Morgan Adler
Mary Stone
Mary Stone

38 Anthony Ku
Sarah Orr
Danny Hurley
Cliff Bramlett
Joe Duty
Henry Bargas, *Amarillo Globe*
Linda Abell

39 Joe Abell
Joe Abell
Tim Quiring
Sarah Orr
John Ater, www.johnater.com
Tim Quiring
Tim Quiring

40 Lana Morgan Adler
Jack C. Smith
Rodolfo Gonzalez
Rodolfo Gonzalez
Mary Stone
Mary Stone
Rodolfo Gonzalez

41 Scogin Mayo
John Davenport, *San Antonio Express-News*
Gary Lawson
John Davenport, *San Antonio Express-News*
Scogin Mayo
John Davenport, *San Antonio Express-News*
Scogin Mayo

42 Brandon Wade
Annalisa Rodriguez Barroso
James D. Smith
James D. Smith
Penny De Los Santos, *National Geographic*, Freelance
James D. Smith
Danny Hurley

43 Ronald W. Erdrich, *Abilene Reporter-News*
Lana Morgan Adler
Mary Stone
Lana Morgan Adler
F. Carter Smith, Polaris Images
Jack C. Smith
F. Carter Smith, Polaris Images

50 Dirck Halstead
Dirck Halstead
Gary Lawson
Gary Lawson
Dirck Halstead
Henry Bargas, *Amarillo Globe*
Gary Lawson

51 Dirck Halstead
Dirck Halstead
Dirck Halstead
Henry Bargas, *Amarillo Globe*
Gary Lawson
Dirck Halstead
Gary Lawson

52 Joshua Trujillo
Joshua Trujillo
Joshua Trujillo
Joshua Trujillo
Joshua Trujillo
Joshua Trujillo
Joshua Trujillo

53 Joshua Trujillo
Joshua Trujillo
Joshua Trujillo
Joshua Trujillo
Joshua Trujillo
Joshua Trujillo
Joshua Trujillo

54 Alicia Wagner Calzada
Rudy Gutierrez, *El Paso Times*
Alicia Wagner Calzada
Alicia Wagner Calzada
Rudy Gutierrez, *El Paso Times*
Alicia Wagner Calzada
Rudy Gutierrez, *El Paso Times*

55 Alicia Wagner Calzada
Alicia Wagner Calzada
John Davenport, *San Antonio Express-News*
Alicia Wagner Calzada
John Davenport, *San Antonio Express-News*
Alicia Wagner Calzada
John Davenport, *San Antonio Express-News*

57 Jerry Lara, *San Antonio Express-News*
Rudy Gutierrez, *El Paso Times*
Jerry Lara, *San Antonio Express-News*
Rudy Gutierrez, *El Paso Times*
Jerry Lara, *San Antonio Express-News*
Jerry Lara, *San Antonio Express-News*
Rudy Gutierrez, *El Paso Times*

58 Craig Robinson
Craig Robinson
Craig Robinson
Craig Robinson
Craig Robinson
Craig Robinson
Craig Robinson

59 Craig Robinson
Craig Robinson
Craig Robinson
Craig Robinson
Craig Robinson
Craig Robinson
Craig Robinson

60 Sean Meyers Photography
Sean Meyers Photography
Sean Meyers Photography
Ronald W. Erdrich, *Abilene Reporter-News*
Ronald W. Erdrich, *Abilene Reporter-News*
Ronald W. Erdrich, *Abilene Reporter-News*
Ronald W. Erdrich, *Abilene Reporter-News*

61 Sean Meyers Photography
Ronald W. Erdrich, *Abilene Reporter-News*
Sean Meyers Photography
Ronald W. Erdrich, *Abilene Reporter-News*
Sean Meyers Photography
Ronald W. Erdrich, *Abilene Reporter-News*
Sean Meyers Photography

62 Michael O'Brien
Michael O'Brien
Michael O'Brien
Michael O'Brien
Chris Dean
Chris Dean
Chris Dean

63 Adam Cunningham
Andrea Heather Becerra
Barbara DeMoulin
Rodolfo Gonzalez
Rodolfo Gonzalez
Scogin Mayo
Rodolfo Gonzalez

67 Tim Fischer, *Midland Reporter-Telegram*
Tim Fischer, *Midland Reporter-Telegram*
Tim Fischer, *Midland Reporter-Telegram*
Sean Meyers Photography
Tim Fischer, *Midland Reporter-Telegram*
Sean Meyers Photography
Tim Fischer, *Midland Reporter-Telegram*

68 Tim Zielenbach
Tim Zielenbach
Tim Zielenbach
Tim Zielenbach
Tim Zielenbach
Tim Zielenbach
Tim Zielenbach

69 Tim Zielenbach
Tim Zielenbach
Tim Zielenbach
Tim Zielenbach
Tim Zielenbach
Tim Zielenbach
Tim Zielenbach

70 Les Hassell
Les Hassell
Les Hassell
Les Hassell
Chris Dean
Chris Dean
Barbara Davidson, *The Dallas Morning News*

71 Barbara Davidson, *The Dallas Morning News*
Dirck Halstead
Dirck Halstead
Danny Hurley
Danny Hurley
Peter A. Calvin
Peter A. Calvin

72 Cheryl Hatch
Cheryl Hatch
Cheryl Hatch
Cheryl Hatch
Cheryl Hatch
Cheryl Hatch
Cheryl Hatch

73 Cheryl Hatch
Cheryl Hatch
Cheryl Hatch
Cheryl Hatch

Cheryl Hatch
Cheryl Hatch
Cheryl Hatch

74 Shelly Katz Photo
Shelly Katz Photo
Shelly Katz Photo
Shelly Katz Photo
Shelly Katz Photo
Shelly Katz Photo
Shelly Katz Photo

75 Shelly Katz Photo
Shelly Katz Photo
Shelly Katz Photo
Shelly Katz Photo
Shelly Katz Photo
Shelly Katz Photo
Shelly Katz Photo

76 Mary Stone
Ronald W. Erdrich, *Abilene Reporter-News*
Ronald W. Erdrich, *Abilene Reporter-News*
Ronald W. Erdrich, *Abilene Reporter-News*
Ronald W. Erdrich, *Abilene Reporter-News*
Ronald W. Erdrich, *Abilene Reporter-News*
Ronald W. Erdrich, *Abilene Reporter-News*

77 Ronald W. Erdrich, *Abilene Reporter-News*
Ronald W. Erdrich, *Abilene Reporter-News*
Ronald W. Erdrich, *Abilene Reporter-News*
Ronald W. Erdrich, *Abilene Reporter-News*
Mary Stone
Ronald W. Erdrich, *Abilene Reporter-News*
Scogin Mayo

78 Alicia Wagner Calzada
Alicia Wagner Calzada
Scogin Mayo
Scogin Mayo
Henry Bargas, *Amarillo Globe*
Henry Bargas, *Amarillo Globe*
Scogin Mayo

79 Chris Dean
Scogin Mayo
Sean Meyers Photography
Sean Meyers Photography
Scogin Mayo
Scogin Mayo
Scogin Mayo

80 Charles L. Mims
Sean Meyers Photography
Rudy Gutierrez, *El Paso Times*
Sean Meyers Photography
Mary Stone
Scogin Mayo
Penny De Los Santos, *National Geographic*, Freelance

81 Les Hassell
Les Hassell
Sean Meyers Photography
Penny De Los Santos, *National Geographic*, Freelance
Tim Quiring
John Davenport, *San Antonio Express-News*
Mary Stone

82 Gary Lawson
Gary Lawson
Gary Lawson
Gary Lawson
Brad Doherty
Brad Doherty
Brad Doherty

83 B'Lan Kao
B'Lan Kao
Scogin Mayo
John Davenport, *San Antonio Express-News*
Scogin Mayo
Scogin Mayo
John Davenport, *San Antonio Express-News*

86 George Fargo
Joe Abell
George Fargo
Chris Dean
Joe Abell
Patrick G Putze
Joe Abell

87 Lance Cheung, *Airman Magazine*
Lance Cheung, *Airman Magazine*
Rudy Gutierrez, *El Paso Times*
Joe Abell
Rudy Gutierrez, *El Paso Times*
Lance Cheung, *Airman Magazine*
Lance Cheung, *Airman Magazine*

89 B'Lan Kao
Beverly R. Schulz
Tim Zielenbach
Tim Zielenbach
F. Carter Smith, Polaris Images
Beverly R. Schulz
B'Lan Kao

90 James D. Smith
Rodolfo Gonzalez
George Fargo
Henry Bargas, *Amarillo Globe*
George Fargo
Scogin Mayo
Henry Bargas, *Amarillo Globe*

91 Roy Mata
Roy Mata
Todd Yates
Todd Yates
Rodolfo Gonzalez
Todd Yates
Ralph Barrera, *Austin American-Statesman*

92 Sean Meyers Photography
Craig Robinson
Sean Meyers Photography
Todd Yates
Sean Meyers Photography
Gary Lawson
Sean Meyers Photography

93 Rodolfo Gonzalez
Sean Meyers Photography
Rodolfo Gonzalez
Sean Meyers Photography
Rodolfo Gonzalez
Sean Meyers Photography
Rodolfo Gonzalez

94 Rodger Prestiy
Cheryl Hatch
Barbara DeMoulin
Rodger Prestiy
Sarah Orr
Rodger Prestiy
Barbara DeMoulin

95 Cheryl Hatch
Barbara Davidson, *The Dallas Morning News*
Cheryl Hatch
Cheryl Hatch
Cheryl Hatch
Barbara Davidson, *The Dallas Morning News*
Henry Bargas, *Amarillo Globe*

96 Kate Stewart
Rodolfo Gonzalez
Scogin Mayo
Kate Stewart
Rodolfo Gonzalez
Kate Stewart
Kate Stewart

97 Rodolfo Gonzalez
Michael O'Brien
Rodolfo Gonzalez
Michael O'Brien
Michael O'Brien
Michael O'Brien
Michael O'Brien

101 Jim Johnston, Sundance Photographic Arts
Tim Zielenbach
Jim Johnston, Sundance Photographic Arts
Peter A. Calvin
Joe Abell
Joe Abell
Tim Zielenbach

102 Brian E. Placette, texgram.com
Brian E. Placette, texgram.com
Louis DeLuca
Louis DeLuca
Louis DeLuca
Brian E. Placette, texgram.com
Louis DeLuca

103 Peter A. Calvin
Louis DeLuca
Peter A. Calvin
Louis DeLuca
Louis DeLuca
Louis DeLuca
Peter A. Calvin

104 Scogin Mayo
Scogin Mayo
Scogin Mayo
Scogin Mayo
Scogin Mayo
Scogin Mayo
Scogin Mayo

105 Scogin Mayo
Scogin Mayo
Scogin Mayo
Scogin Mayo
Scogin Mayo
Scogin Mayo
Scogin Mayo

107 Les Hassell
Tim Fischer, *Midland Reporter-Telegram*
Les Hassell
Tim Fischer, *Midland Reporter-Telegram*
Les Hassell
Charles L. Mims
Tim Fischer, *Midland Reporter-Telegram*

109 Shelly Katz Photo
Shelly Katz Photo
Shelly Katz Photo
Shelly Katz Photo
Shelly Katz Photo
Shelly Katz Photo
Shelly Katz Photo

112 Randy Smith
B'Lan Kao
B'Lan Kao
B'Lan Kao
Les Hassell
B'Lan Kao
Stacy Kendrick

113 Sean Meyers Photography
Sean Meyers Photography
Peter A. Calvin
Peter A. Calvin
Sean Meyers Photography
Sean Meyers Photography
Sean Meyers Photography

114 Peter A. Calvin
Peter A. Calvin
Peter A. Calvin
Peter A. Calvin
Peter A. Calvin
Peter A. Calvin
Peter A. Calvin

115 Peter A. Calvin
Peter A. Calvin
Peter A. Calvin
Peter A. Calvin
Peter A. Calvin
Peter A. Calvin
Peter A. Calvin

116 Brad Doherty
Brad Doherty
Brad Doherty
Joe Abell
Joe Abell
Joe Abell
Joe Abell

117 Joe Abell
Joe Abell
Rudy Gutierrez, *El Paso Times*
Joe Abell
Rudy Gutierrez, *El Paso Times*
Joe Abell
Rudy Gutierrez, *El Paso Times*

118 Andy Biggs
Les Hassell
Penny De Los Santos, *National Geographic*, Freelance
Lana Morgan Adler
Les Hassell
Les Hassell
Les Hassell

119 Les Hassell
Les Hassell
Les Hassell
Mary Stone
Rudy Gutierrez, *El Paso Times*
Sarah Orr
Scogin Mayo

120 Brad Doherty
F. Carter Smith, Polaris Images
Rudy Gutierrez, *El Paso Times*
Joe Abell
Joe Abell
Joe Abell
Peter A. Calvin

121 Joe Abell
Peter A. Calvin
Rudy Gutierrez, *El Paso Times*
Rudy Gutierrez, *El Paso Times*
Sarah Orr
Sarah Orr
Scogin Mayo

126 B'Lan Kao
Peter A. Calvin
Peter A. Calvin
Peter A. Calvin
Peter A. Calvin
Peter A. Calvin
Peter A. Calvin

127 Peter A. Calvin
Peter A. Calvin
Peter A. Calvin
Peter A. Calvin
Peter A. Calvin
B'Lan Kao
Peter A. Calvin

130 Jerry Lara, *San Antonio Express-News*
Jerry Lara, *San Antonio Express-News*
Jerry Lara, *San Antonio Express-News*
Jerry Lara, *San Antonio Express-News*
Jerry Lara, *San Antonio Express-News*
Jerry Lara, *San Antonio Express-News*
Jerry Lara, *San Antonio Express-News*

131 Rudy Gutierrez, *El Paso Times*
Rudy Gutierrez, *El Paso Times*
Rudy Gutierrez, *El Paso Times*
Rudy Gutierrez, *El Paso Times*
Barbara DeMoulin
Rudy Gutierrez, *El Paso Times*
Rudy Gutierrez, *El Paso Times*

132 Peter A. Calvin
Barbara Davidson, *The Dallas Morning News*
Peter A. Calvin
Scogin Mayo
Scogin Mayo
Scogin Mayo
Scogin Mayo

133 Peter A. Calvin
Peter A. Calvin
Peter A. Calvin
Peter A. Calvin
Peter A. Calvin
Sarah Orr
Peter A. Calvin

134 B'Lan Kao
Peter A. Calvin
Chris Dean
Dee G. Crawford
Chris Dean
Penny De Los Santos, *National Geographic*, Freelance
Peter A. Calvin

135 Les Hassell
Peter A. Calvin
Dee G. Crawford
Peter A. Calvin
Peter A. Calvin
Joe Abell
Peter A. Calvin

138 Brad Doherty
Les Hassell
Brad Doherty
Charles L. Mims
Charles L. Mims
Charles L. Mims
Todd Yates

139 Charles L. Mims
Todd Yates
Sarah Orr
Sarah Orr
Brad Doherty
Todd Yates
Todd Yates

140 Penny De Los Santos, *National Geographic*, Freelance
James P. Camp
Brad Doherty
Brad Doherty
James P. Camp
Brad Doherty
Brad Doherty

141 James P. Camp
Brad Doherty
James P. Camp
James P. Camp
James P. Camp
James P. Camp
James P. Camp

142 Stacy Kendrick
Kyle Gerstner
Sean Meyers Photography
Joe Duty
Kyle Gerstner
Cliff Bramlett
Kyle Gerstner

143 Kyle Gerstner
Scogin Mayo
Kyle Gerstner
Scogin Mayo
Kyle Gerstner
Scogin Mayo
Mary Stone

144 Cliff Bramlett
Dirck Halstead
Randy Smith
Kate Stewart
Les Hassell
Todd Yates
Scogin Mayo

145 Tim Zielenbach
Peter A. Calvin
Peter A. Calvin
Peter A. Calvin
Peter A. Calvin
Scogin Mayo
Scogin Mayo

147 Rodolfo Gonzalez
Todd Yates
Rodolfo Gonzalez
Todd Yates
Rodolfo Gonzalez
Rodolfo Gonzalez
Todd Yates

148 Louis DeLuca
Barbara Davidson, *The Dallas Morning News*
Louis DeLuca
Louis DeLuca
Louis DeLuca
Louis DeLuca
Barbara Davidson, *The Dallas Morning News*

149 Todd Yates
Todd Yates
Shelly Katz Photo
Shelly Katz Photo
Shelly Katz Photo
Shelly Katz Photo
Shelly Katz Photo

150 Adam Rendon
Todd Yates
Penny De Los Santos, *National Geographic*, Freelance
Anthony Ku
Annalisa Rodriguez Barroso
Randy Smith
Sarah Orr

151 Randy Smith
Randy Smith
Annalisa Rodriguez Barroso
Annalisa Rodriguez Barroso
Alicia Wagner Calzada
Scogin Mayo
Annalisa Rodriguez Barroso

Staff

The *America 24/7* series was imagined years ago by our friend Oscar Dystel, a publishing legend whose vision and enthusiasm have been a source of great inspiration.

We also wish to express our gratitude to our truly visionary publisher, DK.

Rick Smolan, Project Director
David Elliot Cohen, Project Director

Administrative
Katya Able, Operations Director
Gina Privitere, Communications Director
Chuck Gathard, Technology Director
Kim Shannon, Photographer Relations Director
Erin O'Connor, Photographer Relations Intern
Leslie Hunter, Partnership Director
Annie Polk, Publicity Manager
John McAlester, Website Manager
Alex Notides, Office Manager
C. Thomas Hardin, State Photography Coordinator

Design
Brad Zucroff, Creative Director
Karen Mullarkey, Photography Director
Judy Zimola, Production Manager
David Simoni, Production Designer
Mary Dias, Production Designer
Heidi Madison, Associate Picture Editor
Don McCartney, Production Designer
Diane Dempsey Murray, Production Designer
Jan Rogers, Associate Picture Editor
Bill Shore, Production Designer and Image Artist
Larry Nighswander, Senior Picture Editor
Bill Marr, Sarah Leen, Senior Picture Editors
Peter Truskier, Workflow Consultant
Jim Birkenseer, Workflow Consultant

Editorial
Maggie Canon, Managing Editor
Curt Sanburn, Senior Editor
Teresa L. Trego, Production Editor
Lea Aschkenas, Writer
Olivia Boler, Writer
Korey Capozza, Writer
Beverly Hanly, Writer
Bridgett Novak, Writer
Alison Owings, Writer
Fred Raker, Writer
Joe Wolff, Writer
Elise O'Keefe, Copy Chief
Daisy Hernández, Copy Editor
Jennifer Wolfe, Copy Editor

Infographic Design
Nigel Holmes

Literary Agent
Carol Mann, The Carol Mann Agency

Legal Counsel
Barry Reder, Coblentz, Patch, Duffy & Bass, LLP
Phil Feldman, Coblentz, Patch, Duffy & Bass, LLP
Gabe Perle, Ohlandt, Greeley, Ruggiero & Perle, LLP
Jon Hart, Dow, Lohnes & Albertson, PLLC
Mike Hays, Dow, Lohnes & Albertson, PLLC
Stephen Pollen, Warshaw Burstein, Cohen, Schlesinger & Kuh, LLP
Rick Pappas

Accounting and Finance
Rita Dulebohn, Accountant
Robert Powers, Calegari, Morris & Co. Accountants
Eugene Blumberg, Blumberg & Associates
Arthur Langhaus, KLS Professional Advisors Group, Inc.

Picture Editors
J. David Ake, Associated Press
Caren Alpert, formerly *Health* magazine
Simon Barnett, *Newsweek*
Caroline Couig, *San Jose Mercury News*
Mike Davis, formerly *National Geographic*
Michel duCille, *Washington Post*
Deborah Dragon, *Rolling Stone*
Victor Fisher, formerly Associated Press
Frank Folwell, *USA Today*
MaryAnne Golon, *Time*
Liz Grady, formerly *National Geographic*
Randall Greenwell, *San Francisco Chronicle*
C. Thomas Hardin, formerly *Louisville Courier-Journal*
Kathleen Hennessy, *San Francisco Chronicle*
Scot Jahn, *U.S. News & World Report*
Steve Jessmore, *Flint Journal*
John Kaplan, University of Florida
Kim Komenich, *San Francisco Chronicle*
Eliane Laffont, *Hachette Filipacchi Media*
Jean-Pierre Laffont, *Hachette Filipacchi Media*
Andrew Locke, MSNBC
Jose Lopez, *The New York Times*
Maria Mann, formerly AFP
Bill Marr, formerly *National Geographic*
Michele McNally, *Fortune*
James Merithew, *San Francisco Chronicle*
Eric Meskauskas, *New York Daily News*
Maddy Miller, *People* magazine
Michelle Molloy, *Newsweek*
Dolores Morrison, *New York Daily News*
Karen Mullarkey, formerly *Newsweek, Rolling Stone, Sports Illustrated*
Larry Nighswander, Ohio University School of Visual Communication
Jim Preston, *Baltimore Sun*
Sarah Rozen, formerly *Entertainment Weekly*
Mike Smith, *The New York Times*
Neal Ulevich, formerly Associated Press

Website and Digital Systems
Jeff Burchell, Applications Engineer

Television Documentary
Sandy Smolan, Producer/Director
Rick King, Producer/Director
Bill Medsker, Producer

Video News Release
Mike Cerre, Producer/Director

Digital Pond
Peter Hogg
Kris Knight
Roger Graham
Philip Bond
Frank De Pace
Lisa Li

Senior Advisors
Jennifer Erwitt, Strategic Advisor
Tom Walker, Creative Advisor
Megan Smith, Technology Advisor
Jon Kamen, Media and Partnership Advisor
Mark Greenberg, Partnership Advisor
Patti Richards, Publicity Advisor
Cotton Coulson, Mission Control Advisor

Executive Advisors
Sonia Land
George Craig
Carole Bidnick

Advisors
Chris Anderson
Samir Arora
Russell Brown
Craig Cline
Gayle Cline
Harlan Felt
George Fisher
Phillip Moffitt
Clement Mok
Laureen Seeger
Richard Saul Wurman

DK Publishing
Bill Barry
Joanna Bull
Therese Burke
Sarah Coltman
Christopher Davis
Todd Fries
Dick Heffernan
Jay Henry
Stuart Jackman
Stephanie Jackson
Chuck Lang
Sharon Lucas
Cathy Melnicki
Nicola Munro
Eunice Paterson
Andrew Welham

Colourscan
Jimmy Tsao
Eddie Chia
Richard Law
Josephine Yam
Paul Koh
Chee Cheng Yeong
Dan Kang

Chief Morale Officer
Goose, the dog

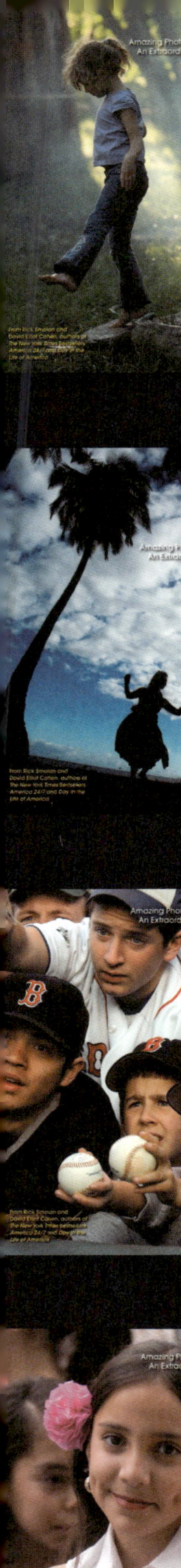
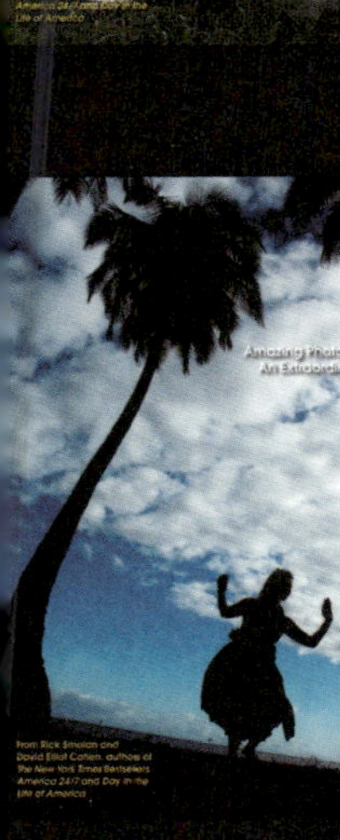
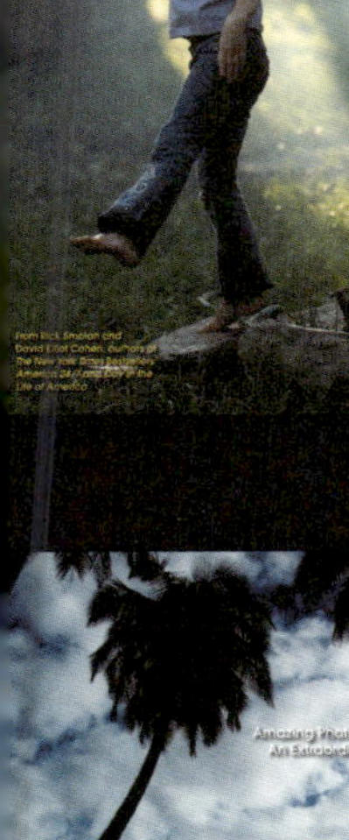
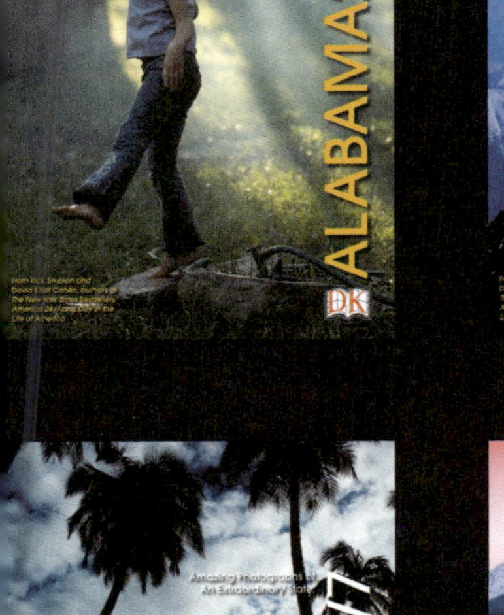
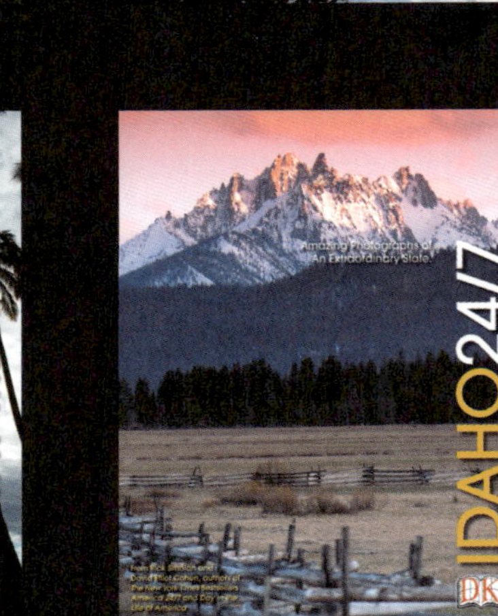
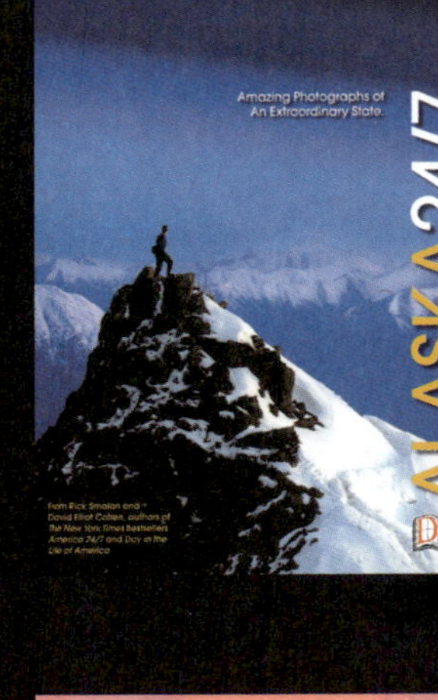
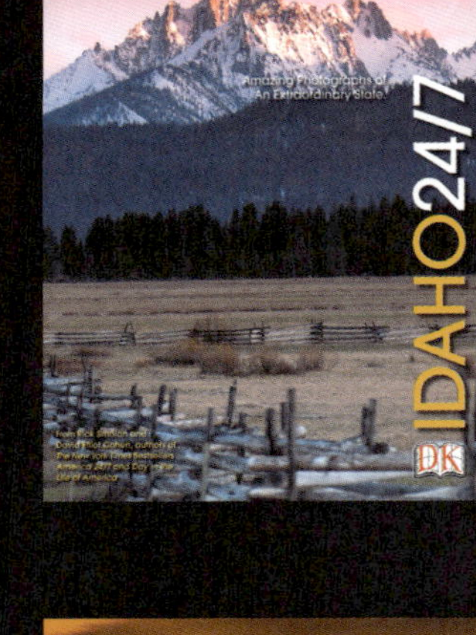
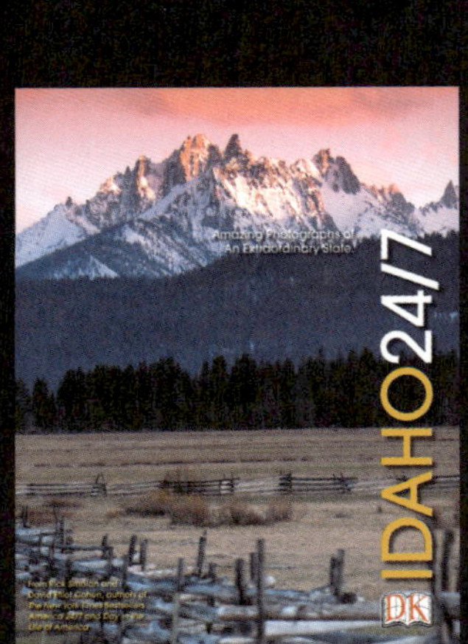
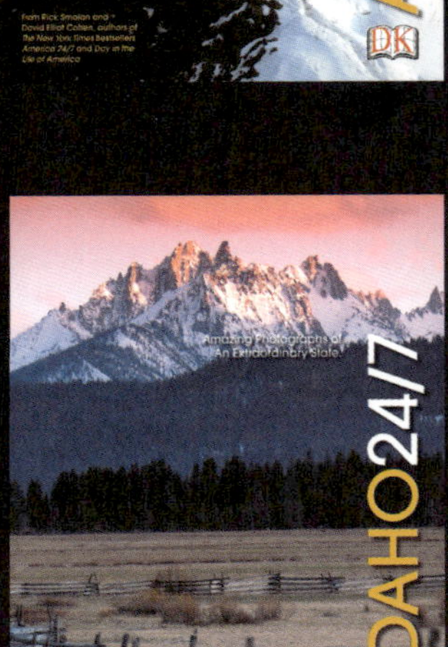
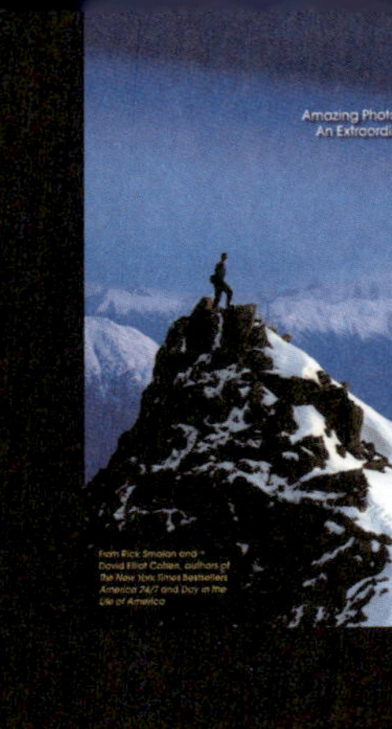
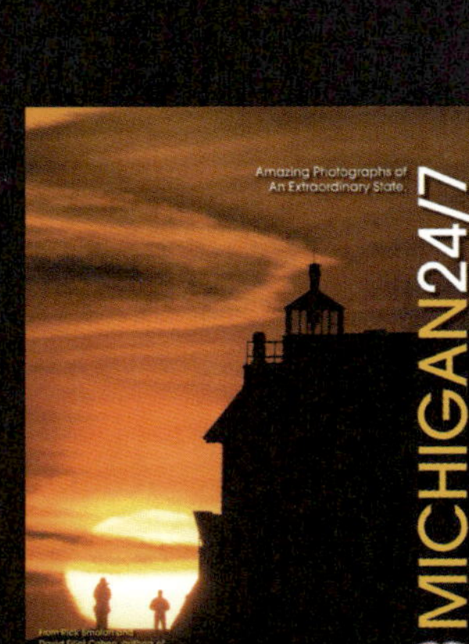
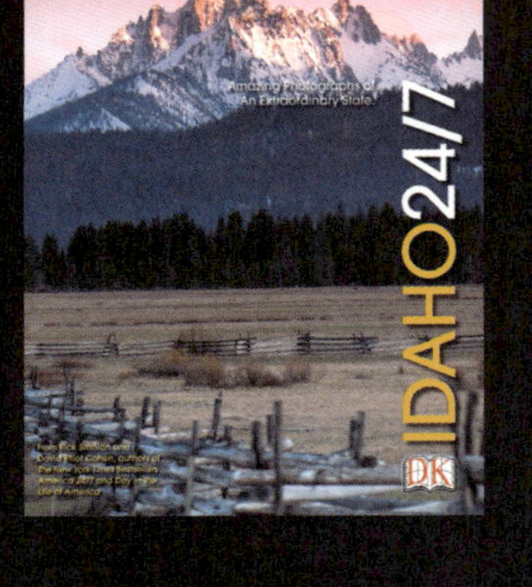
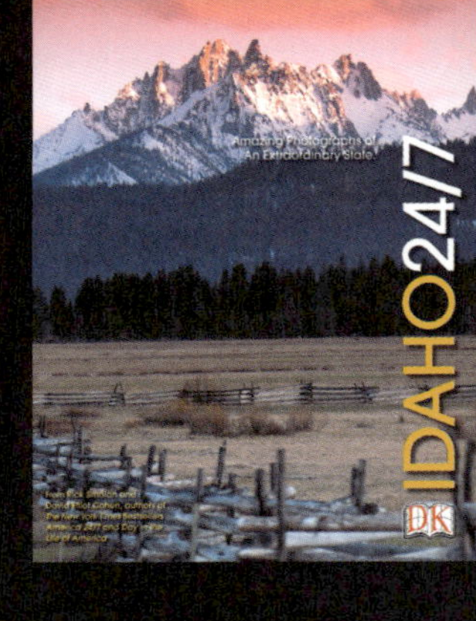
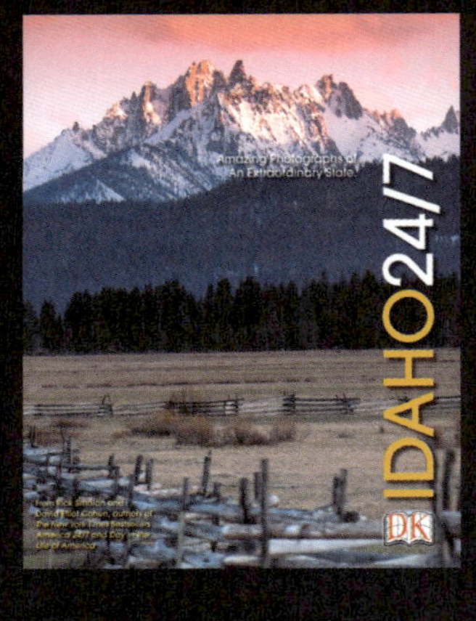
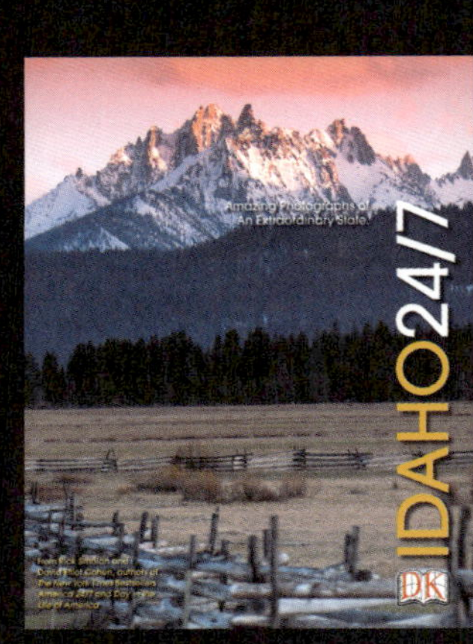
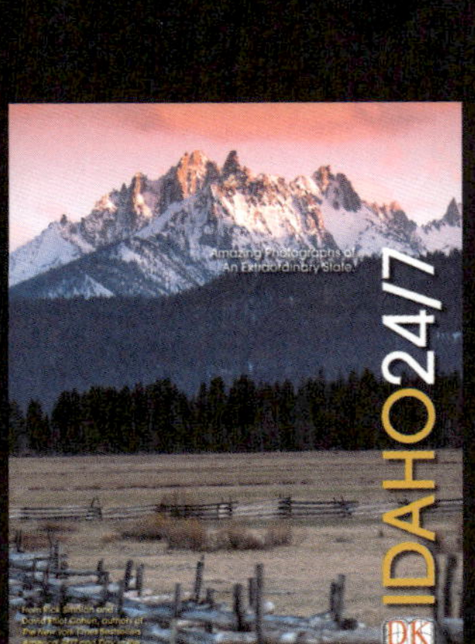
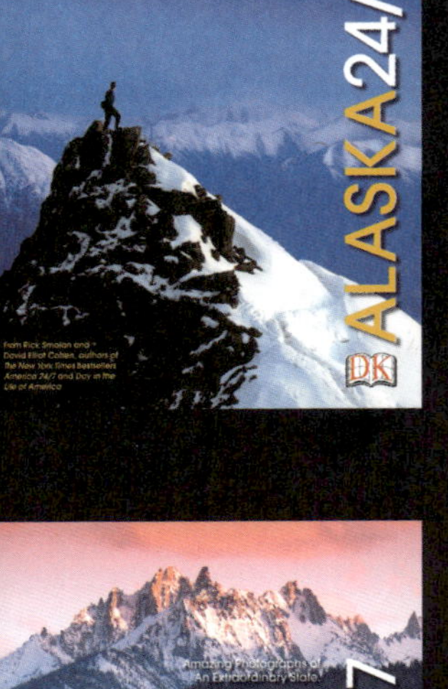
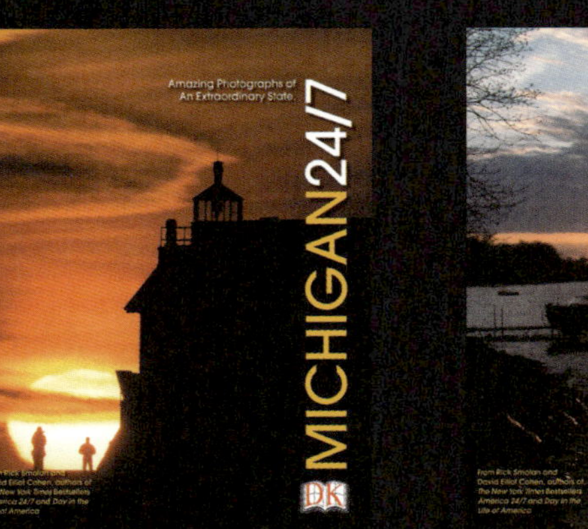
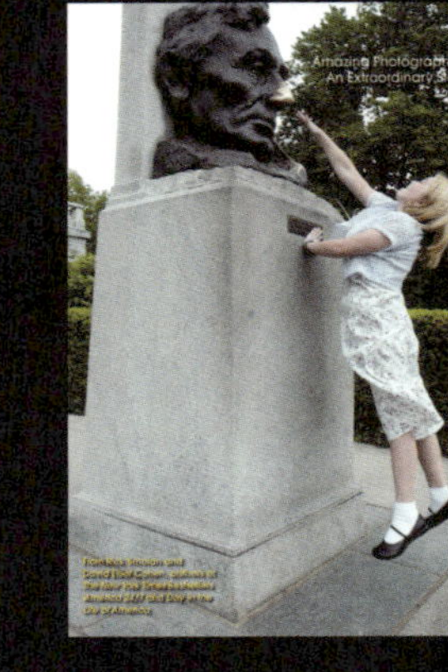
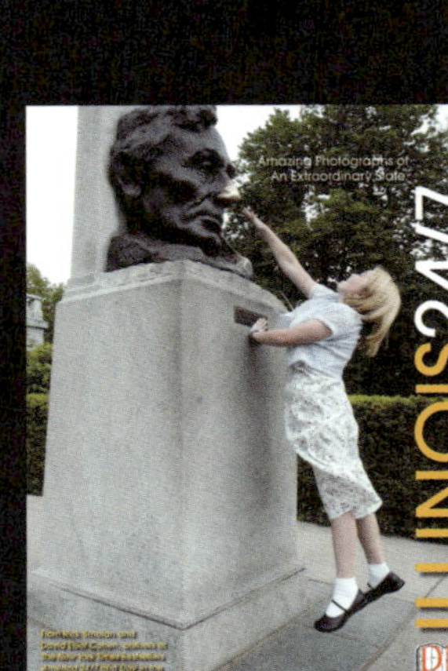
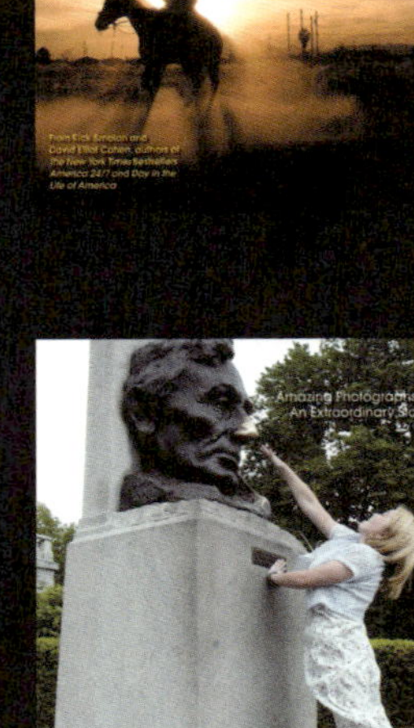
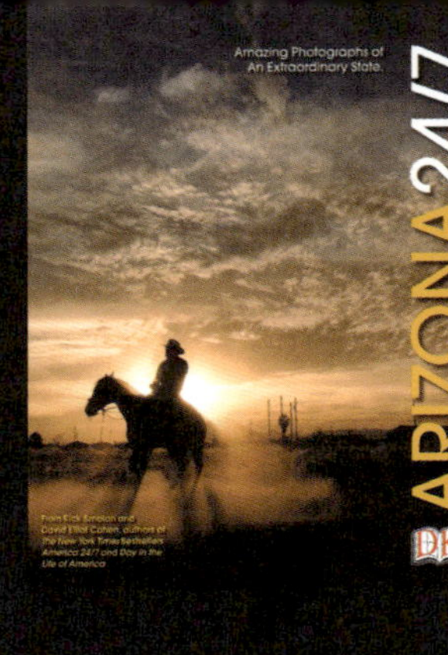
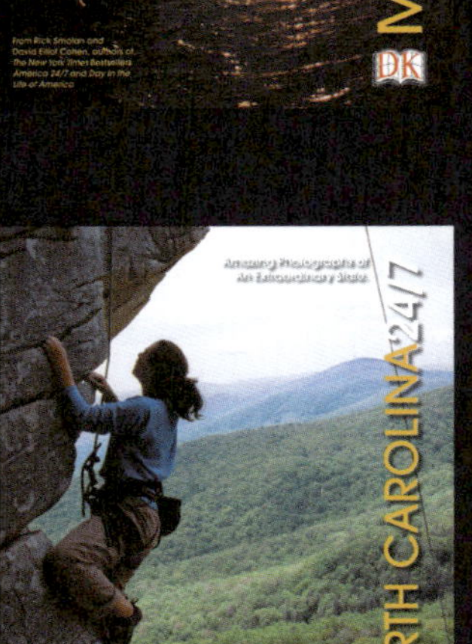
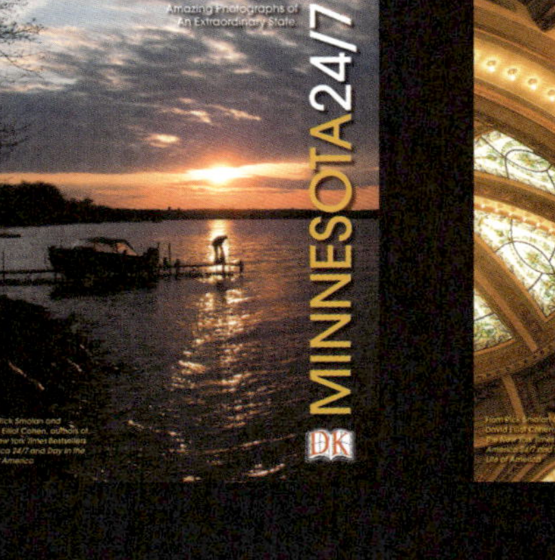
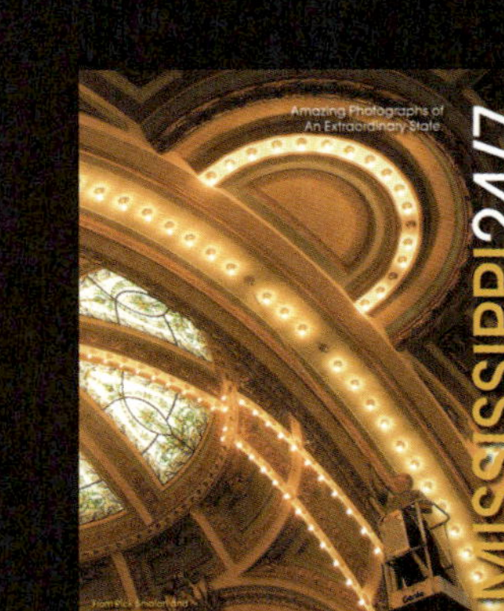
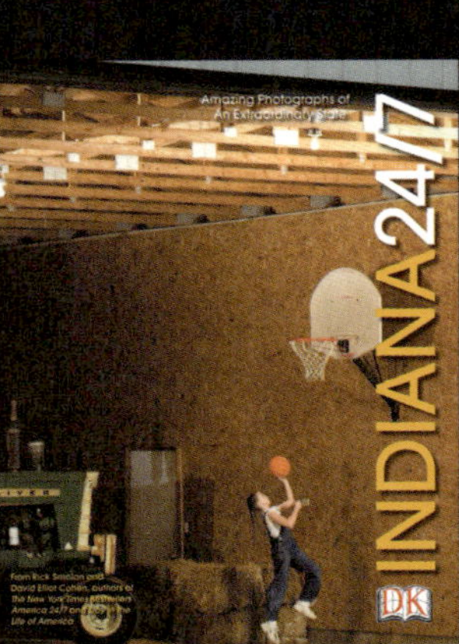
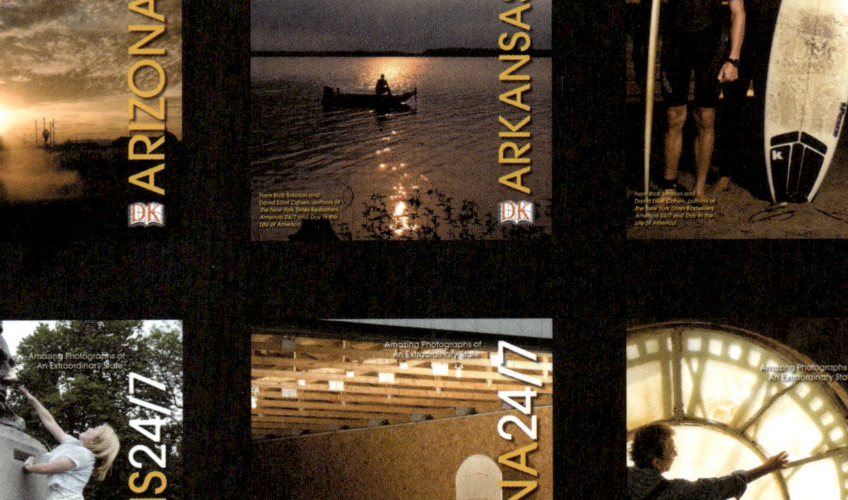
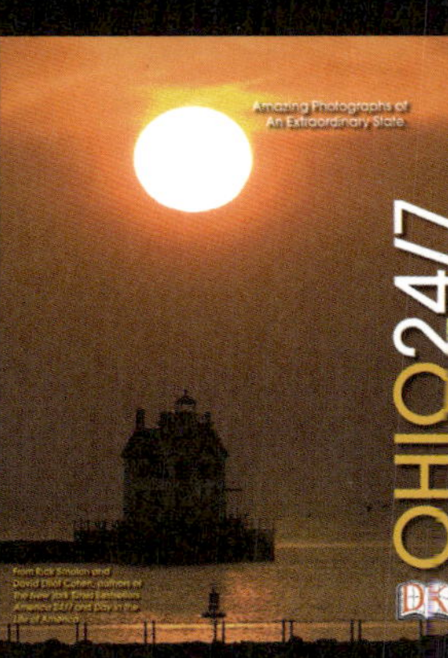

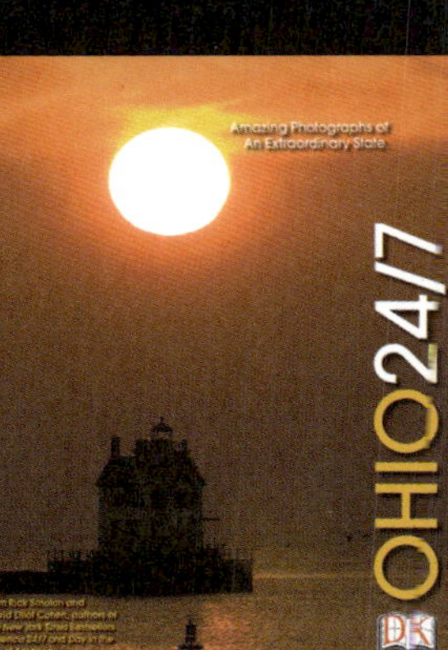
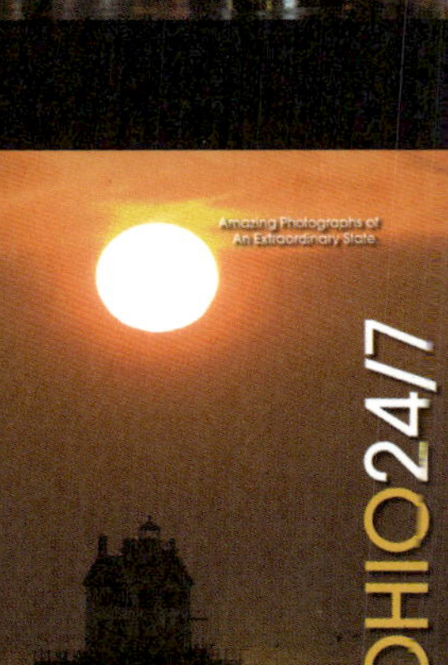
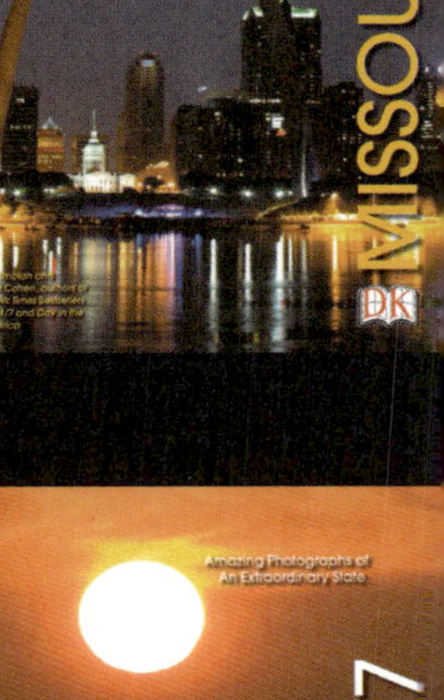
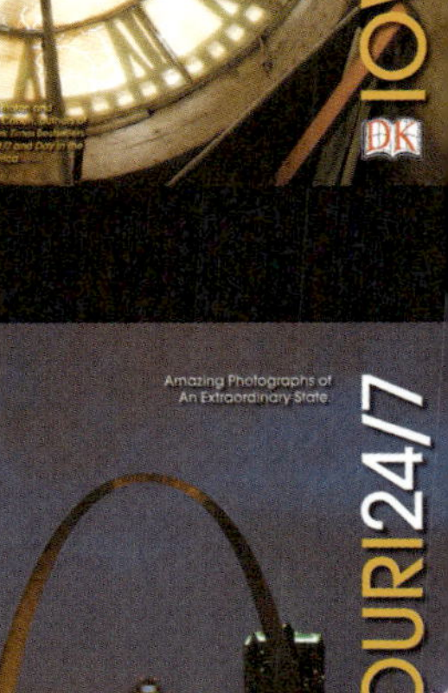
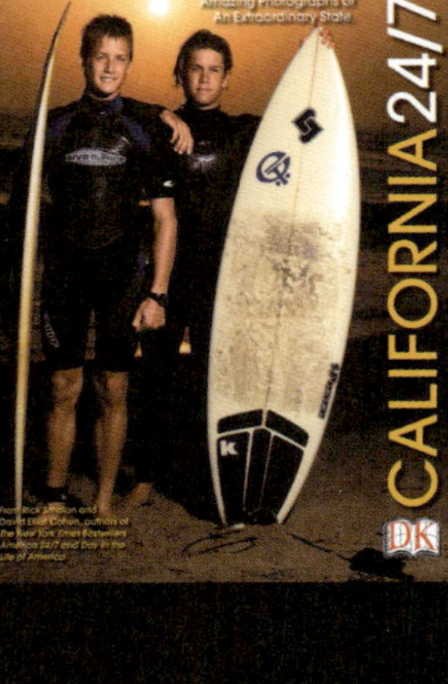

24/7 books available for every state. Collect the entire series of 50 books. Go to www.america24-7.com/store